W9-DJL-683

The Dorsey Series in Political Science

Consulting Editor
Samuel C. Patterson
The University of Iowa

PRESIDENTIAL CAMPAIGN POLITICS

Coalition Strategies and Citizen Response

PRESIDENTIAL CAMPAIGN POLITICS

Coalition Strategies and Citizen Response

JOHN H. KESSEL
Department of Political Science
The Ohio State University

 1980

The Dorsey Press
Homewood, Illinois   60430
IRWIN-DORSEY LIMITED
Georgetown, Ontario   L7G 4B3

ISBN 0-256-02369-7 (paperbound)
ISBN 0-87094-211-5 (hardbound)
Library of Congress Catalog Card No. 79–56080

Printed in the United States of America

1 2 3 4 5 6 7 8 9 0 K 7 6 5 4 3 2 1 0

 Preface

While writing this book I tried to combine flesh-and-blood politics with serious analysis. An attempt to combine substance and method can be awkward and imperfect, but the alternatives are either to shift readers away from the fascinating realm of political maneuver, or to deny readers the real explanatory power of sophisticated methodology. As V. O. Key put it: "Method without substance may be sterile, but substance without method is only fortuitously substantial."

I have tried to make clear that coalition strategies and citizen choice are equally important parts of the same political process. In recent decades, there has been much more research and writing on voting behavior than on political parties. An unhappy consequence has been the appearance of many "electoral" studies that rely almost completely on voting data. Political scientists who wouldn't write a word about voting without a national sample and multivariate analysis unhesitatingly offer off-the-top-of-the-head surmises about party activities. Equally careful analyses of parties and voters are essential to understand the linkage between coalition strategies and citizen response.

I have tried to unite a concern for politics with some attention to the development of theory. I argue that *why* something happens is sometimes explained by internal structure, sometimes by external environment, and sometimes by both. *When* it happens is explained by the temporal pattern of the acting unit. This is a simple theory, but it is sufficiently flexible to be adapted to the subjects. It also permits a comprehensive treatment of presidential nominations and elections within one theoretical framework.

Any book such as this depends as much on the research milieu in which it is written as it does on the thoughts of the author. I have been extremely fortunate in having colleagues at Ohio State with strong research orientations. Those whose work overlaps most with my own—Kristi Andersen, Herbert Asher, Aage Clausen, and Herbert Weisberg—have been more than generous with their time and counsel when I have come to them with questions and puzzlements. Thomas Jackson, Bruce Moon, Barbara Norrander, Stephen Shaffer, Evelyn Small, Gerald Stacy, Kenneth Town, and Steven Yarnell have all been responsible in one way or another for analyses that appear between these covers. Stephen Shaffer and Steven Yarnell made particularly important contributions to Chapter 3, and Stephen Shaffer and Barbara Norrander did so for Chapter 8.

The Elections Studies of the Survey Research Center/Center for Political Studies were made available through the Inter-University Consortium for Political and Social Research. I should like to thank Richard Hofstetter for allowing me to use his 1972 surveys of political activists and voters, Aage Clausen, Doris Graber, Jeane Kirkpatrick, and Herbert Weisberg for allowing me to use some of their data, and the National Science Foundation for Grants GS–2660 and GS–35084 to collect and analyze data on presidential politics. Richard McKelvey was kind enough to send his probit analysis program, and Forrest Nelson and John Aldrich (the latter on repeated occasions) helped me understand how to use probit analysis. Herbert Weisberg helped remove a block from the OSIRIS CLUSTER program so a large input matrix could be used, rewrote a section of the CLUSTER program to assure that each case would end up in the cluster with which it was most closely associated, and coached me on the use of the MDSCAL program. The Polimetrics Laboratory at Ohio State helped me get my data in and out of the computer; James Ludwig and Martin Saperstein aided me time and again when their special expertise was needed. In addition to general gratitude to the authors of the OSIRIS and SPSS programs, a special word of thanks ought to go to Norman Nie and his SPSS colleagues for the COMPUTE (and other similar) statements that allow nonprogrammers to manipulate data to meet particular needs.

Kristi Andersen, Richard Fenno, and Fred Greenstein all offered helpful reactions as the book was taking shape. Philip Converse, Richard Niemi, and Herbert Weisberg provided illuminating criticisms of the section on the Citizen in Presidential Elections. John Bibby, Stephen Brown, and Samuel Patterson read the entire manuscript and showed me many ways in which it could be improved. No one named in these paragraphs is responsible for the interpretations in this book, but all should be given credit for trying to make it better.

Finally, and above all, my thanks go to Maggie for 25 years of love and understanding.

Columbus, Ohio   **John H. Kessel**
November 19, 1979

 Contents

Part III
CAMPAIGN STRATEGIES

Part IV
THE CITIZEN IN PRESIDENTIAL ELECTIONS

Part V
CONCLUSION

PRESIDENTIAL CAMPAIGN POLITICS
Coalition Strategies and Citizen Response

part I

NOMINATION POLITICS

chapter 1

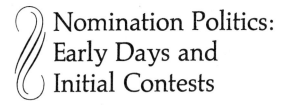

Nomination Politics:
Early Days and
Initial Contests

A MATTER OF TIME

May 1979 saw the announcement of two Republican presidential candidacies and indications of trouble in two other GOP nomination efforts. George Bush, a former Texas congressman who had held a series of foreign policy posts in the Nixon and Ford administrations, promised stable leadership in his May 1 declaration. Three days later, Representative Philip M. Crane of Illinois fired his campaign manager, accepted the resignations of four more aides who quit in protest, and was reported to be worried about a campaign debt of over $800,000. Senator Robert Dole traveled to his home town, Russell, Kansas, to announce his candidacy. Dole said that he cared about the American people and wanted them to believe in themselves. On May 17, Senator Lowell Weicker of Connecticut dropped out of the presidential contest, revealing that a Connecticut survey showed 26 percent of the state's Republicans preferred former President Gerald Ford, 21 percent former California Governor Ronald Reagan, and 13 percent Senator Weicker. "Third is not good enough," the senator said. "I can't ask the people in New Hampshire, Vermont or Florida to support me if I don't even have the support of my own state."

There had been earlier announcements, and there were more to come. Former Treasury Secretary John B. Connally of Texas had made his formal entry into the race early in the year. John Anderson of Illinois, a moderate Republican who had been chairman of the House Republican Conference, made his announcement on June 8. Senate Minority Leader Howard Baker was delaying his formal announcement because of the then pending Senate

3

debate on the SALT II treaty with the Soviet Union, and Ronald Reagan was delaying his in order to continue a profitable radio series. Two minor candidates, onetime Minnesota Governor Harold Stassen and Los Angeles businessman Benjamin Fernandez, had also announced. Gerald Ford had indicated he would be willing to accept the 1980 Republican nomination, but had no immediate plans to campaign.

Of the nine active contenders, Ronald Reagan had the most support among Republicans contacted in nationwide surveys. Howard Baker was favorably regarded by those who knew him, but was not as widely known as former Governor Reagan. But support among all Republicans is not as important as support by those who take part in the selection of delegates. Here the situation was not as clear cut. For instance, a poll of Iowa Republicans attending a fund-raising dinner in Ames showed George Bush with 40 percent, Ronald Reagan with 26 percent, Howard Baker with 14 percent, and John Connally with 11 percent. Speaking for themselves, all of the aspirants said they expected to do well in the early contests for delegates, and to go on to win the nomination.

On the Democratic side, polls by Gallup, *New York Times*/CBS, NBC/AP, and anyone else who asked, found President Carter's standing with the voters lower in May 1979 than it had been at any previous point in his administration. Cleveland, Ohio, Democrats met and passed a resolution calling for the nomination of Senator Edward Kennedy. On May 21, five Democratic congressmen—Richard Ottinger of New York, Richard Nolen of Minnesota, John Conyers of Michigan, Fortney Stark of California, and Edward Beard of Rhode Island—announced a campaign to draft Senator Kennedy. "There is tremendous unhappiness with Carter's policies," explained Congressman Ottinger. "Also, I think the public's perception of Carter's performance is not high, and we'd like to see a Democratic victory next year." A couple of weeks thereafter, a national meeting of Democratic politicians who wanted to replace Jimmy Carter with Edward Kennedy was held in Minneapolis. Senator Kennedy let it be known that he had told President Carter in March that he was likely to support him, and was still reiterating his public position that he expected President Carter to be the nominee and that he expected to support him. If Senator Kennedy was not anxious to run against President Carter, Governor Jerry Brown of California was more than anxious. However, when the respected California Poll asked Golden State natives about their presidential preferences as of May 1979, Senator Kennedy had by far the most support, then President Carter, and only then Governor Brown. Further, at least some of the pressure on Senator Kennedy to run was because many Democratic leaders were not fond of Governor Brown.

There were reminders in all this of changes that have crept into nomination politics. Two decades ago, there would not have been this much visible activity this early. But Theodore White had begun chronicling the long preconvention campaigns of aspirants in 1960, and both George McGovern and Jimmy Carter had been successful with campaigns that had begun very early. Two decades ago, there would not have been this much overt opposition to an incumbent president in his own party, but Lyndon Johnson had been challenged in 1968, Richard Nixon in 1972, and Gerald Ford in 1976. The seriousness of these challenges varied with the incumbent's strength, but the taboo against running against the leader of one's own party seemed to have vanished.

The most unusual action in May 1979 was the departure of Senator Weicker from the roster of announced candidates. Goodness knows how many governors, senators, and other public figures dream privately of becoming president. Most, however, take careful soundings to determine likely support before they announce their candidacies. If they reckon it is inadequate, we never hear from them. Lowell Weicker's action was unusual in that he apparently did it the other way round.

Otherwise, all was customary. George Bush pointed out that he was a lifelong Republican, by way of distinguishing himself from former Democrats John Connally and Ronald Reagan. Robert Dole began his campaign with a well-publicized trip back to Kansas, a careful hedge against misfortune in his presidential bid. His Senate term was due to expire in 1980, and if he did less well than he hoped in his pursuit of the White House, he could concentrate on winning another term as the senior senator from Kansas. Democrats were responding to Jimmy Carter's unpopularity by yearning for Edward Kennedy as their nominee, just as Democrats responded to Harry Truman's unpopularity by yearning for Supreme Court Justice William O. Douglas as his replacement.

All in all, the most salient fact was that it was May 1979—more than a year before either party's 1980 convention. Some perspective can be obtained by asking what was taking place at this point in previous campaigns. In May 1975, a little known ex-governor of Georgia, Jimmy Carter, was touring Japan, and President Gerald Ford still believed that Ronald Reagan would not run against him. In the spring of 1963, New York Governor Nelson Rockefeller was running ahead of Arizona Senator Barry Goldwater 43 percent to 26 percent among Republicans, but on May 4 he married Mrs. Margaretta ("Happy") Murphy, a recently divorced mother of four young children, and a late-May Gallup Poll showed Goldwater running 35 percent to 30 percent ahead of Rockefeller. In May 1951, General Dwight Eisenhower was in France organizing NATO forces. Domestic political news was dominated by Senate hearings on the recent relief of General MacArthur by President Truman, and by arguments before the Supreme Court on whether Truman had acted unlawfully in nationalizing the steel industry. Contemplating these events gave hints—but only hints—of the shape of nomination politics in the year to come. It was still Early Days.

Early Days

Nomination politics passes through a series of stages, at least four of which can be distinguished. The first is Early Days, the period between the mid-term election and the initial selection of delegates. There may be some gentle campaigning before the mid-term election to help build name recognition for the candidate, and the candidate often helps those seeking other offices during the mid-term election in anticipation of potential help from them later. Still, it is too early for much serious organizing. For one thing, no one can be certain who will survive the election. If a senator or governor wins by a large margin, it may set the stage for a presidential bid two years later. On the other hand, candidates retired by the voters of their states may not even be in a position to influence their own state delegations. Without information on the identity of the players one can make tentative plans but that's about all.

What happens during Early Days depends on whether a decision has been made to make an active bid for the White House. Barry Goldwater, for example, had not made his decision during 1963 nor had Nelson Rockefeller during 1967. If this decision has not been made, then the candidate spends a lot of time listening to the importunings of persons who would like to see an active candidacy, and a lot more time trying to figure out whether these urgings reflect the interests of the people doing the coaxing or are in fact grounded in genuine public support.

If the potential candidate is even thinking seriously about running, an early step will now be the creation of an exploratory committee that is empowered to receive contributions. This is because of the Federal Election Campaign Act of 1974 (actually, amendments to the 1971 Act) that created federal financing of presidential campaigns. This has had a number of consequences. First, a candidate must raise $5,000 in amounts of not more than $250 in each of 20 states. One hundred thousand dollars is not a lot of money as national campaign expenses go, but it does require the creation of an organization to raise money over a wide area. Second, the federal fund will provide up to 50 percent of $10 million (plus an inflation allowance). Since the federal fund matches money raised by the candidate, this doubles any disparity that may result from fund-raising capacity. In other words, if Candidate A raises the minimum $100,000 and Candidate B raises $1 million, the matching funds will give Candidate B a financial advantage of $2 million to Candidate A's $200,000. Third, this may lead candidates to take stands that will stimulate gifts from donors, and it does stimulate much more organized Early Days activity. Serious contenders are forced into early fund raising if only to keep from entering the race too far behind their competitors.

If the decision to run has been made, then Early Days revolve around planning and organizing. At least the outline of a strategy is needed. Which primaries will be entered? What stands will the candidate take? An initial staff must be recruited. In addition to the aforementioned need for a fund raiser, an absolute minimum is someone to handle the media and someone to organize the campaign. Once these essentials are in hand, then the candidate begins making forays into those states in which the first delegates are to be chosen, and begins to set up campaign organizations in those states. These activities are intertwined with one another. The staff members are very likely to take part in initial strategy discussions, and residents of early primary states who tell a campaigner how impressed they are may well find themselves recruited into the candidate's state campaign organization.

Early Days is also marked by a lack of information about the opposition. If a potential candidate has not decided whether to run, others certainly don't know. And even among announced candidates, it is too soon to know how well organized they are, how well financed they will be, or how attractive to the voters. Consequently, only preliminary judgments can be made about who the strong contenders will be and who will soon disappear for lack of support.

Initial Contests

The Initial Contests are, of course, the first campaigns for delegates. New Hampshire has traditionally held the first primary election, although a number of other states have scheduled early primaries in recent years. Iowa has also gained attention recently by holding the first party caucuses in which delegates are selected. Considerable attention has been paid to New Hampshire and Iowa just because they are first; but the crucial point is whether or not they are contested, especially by those regarded by the media as strong candidates. As long as New Hampshire is first and contested, it will be an important primary; but if a New Hampshire governor were to run as a favorite son and other candidates stayed out, attention would shift elsewhere.

The number of states in which a candidate seeks delegates depends on his or her strength and resources. If an aspirant has the funds and organization to make it feasible, he or she may enter a large number of primaries and seek delegates in several caucus states. With this kind of strategy, the Initial Contests phase is not so critical. Obviously it helps to win, but a defeated candidate who is confident of support that can be picked up later in other parts of the country can afford to take a more detached view. For less well supported candidates, however, success in the Initial Contests is imperative. Their hope is that they can generate some enthusiasm among the voters, which in turn will produce the resources that will enable them to enter later primaries. If support from the voters is not there, the only option is to drop out of the race.

The Initial Contests are watched very closely by the media. The three national networks broadcast 100 stories on the New Hampshire primary in 1976 in which 38 delegates were being chosen, compared with 30 stories on New York's April 6 primary in which 428 delegates were being chosen (Robinson, 1976). Whether a candidate has won or lost becomes less important in media interpretation than how the candidate's performance measures up against expectations. Needless to say, campaign organizations go to great efforts to establish low expectations so they can be "pleasantly surprised" by the actual results. Reporters, however, are equally interested in establishing more objective standards. Among other things, they refer to historical standards (how well the candidate has done in the state on previous occasions), preprimary polls, geographical propinquity (whether the candidate comes from a nearby state), and the investment of time and resources made by the candidate (Matthews, 1978; cf. Arterton, forthcoming). If a candidate does better than expected, it is hailed as a victory and the candidate gains precious momentum. If a candidate does about as well as expected, not too much attention is paid. If a candidate falls below expectation, then articles are written analyzing the failure of the campaign.

There have been complaints about this measurement of performance against expectation. By this logic, Senator Edmund Muskie was said to have lost the 1972 New Hampshire primary, although he won 46.4 percent of the vote to Senator George McGovern's 37.2 percent, because Muskie had been expected to do better. Similarly, Senator McGovern's campaign was not harmed by the results of the subsequent Florida primary, where he got only 6.2 percent of the vote, because no one expected him to do much better. This seems perverse, but in the absence of "hard" information about the progress of coalition building, the expectations developed by the media probably provide better standards of comparison than the claims of the candidates.

Mist Clearing

The third phase of nomination politics is hardest to pinpoint at a particular point in time, but it usually occurs while the delegates are still being chosen. It is marked by a reduction of the uncertainty which has thus far attended the nomination process, and in this sense is akin to the clearing of a mist that allows one to see the pine trees some distance across a woods or cars several hundred yards down the road. Whereas vital pieces of information are missing during Early Days, and subjective impressions of reporters provide the best standards for judgment during Initial Contests, Mist Clearing allows one to know how many serious contenders there are for the nomination, and what their strength is vis-à-vis one another. Some candidates who have failed to gain much support may remain formally in the race to act as spokesmen for a point of view (or to collect federal matching funds to pay off campaign debts), but effective campaigning will be carried on by the serious contenders for the nomination.

The principal shift in campaigning from Initial Contests to Mist Clearing is from a desire to create an impression of movement to a prevailing concern with the acquisition of delegates. A shift from the first 20 delegates to, say, 200 delegates implies a change in the method of campaigning as well as a more complex campaign organization. Whereas the earlier appeal had to be on the grounds that the candidate was the most attractive among half a dozen or more declared aspirants, the appeal now can be that while the candidate may not be ideal, he is one who comes close to the stands the delegate would prefer *and* has a real chance of winning. If the candidate has already attracted 200 delegates, then there is a coalition in being. The groups of delegates who make up the coalition do not all have identical views, and a certain amount of organizational effort is needed to hold the coalition together at the same time that additional groups of delegates are being recruited.

Relationships between the candidates and reporters are also rather different in this phase of nomination politics. Early on, the candidate was anxious to create news and made himself available to the few reporters whose organizations took the trouble to cover the campaign. By the Mist Clearing stage, the candidate's success has made him a prime news source and there is now a much larger press entourage. This shift gives the campaign staff a better opportunity to control the news by rationing the candidate's time among the greater number of reporters who want to see him. On the other hand, what the candidate says will now be subject to much greater scrutiny. When he was one of several candidates during Initial Contests, not much space could be devoted to his issue statements or those of any one candidate. Now that the candidate is one of two or three who may be a major party nominee, statements on foreign policy or economics or whatever will be more carefully analyzed.

There will sometimes be a flurry of activity during this phase on the part of a late entrant in the race. Pennsylvania Governor William Scranton did not declare his candidacy until June 1964; New York Governor Nelson Rockefeller did so in May 1968 after having announced earlier that he would not run; Governor Jerry Brown of California and Senator Frank Church of Idaho had made their decisions in March 1976, but the first contests they were able to enter did not take place until May. The late entrant is likely to get a fair amount of media attention; he does enliven what may be an all-but-decided contest. But the late entrant is likely to be giving voice to different attitudes than those held by the likely winning coalition, or he may be simply attracting publicity with an eye on a future campaign. Unless there are very unusual circumstances, there are just too few delegates remaining to be chosen to give the late entrant any real chance of building a winning coalition.

The Convention

In recent decades, conventions have ratified decisions made earlier by nominating the leading presidential candidate on the first ballot. The last multi-ballot conventions were in 1952 for the Democrats, and in 1948 for the Republicans. The last truly deadlocked conventions were in 1924 for the Democrats, and in 1920 for the Republicans. It is always possible that we might see another multi-ballot convention, especially if there should be two strong coalitions, each strong enough to keep its rival from getting enough votes to win, but without the leverage needed to pick up the few votes needed to achieve victory. The dominant pattern, though, is one of first-ballot nominations. The wide publicity now given to the primaries and caucuses in which the delegates are selected give ample indication of the likelihood that one candidate or another will win. The "tests of strength" that took place on early ballots of multi-ballot conventions are no longer as essential to provide clues about this.

Even so, the Convention is a consequential stage in the nominating process. There are a series of decisions made by the convention before the nomination of the presidential candidate. These are taken by voting to approve (or amend, or reject) reports from several committees. The first is a Committee on Credentials, which makes recommendations on what delegates are to be seated. The second is a Committee on Permanent Organization, which suggests permanent officers to replace the temporary officers who will have guided the convention in its opening sessions. Next comes a Committee on Rules, which proposes rules to govern the present convention, authorizes a National Committee to transact party business during the next four years, and sets forth the procedure for calling the next convention. Finally, a Committee on Resolutions presents the party platform for adoption. These are important decisions. Credentials, Permanent Organization, and Rules are important in the short term of the convention itself. By seating certain delegates—for example, by seating McGovern delegates rather than Humphrey delegates from Illinois and California in 1972—one can create a majority in favor of one candidate. The rules may favor one side or another, and the permanent chairperson may enforce the rules so as to give an advantage to one of the contenders. Rules and the Platform have long-term consequences as well. Both parties have adopted rules at recent conventions that have mandated reforms in the composition or procedures of future conventions. For instance, the McGovern-Fraser Commission, which recommended a new set of procedures for the selection of delegates to the 1972 Democratic Convention, was appointed under the authority of a rule adopted in 1968. And a careful study of party platforms over a 24-year period has shown that 80 percent of the pledges were implemented by the party winning the White House (Pomper, 1968, chap. 8).

These Convention votes also play a role in the contest over the presidential nominee. What happens in any particular Convention depends on the strength of the contending coalitions. Let's say there is a winning coalition that does not have too many votes to spare, and at least one reasonably strong challenging coalition. This has been a reasonably common situation in recent conventions. In these circumstances, the challenging coalition will try for a test vote on an issue that will maximize its strength. It may come, for example, on the adoption of a rule that the challenging coalition thinks would be attractive to uncommitted delegates, or it may come on a platform plank that will tend to split the winning coalition. Whatever the topic, the object is to pick an issue that will attract more votes than the challenging coalition can muster in behalf of its candidate. The winning coalition, on the other hand, will be more interested in the presidential roll call to come, and may just accept the proposed change as long as coalition leaders think they can live with it. If the winning coalition is in a very strong position, they will have the votes to beat back any challenges. In these circumstances, motions challenging credentials, rules, or platform are likely to be made only by those who feel strongly about the issue as a matter of principle.

In view of the possibility of contests on a number of issues, the coalition leaders must have some way of communicating with their groups of delegates. When the convention is not in session, the delegates will be lodged in hotels all over the city. Some person will normally be designated as the contact for each coalition's delegates in each state, though communication is at best awkward when delegates are spread all over a large metropolitan area. On the convention floor, the key coalition leaders will usually be in some central location (often in a trailer parked outside the convention hall) which provides telephone or walkie-talkie communication with the state delegation leaders. This allows rapid dissemination of a decision to try to beat back a challenge, to accept it, or to take no position on it.

Finally, the Convention is both the conclusion of nomination politics and the beginning of electoral politics. These differ in fundamental ways. The prime objective of the former is to attract enough delegates to win the nomination; the prime objective of the latter is to convince voters to support the candidate in November. But the conventions are widely reported by press and television, and while the delegates are listening to speeches and casting votes, citizens are making up their minds about the coming general election. Just over a quarter of presidential voting decisions in the elections since 1948 have been made during the conventions (Flanigan and Zingale, 1979, pp. 172–73). There have been conventions— such as the 1964 Republican Convention when Governor Nelson Rockefeller was booed when addressing the delegates, and the 1968 Democratic Convention with a bloody confrontation between Chicago police and antiwar demonstrators—which seriously handicapped the parties in the fall campaign; and even without events as dramatic as these, the identity of the nominee, the vice presidential candidate he selects, and the issue positions are important considerations in the citizen's own presidential choice.

The Temporal Pattern in Nomination Politics

These four phases—Early Days, Initial Contests, Mist Clearing, and the Convention—blend into one another. Time is continuous. The campaign forays of Early Days and the skeleton organizations that are set up in Iowa, New Hampshire, and elsewhere set the stage for the Initial Contests. Victory in the Initial Contests provides pledged delegates, and delegates continue to accumulate gradually until the genuine strength of one or more coalitions is discovered in the Mist Clearing phase. And while appointments to the convention committees are not formally made until the convention opens, the decisions about who is going to be appointed are made well in advance, and preliminary meetings of the Platform Committee (or at least of a drafting subcommittee) take place while the competing coalitions are still seeking delegate support.

Even so, it is useful to consider these phases separately. Each can be distinguished on the basis of characteristic behavior patterns. To see this, we shall briefly review four nomination contests as they passed through these stages: Carter, 1976; Goldwater, 1964; Ford versus Reagan, 1976; Eisenhower versus Taft, 1952. The first two contests typify those in which there are several potential nominees during Early Days and the eventual victor gradually pulls away from the field. The latter are the two modern examples of two candidate struggles that last from Early Days on through the Convention.[1]

EARLY DAYS

Carter, 1976   Jimmy Carter announced his candidacy for president early, December 12, 1974, but his planning and organization had begun

---

[1] These are two of the three modern patterns of nomination. The third pattern is that in which the identity of the probable nominee is known from the start, as with Lyndon Johnson in 1964 or Richard Nixon in 1972. This hardly requires any analysis.

even earlier. His own decision had been made in the fall of 1972, and his aide Hamilton Jordan had written a memorandum setting forth a detailed strategy. "The New Hampshire and Florida primaries provide a unique opportunity for you to demonstrate your abilities and strengths at an early stage of the campaign." The memorandum went on to point out that New Hampshire was a small rural state that would be receptive to a candidate of Carter's background and campaign style, and that Florida had advantages for a southern candidate. It also urged that Carter use the governorship to establish contacts, begin to read the *New York Times* and *Washington Post* regularly, and travel abroad to be able to claim familiarity with foreign affairs (Schram, 1977, pp. 52–71).

The most important contact Carter made was with Robert Strauss. The Democratic national chairman visited Atlanta in March 1973, and the conversation led to an invitation for Carter to serve as chairman of the 1974 campaign. Hamilton Jordan moved to Washington in May, and Governor Carter spent much of 1974 traveling around the country in behalf of Democratic candidates, and making the contacts with Democrats that were to be the basis of his own presidential campaign. (Senator George McGovern had a similar opportunity to become known in party circles in 1969–70 as chairman of the McGovern-Fraser Commission that wrote the rules that were to govern 1972 delegate selection. Party activity is a very important part of the answer to the question, "Where did such an improbable candidate come from?")

By 1975, Jimmy Carter was ready to spend a lot of time in Iowa, New Hamphire, and Florida. Seven aspirants were invited to a celebration of Marie Jahn's 37 years as Plymouth county (Iowa) recorder in February 1975. Only Jimmy Carter came. While he was there, he also taped a show on the local radio station, had interviews with the *LeMars Daily Sentinal* and a nearby college newspaper, and within two weeks all the local Democrats he had met had received personal letters from him. The Plymouth county Democrats, and others whom Carter had met on his 21 trips to Iowa that year, were contacted soon thereafter by Tim Kraft, a New Mexico Democrat who was coordinating Carter's Iowa activities, and in due course there was a 20-person Iowa Carter for President Steering Committee (Lelyveld, 1976c).

Reporters were not paying much attention to Carter's Early Days activities, but this ended with a straw poll taken at a Democratic dinner in Ames, Iowa, on October 25. Acting on a hunch that someone would take a straw poll, Tim Kraft urged Carter Steering Committee members to get as many supporters as possible to come to the dinner, and to persuade others attending to vote for Carter. The *Des Moines Register* did take a poll; Carter got 23 percent; no one else got over 12 percent (Schram, 1977, p. 16). On this basis, the *New York Times*'s respected R. W. ("Jonny") Apple wrote a front-page story headlined, "Carter Appears to

Hold a Solid Lead in Iowa . . .," and this caused a good deal of media attention for the hitherto neglected ex-governor of Georgia (Arterton, 1979, p. 39).

Jimmy Carter was not the only aspirant to make an early decision to run, but he was the only one who decided early, and who also concentrated on building a base in Iowa, New Hampshire, and Florida. Senator Henry Jackson of Washington had formed an exploratory committee, and had raised over $1 million in 1974, but his strategy was keyed toward winning a lot of delegates in the New York primary. Arizona Congressman Morris Udall had made his decision to run in mid-1974 after he had been approached by two liberal Democratic representatives from Wisconsin, David Obey and Henry Reuss. He announced in November 1974, and began focusing on New Hampshire (Ivins, 1976). Senator Birch Bayh of Indiana waited through much of 1975 before making any decision, and by the time he did announce his candidacy, in September, other candidates had spent months planning, organizing, and campaigning in the early states (Witcover, 1977).

Goldwater, 1964   There was one man that conservative Republicans wanted as their candidate in 1964: Senator Barry Goldwater of Arizona. His had been a leading voice for conservative positions, and he had been willing to work within the Republican party. He had been chairman of the Senate Republican Campaign Committee, but had done far more than that position required in the way of party service. He had made 225 appearances at party functions in 1961 and even more in 1962 until he had cut his schedule back to keep from creating an undesired impression of seeking the presidency. Barry Goldwater was a warm, attractive human being, and he left friends wherever he spoke. (His eventual running mate, William E. Miller, was working these same vineyards as chairman of the Republican National Committee. As with Carter and McGovern, Goldwater and Miller provide additional examples of "out of nowhere" nominees who were busy in party circles during Early Days.)

A group of Goldwater supporters under the leadership of F. Clifton White, a onetime president of the Young Republicans, had met in Chicago in late 1961, again after the 1962 elections, and then announced themselves as the National Draft Goldwater Committee in April 1963. For his part, Barry Goldwater was not at all sure he wanted to run for president. He asked his old friend Arizona attorney Denison Kitchell to come to Washington and to make preparations for whatever campaign he found himself engaged in, whether for president or for another term in the Senate. Eventually, he was persuaded to run for president, and, in his January 1964 announcement, he promised an "engagement of principles" that would offer "a choice, not an echo."

The only other Early Days activity was on behalf of New York Governor Nelson Rockefeller. Though considerably weakened by his remarriage, he had been twice elected governor of the Empire State by margins of over half a million votes, and had assembled an exceptionally skilled group of political craftsmen to work in his behalf. Rockefeller assumed that his best chance lay in demonstrating his popularity with the public, and so focused on the New Hampshire primary. Among other aspirants, Richard Nixon had not been available to speak at party affairs, had been defeated for governor of California, and was establishing a law practice in New York. Henry Cabot Lodge was in Saigon as American ambassador to Vietnam, and William Scranton and George Romney were just beginning gubernatorial terms in Pennsylvania and Michigan.

Ford versus Reagan, 1976   There had been talk for some time about a Ronald Reagan candidacy in 1976, but many of Gerald Ford's advisors did not seem to believe it. In common with many organization Republicans, Ford advisors were worried about the harm conservative ideologues could do to the party in a general election, but seemed to think that if enough gestures were made in their direction they would stop acting as ideologues and support moderate candidates in the interest of party unity. Ford's first gesture—coming at about the same time as his summertime announcement of candidacy—was the appointment of former Army Secretary Howard ("Bo") Callaway to head the President Ford Committee. Callaway had achieved some success in Georgia politics (a term in Congress, a near miss for the governorship), but had no national experience, and at once began talking about the possibility that Vice President Nelson Rockefeller would be dropped in 1976. The eventual result of this was that Rockefeller departed from the ticket, but conservatives kept right on supporting Ronald Reagan.

In other respects, the Ford Early Days posture was a classic strategy for an incumbent: try to demonstrate to any potential opponent that the president has enough support in his party to make opposition impractical. Some moves in the service of this strategy were important. Republican parties in large states—Ohio, New York, Pennsylvania, and Michigan—endorsed the president for reelection, as did several prominent California Republicans. Two important personnel appointments were made in the fall. Professional campaign manager Stuart Spencer and newspaperman Peter Kaye, both long active in California Republican politics, were brought in as director of organization and as press secretary of the President Ford Committee. Spencer also lacked national campaign experience, but brought real expertise to the committee, and at once turned to the task of creating a good New Hampshire organization along with Congressman James Cleveland (Witcover, 1977, chaps. 4,6).

The serious conversations about a Reagan candidacy took place between the governor and several advisors who had been close to him in his California administration: Lyn Nofziger, Michael Deaver, Peter Hannaford, James Lake, and others. In 1974, they expanded their group by recruiting a campaign director, John P. Sears. Sears, a lawyer who had gained delegate hunting experience in the successful 1968 Nixon campaign, and who had opened a Washington office after a brief stint on the White House staff, was an able and resourceful tactician. He brought a skill level to the Reagan campaign that matched the ability Stuart Spencer brought to the Ford campaign.

With a new Republican president in the White House, Ronald Reagan was not at all sure he wanted to run. His personal decision was not made until the spring of 1975, and even then he delayed any public announcement. John Sears and Lyn Nofziger started letting conservatives know that Reagan would run, recruited Nevada Senator Paul Laxalt as national chairman, and put together a New Hampshire committee headed by ex-Governor Hugh Gregg. When Reagan was ready to announce in November, the manner of doing so showed the strength of the challenge he was to make. The night before, he answered questions in New Hampshire, then flew to Washington's National Press Club for the announcement itself, then on for press conferences in Florida, North Carolina, and California. Ronald Reagan was a highly articulate conservative, and three of the early primaries—New Hampshire, Florida, and North Carolina—were to be held in states where a conservative should garner a lot of Republican votes.

Eisenhower versus Taft, 1952   It was not always the case that there had been such extensive Early Days activities. In 1951, the only visible effort was on behalf of Ohio Senator Robert A. Taft. Taft had a brilliant mind (he had been first in his class at Harvard Law School), and was the acknowledged leader of Senate Republicans. He had tried for the GOP nomination in 1940 and 1948, and had been active in behalf of Ohio Governor John W. Bricker in 1944. Taft's 1950 reelection to the Senate by a 437,000 vote margin set the stage for another attempt by this leader of Republican conservatives.[2] David Ingalls, a cousin of Taft's from Cleveland, and Ben Tate, also from Cleveland, set out to visit Republican leaders around the country—with the ostensible purpose of determining whether there was enough support for Taft, and the actual purpose of putting together a Taft campaign organization. To no one's surprise, they located enough support, and Senator Taft announced his candidacy on October 16, 1951. The Taft effort was headed by Ingalls, Tate, former national chairman John D. M. Hamilton, and Thomas E. Coleman, Wisconsin's highly regarded Republican state chairman.

---

[2] The words "liberal" and "conservative" change meaning so often that it would be hard to know what positions Taft took from the fact that he was a conservative. He generally opposed American involvement overseas; but on domestic matters he favored federal aid to education, and federal aid for housing and hospital construction. Taft had the solid support of conservatives, but on domestic issues he often took positions that were much more progressive than those of his followers.

Two more announcements came toward the end of the year. California Governor and 1948 vice presidential candidate Earl Warren offered his name in a brief statement in November, and former Minnesota Governor Harold Stassen (still a credible candidate because of a strong 1948 effort) did so just after Christmas. But leaders of the coalition that had supported New York Governor Thomas E. Dewey, the Republican nominee in 1944 and 1948, had made it clear they preferred General Dwight Eisenhower. He was in France throughout the year and remained quite silent about his political aspirations, or even whether he was a Republican or a Democrat. Then on December 17, 1951, New Hampshire Governor Sherman Adams wrote Massachusetts Senator Henry Cabot Lodge, who was known as a leader of those favoring Eisenhower, urging that the general declare himself to be a Republican so his name could be entered in the New Hampshire primary.

INITIAL CONTESTS

Carter, 1976   Once the Initial Contests begin, something is known about the structure of competition. The relative strength of the candidates is hard to determine this early, but the ideological positioning of the candidates can be discerned from the policy statements they make; and surveys soon reveal the types of voters the various candidates are likely to be able to attract. Speaking very generally, the initial Democratic structure of competition found former Oklahoma Senator Fred Harris on the far left; Birch Bayh, Morris Udall, and 1972 vice presidential candidate Sargent Shriver on the moderate left; Henry Jackson and Jimmy Carter in the center; and Alabama Governor George Wallace on the right.[3] Bayh, Udall, and to a lesser extent Harris and Shriver were competing for the same constituency: young, liberal, college educated, white-collar. Jackson's appeal was supposed to be to union members and blue-collar workers, although it turned out to be to Jewish voters and older persons. Jimmy Carter was positioned so he could attract different voters from state to state depending on the nature of the opposition. There was considerable difference in the Carter constituencies in the North and South. In the North, his constant supporters were less educated, black, rural, and Protestant; in the South, he attracted a much wider following. The Wallace constituency was motivated by mistrust of government. They were conservative, law and order types with high school educations, and tended to be middle aged with average incomes (Orren, 1978).

The general structure of competition is less consequential in the Initial

---

[3] Other announced candidates were Pennsylvania Governor Milton Shapp, Duke University president Terry Sanford, Texas Senator Lloyd Bentsen, and anti-abortion candidate Ellen McCormack. California Governor Jerry Brown and Idaho Senator Frank Church entered later.

Contests, though, than who is entered in each state. In Iowa, as we have seen, Carter had been campaigning for a year. Fred Harris had also been working for some time, although there was less popular support for the populist positions he was taking. When Birch Bayh made his late decision to run, he elected to make an effort in Iowa, and Morris Udall reversed his decision to have his early focus in New Hampshire and made a last minute effort in Iowa. Sargent Shriver, the only Catholic candidate, hoped for some support in Catholic areas. This meant that Harris, Bayh, Udall, and Shriver were all competing for the liberal vote, and Jimmy Carter was the only one appealing primarily to the moderate and conservative voters. "Uncommitted" won, receiving 37 percent of the precinct vote to Carter's 28, Bayh's 13, Harris's 10, and Udall's 6. "Uncommitted," however, was unavailable to appear on network television, whereas Jimmy Carter was in New York City, and appeared as the Iowa winner on NBC's "Today," ABC's "Good Morning America," and "CBS Morning News" the following day (Drew, 1977, p. 16).

The field of candidates was identical in New Hampshire. The principal difference in campaigns was that both Carter and Udall were well organized. The Udall campaign was headed by David Evans, a 1972 McGovern worker, and Maria Currier, the 1972 state coordinator for Muskie. They organized a thorough canvass, that is, contacting voters to ask who they supported and thus learn who was likely to vote for you. The Carter campaign had both a door-to-door canvass and a telephone canvass. The Bayh campaign tried using volunteers over the weekend to canvass, but couldn't match Carter and Udall (Witcover, 1977, chap. 16). Fred Harris had been helped by a small band of faithful supporters, and Sargent Shriver hoped to do better because of the Kennedy reputation in New England (he was married to Eunice Kennedy) and because of the larger Roman Catholic population. But the structure of competition was again Udall, Bayh, Harris, and Shriver competing for the liberal vote, and Carter appealing to moderates and conservatives. Udall was the best organized of the liberals and did better than other liberals; but the vote was 30 percent for Carter, 24 percent Udall, 16 percent Bayh, 11 percent Harris, and 9 percent Shriver. Jimmy Carter again appeared as the victor on television, and now predicted a first ballot nomination.

The structure of competition was different in Florida. This time the major candidates were Henry Jackson, relatively liberal on everything except foreign policy, Jimmy Carter in the center, and George Wallace on the right. The Wallace vote was assumed to be reasonably fixed because of Wallace campaign efforts in Florida in past years, and because large numbers of Florida immigrants come from Alabama. The question was how the non-Wallace vote would be split between Jackson and Carter. And it happened that there were quite a few Georgians who had moved to Florida (Gatlin, 1973), and Carter had been busy campaigning for a year. In the campaigning just before the election, Jimmy Carter became particularly critical of Henry Jackson because both were fighting for the same vote. And it turned out that the non-Wallace vote was larger in 1976 than it had been earlier, and Jimmy Carter got more of it than Henry Jackson. Carter ended up with 34 percent of the vote, Wallace with 31, and Jackson with 24.

The Carter strategy had been an Initial Contests strategy. Virtually all of their resources—campaign time, organization, money—had been committed to the early contests in Iowa, New Hampshire, and Florida. Carter national finance director Joel McCleary later explained, "We had no structure after Florida; we had no organization. We had planned only for the short haul. After Florida, it was all NBC, CBS, and the *New York Times*" (Arterton, forthcoming). If this Initial Contests strategy had not worked out, the Carter campaign would have been in serious difficulty, but luck had been with them, and at the end of this phase Jimmy Carter had established himself as a significant contender.

Goldwater, 1964 New Hampshire, the only consequential early primary in 1964, should have been a state where Barry Goldwater could have done very well. Many of his positions were appealing to conservative New Hampshire Republicans, and important Republicans leaders—Senator Norris Cotton, a former governor, the Speaker of the House, and the Senate President—all identified themselves with Goldwater. But quarrels developed between responsible persons, such as Senator Cotton, and volatile right-wing types, such as *Manchester Union-Leader* publisher William Loeb; Senator Goldwater himself was in some pain from recent surgery on his heel; and Goldwater made a number of politically vulnerable statements, such as "most people who have no skills have no education for the same reason—low intelligence or low ambition."

Nelson Rockefeller was disappointed so many leaders were working for Goldwater, but put together a reasonably strong slate of his own, and visited no less than 82 communities between the time of his announcement and the March 10 primary. Rockefeller and the skilled publicists working for him took advantage of Senator Goldwater's gaffes, stating, for example, that imperfect operation of the economic system was to blame for unemployment rather than the laziness or stupidity of those who were out of work. Rockefeller's efforts were reflected in polls, which showed him catching and then passing the senator from Arizona.

While the conservative Goldwater and the liberal Rockefeller were the only actively campaigning candidates, they did not represent the entire structure of competition. There were two serious write-in efforts on behalf of moderate Richard Nixon and liberal Henry Cabot Lodge. The expensive Nixon campaign, led by former Governor Wesley Powell, did not produce too much. The Lodge campaign did. Henry Cabot Lodge was unpopular with Republican leaders but popular with voters. His campaign was conducted by volunteers. A mailing was sent to an old list of known Republicans and this elicited 10,000 pledge cards. The 10,000 were sent instructions on how to write in Lodge's name, and asked to contact friends. The media paid very little attention to all this, and were consequently quite surprised when Lodge received 36 percent of the vote, compared with 21 for Goldwater, 20 for Rockefeller, and 17 for Nixon.

Henry Cabot Lodge was helped by these results, but was unwilling to come home from Vietnam to campaign. Hence the New Hampshire primary was not a decisive event, but one that indicated to Goldwater and Rockefeller that they would have to seek success elsewhere. Senator Goldwater turned his attention to a restructuring of his staff and strategy, and Governor Rockefeller went back to Albany to deal with the state legislature (which was then in session) and to lay plans for the Oregon primary.

Ford versus Reagan, 1976   There is little puzzle about the structure of competition in a two-person race. Here it was moderate versus conservative, although it wasn't quite a straight ideological contest. Gerald Ford won some support from conservatives because he was president, and Ronald Reagan had some appeal to middle-of-the-road Republicans because of his platform skill. Still, both camps placed great importance on the Initial Contests, and both tried to rob the opponent of credibility. The Ford campaign sought to depict Ronald Reagan as given to irresponsible ideas, and the Reagan campaign sought to convey the idea that President Ford was not an effective leader.

Many early polls in New Hampshire gave Reagan a lead, and the Reagan campaign tried to hold this lead with "Citizens' Press Conferences," in which members of the audience (rather than experienced reporters) asked questions. In his replies, Reagan did not attack Ford directly, but placed himself on the side of "the people" as opposed to "the government." Defense spending? "Well, here again, is where I believe a president must take his case to the people, and the people must be told the facts." Angola? "The government has left the American people in complete ignorance." He stressed that he was an outsider, "not part of that Establishment in Washington, and therefore not part of that buddy system that goes on." Reagan spent 15 days in the state, and the applause lines from the Citizens' Press Conferences were used in television commercials.

That Reagan was unable to hold his lead over Ford was partly due to an improvement in the economy, which helped the incumbent, and partly due to the skill of Ford campaigners, especially Stuart Spencer. In September, Ronald Reagan had given a speech in Chicago that included the claim that "transfer of authority in whole or in part [in welfare, education, housing, food stamps, Medicaid, community and regional development, and revenue sharing] would reduce the outlay of the federal government by more than $90 billion." Not much attention was paid at the time, but it caught Spencer's eye and he had some research done on its implications. Peter Kaye, the press secretary, made arrangements for the New Hampshire Speaker of the House and the Senate President to hold a press conference denouncing the plan on Reagan's first trip into New Hampshire, and the issue dogged Reagan throughout the campaign. Later, Reagan made a comment about investing social security funds "in the industrial might of the country," and Commerce Secretary Elliot Richardson promptly interpreted that as a suggestion to risk social security funds in the stock market (Witcover, 1977, chap. 25; Arterton, forthcoming). The improvement in the economy and television ads showing Gerald Ford at work in the Oval Office made the incumbent look a little better; questions raised about Ronald Reagan's proposals made him look a little less responsible; New Hampshire voters gave the president 50.6 percent of their vote.

The Florida primary was another in a conservative state that was won by the moderate Mr. Ford. Three things helped Ford here. First, Stuart Spencer had hired the other half of the Spencer-Roberts campaign management firm, Bill Roberts, and had placed him in charge of the Florida campaign. Second, the president, having won New Hampshire by however narrow a margin, seemed stronger, and this impression was helped by uncontested victories in Vermont and Massachusetts. Third, Ford began to remind people he was the head of the federal government, announcing such things as a missile contract award to a Florida firm and the completion of an interstate highway. On election night, the president got 53 percent of the vote, and the next day the *New York Times*'s R. W. Apple wrote that Reagan's loss had drastically reduced his chances. "With only two contestants, a consistent loser soon finds himself without the funds and the campaign workers to keep him fighting."

Eisenhower versus Taft, 1952   Any doubt about the structure of competition in the 1952 Republican contest ended on January 6 when Senator Henry Cabot Lodge told a news conference, "I have been asked by Governor Sherman Adams of New Hampshire to enter General Eisenhower as a candidate for the presidency on the Republican ticket in the New Hampshire primary." Lodge said that he would do so, and added, "I am speaking for the general and I will not be repudiated." This promised that most of the groups that had made up the Dewey coalition in 1948 would support the popular World War II commander, and that the groups supporting Taft would once again rally behind their "Mr. Conservative."

John D. M. Hamilton, Taft's eastern campaign manager, had already been in New Hampshire, and had organized conservative Republicans, including *Manchester Union-Leader* publisher William Loeb, Wesley Powell (then administrative assistant to Senator Styles Bridges), and others. The Taft committee was chaired by Mayor Shelby Walker of Concord and Frederick Johnston, a veteran leader in Manchester. Taft campaigned on his own behalf.

Governor Adams had lined up seven former governors, Lane Dwinell, then Speaker of the House, Congressman Norris Cotton, and others on the Eisenhower side. The general did not campaign as he was still in France, but was represented by Senators Leverett Saltonstall, James Duff, Frank Carlson (and Lodge, of course), Congressmen Hugh Scott, Christian Herter, Walter H. Judd, and others associated with the internationalist wing of the Republican party. On election day, the absent Eisenhower received 57 percent of the vote, a sufficiently large margin to sustain his supporters' claim that he was electable.

Ten days later, after a five-day amateurish campaign, General Eisenhower received over 100,000 write-in votes in Minnesota, coming close to beating Harold Stassen who was listed on the ballot. This was hailed by *Time* (which was supporting Eisenhower along with the *New York Times* and the *New York Herald-Tribune*) as "a striking and momentous demonstration that an Eisenhower boom of tremendous proportions is sweeping across the land" (Keech and Matthews, 1976, p. 131). Not quite. In state conventions, Taft and Eisenhower had split the delegates elected in Oklahoma and North Carolina, and Florida had elected 14 Taft delegates to only one for Eisenhower.

Summary

In this chapter we have reviewed the first two stages of the nomination process, Early Days and Initial Contests. Both are necessary preludes for the activity that is going to take place, but neither reveals much about the ultimate outcome. For example, there was a good deal of Early Days activity in the summer of 1979. In the face of polls showing lower popularity ratings than any of his predecessors, Jimmy Carter took counsel with leaders in various fields who were summoned to Camp David. On his return to Washington, the president accepted the resignations of some cabinet members whose competence was not questioned but whose loyalty was. He stated that he was going to spend more time out listening to the people; then his first two trips were to Kentucky and Iowa, states where he had found support in 1976. Tim Kraft, a skilled organizer, was dispatched from the White House staff to become campaign director of the Carter-Mondale Reelection Committee. At the same time, Senator Edward Kennedy began putting more distance between himself and the Carter administration, and leading Democrats in New England states with early primaries announced plans to run as stand-in candidates for Senator Kennedy. None of this summer activity foretold whether Senator Kennedy was going to challenge President Carter for the Democratic nomination, but both men were positioning themselves for a contest which was a distinct possibility.

Much the same thing can be said about the Initial Contests. There is more information at this point about the structure of competition. By this point, you know who has decided to enter the lists and who is remaining on the sidelines. But the Initial Contests may not be very consequential. Few observers, for instance, were predicting the nomination of Senator Goldwater after the New Hampshire primary in 1964. There are two kinds of conclusions one can draw after the Initial Contests. One concerns the weakest candidates in a multi-candidate race who are forced out after the Initial Contests for lack of support. The other is that if there are two strong candidates with support across the country, and both do reasonably well in the Initial Contests, then it is likely (but not yet certain) that there will be a stable two-candidate race that will last through the Convention. For more than this, one has to wait for Mist Clearing, and it is to this stage of nomination politics that we now turn.

chapter 2

Nomination Coalitions: Mist Clearing and the Convention

MIST CLEARING

Carter, 1976 By the time the Pennsylvania primary approached, the Democratic structure of competition could be much more clearly perceived. There were fewer competitors, and enough delegates had been won so that one knew something about the relative strengths of the candidates, in addition to the ideological positioning. Birch Bayh had dropped out after the Massachusetts primary; Pennsylvania Governor Milton Shapp (he was not a major candidate, but if he had shown any strength at all, he might have figured more prominently in his home state primary) dropped out after Florida; Sargent Shriver after Illinois; Fred Harris after Wisconsin. George Wallace did not end his campaign, but he was not a serious candidate after Carter had beaten him in Florida, Illinois, and North Carolina. This left Morris Udall on the left, and Henry Jackson and Jimmy Carter in the center. The Carter coalition had 267 delegates at this point, Jackson 175, and Udall 150. Carter had only 18 percent of the 1,505 delegates needed for the nomination but 28 percent of those chosen thus far. Jackson, his nearest rival, had only 18 percent.

Senator Jackson had been pursuing a large state strategy. He had won in Massachusetts, and had won again in New York. Pennsylvania was the next state on his list. Since Jimmy Carter and Morris Udall were also on the ballot there, this race was watched very closely. Carter got 37 percent of the Pennsylvania vote to 25 for Jackson, and won 64 delegates to 24 for Udall and 14 for Jackson. Senator Jackson had been counting on organized labor, regular Democrats, and a good media campaign. Jimmy

Carter had actually done better with organized labor; the regular Democrats preferred noncandidate Hubert Humphrey; and because of heavy spending in earlier primaries and lack of federal matching funds (due to a Supreme Court decision), money wasn't available for the media campaign. The Carter managers had carefully set money aside for a Pennsylvania media campaign. Governor Carter did well throughout the state, benefiting especially from Protestants and small town–rural voters, both of whom are numerous throughout the Keystone State.

Hubert Humphrey now came under considerable pressure to become an active candidate. Two days after the Pennsylvania primary, Senator Humphrey called a press conference to say, "I shall not seek it. I shall not compete for it. I shall not search for it. I shall not scramble for it." Over the weekend, Senator Jackson withdrew. This left Jimmy Carter and Morris Udall, and Carter had twice as many delegates.

There were further developments. Governor Jerry Brown and Senator Frank Church became active candidates and both won some primaries. But the effect of their entry after Pennsylvania was to create a structure of competition, with Jimmy Carter in the center with 331 delegates, and on the left Morris Udall (174 delegates), Frank Church (0 delegates), and Jerry Brown (0 delegates). In fact, Carter did much less well in the post-Pennsylvania primaries; but with this structure of competition, it didn't make any difference.

Goldwater, 1964   "I must have goofed up somewhere" was the characteristically direct comment made by Barry Goldwater after New Hampshire, and his was the only campaign that changed much. The number of careless statements was reduced by the addition of good speech writers, and a policy that questions wouldn't be answered unless submitted in writing in advance. Even more important, an emphasis was placed on conventions rather than primaries, and an experienced delegate hunter, F. Clifton White, was added to the core group of inexperienced Arizonans. Others didn't alter their postures. Nelson Rockefeller kept trying as hard as he could, Henry Cabot Lodge remained in Saigon, and unpublicized efforts continued for Richard Nixon.

With Goldwater busy elsewhere and Lodge an absent candidate, Nelson Rockefeller was the only active candidate in the Oregon primary. His campaign was very well organized, and the results were the reverse of New Hampshire. Lodge had been running well ahead of Rockefeller (and everybody else) in the polls; but Rockefeller overtook Lodge and got 33 percent of the vote, to Lodge's 28. Goldwater and Nixon ran third and fourth, with just a little more and a little less than 17 percent, respectively. The Oregon results effectively ended the Lodge campaign, which had been sustained only by Lodge's popularity with the voters, and reestablished Rockefeller as a credible candidate.

Conventions were another story. In the West, for example, Arizona had met first, on April 18, and had of course elected a solid Goldwater delegation. In Nevada, April 24–25, Goldwater efforts had been led by Lt. Gov. Paul Laxalt, and all delegates were for Goldwater. Another Goldwater delegation was picked by the Wyoming convention on May 8–9. A Rockefeller delegation did win in Alaska, meeting just after the Oregon primary—but that was all (White, 1965). The net of convention work around the country was that by the end of May Goldwater had 368 publicly committed delegates. Eighty-six more were to be selected in California's June 2 primary. If Goldwater won these, then his coalition would be so large that there would be no effective way of stopping him. Three hundred and thirty-five delegates were to be selected after California, many in conventions that had been scheduled then by state leaders so they would have an idea how things were going to turn out. If Goldwater won in California, it was certain he would win enough more delegates to have a majority. If Rockefeller won in California, the outcome was open to question, but it was possible that Goldwater might be stopped short of a majority. So California was crucial.

Essentially, Rockefeller had a little more support among the voters; but it was quite soft, whereas the Goldwater support came from dedicated believers. Rockefeller campaigners, in the able hands of the Spencer-Roberts firm, did what they could, while Goldwater volunteers concentrated on classic precinct work. All the surveys, including Goldwater's, showed Rockefeller with a narrow margin among the voters; but Rockefeller only had 2,000 volunteers across the state, while Goldwater had 11,000 in Los Angeles county alone. Nelson Rockefeller did well, carrying 54 of California's 58 counties; but Barry Goldwater's majorities in the other counties, particularly in Los Angeles and Orange counties, were so large that Goldwater carried the state by a narrow margin.

Ford versus Reagan, 1976   Ronald Reagan's campaign did not look too strong after his defeat in the Initial Contests, and Ford sympathizers began to urge him to drop out of the race. There was one meeting between John Sears and new President Ford Committee chairman Rogers Morton about some conditions under which a withdrawal might take place (Witcover, 1977, p. 413). Three things, however, combined to revive the Reagan campaign. First, Ronald Reagan began to focus on three international involvement questions—detente, the Panama Canal, and Secretary of State Kissinger—on which his surveys had uncovered a fair amount of criticism of the Ford administration among Republican activists (Moore and Fraser, 1977, p. 46). Second, there was a nationally televised speech by Governor Reagan that brought in contributions at a time when the campaign was badly in debt. Third, many of the later primaries were scheduled in states where conservatives were quite strong.

Mist Clearing took place very rapidly. In the Texas primary, May 1, Ronald Reagan carried every congressional district and picked up 96 delegates. Even Senator John Tower, running as a Ford delegate, was defeated. In the Alabama, Georgia, and Indiana primaries on May 4, Ronald Reagan got 130 delegates to Gerald Ford's 9. This brought the strength of the Reagan coalition to 313 delegates to 241 for the incumbent president. These figures did not reflect the large New York and Pennsylvania delegations, formally uncommitted though likely to support Ford; but with many remaining primaries in conservative states, it was clear that this was a contest between two strong coalitions. It was not clear which would win.

Eisenhower versus Taft, 1952   If there had ever been any doubt that the 1952 contest would be between two equally matched coalitions, it should have vanished by the end of April. Supporters of General Eisenhower did reasonably well in the two primaries in which both Eisenhower and Taft were on the ballot. The general had won by nearly two-to-one in New Jersey, and by better than two-to-one in Massachusetts. Eisenhower also had fared well in an uncontested Pennsylvania primary, although the delegation was split three ways. These contests were in the East, though. Taft had won a write-in effort in Nebraska and had picked up a substantial number of delegates at the same time he was winning an uncontested primary in Illinois. In convention states, an Eisenhower delegation was selected from his native Kansas, a split delegation was picked in Iowa, and an uncommitted delegation was selected in Michigan. On April 30, the Associated Press delegate count stood at 274 for Taft, 270 for Eisenhower, 22 for Harold Stassen, 6 for Earl Warren, 2 for General MacArthur, and 141 whose preferences were unknown. The equal strength of the two coalitions was clear; the possible outcomes at this point included an Eisenhower nomination, a Taft nomination, and a deadlock.

THE CONVENTION

Carter, 1976   With the Carter coalition in firm control, there were no challenges to their leadership. Platform Committee members meeting in Washington in June were supplied with a 37-page statement of Carter's positions; Carter issues specialist Stuart Eizenstat was in attendance to handle the few questions that did come up; the Platform, which was adopted by the convention without controversy, did not contain any statements that were unacceptable to Jimmy Carter. The closest thing to a fight came on Rules Committee recommendations on representation at future conventions. A number of women wanted a requirement of equal numbers of male and female delegates, but the National Women's Political Caucus (not part of the convention, but influential with feminist delegates) voted to accept a Carter-proferred compromise that would encourage states to promote equal numbers of men and women in their delegations.

The only question of any consequence was who would be chosen as the vice presidential nominee. Governor Carter considered this with unusual care. In the weeks before the convention opened, information was gathered about potential running mates, the most promising were interviewed by Carter associates and then Carter himself interviewed the "finalists" either in Plains, Georgia, just before the convention or in New York City after his arrival at the convention site. The three to whom most serious consideration was given were all northern senators: John Glenn of Ohio, Edmund Muskie of Maine, and Walter Mondale of Minnesota. The choice went to Mondale because he was bright, the personal chemistry between Carter and Mondale was good, and Mondale had links to groups in the Democratic party where Carter himself was not strong. By attracting liberal support, Mondale broadened the Carter coalition as it moved from nomination politics to electoral politics.

Goldwater, 1964   The Goldwater coalition had the votes to win at San Francisco, but they did not escape challenge. Pennsylvania Governor William Scranton had mounted a last-minute campaign, which had the effect of giving moderate Republicans a rallying point. The Scranton coalition came from areas where the moderate wing of the party had been strong: the East, Michigan, Minnesota, Oregon. (Some of the votes from these states were cast for other candidates, but the moderates were working together.) The reason for the moderate challenges was not just that they disagreed with Goldwater positions. They disagreed all right; but, in addition, surveys had told them that Goldwater would be a real drag on all Republican candidates in the fall. Therefore they needed to distinguish themselves from Goldwater and Goldwater positions.

"We need a battleground," said a Scranton leader, "but they've got the screws turned down real tight." In fact, instructions to the Goldwater delegates were simply to support anything brought to the floor by those in charge of the convention. This was a classic posture for a winning coalition. They were more interested in preserving their strength for the presidential roll call than in taking part in ancillary skirmishes; but this also meant that the moderates were challenging convention leaders who were more likely than Goldwater leaders to come from the center of the party. Thus, when the moderates decided to make their fight on some platform planks, they were taking on one of the strongest Republican leaders, Congressman Melvin Laird of Wisconsin. Three issues were picked: extremism, civil rights, and nuclear responsibility. Each of these were issues on which the moderates were especially anxious to distinguish themselves from Senator Goldwater. The senator had said that he had been impressed by the type of people who belonged to the right-wing John Birch Society; he had voted against the Civil Rights Act of 1964, which had written the 1960 Republican platform statement on civil rights into law; he was hawkish on foreign policy, and was thought to look with favor on the use of nuclear weapons. But regardless of the issue, and regardless of the form in which the question was posed, the delegates rejected the moderate proposals by decisive votes. If the Goldwater coalition had wished to reach an accommodation with the moderates, it would have been simple enough. Certain of the moderate resolutions were deliberately worded so they could be reconciled with previous Goldwater statements.

On the presidential roll call the following evening, the Senator from Arizona received just over two-thirds of the votes. Governor Scranton moved to make the nomination unanimous, saying, "We must now be about the business of defeating the Democrats. . . . [L]et it be clearly understood that this great Republican party is our historic house. This is our home; we have no intention of deserting it." Rather than accepting this offer when he made his acceptance speech the next night, Senator Goldwater declared, "Anyone who cares to join us in all sincerity, we welcome. . . . I would remind you that extremism in the defense of liberty is no vice. And let me remind you that moderation in the pursuit of justice is no virtue." Clearly, the voices to be heard in the Goldwater campaign were to be those of unalloyed conservatism.

Ford versus Reagan, 1976   When the last delegate had been selected, the Reagan forces were in real difficulty. They had mounted the strongest challenge to an incumbent president in over half a century, but the *Washington Post* delegate count showed Ford with 1,093, Reagan with 1,030, and 136 uncommitted. With 1,130 needed to nominate, Ford stood a much better chance of getting the few uncommitted delegates. Furthermore, almost all of the ideological conservatives were already supporting Reagan. There was no further move open which would please his conservative supporters and impress uncommitted delegates. "What we direly needed," John Sears said later, "was some way to carry the fight, to get some maneuverability again. At this particular juncture, the perception was growing that if things stayed as they were, we were going to get counted out of the race" (Moore and Fraser, 1977, p. 48). What John Sears proposed, and Ronald Reagan accepted, was the announcement that if Reagan were nominated, moderate Pennsylvania Senator Richard Schweiker would be tapped as his running mate. As things turned out, this did not gain additional delegates for Reagan; but the unhappiness it caused within the Reagan coalition, specifically in the Mississippi delegation, ultimately led to an advantage for Ford.

John Sears selected a rules proposal as the vehicle for the Reagan coalition's principal tactical challenge. The proposal, known as Rule 16–C, would have required that presidential candidates make their vice presidential choices known before the balloting for president. There were two reasons for this selection. First, the uncommitted delegates were not ideological conservatives, and so might be more easily persuaded to support a "neutral" procedural point. Second, it was hoped that Ford's choice would cause some unhappiness within the Ford coalition, so that some Ford delegates could be wooed by Reaganites. This proposal was rejected on a 59 to 44 vote within the Rules Committee itself, but the decisive vote was to come on the Convention floor. At the end of that roll call, the vote stood 1,041 in favor of Reagan's 16–C motion and 1,112 against. Neither side had the 1,130 votes for a majority. Then Florida, where Ford had won an early primary, cast 28 votes for and 38 votes against, and Mississippi, the object of intense effort by the Ford leaders ever since the Schweiker ploy, cast 30 votes against. The principal Reagan challenge had been turned back.

There was one more vote to come. There were some determined conservatives, such as North Carolina Senator Jesse Helms, who had not been responsive to the Reagan leadership. They thought it would have been better to have the decisive vote on a "red meat" conservative policy issue, and presented a "Morality in Foreign Policy" amendment to the report of the Platform Committee. This was intended to symbolize the conservative belief in Moral Purpose, as opposed to the realpolitik of Secretary of State Henry Kissinger, but the amendment was stated in very general language and the Ford leaders decided not to oppose it.

Ford received 1,187 votes on the presidential roll call to Reagan's 1,070. The regional nature of their support was quite apparent. President Ford got 73 percent of the votes cast by eastern and midwestern delegates; Governor Reagan got 72 percent of the votes cast by southern and western delegates.

Reagan had agreed to a meeting with Ford afterward on condition that he not be offered the vice presidential nomination. Ford mentioned other persons he was considering, and Reagan said he thought Senator Robert Dole would be acceptable. The others who were given the most serious consideration—both before the Convention and in an all-night meeting between Ford and his advisors after he was nominated—were former Deputy Attorney General William Ruckelshaus, Senator Howard Baker, and Anne Armstrong, the ambassador to England. None were flaming liberals, but each would have broadened the ticket. In the end, it came down to Dole. Ford was comfortable with him; he was popular within the party; his nomination could be got through a conservative and unpredictable convention. In a sense, the selection of Dole was comparable to Carter's selection of Mondale and Reagan's of Schweiker. In each case, the presidential contender was reaching out for a vice presidential candidate who was representative of the other wing of the party. The difference was that when Carter, a moderate Democrat, picked a liberal Mondale, or when Reagan, a conservative Republican, said he would choose Schweiker, the tickets' chances in the general election were strengthened, whereas when moderate conservative Ford chose conservative Dole, the appeal of the ticket was narrowed.

Eisenhower versus Taft, 1952 When the 1952 Republican Convention met in Chicago, Senator Robert Taft had a lead in uncontested delegates. There were 458 uncontested Taft delegates, 406 uncontested Eisenhower delegates, 131 pledged to other candidates, 118 who were uncommitted, and 96 delegates whose credentials were challenged.[1] The most important of the contested delegates were 68 from Georgia, Louisiana, and Texas. In these states, rival delegations had been selected favoring Taft and Eisenhower. Seating the 68 Taft delegates would have given the senator a lead of 526 to 406. Seating the 68 Eisenhower delegates would produce a majority for the general of 474 to 458.

This looked as though it were a question to be settled tentatively within the Credentials Committee and finally by a floor vote on that committee's report.[2] Two moves were made in this direction. Senator Taft proposed a resolution of the disputed Texas delegates on a district by district basis that would have given him 22 and Eisenhower 16. Ex-President Herbert Hoover proposed that both sides appoint "an eminent citizen, not one of their own managers, to sit with me and see if we could find the basis of an agreement." Henry Cabot Lodge rejected the Taft offer, saying that "General Eisenhower is a no-deal man," and turned down the Hoover suggestion on the ground that it would be undemocratic for three men sitting in a room to make the decision. Then a manifesto was issued by 23 of the 25 Republican governors, most of whom were supporting Eisenhower, calling for a "Fair Play" rule under which all disputed delegates would be prevented from voting on any disputed delegate. (Otherwise the contested but temporarily seated Louisiana and Texas delegates would vote on which Georgia delegates to seat; Georgia and Texas would vote on Louisiana; Georgia and Louisiana would vote on Texas.) So the first test vote was to come not on the Credentials Committee report itself, but on a rule governing how the vote was to be cast.

With the "Fair Play" rule the Eisenhower leaders adopted high moral ground, portraying the Taft leaders as wanting to make deals behind closed doors. It also had important tactical advantages: it would reduce

---

[1] The careful reader may have noticed that the number of delegates differs from convention to convention. For example, 1,130 votes were needed for a majority in the 1976 Republican Convention, but only 605 votes were needed for a majority in the 1952 Republican Convention. In general, the number of delegates has been increasing over time, and Democrats have more delegates at their conventions than Republicans.

[2] Credentials Committees exist because there are sometimes fights between rival factions of local organizations, and both send delegations to the national convention. It is the job of the committee to determine which of the claimants have been properly selected according to the laws and party rules in that state.

the size of the Taft coalition on the critical vote, and was an issue on which the Eisenhower coalition could hope for support from uncommitted delegates and those pledged to other aspirants, such as California Governor Earl Warren. The "Fair Play" rule was rejected in the Credentials Committee, but this was not decisive. Convention committees have equal representation from each state (as does the U.S. Senate), but more populous states have larger delegations on the floor. When the crucial vote came, the Eisenhower coalition won 658 to 548.

While making preparations for the vote on seating the contested delegations, Eisenhower managers had also been busy recruiting other delegations to their coalition. Maryland delegates were picked up when Governor Theodore McKeldin agreed to nominate Eisenhower, and Pennsylvania delegates led by Governor John Fine, and Michigan delegates led by national committeeman Arthur Summerfield both decided to support Eisenhower. With the addition of these three groups and those from Georgia, Louisiana, and Texas, the Eisenhower coalition led the Taft coalition by a vote of 595 to 500 at the end of the first ballot.[3] Minnesota, which had cast 19 votes for their ex-Governor Harold Stassen, switched all their votes to Eisenhower, and it was all over.

THE STRUCTURE OF COMPETITION

How did we end up with these two candidates? Can't America do better than Ford and Carter? Or Nixon and McGovern? Or whoever the major party nominees happen to be in 1980? This question is asked constantly during presidential election years. It reflects dissatisfaction with the quality of the nominees; but it may also reveal a lack of understanding of what the nominees represent. Our president is a symbol for our country. He is treated with respect; we speak of his wife as the First Lady. There is an implication here that he should be the best among all Americans. This isn't necessarily so. The best person, depending on the context, may be a pathbreaking scientist, a skillful surgeon, an accomplished musician, or someone who has demonstrated his or her talent in any of a dozen different pursuits. What we need from a president is not talent or virtue measured on some absolute scale but political leadership. Specifically, he should advocate policies that are acceptable to a majority of citizens, and have the competence to get these policies accepted and implemented. It follows that a presidential nominee should represent policies that are acceptable to a majority of the members of a political party, and that the party members think he or she can do the job.

---

[3] The Eisenhower coalition had 80 percent of the delegates from the East while the Taft coalition included 62 percent of those from the Midwest. Taft had a slight edge in the South, 52 percent to 45 percent, and western delegates were evenly split between Eisenhower, Taft, and Governor Earl Warren of California.

Acceptable policies and personal competence are not unrelated to winning the nomination, but they are tested by the candidate's ability to win delegates. As we have seen, this means that a great deal depends on the structure of competition. Suppose there had been a moderate midwestern governor in 1976 who had split the moderate Democratic vote with Jimmy Carter in Iowa and New Hampshire. This would have meant that Birch Bayh would have gotten the most delegates in Iowa, and that Morris Udall would have been the winner in New Hampshire. Or suppose that Henry Cabot Lodge had not been entered as a write-in candidate in New Hampshire in 1964. This would have meant that the liberal Republican vote would not have been split between Lodge and Rockefeller, and Nelson Rockefeller would have emerged as a credible candidate from the first primary. We can't be sure of these "might-have-beens," but we can be certain that winning or losing a presidential nomination does not depend on the intrinsic merit of the candidate. *Success in nomination politics does depend on both the strategy that is followed and on the structure of competition.*

Frank Mankiewicz, Senator George McGovern's 1972 campaign director, compared the success of the McGovern strategy to bidding a grand slam in bridge. "You get to the point where your partner puts his cards down and you see it can be won, but only if the trumps break right, if the queen is where you want it and all the finesses work" (Lydon, 1972). The 1972 structure of competition had McGovern and New York Mayor John Lindsay on the left, Senators Hubert Humphrey and Edmund Muskie in the center-left, Senator Henry Jackson and Congressman Wilbur Mills, long-time chairman of the Ways and Means Committee, in the center-right, and Governor George Wallace on the right. McGovern was stronger on the left than Lindsay (who dropped out after Wisconsin), and Wallace was more popular in the South than Mills. The Muskie campaign collapsed midway through the primaries, and Jackson did not prove to be a strong candidate. Consequently, the final structure of competition had McGovern on the left, Humphrey center-left, and Wallace on the right. There were votes on the right, but not enough to nominate Wallace, and given the 1972 delegate selection procedures (Lengle and Shafer, 1976), McGovern got more delegates than Humphrey. Did this prove that George McGovern was the best Democrat who could have been nominated in 1972? Not at all! It is simply another illustration that winning the nomination means that the candidate's strategy has been successful in view of the structure of competition in the party that year.[4]

A second major point we have seen in this chapter is that *there is a fundamental difference between a multiple-candidate structure of competi-*

---

[4] The success of the strategy implies, of course, that a goodly number of Democrats approved of McGovern's policies and thought him competent. Otherwise, he would not have been able to win the requisite delegate support.

tion and a two-candidate structure of competition. We have seen multiple-candidate structures of competition in the cases of the Carter and Goldwater nominations, and two-candidate structures of competition in the cases of the Ford and Eisenhower nominations. In the Carter and Goldwater instances, it was not at all clear during Early Days which candidates would emerge from the nomination process. Once Carter and Goldwater did emerge during Mist Clearing, though, the odds were against anyone else being able to mount a challenge against them. In the Ford versus Reagan and the Eisenhower versus Taft cases, the structure of competition remained very much the same from Early Days on through the Convention itself. Eisenhower was actually behind in committed delegates when the 1952 Convention opened, and it was very late before President Ford finally got enough delegate pledges to secure his 1976 nomination.

John Aldrich, who has developed a formal model of the nomination process (1979), has found that a multiple-candidate structure of competition is inherently unstable. His reasoning is this. Each candidate (and the reporters covering them) develops expectations about how well he should do. If they do better than expectations, they have positive momentum. If they just meet expectations, there is a "that's just what they were expected to do" reaction. If they do less well, then their campaign is in trouble. "The larger the number of candidates," Aldrich writes, "the greater the number who cannot possibly meet . . . expectations. Thus, very early in the contest, we should expect the field to be 'winnowed-down' to a much smaller number of viable candidates" (p. 40). In other words, Fred Harris, Sargent Shriver, Birch Bayh, and Morris Udall could not possibly get the same liberal Democratic votes in 1976, and Ronald Reagan, John Connally, Robert Dole, and Philip Crane were all fighting for the same conservative Republican votes in 1980. With a two-candidate contest, on the other hand, both coalitions could have legitimate expectations of getting about half of the delegates over time. These expectations have a better chance of being borne out, and if they are successful this structure of competition can remain stable from Early Days on through the Convention.

A third conclusion about the structure of competition is that *the four stages of nomination politics can be understood in terms of increasing information about the structure of competition.* During Early Days, we do not even know who all the competitors will be. Some plausible candidates may consider making the race, then decide not to do so. When Initial Contests begin, we know who the candidates are and who is likely to be fighting for liberal, centrist, and conservative votes, but we do not yet know which of the candidates will be successful in attracting this support. By Mist Clearing, information about the delegate strength of the surviving coalitions can be added to the left-right positioning of the candidates. This gives much more substantial information about the structure of competition than earlier guesses based on the momentum a candidate is thought to have established. Finally, test votes at the Convention provide nearly complete information about relative coalition strength. Even the absence of a test vote may suggest that a winning coalition is in too strong a position to be challenged.

Knowing that the structure of competition is important leads to a more general point. Structure is important. The structure of competition is only one part of the structure that shapes nomination politics. What we have seen in these brief sketches of four nominations is the gradual organization of a winning coalition around the successful candidate. These coalitions have both *internal structure*, which depends on their composition, and *external structure*, which includes those activities the coalition must carry on to reach audiences whose support is necessary and those activities that are shaped by the context in which the coalition finds itself. It is also the case that both internal structure and external structure change as the coalition moves through the four stages of nomination politics. The internal structure becomes more complex, and the external structure varies as the context changes. To see this, we shall look in a little more detail at internal structure and external structure.

INTERNAL STRUCTURE

The idea of internal structure follows from an observation made by Herbert Simon (who won the Nobel Prize in economics for his work on decision-making) in 1952: "Complexity in any body of phenomena has generally led to the construction of specialized theories, each dealing with the phenomena at a particular 'level.' Levels are defined by specifying certain units as the object of study and by stating the propositions of theory in terms of intra-unit behavior and inter-unit behavior. (Compare the sequence of elementary particle-atom-molecule in physics and the sequence: gene-chromosome-nucleus-cell-tissue-organ-organism in biology)" (pp. 1030–31). Levels of analysis may thus be understood as nested concepts. The unit on any particular level is made up of smaller components from a less-inclusive level. The same unit is also contained within a larger unit on a more-inclusive level. Atoms are made up of elementary particles, and are contained within molecules. Similarly, groups are made up of individuals, and are contained within coalitions.

For our purposes, a coalition will be understood as having three analytical levels, each with its own set of attitudes and behavior. At the first level, there is the *activist*, a citizen who is active in politics. The activist's attitudes are a set of valenced cognitions about political objects;

and the set of behaviors include those appropriate to nomination politics, electoral politics, or whatever form of politics the activist is engaged in. The concept on the next level is the *group*, which is defined as a set of activists. The group attitudes are those shared attitudes on such topics as the group's goals, norms, and environment; the group behaviors are those that fall into a reasonably stabilized pattern of interaction. A *coalition* is composed of a set of groups. The most important coalition attitudes are those that fall into the intersection of the sets of attitudes of member groups. Coalition behaviors need not be overtly coordinated, but the member groups are dependent on each other for achievement of the coalition goals.

The social sciences have developed rich theories of individual behavior, group behavior, and coalition behavior, and these definitions follow from these theories. There are also implications that flow from the definitions. A coalition is not just a collection of individuals. Rather, one must consider the groups to which the activists belong, and understand how the shared attitudes of the groups modify individual behavior, and consider which coalitions could be constituted from the existing groups. For example, the Carter coalition at the 1976 Democratic Convention included groups originally elected as Jackson delegates, and groups originally elected as Wallace delegates. Neither the Jackson delegates nor the Wallace delegates shared the enthusiasm for Jimmy Carter of the larger number of groups originally elected as Carter delegates, and the Jackson delegates and Wallace delegates did not agree with each other about a number of policies. In the 1976 Republican Convention, there was a group of doctrinaire conservatives who were responsive to the leadership of Senator Jesse Helms and thus unwilling to cooperate with the strategy suggested by leaders of the Reagan coalition. Thinking this way about the composition of a coalition suggests where tensions are apt to develop and thus helps to understand coalition behavior.

How does the internal structure of a coalition develop in the four stages of nomination politics? Until the candidate decides to seek the nomination in Early Days, there isn't any meaningful distinction between internal and external structure. At most, there are groups of potential supporters. These may include enthusiasts without any close ties, such as the liberal Republicans who wanted to get Eisenhower to run in 1952, or the liberal Democrats who were anxious for Edward Kennedy to run in 1980. There is also likely to be a group of close advisors with whom the candidate takes counsel, and who may perceive a possible candidacy when it is invisible to everyone else. The tiny group of Georgians who began thinking about the possibility of a Carter candidacy is an example of this.

Depending on the skills contained within this core group, they may constitute all the structure there is for a while, or they may recruit a few key persons, such as a press aide, fund raiser, and so on. The next groups likely to be created are those who will run the campaign in those states where the Initial Contests will take place. If the campaign does not meet expectations, the structure—as the candidacy itself—may collapse at this point. Otherwise, the initial group of delegates is acquired and coalition building begins.

The first groups of delegates are likely to admire the candidate and to be in close agreement with the candidate on policy questions. By the Mist Clearing stage, this may not be so. Assuming the candidacy is still viable, two closely related things are likely to have happened. The appeal of the candidate is likely to have changed from "Our Governor is the perfect candidate for you" to "Our Governor may not be the *perfect* candidate for you, but he's certainly better than any of the other candidates and he stands a real chance to win." Morris Udall used a version of this argument in the spring of 1976 when he said he was the only horse the liberal Democrats had to ride. If the candidacy continues to be successful, though, different groups of delegates are going to be attracted—groups whose first choice was some other contender and who are not likely to be in full agreement with the candidate on policy questions. Therefore coalition management becomes more of a priority, both because of the greater number of groups in the coalition and because of the increasing diversity of the groups.

By the time of every recent convention, there has been a winning coalition in being. This means, of course, that the leaders of the winning coalition need to stay in touch with all of their member groups, and keep them on board. Leaders of challenging coalitions want just the opposite. This means that appeals will be focused toward those groups thought to be unhappy for one reason or another, and on issues that the groups are unhappy about. Thus the Ford coalition began to woo Mississippi delegates just as soon as Ronald Reagan announced that he was going to tap Richard Schweiker as his vice presidential nominee. And when a story appeared in the *Birmingham News* on the night of the crucial 16–C vote, headlined "Ford Would Write Off Cotton South?", President Ford himself called Clarke Reed, Mississippi Republican chairman, to deny that such a strategy was being considered. The Ford leaders did not want to hand that issue to the Reagan coalition and give them a chance to appeal to groups of Ford delegates in the South.

The composition of the coalitions has a great deal to do with the policies endorsed by the convention when the platform is adopted or a candidate is nominated. In 1968, for example, James Clarke and John Soule found that 85 percent of the Democratic delegates and 90 percent of the Republican delegates said that the most important attribute for a presidential candidate was agreement in principle between the candidate and the delegate (Clarke, 1970). In 1972, Jeane Kirkpatrick reported that 90 percent of the Democratic delegates and 81 percent of the Republican delegates said that a chance to influence the party on policy was either an extremely important or a quite important reason for their participation in politics (1976, p. 101).

Not only are policies important, but there is some consistency over time in the groups that join liberal and conservative coalitions. A study of five contested Democratic conventions since 1952 found that the state delegations with the most liberal voting records were Wisconsin, Oregon, Arizona, New Hampshire, Michigan, Massachusetts, Iowa, South Dakota, Vermont, and New York; those with the most conservative voting records were South Carolina, Louisiana, North Carolina, Texas, Delaware, Arkansas, Florida, Kentucky, Missouri, and Georgia. A parallel study of six contested Republican conventions since 1940 shows the states with the most moderate voting records were Connecticut, New York, New Hampshire, Oregon, Vermont, Maine, New Jersey, Michigan, Massachusetts, and Maryland. The state delegations with the most conservative voting records were: Texas, Mississippi, California, Alabama, North Carolina, Idaho, Louisiana, Ohio, New Mexico, and Oklahoma (Costain, 1978, app. 2). In the three Republican nominations we reviewed, the moderate states all voted for Eisenhower in 1952, for Scranton (or another non-Goldwater candidate) in 1964, and for Ford in 1976. The conservative states all voted for Goldwater in 1964, and for Reagan in 1976.[5]

The Republican coalitions have been a little more stable from convention to convention than the Democratic. There has been a strong tendency for southern Republicans to be conservative, and for the East plus Michigan, Minnesota, and Oregon to end up in moderate coalitions. Still, comparison of these findings with an earlier study (Munger and Blackhurst, 1965) indicates that recent coalitions are less regional in character. The left coalition in the Democratic party includes groups of delegates from all regions except the South. The right coalition in the Republican party includes groups from all regions except the East. Increasingly, Democratic conventions are ending up as contests between left and non-left coalitions, and Republican conventions as struggles between right and non-right coalitions (Costain, 1978). Hence, the change in internal structure from

---

[5] There is one exception, and it is instructive. Ohio voted for President Ford in 1976 (and Governor Rockefeller in 1968). Ohio's position as a stalwart in conservative coalitions in earlier conventions was because Ohio's Senator Taft had so often been the conservative candidate. While we can generalize, each nomination is a fresh contest. There are changes in both states and delegates. The California Republican Assembly whose hero in 1976 was Governor Ronald Reagan was a very different group than the California Republican Assembly in 1952 whose hero was Governor Earl Warren. There is also a high rate of delegate turnover. From 1944 through 1968, 65 percent of Republican delegates and 64 percent of Democratic delegates were attending their first conventions (Johnson and Hahn, 1973, p. 148).

Early Days to the Convention is apt to be a transition from a group composed of the candidate and his closest advisors to a coalition whose groups have been drawn from all parts of the country.

EXTERNAL STRUCTURE

Each coalition exists in a specific institutional context, and each institution has certain functions. In order to carry out these functional requirements, the coalition must be able to attract the attention and support of certain audiences. For a nomination coalition to succeed, it must be able to gain delegates. To do this, the coalition must be able to reach *reporters, voters in primary election states,* and the *delegates* themselves. Their chances of successfully doing so are affected by the *structure of competition,* the *legal requirements that set the dates and conditions of delegate selection,* and the *convention rules.* In nomination politics, external structure is focused on these half-dozen elements. More generally, it embraces the structured activities carried forward to reach audiences whose support is essential, and those constraints that delimit the coalition's ability to do so.

In truth, it should be added that external structure is much harder to define satisfactorily than internal structure. A coalition is put together from the less-inclusive levels of analysis. So long as one knows which activists are included in which groups, and which groups are included in which coalition, the internal structure is completely specified. Looking outward from the coalition, virtually everything can be considered as part of its environment. The number of elements must be limited somehow or external structure would include so many things that it would be useless as a concept. Our way of limiting it will be to focus on those activities that are necessary for a coalition to carry out its institutional functions, and on the constraints that facilitate or inhibit it from doing so.[6]

We have already looked at one very important element of external structure—the structure of competition—in some detail. Clearly, it makes a difference whether a candidate is the only one who is appealing to a segment of party supporters or if the candidate is one of four fighting for the same votes. Now what else is there? From the time of the Early Days decision to enter until at least through the Initial Contests, perhaps the most important element of external structure is the media. There are two phrases used to refer to the traveling press corps: "surrogate audience" and "alternate audience." The former refers to the reporters' view of themselves; the latter to the politicians' view of the reporters (Arterton, forthcoming).

---

[6] External structure corresponds to what has been variously called contextual or institutional properties, or environmental constraints, except that temporal effects are separated out for distinct treatment.

The view of the reporters as surrogates implies that they are substitutes for citizens who are busy elsewhere, and that the reporters' task is to ask questions on behalf of the general public. The national political reporters who travel with the candidate during Early Days and prior to the Initial Contests are quite conscious that they constitute a screening committee who play an important part in the winnowing process (Broder, 1970, pp. 11–14). They carefully consider problems in reporting past campaigns—such as neglecting long-shot candidates who turn out to do quite well, putting too much attention on the "horse race" aspects of the campaign, not providing enough information about candidates so readers could make judgments about their character, not examining issues in enough detail—and do their best to prevent these problems from reoccurring (Matthews, 1978). The reporters' goal was to bring the public solid information about the serious candidates.

The campaigners, however, treat the reporters as an alternate audience, that is, one to be treated differently than the voters to whom candidate image and issue positions are being projected. The coalition leaders observe that the media gives greater coverage to "serious" candidates; therefore, they spend a great deal of time trying to convince the press that their candidate is "serious." Part of this is done by arranging the schedule of the candidate or campaign spokespersons, or both, so they can spend time with the press. Part of it is done by trying to manipulate press expectations so the candidate will meet them. For example, as a standard part of his itinerary in any community, Jimmy Carter met with newspaper editorial boards. Also, in New Hampshire, the Carter entourage consistently talked of New Hampshire as a race between Carter and Udall, thus distracting attention from the structure of competition advantage Carter had as the only center-conservative candidate in New Hampshire. The most advantageous thing that can be done, of course, is to be available at a time when there is hard evidence that the candidate had met the expectations of a serious candidate. Thus, instead of leaving to campaign in upcoming primaries in Massachusetts and Florida, Jimmy Carter stayed in New Hampshire to be available to the press when favorable returns came in. The result was that he was on all three television networks, and on the covers of *Time* and *Newsweek*.

When the Mist Clearing stage arrives, the surviving candidates have a changed relation with the press. First, they are now indisputable news sources and they will receive coverage without having to make special arrangements to make themselves available to reporters. For example, from the week of the Nebraska primary (just after the Texas, Indiana, Georgia, and Alabama primaries where he had done very well) until the primaries were over, Ronald Reagan received more coverage in the *Washington Post* than Gerald Ford (Aldrich, Gant, and Simon, 1978). Second, the size of the traveling press corps increases and there are more requests for information and interviews. This requires additional staff to handle the reporters. These two developments, the greater prominence of the candidate as a news source and the increasing number of requests for interviews, give the campaign somewhat more control over what is written. At the same time, when an aspirant is viewed as a likely nominee, his or her statements may be scrutinized more closely. For example, Jimmy Carter had been troubled for some time by a charge that he was fuzzy on the issues, a charge not unrelated to a Carter strategy that chose not to talk about the details of policy; but after his Pennsylvania victory, he began getting questions about where he stood on specific pieces of federal legislation (Matthews, 1978; Arterton, forthcoming; Witcover, 1977). This closer scrutiny after Mist Clearing means that a candidate may have more difficulty with issue positions he or she takes than heretofore in the campaign.

Another change in external structure at the Mist Clearing stage is a greater concern with the acquisition of delegates. Obviously, there has been some concern with this all along, but so few delegates are at stake in the early primaries that impressions of probable success are more important. Impressions, however, cannot move a candidate from the 200 or 300 delegates that establish her or him as a formidable contender to the 1,500 needed to nominate.[7] For example, Jerry Brown beat Jimmy Carter in Maryland by 48 percent to 37 percent. These results were described as "devastating" to Carter; but Carter had delegates running and Brown did not, and as a result, 44 of Maryland's 53 votes were cast for Jimmy Carter.

Delegate acquisition means the coalition must be able to work state (and district) conventions, and put on primary campaigns. In 1976, 22 states selected their delegates in some combination of caucuses and conventions. Missouri, Minnesota, Virginia, and Washington were the largest of the states doing so. But 76 percent of the Democratic delegates and 71 percent of the Republican delegates that year were selected in primary elections, so the ability to put on a primary campaign that impresses the voters in a state is now more important than the capacity to bargain with state political leaders who are presumably influential in conventions. This, in turn, calls attention to another important feature of external structure in nomination politics: the rules that specify how delegates are going to be allocated to one candidate or another. There are three basic forms of primary elections used: a winner-take-all system, in which the candidate with the largest number of votes gets all of that state's delegates; a proportional scheme, in which each candidate who gets more than some minimum number of votes receives a proportionate share of

---

[7] These numbers are simply illustrative. As already noted, the actual numbers of delegates vary from one convention to another.

the state's delegates; and a district plan, in which delegates are divided among candidates depending on who gets how many votes within congressional districts. The rules that were used vary from state to state, but each had some variation of these basic forms. The rules did have an effect in 1972. Senator Hubert Humphrey, not Senator George McGovern, received the largest number of votes in the Democratic primaries. If winner-take-all rules had been in effect, Humphrey would have gone into the California primary well ahead of McGovern in the number of delegates (Lengle and Shafer, 1976). The voting rules did not affect the outcome in 1976. Both Ford and Carter would have obtained the largest number of delegates under winner-take-all, plurality, or districted rules (Pomper, 1977; Gerston, Burstein, and Cohen, 1979); but the voting rules remain as potential influences, depending on which rules are in effect and how close the race is.

The Convention is the stage of nomination politics that has the most elaborate set of rules. A Convention organizes itself by receiving a series of committee reports: credentials, permanent organization, rules, and platform. In our brief review of four nomination contests, we have seen battles waged over three of these. There was a fight over the rules governing which credentials would be accepted (the "Fair Play" amendment in 1952); there was a fight over platform planks on foreign policy, civil rights, and extremism in 1964; there was a fight over rules governing when a vice presidential designee must be announced (Rule 16–C) in 1976. These were fights for tactical advantage. The challenging coalition wanted to have a contest on an issue where it might pick up extra votes, and the winning coalition wanted to preserve its strength for the presidential balloting, but these contests had intrinsic significance as well. The rules lead the competing coalitions to take various actions, and may favor one coalition rather than another. One rule that does favor certain delegates—Congress members—is a rule that states that the Convention shall proceed under the rules of the House of Representatives. The House rules are designed to allow business to be transacted in a large body, and this of course is what a National Convention is; but the House rules are different than the more familiar *Robert's Rules of Order*, and the Congress members who know which motion is proper to make enjoy a real advantage in a hotly contested floor fight. The platform does not affect the Convention itself, but has been shown (Pomper, 1968) to have real consequences for the actions of the executive and legislative coalitions to come.

Internal Structure, External Structure, and Time

Some actions taken by a coalition are due to its internal structure, to the activists who belong to the coalition, and to the groups into which their shared attitudes and behavior patterns assemble them. Other actions of a coalition are compelled by its external structure, by the activities necessary to gain support of those who will allow them to achieve their goals, and by the constraints fixed by the rules of the game.

The levels of analysis within a coalition (activist-group-coalition) remain constant across institutions (although *who* is recruited into the coalitions may vary), but the external structure of a coalition will differ from one institutional domain to another. In nomination politics, internal structure grows more complex as one moves from Early Days to the Convention, and external structure is different from stage to stage depending on the context. The actions of a coalition must be consistent with the demands of both internal structure and external structure. Perhaps the best example of this was Ronald Reagan's designation of Richard Schweiker as his prospective running mate. This was perfectly consistent with external needs—specifically the need to gain additional delegates among uncommitted moderates and the desirability of broadening the appeal of the ticket in the fall. But this was inconsistent with the shared attitudes of some groups within the Reagan coalition, most particularly the Mississippi delegation.

The view of a political party taken in this book is that what we can observe is a coalition in a specific institutional setting. There are other definitions—the party as a unifying symbol, for example—but we want to explain what a party does. The principal activity we want to explain, to understand, is the strategy adopted by a party, and for this purpose, coalition-in-institution is what we have to consider. Our general argument will be that *why* a coalition takes a particular action will sometimes be explained by its internal structure, sometimes by its external structure, and sometimes by both. *When* it takes a particular action will be explained by the temporal pattern of the institution in question.

Summary

Substantively, this section of the book has covered the two principal patterns of contested presidential nominations: the relatively stable two-candidate race, in which two strong contenders struggle from Early Days through the Convention itself, and the less-stable multi-candidate contest in which one candidate pulls away from the field. We have seen two examples of both of these. Ford versus Reagan in 1976 and Eisenhower versus Taft in 1952 both followed the classic two-candidate pattern. Carter in 1976 and Goldwater in 1964 are two examples of races in which one candidate was able to do so well that he was established as the probable nominee by the Mist Clearing stage. There is of course variation from one nomination to another, but if you understand these two basic patterns you ought to be able to explain future nominations.

Conceptually, this chapter has set forth the ideas of internal structure, external structure, and time. In nomination politics (as in other institutional domains), the internal structure of a coalition is made up of activists who are aggregated into groups. The external structure of a nomination coalition consists of the activities necessary to reach voters, reporters, and delegates, the structure of competition, the rules that determine how delegates will be allocated, and the rules and procedures of the Convention. The four stages of the temporal pattern are Early Days, Initial Contests, Mist Clearing, and the Convention. By using these concepts, you ought to be able to understand the strategies employed by those seeking presidential nominations.

part II

ELECTORAL
POLITICS

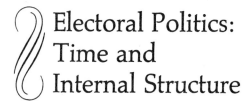

chapter 3

Electoral Politics: Time and Internal Structure

Introduction

There are substantial differences between nomination politics and electoral politics. Nomination coalitions are made up of those groups willing to give their all for a particular candidate, whereas electoral coalitions are usually made up of all groups in the party. Nomination campaigns are aimed at getting delegates; electoral campaigns are aimed at winning votes.

Primary elections begin in late February and last until early June. The general election takes place in every single state on the same day in November. The planning and organization for nomination politics begin a couple of years before the convention. All of electoral politics is compressed into the few months between the convention and the general election. In brief, electoral politics is partywide, nationwide, and short.

There are some hints of the nature of electoral politics in the closing hours of the national convention when the nomination has been captured and electoral politics has begun. After the acceptance speeches, division is put aside and the assembly is transformed into a victory rally. The presidential candidate is joined by the vice presidential candidate, and both are joined by their families. The cheers continue and traditional pictures are taken. Then other party leaders come forward—those who have played key roles and others who have sought the nomination themselves. At the 1976 Democratic Convention, the Carters and the Mondales were joined by so many prominent figures—Hubert

Humphrey, Henry Jackson, Morris Udall, national chairman Robert Strauss, and so on—that special efforts had to be made to get some people *off* the platform for fear the temporary structure might collapse. At the Republican Convention in Kansas City a few weeks later, President Ford was joined simultaneously by vice presidential nominee Robert Dole and outgoing Vice President Nelson Rockefeller. Then, after considerable public coaxing, Ronald Reagan came to the rostrum as well. The congregation of all the leading Democrats on their platform, and the simultaneous presence of the moderate Rockefeller and the conservative Reagan on the Republican platform, symbolized the partywide backing to be given to the nominees in the fall campaign.

In part, this demonstration of unity is aimed at the millions of voters watching on television across the nation. While coalitions have been struggling for the nomination, citizens have been making tentative voting decisions. From 1948 through 1976, an average of 39 percent report they have made their presidential choices before the conventions. Another 26 percent say they made up their minds during the conventions (Flanigan and Zingale, 1979, pp. 172–73). The remaining third of the electorate includes many who have only a minimal interest in politics. The faces on the convention stage constitute the image the party will present as they strive to gain the attention and win the support of these voters in November.

It would be a mistake, though, to think of this victory rally as *only* a public show. There is an affective unity—an emotional sense of belonging akin to that felt by a team of athletes—within a political party during an election campaign. The cheers of the delegates help to cement this feeling. Those who have supported the successful candidate experience the thrill of seeing him as the party nominee. Those who have worked just as hard for an unsuccessful aspirant get a chance for a few personal cheers when he comes to the stage. This common experience helps unify the party and set the stage for the campaign to come. After all, there is a great deal of work to be done by the party activists, and the time is very short.

In the preceding two chapters, we saw something of the patterns of nomination politics. In this chapter, we will focus on the temporal pattern of electoral politics and the internal structure of electoral coalitions. Then in the next chapter, we will turn to the external activities that are required to conduct an election campaign.

THE TEMPORAL PATTERN

THE STERN LIMITS OF TIME

The first thing mentioned by McGovern campaign director Gary Hart in his discussion of the differences between nomination politics and a general election campaign is that the latter "is a much briefer, more compact experience" (1973, p. 249). Of the various forms of politics, electoral politics has the most truncated time frame. Depending on when the national convention has been scheduled, there may be as much as three-and-a-half months between the convention and the general election or as little as two months. There is some plasticity in the limits within which one must work, but even if the party has opted for an early July convention, more must be accomplished in less time than in any other political setting.

It might seem that the campaign strategists would look ahead to this situation, and try to prepare for it by making plans for the election campaign. But this overlooks what the candidate and his closest advisors are doing prior to the convention. Winning the nomination itself has been the goal to which their actions have been directed for a good many months. It may be that there are real questions about winning the nomination. How would the Credentials Committee fight turn out in the 1972 Democratic Convention? Would McGovern get the disputed California delegates or would he have to split them with Humphrey, making things much closer? Would Ford be able to withstand the 1976 Reagan challenges on convention rules, and would his very narrow margin in delegate support hold up? And even if the candidate appears to have a large enough nomination coalition to win, obtaining these delegates has been the focus of attention of the candidate's strategists for a good many months, and they are likely to continue to organize their thinking around the imperatives of nomination politics. Questions about how the nomination is going to be insured—for example, Do you have good communication to the delegates on the floor?—occur to them more quickly than questions about what is to be done in an ensuing fall campaign.

There are, of course, some presidents who can look forward to their own renomination. (This is a smaller number than all incumbents. Some cannot seek another nomination because of the Twenty-second Amendment; others are subject to serious challenges from within their own party.) In this case, their attention may well be focused on the imperatives of executive politics. If they have a foreign policy crisis on their hands, or if the economy is shaky, they are going to give more attention to the troublesome policy area and not worry about the relatively distant general election campaign.

The implication is that the only candidates who can "expand" the time available for electoral politics are those who manage to assemble a winning nomination coalition early on, and who are themselves free from the responsibilities of office. In recent years, this would be only Nixon in 1968 and Carter in 1976. Another way in which some effective advance planning could be done would be for a politically strong incumbent president to authorize his campaign committee to take the necessary steps. Eisenhower did this with the Republican National Committee in

1956. The work done in advance of the conventions in these cases—for example, the careful selection of Walter Mondale as Jimmy Carter's running mate in 1976—has been important to the success of the general election campaigns. Still, such advance planning requires special circumstances. Since 1952, most of the electoral coalitions have not been able to focus on the fall campaigns until after the convention. The normal pattern forces them to work within tight, fixed time limits.

The sense of working within a very short period of time is reinforced by polls that repeatedly announce the candidates' standings. These serve as reminders that only so many weeks remain until the election—and in the elections from 1964 through 1976, these tidings were particularly ominous for one candidate or the other. In 1964 and 1972, the challengers began their campaigns far behind incumbent presidents; and while they made progress, they could not close gaps of such magnitude. The first postconvention poll in 1964 gave Goldwater all of 31 percent. This rose only to 39 percent by election day. In late August 1972, the Gallup Poll gave McGovern only 30 percent (excluding 6 percent undecided), and he, too, ended up with 39 percent in the election. In 1968 and 1976, candidates of the out party had commanding leads at the beginning of the campaign, but then saw them dissolve as the campaigns progressed. On Labor Day weekend in 1968, Richard Nixon had 43 percent of the vote to 31 percent for Hubert Humphrey and 19 percent for George Wallace. Come election day, Nixon received 43.4 percent of the vote, but Humphrey got 42.7 percent. After the 1976 Democratic Convention, the Gallup Poll gave Jimmy Carter a 62 percent to 29 percent lead over Gerald Ford; but in the election, Carter received just a shade over 50 percent while Ford got 48 percent. The challenging senators, Goldwater and McGovern, were trapped by time. The election was only a short way off, and in spite of their best efforts there seemed to be little they could do to convince the voters to move in their direction. In the 1968 and 1976 elections, supporters of the candidate whose lead was evaporating felt the election too far away. Still, all they could do was hope that the front-runner's lead would hold up until election day. From the Humphrey and Ford viewpoints, of course, the hope was that they would be able to gain fast enough to pass their rivals. But regardless of their position, all had their eyes on the calendar, and all knew that the season of passionate appeal to the electorate would be short.

One often hears pleas that American election campaigns be further shortened. The basis of the argument is that, especially after protracted nomination contests, the candidates are exhausted, campaign debts have been run up, and the voters are bored. There is something to this, and such an argument often is made by a weary campaign manager or a journalist who has gotten up at 6:00 A.M. time and again to cover another full day of campaigning. What the argument for a shorter electoral period overlooks, I think, is the number of things that must be done to conduct a presidential campaign on a subcontinental scale. Just as is true of nomination politics, there are a number of stages to a typical campaign, and it is hard to see how any of them could be omitted.

ORGANIZATION AND PLANNING

Organization and planning go on more or less simultaneously in the weeks following the national convention. The first question is who is going to fill the top jobs in the campaign organization. Not infrequently, more people feel they ought to be given top jobs than there are top jobs to fill. In 1964, for instance, Barry Goldwater decided that his long-time friend Denison Kitchell would be "head honcho," and that Dean Burch would be the chairperson of the Republican National Committee. But F. Clifton White, who had played an important role in rounding up delegates, very much wanted to be national chairperson, and so something had to be done about him. He was persuaded to accept the chair of Citizens for Goldwater-Miller. In 1972, George McGovern promised three people—Jean Westwood, Larry O'Brien, and Pierre Salinger—that each would be chairperson of the Democratic National Committee. It took some time to find assignments that O'Brien and Salinger were willing to accept after Westwood got the job.

Selection of a national chairperson is only the beginning. As we will see in Chapter 4, there are four principal activities that must be carried on by a campaign staff: campaign operations, public relations, research, and finance. Individuals must be recruited who have the skills and contacts to handle each of these responsibilities. And once the national appointments have been made, the head of the campaign division must locate regional coordinators, each of whom will handle the campaign in several contiguous states. The regional coordinators, in turn, must tap state coordinators.

The staff needed to run in successive primary campaigns is much smaller than the nationwide organization required for a general election campaign. As Hamilton Jordan recalled the 1976 Carter campaign: "Early on, we had three very talented people that we just rotated in the primary period from Iowa to Massachusetts to Ohio to Florida to Wisconsin to Maryland and then to New Jersey. Of the 45 or 50 state coordinators in the general election, only 5 or 6 had been involved in our campaign previously" (Moore and Fraser, 1977, p. 132). Where do the other 40-odd state coordinators come from? Some have been involved in the nomination campaigns of losing aspirants. Some have been identified in the course of spring contests, especially if the nominee had been entered in the primary in that state. Some come from other states. (The Kennedy organization in 1960 and the Carter organization in 1976 picked their state chairpersons from states other than those for which they had responsibility.) Perhaps the most fertile sources of leaders for the state campaigns are the regular party organizations in the state. Wherever the state chairpersons come from, the appointment will be cleared with the state party organization unless the circumstances are very unusual.

Finally, the state leaders have to recruit county leaders (or town leaders in New England). As we will see later in this chapter, the heads of presidential campaigns at the county level are largely Republican or Democratic activists who have been involved in previous presidential campaigns.

The organization of the campaign committees from nation to region to state to county has two consequences. The first is that there is a progressively greater overlap between the presidential campaign committees and the regular party organizations as one moves from the national to the county levels. While the Republican National Committee and the President Ford Committee had separate staffs located in separate buildings in Washington, D.C., the chairpersons of the Republican party and the President Ford Committee in Franklin county, Ohio, were well known to each other. Second, and more germane to our concern with the temporal pattern of electoral politics, all this organization takes time. The national chairperson has to pick a campaign director; the campaign director has to pick regional coordinators; the regional coordinators have to select state directors; state directors have to tap county leaders. Assignments must be made in research, public relations, and finance as well. Since each person selects his or her subordinates in consultation with other party leaders, the process goes on sequentially. Finally, all those who have been selected have to get to know one another and establish working relationships. It takes just as much time for a collection of individuals to become a functioning organization in electoral politics as in any other sphere of life. There is no way of rushing the creation of a nationwide campaign organization.

Planning begins as soon as individuals know what responsibilities they are going to have in the campaign. This involves decisions about geographic concentration, positions to be taken on issues, media use, how the candidate is to be portrayed, how the opposition candidate is to be attacked and by whom, what themes will tie all this together, and so on. Some of these things cannot be worked out in all detail in advance, but they are going to be decided *somehow*. It may be that a key decision will be made when a reporter asks the candidate a question, the candidate answers off the top of his head because he thinks an answer is required, and thus goes on the record with an issue statement or a characterization of his opponent. It may be that a partial plan will be thrown together hurriedly, as Joseph Napolitan did once Hubert Humphrey had won the Democratic nomination in 1968. "I'm writing the campaign plan," he told Theodore White. "Do you know there isn't *any* campaign plan? I have to get this ready by tomorrow!" (White, 1969, p. 338.) Or the plan may be quite comprehensive. The Ford strategy plan in 1976 ran 120 pages plus appendices, and went through eight drafts before it was presented to President Ford for his approval (Moore and Fraser, 1977, p. 118; Witcover, 1977, p. 530). There is considerable variation here; what is improvised in one campaign will be systematically planned in another. In one way or another, though, decisions will be made.

The Organization and Planning stage is not very visible to the general public. After the 1976 campaign, Hamilton Jordan was asked why the Carter people let so much time go by after the Democratic Convention without active campaigning. He replied: "Carter was in Plains most of the time with an occasional trip out, but we were busting our ass to put the fall campaign together. Tim Kraft and Phil Wise assembled a first rate field organization, and we got control of our budget. Rafshoon was working on the media, and Pat Caddell started doing surveys in critical states. The time was well spent" (Moore and Fraser, 1977, p. 130). What he could have added was that the Carter forces had time available to do this because the Democratic Convention had met in the first half of July. When a convention is held in late August, then the Organization and Planning stage is forced into the early weeks of the campaign proper. Whenever it comes, though, and however thoroughly or hastily it is handled, Organization and Planning is a necessary prelude to the rest of the campaign.

GRAND OPENING

The Grand Opening is the stage of the campaign when the efforts that follow from the plans made during the preceding stage first become visible to the public. This stage includes all those activities that have been designed with an eye to sustaining and increasing the candidate's standing with the voters. Just as the grand opening of a commercial venture is intended to bring customers to the establishment, and just as the opening night of a play is intended to spur lines at the box office, so the Grand Opening of a campaign should help maintain a front-runner's lead in the polls, or allow an underdog to catch up.

Grand Opening certainly includes the initial major speech and the first campaign swings. For instance, Democratic candidates have often given their first speeches in Cadillac Square in Detroit on Labor Day, and have then gone on about the country. Jimmy Carter chose to open his 1976 campaign on Labor Day with a speech at Franklin Roosevelt's "Little White House" at Warm Springs, Georgia, and then began a ten-state swing that took him to the Deep South, New York, Connecticut, Pennsylvania, the Midwest, and Florida. Incumbent presidents often stay close to the White House during the Grand Opening. Gerald Ford followed this pattern during September 1976, when he made any number of Rose Garden appearances. These were designed to keep the media spotlight on Jimmy Carter and permit Ford to appear presidential. The Grand Opening also includes any initial advertising. Carter media advisor Gerald Rafshoon had found during the primaries that when Carter advertising started before the opposition's, the campaigns could survive any anti-Carter advertising. Therefore the Carter campaign began their media campaign during the Grand Opening (Moore and Fraser, 1977, p. 128).

How long the Grand Opening lasts depends on whether the campaign strategy appears to be leading toward the hoped for results. Essentially, this stage of the campaign lasts as long as it is successful. Occasionally, a Grand Opening goes so well that it lasts for most of the campaign. Such was the case with the 1972 Nixon campaign. Even if the hopes of the campaign strategies are not being met, Grand Opening activities last for much of September. It takes at least that long to discover that things are not going well, and to devise an acceptable substitute course of action.

CAMPAIGN ADJUSTMENTS

The next stage of a campaign does not occur at a specific point in time, but when the need for adjustment becomes obvious. There are two general types of alteration: Tactical Adjustment and Strategic Adjustment. Tactical Adjustment is much the simpler of the two. It is a response to some event. This may be a news bulletin that calls attention to a policy area and therefore suggests the desirability of a demonstration of the candidate's competence to deal with the question. It may be some troubling development within the campaign organization, or an awkward statement by the candidate himself, such as Gerald Ford's reference to no Soviet domination of Eastern Europe in the second debate in 1976. The Tactical Adjustment in this last case included a public statement by the president that he knew there were divisions of Russian troops in Poland, a telephone call to Aloysius Mazewski, the president of the Polish-American Congress, and some meetings with ethnic group leaders. A Tactical Adjustment is focused on the original event, contained in time, and does not involve any general changes in campaign strategy.

A Strategic Adjustment is a somewhat more serious matter. It suggests the campaign may be in real difficulty. If a projection of poll results shows a probable election loss, then groups in the electoral coalition are going to make their unhappiness known. If there is enough expression of discontent, then the campaign strategists are likely to try some new approach. In part, this is because they can see the same difficulties as the members of the supporting coalition, and in part because they need to do something to convince workers that an effort is being made to extricate the campaign from its difficulties. A 1972 shift on the part of George McGovern from positive presentations of his own ideas to negative attacks on Richard Nixon is an example of the Strategic Adjustment intended to bolster the sagging fortunes of that campaign.

A Strategic Adjustment cannot be devised very quickly. It takes some time for complaints to work their way up through the campaign structure, and it takes more time for the strategy group to realize that the Grand Opening (in which they have some psychological investment since they approved it) is not bringing about the desired results. It requires still more time for the strategy group to agree on the nature of the adjustment. The Grand Opening probably represented the satisficing agreement (that is, one acceptable to all group members) they could reach most easily, and some time would be required to discover an alternative approach that is acceptable to coalition members and has some promise of persuading voters. In fact, enough time is needed to realize that a Strategic Adjustment is called for, and then to figure out what to do, that not more than one or two real Strategic Adjustments can occur in a campaign.

TIME'S UP

The last stage of a campaign is usually referred to by the media as the final drive or the climax of the campaign. It would be more accurate to call it the Time's Up stage. It is one of the ironies of electoral politics that the period just before the election is the time when the candidates have a chance to reach the largest possible audience because of the intense pre-election coverage, and is also the time when the strategists have the least control over what is happening. The meaning of Time's Up is that it is too late to make any more television commercials, too late to buy any more television time, too late to implement any new campaign emphases, too late to do the necessary advance work to prepare for additional campaign appearances. Too late, in sum, to do much more than carry out the plans that already have been made, and hope that these efforts will be rewarded when the voters reach the polls.

The manifest tone of the campaign in the Time's Up phase depends on the probable outcome of the election. If the candidate is far in front, then his public appearances will have the aura of triumph. Other candidates will jostle for the honor of appearing at his elbow. The candidate may be weary, but the adrenalin stimulated by being at the top of a career in politics is enough to keep him going through the final days. If the candidate is far behind, we are likely to hear some bitter comments about the voters' failure to understand or his coalition's inability to work hard enough. He is tired, knows he has done what he can, and needs to steel his ego against the bruises of defeat. If the race is close, then extra physical effort is put forth. It is hard to say where the reserves of energy that allow this come from. The extra bit of energy expended on the campaign trail means the candidate's voice sometimes fails, and he is bone weary. But in the Time's Up stage, it is too late to make any further plans or implement any new strategies. And since the extra bit of effort may make the difference, he gives it willingly.

Summary

Of all the major forms of politics, electoral politics has the shortest time span. The limits vary from three-and-a-half months to a little more than two. Organization and Planning, Grand Opening, Adjustments, and Time's Up stages follow one another in rapid succession. The hope that nominees bring from their Convention triumphs leads to electoral glory for one and weary defeat for the other.

INTERNAL STRUCTURE OF ELECTORAL COALITIONS

Introduction

Toward the end of Chapter 2, we saw that internal structure is defined in terms of three analytical levels: activists, groups, and coalitions. Now we want to see who the activists are that are involved in electoral politics, which groups their shared attitudes lead them to, and how these groups coalesce. Our purposes are more than descriptive, though. This analysis calls our attention to a series of important political questions. How long have the activists been involved in politics? Are they more interested in patronage or in the direction of public policy? Are their issue preferences representative of the communities where they live or are they closer to the preferences of fellow party members? Do the activists' shared attitudes make it more appropriate to think of parties as being made up of issue groups or of demographic groups? Do the coalitions that are formed by the groups tend toward the center of their respective parties or in a more polarized direction? The answers to these questions lead to very different kinds of political parties. If, for example, the activists are more interested in their own jobs, are simply spokespersons for their own communities, share attitudes with others in the same demographic categories (that is, union members, farmers, and so on), and form coalitions that tend toward the center of the political spectrum, then we have sluggish political parties that offer few choices to citizens. If, on the other hand, we have activists who are interested in issues, combine with others taking similar positions, and tend to form liberal or conservative coalitions (depending on the party), then the citizens are being presented with some policy choices to make.

CORE GROUPS AND STRATEGY GROUPS

The most important activists are those who belong to the *core group* and to the *strategy group*. The core group consists of the candidate's own confidants, persons he has known well or worked closely with for some years. In Jimmy Carter's case, this would certainly include Atlanta attorney Charles Kirbo, and both Hamilton Jordan and Jody Powell, who had been with Carter since his days as governor of Georgia. In Barry Goldwater's case, the most important members of the core group were Denison Kitchell, general counsel of Anaconda Copper and a close personal friend, and Dean Burch, the senator's administrative assistant who became Republican national chairman. If the candidate's wife is politically active, she would obviously be a member of this core group. For example, Rosalynn Carter and Eleanor McGovern would be among the most important of their husbands' political confidants, but Pat Nixon apparently was somewhat less active.

The strategy group is made up of those persons who are making the basic decisions about the campaign. Its membership is quite restricted, and it should not be confused with a publicly announced "strategy committee," some of whose members are likely to be key decision-makers while others are included because their status calls for some kind of recognition. There is likely to be at least a partial overlap between the core group of confidants and the strategy group of decision-makers. If the candidate himself is not present when the key decisions are being made (and he may be off campaigning somewhere), there must be persons present who know the candidate well enough to speak for him. There are also likely to be members who have important operating responsibilities in the campaign, but who *may* not be as well acquainted with the candidate. These opposite tendencies are illustrated by the two 1976 strategy committees. The Carter strategy group was virtually an extension of the core group. Kirbo, Jordan, and Powell were members, as were media consultant Gerald Rafshoon, pollster Pat Caddell, attorney Robert Lipshutz, issues specialist Stuart Eizenstat, Senator Mondale, and his ranking aide, Richard Moe. This strategy group was almost completely Georgian, and, with the exceptions of Mondale, Moe, Eizenstat, and Caddell, completely lacking in national campaign experience. The principal members of the Ford strategy group, on the other hand, consisted of White House chief of staff Richard Cheney, President Ford Committee chairperson James Baker, Ford Committee organization director Stuart Spencer, media consultant John Deardourff, and pollster Robert Teeter.[1]

---

[1] Robert Teeter has provided a very nice description of the Ford strategy group. "The week spent at Vail [Colorado] right after the convention was the key to the development of the fall campaign. . . . We came out of the Vail meeting a small group of men who got along, who knew and understood each other, who had a

Cheney, who as a graduate student had co-authored an elegant analysis of congressional policy dimensions (Clausen and Cheney, 1970) and who was later to be elected to Congress himself, and Baker, a Houston attorney who had been in charge of the Ford delegate hunt during the primaries, had not been through a national campaign before. But Robert Teeter had considerable experience in political polling with the Detroit firm of Market Opinion Research, and Stuart Spencer and John Deardourff were two of the best professional campaign managers in the country. Between them, they could put together about 50 years of campaign experience. Where the Carter strategy group was unusual in being composed almost entirely of persons who had known Carter for some time, the Ford strategy group was unusual in its professional orientation. Both elements are needed. A strategy group must include members trusted by the candidate if he or she is to concur with their decisions; it must include experts if the group is to appraise political conditions correctly. The common pattern is to have some balance between persons with each of these qualifications.

While core groups and strategy groups are fundamental, they are no more than the essential beginning of a campaign organization. The strategy groups make decisions about campaign emphases, but they cannot carry them out themselves. And they certainly are not a party-wide coalition capable of reaching a national constituency.

ACTIVISTS

The 1972 Hofstetter Study

The *only* nationwide study we have of campaign activists was conducted by Richard Hofstetter in 1972 as part of a broader investigation of television coverage of the Nixon-McGovern campaign (Hofstetter, 1976). The persons to be interviewed were selected the same way the leaders themselves were chosen: by nomination downward. The names of state campaign directors were obtained from the national offices of the Committee to Re-elect the President and of the McGovern-Shriver Committee. The state leaders were then asked to supply names of the persons in charge in counties that were part of a national sampling frame.

---

strategy in mind for the campaign. . . . Jim Baker, Dick Cheney, Stu Spencer, John Deardourff, and I were five people who got along as one unit and had a strategy in mind for what we were going to try to accomplish in the campaign" (Moore and Fraser, 1977, p. 123). Teeter did not use the formal language of a group theory, such as David Truman's—"These interactions . . . because they have a certain character and frequency, give the group its molding and guiding powers." From "interactions in groups arise certain common habits of response, which may be called norms, or shared attitudes. These afford the participants frames of reference for interpreting and evaluating events and behaviors" (1971, pp. 24, 33).—but his reference to five individuals "who got along as one unit" is precisely why group theory is a useful way to analyze politics.

One hundred ninety-seven Democratic and 204 Republican county leaders were contacted and interviewed. One series of questions dealt with the activists' backgrounds, motivations, and activities. Another dealt with their issue positions, their perceptions of the candidates, and their perceptions of the preferences of voters in their counties. This latter series of questions was identical to questions being put to citizens who lived in the same counties. The first set provided information about the county leaders' attitudes and activities; the second set told us how representative they were.

Since the findings to be discussed in the balance of this chapter rely on the Hofstetter study, the reader ought to be warned about the limits of this data set. We have a limited number of interviews; they are now eight years old; they come from a single election year. This does not mean that inferences cannot be drawn about the electoral parties. As we shall see shortly, there are substantial reasons to believe that the 1972 activists were not atypical. But with only a single study, we don't know how representative the 1972 sample was of the Republican and Democratic electoral parties over time.[2] There undoubtedly has been some change between 1972 and 1980. The problem is that we don't know *how much*, and therefore we ought to be careful in drawing inferences.

WHO ARE THE ELECTORAL ACTIVISTS?

Since delegates to national conventions have been extensively studied (McClosky, Hoffman, and O'Hara, 1960; Niemi and Jennings, 1968; Soule and Clarke, 1970; Soule and McGrath, 1975; Johnson and Hahn, 1973; Sullivan, Pressman, Page, and Lyons, 1974; Kirkpatrick, 1976; and many others), it is useful to compare the county campaign leaders with convention delegates. The background characteristics of activists in the two institutional domains are shown in Table 3–1. There were a few differences. Among convention delegates, Democrats were more likely to be young and nonwhite than Republicans. Democratic campaign leaders were more likely to be young and to have lower incomes than any other category. (The largest proportion of Republican campaign activists, 45 percent, fell into the 30–45 age bracket.) Campaign leaders were more likely to have professional or managerial occupations than convention delegates (although this difference is slightly exaggerated in Table 3–1 due to coding variations). But what is most striking about these data is that regardless of the background characteristic and regardless of the category of activist, almost all come from upper socioeconomic strata.

---

[2] My *guess* is that this sample is least representative of the Democratic party in the South because of limited support there for Senator McGovern. I also *suspect* that the sizes of the Democratic issue groups called "Democratic moderates" and "coercive individualists" (to be discussed later in this chapter) are somewhat underestimated.

TABLE 3–1

Comparison of Selected Background Characteristics: 1972 Convention Delegates and Electoral Activists

Background Characteristic*	Convention Delegates		Electoral Activists	
	Republicans	Democrats	Republicans	Democrats
Under 30	8%	22%	8%	48%
Professional or manager	71	73	90	91
Income over $10,000	94	87		
Income over $12,000			86	66
Attended college	87	87	84	91
Caucasian	94	80	97	93
Political generation				
Pre–1945	14	7	10	5
1946–1959	41	32	35	18
1960–1967	36	31	33	28
1968–1972	9	30	22	49

* Cell entries are percentages of persons having characteristic.
Data sources: Convention Delegates, adapted from Tables 3.1, 3.2, 7.7, and 7.8 in *The New Presidential Elite*, by Jeane Kirkpatrick, © 1976 by The Russell Sage Foundation, New York. Electoral Activists, 1972 Hofstetter study.

What one makes of these characteristics is a matter of perspective. On the one hand, politics is a complicated business. If one is to keep track of the various motions being voted on at a national convention, or if one is to run a county campaign, stay in touch with workers, coordinate activities with state and county organizations, and so on, organizational and communication skills are necessary. These are most often associated with higher education and white-collar jobs. Moreover, college educations and professional status are not particularly unusual in modern American society. On the other hand, persons who have these advantages are less likely to have been unemployed, or to have faced the problems of feeding one's family on food stamps. Since they lack the personal experience of making ends meet on a very limited income, they *may* be less sensitive to issues affecting poor people.

When we turn to the question of experience, there are pronounced differences between the convention delegates and the electoral activists. To begin with, the data on political generation in Table 3–1 show that much larger proportions of county campaign leaders in both parties had their political initiations during the 1968–72 period. But it is the convention delegates, not the campaign activists, who are less experienced at what they are doing. A high rate of delegate turnover has long been one of the most important facts about national conventions. An examination of the delegate rosters showed that from 1944 through 1968, 64 percent of the Democratic delegates and 65 percent of the Republican delegates were attending their first conventions. Another 22 percent of the Democrats and 21 percent of the Republicans had only attended one prior convention (Johnson and Hahn, 1973). The convention delegates tend to be experienced politicians, and are often fairly important figures in their home communities; but at the convention itself, most of them are seeking their footing on unfamiliar terrain.

In contrast, most of the county campaign leaders are experienced in presidential campaigns. Most of them began that way. A majority of both parties—50 percent of the Republicans and 62 percent of the Democrats—reported that their first campaigns were presidential campaigns. Four times as many began in presidential campaigns as in *any* other type. Furthermore, the second most frequent form of political initiation was in gubernatorial politics. Twelve percent of the Republicans and 15 percent of the Democrats started this way. Clearly, these activists are attracted to high-visibility executive politics.

The Formal Party Organization

In this book a political party is not considered as a whole, but is broken down into observable units. The acting unit is the coalition-in-institution. The coalition is composed of specific groups of actors and carries out its business in a given setting. Thus, an electoral coalition is constrained by the need to reach voters in a certain context. How does this correspond to the formal party organization?

The simplest answer is that the two definitions—coalition-in-institution and formal party organization—refer to different sets of actors. We are concerned with those who are involved in presidential campaigns. The formal party organization, on the other hand, consists of those who hold office or take part in the national, state, county, ward, and precinct committees.

There is considerable overlap between these sets of actors. In the past, the presidential campaigns have often been led by the national committee staffs. They are now excluded from this by the Federal Election Campaign Act of 1974, but both the Republican National Committee and the Democratic National Committee raised funds, and conducted voter identification and turnout drives in 1976, and the Republican National Committee provided research on Governor Carter. These activities were very much part of the presidential campaign.

There is also considerable overlap between the electoral coalitions and the formal party organizations on the state and county levels. Five-eighths of the Republican campaign activists and half of the Democratic campaign activists held some party office in 1972, and 76 percent of the Republicans and 69 percent of the Democrats had held some party position in the past (Howell, 1976). Other members of the formal party organization were doubtless active in gubernatorial, senatorial, congressional, and other campaigns. These persons would be germane to an analysis of those efforts, though not to a consideration of presidential politics. Then there are party officials who cling to formal power, but don't take part in any campaigns. They can be safely discounted as political ciphers.

The average experience of the county campaign leaders was 14 years for the Republicans and 10 years for the Democrats. When this is added to origins in presidential politics and their relative youth, the modal pattern seems to be one of a person who was attracted to presidential politics while in his or her late teens or twenties, and who had been around politics for a while before being given the responsibility of running a county campaign.

Another important fact about the electoral activists is the number of them who began their political careers in presidential campaign years. Two thirds of the Republicans and 72 percent of the Democrats began in such a year. The years are portrayed in Figure 3–1. The activists who

FIGURE 3–1

Presidential Parties as Residues of Past Campaigns: Proportions of Electoral Activists with First Experience in Presidential Campaign Years

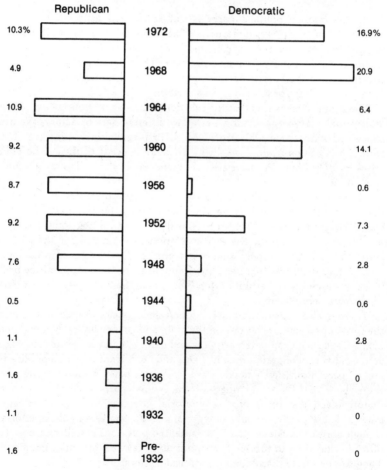

Republican		Democratic
10.3%	1972	16.9%
4.9	1968	20.9
10.9	1964	6.4
9.2	1960	14.1
8.7	1956	0.6
9.2	1952	7.3
7.6	1948	2.8
0.5	1944	0.6
1.1	1940	2.8
1.6	1936	0
1.1	1932	0
1.6	Pre-1932	0

were working in behalf of George McGovern and Sargent Shriver in-
cluded significant numbers who had been brought into politics during
the campaigns of Lyndon Johnson, John Kennedy, Adlai Stevenson,
Harry Truman, or Franklin Roosevelt. The Committee to Re-elect Richard
Nixon as President included those who had rallied to the banners of
Dwight Eisenhower, Thomas Dewey, Wendell Willkie, or even Herbert
Hoover. In fact, the activist with the longest experience who turned up
in the sample had begun his political career working for Charles Evans
Hughes over half a century earlier!

This suggests a conclusion of some significance: *a presidential party
at any time is a residue of its past campaigns.* This has some consequences
for the inferences we can draw from these 1972 data. We can be certain
that the activists who were working for the Committee to Re-elect the
President and the McGovern-Shriver Committee were not wildly atypical
of Republicans and Democrats in other campaigns because 90 percent
of the Republicans and 83 percent of the Democrats had begun in earlier
campaigns. At the same time, we know that the parties in 1980 will be
somehow different from the 1972 parties because of the new cohorts of
activists brought into politics by the 1976 and 1980 campaigns.[3]

ADVOCACY PARTIES

The activists' characteristics hint at the nature of the campaign organizations they might form. The educational and occupational characteristics suggest they might be more sensitive to middle-class issues.
Their initial attraction to high-visibility executive politics hints at a
greater concern with policies followed by the government after the election than with patronage in the county auditor's office. The experience
of the activists implies some organizational continuity in spite of any
unique policy tendencies exhibited by a nominee.

Half a dozen questions in the 1972 study dealt directly with the activists'
attitudes about engaging in, or avoiding, certain types of party activity.
Two of these questions concerned the importance of issues, two tapped
the importance of prior party service in candidate selection or patronage,
and two dealt with discipline that ought to apply to party leaders or the
activists themselves.

An analysis of the responses to these queries about party norms appears in Table 3–2. The higher the difference score for a given item, the
greater the obligation the activists felt to engage in that behavior. There

---

[3] This recruitment process spells out limits to the hopes of such groups as the
moderate Republicans, who wanted to go back to "normal" pre-Goldwater politics
after 1964, and the "Coalition for a Democratic Majority," which wanted to repudiate
the "New Politics" of George McGovern after 1972. A party is never completely taken
over by the new arrivals who come into politics in a given campaign, but it never
goes back to being what it was before that campaign either.

TABLE 3–2
Activists' Feelings of Obligation about Party Work

Activity about Which Attitude Is Held	Difference Score*	
	Democrats	Republicans
Hold strong personal beliefs about a number of different issues	72.3	54.4
Select nominee strongly committed on variety of issue positions	73.0	46.5
Weigh party service very heavily in selecting candidate for nomination	3.2	23.0
See that those who work for party get help in form of job and other things if needed	6.5	23.2
Keep elected officials strictly accountable to party organization	4.4	13.2
Follow decisions of party leaders even when you disagree	−9.4	0

* Higher scores mean greater obligation to engage in activity. For details, see Appendix A–3.1.
Data source: 1972 Hofstetter study.

were noticeable differences between the parties. Issues were more important to the Democrats, both in their belief that they ought to have strong views themselves and in their belief that the nominee ought to be strongly committed on a number of issues. Republicans were more likely to emphasize organization. This is reflected in the higher scores for consideration of prior party work in candidate selection and patronage. The item on which the activists of both parties were in closest agreement was on the inappropriateness of party discipline as it applied to them.

Important as these party differences are, the similarities between the parties are more consequential. As you read down either party column in Table 3–2, it is clear that much more emphasis is placed on issues than on any other activity. The next most important party norms, those concerning party service and patronage, come a long way back of the issue items. As of the 1970s, most activists in electoral politics have a strong interest in the policies followed by the government once the election is over. It would be too much to say that an interest in issues draws them to political life in the first place. The activists are likely to speak of their motivations in global terms; they are attracted to politics per se. But it is also clear that an interest in issues is an important component in the attraction to politics, and in the way they participate once they become involved.[4]

Electoral activists agree with their party colleagues to a greater degree

[4] Of the many types of local politicos reported in the literature, these electoral activists most closely resemble the citizen politicians in Western cities such as Los Angeles and Tucson (Marvick, 1973; Arrington, 1975). Here, too, one finds an emphasis on issue politics, and relative disinterest in patronage.

than they agree with their constituents. This was a rather surprising finding since parties are often thought of as representative institutions that articulate the preferences of less-involved members of the public. Party activists are assumed to be persons with distinctive skills in knowing what their constituents want, and being able to assemble these preferences in packages that win votes at election time. Yet the data indicate that this is *not* what these electoral activists are doing.

One of the advantages of the Hofstetter study was that voters living in the same counties as the party activists were also interviewed, thus presenting the opportunity to address parallel questions to both sets of respondents. There are two ways in which the activists might represent their constituents. One is through what Aage Clausen calls "involuntary representation," a process in which the personal attitudes of the party leaders happen to coincide with the views of their fellow citizens. The party leaders have the same attitudes, presumably through having lived in the community and having been exposed to the same influences; but the linkage is as unconscious as other involuntary processes, such as breathing. The other type of representation does not call for any such coincidence between the leaders' attitudes and those of their fellow citizens, but does assume that the leaders are able to perceive their constituents' attitudes accurately.

It is possible to determine the coincidence of attitudes between leaders and constituents, and the extent to which the leaders' perceptions coincide with constituents' attitudes, by calculating agreement scores.[5] When this is done, it becomes evident that neither of these possible modes of representation is working very well. Considering both parties together, involuntary representation is working a little bit better. The scores reflecting attitudinal agreement are 17 percent better than one would expect by chance, and the scores reflecting perceptual accuracy are only 2 percent better than random chance.

The average agreement score for similarity of attitudes was .22 for Republicans and .12 for Democrats. (This means 22 percent better than chance for Republicans and 12 percent better than chance for Democrats.) The average agreement scores for perceptual accuracy were 0 for Republicans and .05 for Democrats (Yarnell, 1975). The similarity of attitudes between activists and constituents is not impressive, and the political leaders' presumed competence at knowing what their constituents prefer is nonexistent.

---

[5] Agreement scores indicate the degree to which two persons take the same positions. If both persons give the same answer to every question they are asked, they will have an agreement score of 1.0. If their agreement is no better than chance, the agreement score will be 0. Thus, the agreement score between two political activists (or in this case, between a county leader and the average response of citizens in that county) represents that extent of agreement beyond what would be expected by chance. For further details, see Appendix A–3.2.

In contrast, the average agreement score among all Republican activists in 1972 was .29, and that among all Democratic activists was .30. These figures are almost identical for both parties, and denote agreement among activists about 30 percent beyond what one would expect by chance. Even more important, these scores tell us we can know more about activists' attitudes by learning whether they are Republicans or Democrats than by knowing anything about attitudes in the communities from which they come.[6] The implication is that they are not giving voice to their constituents' views. Rather, they are urging policies that their party colleagues think wise. Our electoral parties are not representative entities, but *advocacy parties*.[7]

GROUPS

REPUBLICAN ISSUE GROUPS

In choosing concepts to analyze the internal structure of coalitions, we have assumed that groups composed of activists with shared attitudes would be important. When we put this assumption together with the finding that the issues are central to the thinking of political activists, it follows that issue groups composed of persons with shared attitudes on public policy ought to be a useful way to understand political parties. The characteristics of such groups should tell us what the party is agreed about, what questions divide it, and something of the dynamics by which the party determines its positions on issues that cause internal division.

Issue groups of this kind have been isolated by means of a cluster analysis. The details of this procedure are set forth in Appendix A–3.3, but the essential point is that each activist is assigned to the issue group with which he or she has the highest average agreement score. If an activist fails to meet the stipulated level of agreement with any group,

---

[6] Notice, however, that this conclusion depends on the lack of agreement between Democrats and residents of their counties in 1972. The agreement score between Republicans and citizens of their communities in 1972 was .22, and the agreement score among all Republicans was .29. This difference is not great, and it is not inconceivable that both parties might be as representative of their communities in some future campaign as the Republicans were in 1972.

[7] There are choices that the county leaders can make about issues, particularly in selecting which issues to emphasize and which to ignore in their local campaigns. As we shall presently see, their attitudes about issues do have consequences in the choices they make and on the strategy which the electoral party implements across the country. However, the full range of their activity is better understood as activity in behalf of a candidate with known issues positions than as full-time espousal of issues. This is better stated by the verbs "to support" or "to back" than "to advocate." The reason for choosing the term "advocacy parties" has to do with the lack of a better adjective. "Supportive party" doesn't suggest much of anything, and there isn't an adjective form of "to back." "Advocacy party" has the right connotations, but its meaning should be understood in the light of this explanation.

then he or she is treated as an isolate. Thus we can be sure that we have groups whose members share common outlooks on questions of public policy, and a number of activists who do not belong to any group because their own views are unique.

There were four Republican issue groups in 1972, and seven Democratic groups.[8] The sizes and *approximate* locations of the groups with respect to each other are depicted in Figure 3–2. The word approximate is stressed

FIGURE 3–2
Republican Issue Groups

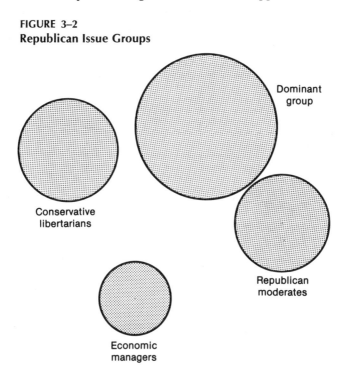

The size of the circles corresponds to the size of each group. The location suggests the *approximate* location of each with respect to the others in issue space. For details, see Appendix A–3.4.

because the issue space is multidimensional. There are four policy areas. International involvement concerned the extent of American involvement overseas: foreign commitments, defense spending, foreign aid, and (in the late 1960s and early 1970s) Vietnam. Economic management deals with the use of the federal government to direct the economy: the level of spending, the use of economic controls, and views of the power of the federal government. Social benefits includes those programs that

---

[8] The analysis of group characteristics is based largely on a memorandum written by Stephen D. Shaffer.

shelter individuals from adverse circumstances: health care, social security, education, and so forth. Civil liberties deals with civil rights, police power, busing, and life-style questions. Since there are four policy areas, one group might agree with a second on international involvement but disagree on economic management, and might agree with a third on international involvement and economic management but disagree on civil liberties, and so on. Therefore, no *two*-dimensional analysis (such as Figure 3–2) is going to be able to depict all of the relationships between the issue groups. The positions of the Republican issue groups in all four policy areas are summarized in Table 3–3.

All four Republican issue groups take moderate positions on public policy questions. The dominant group is poised on the boundary between moderate and moderate conservative. Within this group, there was likely to be disagreement on individual questions relating to international involvement and economic management. For example, about a quarter of the members—a larger proportion than any other GOP group—were willing to entertain the idea of bringing some American troops back from overseas. As with other Republican groups, there was some disagreement on social benefits, and considerable consensus on civil liberties.

TABLE 3–3
Republican Issue Groups: Varieties of Moderation

Group	Position in Policy Area*				Percent of Activists in Group
	International Involvement	Economic Management	Social Benefits	Civil Liberties	
Dominant group	Moderate (3.5)	Moderate (3.6)	Moderate (3.5)	Moderate conservative (3.2)	29.8%
Conservative libertarians	Moderate conservative (3.2)	Moderate conservative (3.3)	Moderate conservative (2.7)	Moderate (3.8)	14.9
Economic managers	Moderate (3.8)	Moderate liberal (4.9)	Moderate (3.5)	Moderate conservative (3.3)	7.7
Republican moderates	Moderate (4.1)	Moderate (3.7)	Moderate (4.3)	Moderate conservative (3.3)	11.6
Isolates	Moderate (4.4)	Moderate (4.1)	Moderate (3.6)	Moderate (3.5)	35.9

* The figures in parentheses are median positions on scales that vary between 1 and 7. In general a high score (7) represents a dove position in international involvement, and a willingness to use government power and resources in the domestic policy areas. A low score (1) represents the opposite.

The convention followed for substantive interpretation of the scale scores was: values from 1 to 2.4 , conservative; 2.5 to 3.4, moderate conservative; 3.5 to 4.5, moderate; 4.6 to 5.5, moderate liberal; 5.6 to 7, liberal. This classification is nothing more than an aid to understanding, and should not be taken as a precise denotation. Note, for example, that if the upper boundary of moderate conservative had been moved from 3.4 to 3.5, there would have been 10 moderate conservative scores rather than 6.

Data source: 1972 Hofstetter study.

This high rate of agreement on civil liberties, an agreement that tends slightly in a conservative direction, may reflect the large number of southern Republicans in this group. Half of the southern Republican activists belonged to the dominant group. This was the *only* case in *either* party where a majority of those from *any* region could be found in a single group.

The conservative libertarians[9] had slightly more conservative positions on international and economic matters, and much more conservative preferences on social benefits. On civil liberties questions, though, they depart from the other Republican groups in the opposite direction. The conservative libertarians are more skeptical about the wisdom of increasing police authority, and are much more in favor of open housing. It is in this group that one hears the strongest echo of the historic Republican position in favor of civil rights.

The economic managers are the smallest Republican group, and depart from the dominant group's issue profile primarily on economic questions. They are slightly less in favor of cutting spending, and are far more willing to use federal instrumentalities to regulate the economy than any other Republican group. Not only do they provide the single example of the GOP group taking a moderate liberal position, but the economic managers are less worried about the power of the federal government than any Democratic group.

The Republican moderates are close to the dominant group's positions on economics and civil liberties, but take more liberal positions with respect to international involvement and social benefits. The Republican moderates are much more in favor of foreign aid than any other Republican group. It is the only GOP group in which a majority is open to the idea or supportive of increasing welfare payments, and the only one that is united in favor of a social security increase.

The isolates are also essential to an understanding of the internal structure of the Republican party. Consider the information in Table 3–3. There are more Republicans who are isolates than there are in any one of the Republican groups. Furthermore, their policy preferences are moderate in all four policy areas. Since the isolates are more numerous and relatively liberal, it would *seem* that they ought to be able to move the Republican party somewhat to the left. Yet they haven't been able to do so. Why not?

The explanation is that the isolates are not members of any group.

---

[9] The names I have given these issue groups can only suggest their policy tendencies, not serve as complete descriptions. With four different policy areas, names that stated the group's full set of preferences would be too long to be useful. The problem is the same with your family name. Your genetic inheritance comes equally from all four grandparents, but for the sake of convenience, your paternal grandfather's name is used as your family name.

The workings of the computer program through which these groups were found are such that if an activist had agreed with even one other activist (at the stipulated level), they would have been joined into a two-person group. Therefore we know these persons tend to be isolated from each other. Since they lack allies, it is hard for them to move their party in any direction. This is the reason for the political impotence of the relatively small band of Republican liberals. Not only are they outnumbered, but they disagree among themselves.

DEMOCRATIC ISSUE GROUPS

The Democratic issue groups are portrayed in Figure 3–3, and their issue preferences are summarized in Table 3–4. The issue space is again multidimensional, but because Democratic disagreements in 1972 were focused on international questions and economic matters, it is possible to think of the vertical dimension as being related to international questions, and the horizontal dimension as being related to domestic matters. This analogy should *not* be pressed very far; some groups are out of place with respect to some other groups in certain policy areas. But the upper left-hand group, the liberal pacifists, are the most dovish and the most liberal

FIGURE 3–3
Democratic Issue Groups

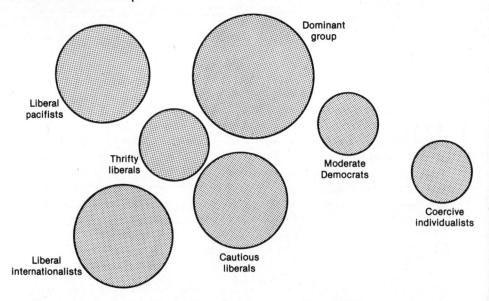

The size of the circles corresponds to the size of each group. The location suggests the *approximate* location of each with respect to the others in issue space. For details, see Appendix A–3.4.

on domestic questions, while the group farthest to the right, the coercive individualists, tends to be conservative hawks.

The dominant group in 1972 took prototypical Democratic positions. It was united in favor of social benefits, and in favor of protecting the civil liberties of minorities. On foreign policy it opposed defense spending, but was divided on questions of foreign aid and keeping American troops overseas. On economic matters it contained some skeptics about continued reliance on the federal government, and showed real division on federal spending.

The liberal pacifists and liberal internationalists both took even more liberal positions on social benefits, but these two groups departed from the dominant group on international matters in opposite directions. The liberal pacifists wanted to bring American troops back home, did not want to spend for defense, and had doubts about foreign aid.[10] This group represents a tradition in the Democratic party that goes back to Henry Wallace and William Jennings Bryan. The liberal internationalists were split on the question of bringing troops home, but were solidly in favor of defense spending and foreign aid. This group represents those favoring international involvement who have found spokesmen in John F. Kennedy, Dean Acheson, and Franklin D. Roosevelt.

The other Democratic groups all depart from the dominant group in a conservative direction in one or more issue areas. The profile of the cautious liberals is quite similar to that of the dominant group, but a shade more conservative on several items. The cautious liberals are more willing to spend for military purposes, much more divided on the wisdom of national health care, and perceptibly more favorable to the police. It is this last difference that moves the cautious liberals from "liberal" to "moderate liberal" on civil liberties.

The thrifty liberals take positions similar to the dominant group except on economic questions. Here the departure is quite pronounced. For example, the dominant group is split on the question of cutting government spending. All the thrifty liberals think that government spending should be reduced.

The Democratic moderates are the smallest Democratic group, and while they have similar international positions as the dominant group, they take more conservative positions in all of the domestic policy areas. Along with the thrifty liberals, all the Democratic moderates favor a

---

[10] In our coding decisions, we called these dovish positions "liberal," and the positions taken by the "liberal internationalists" were called "moderate." In so doing, we followed the usage of most commentators on the 1972 election. These coding decisions had no bearing on the structure we found. However we had decided, there would have been one Democratic group departing from the dominant group in the direction of further overseas participation, and one in the direction of withdrawing.

TABLE 3–4
Democratic Issue Groups: Varieties of Liberalism

Group	International Involvement	Economic Management	Social Benefits	Civil Liberties	Percent of Activists in Group
	Position in Policy Area*				
Dominant group	Moderate liberal (5.1)	Moderate (4.4)	Liberal (5.8)	Liberal (6.5)	22.0%
Liberal pacifists	Liberal (6.1)	Moderate liberal (5.0)	Liberal (6.4)	Liberal (6.5)	14.3
Liberal internationalists	Moderate (4.3)	Moderate (4.5)	Liberal (6.2)	Liberal (6.5)	14.8
Cautious liberals	Moderate liberal (4.8)	Moderate (4.5)	Liberal (5.7)	Moderate liberal (5.2)	14.3
Thrifty liberals	Moderate liberal (4.6)	Moderate conservative (3.3)	Liberal (5.7)	Liberal (6.3)	7.1
Democratic moderates	Moderate liberal (5.1)	Moderate conservative (3.4)	Moderate (4.5)	Moderate liberal (5.1)	5.5
Coercive individualists	Moderate (4.0)	Moderate conservative (3.2)	Moderate liberal (4.6)	Moderate (3.8)	6.0
Isolates	Moderate (4.1)	Moderate (4.3)	Liberal (5.9)	Moderate liberal (5.0)	15.9

* The figures in parentheses are median positions on scales that vary between 1 and 7. In general a high score (7) represents a dove position in international involvement, and a willingness to use government power and resources in the domestic policy areas. A low score (1) represents the opposite. For the convention followed in giving substantive interpretations to these scores, see the explanation at the bottom of Table 3–3.
　Data source: 1972 Hofstetter study.

reduction in government spending. They are also less enthusiastic about social programs and protecting minority rights than the dominant group. As a matter of fact, a majority of the moderates opposes any increase in welfare payments.

　The coercive individualists, so called because they want the government to let them alone to conduct their business affairs but are willing to use the military abroad and the police at home to intervene in the lives of others, mark the Democrats' conservative perimeter. The coercive individualists are about as hawkish as the liberal internationalists, but oppose foreign aid as well. They are almost as opposed to federal spending as the thrifty liberals, and more resistant to a strong federal government. Some 55 percent of this group opposed national health care, whereas only 20 percent of the Democratic moderates did so. And the coercive individualists were the only group of Democratic activists who maintained that the police should be given increased authority. In every single-policy area, the coercive individualists took the most conservative Democratic position.

The Democratic isolates are mirror images of the Republican isolates. Both hold minority views within their own parties. The Republican isolates are relatively liberal; the Democratic isolates are relatively conservative. Neither set of isolates is very influential because of lack of agreement among themselves or with any of the issue groups. The only contrast is that the Democratic isolates are less important to an understanding of the Democratic structure because they are so much less numerous.

A NEW VIEW OF ELECTORAL PARTIES

The character of these issue groups is clear. They may be understood in terms of their size, the generally moderate positions taken by the Republican groups, and the generally liberal positions taken by the Democratic groups. This is a different interpretation of party groups than is usually offered. The standard view, especially of the Democratic party, is that the party is made up of demographic groupings. For example, Robert Axelrod (1972) names the Democratic groups as the poor, the blacks, union members, Catholics, southerners, and central city residents. Andrew Greeley writes that the political party "is comprised of voluntary associations (such as trade unions), interest groups (civil rights organizations), strictly political groups (Cook County Democratic party), and major proportions of population groups (blacks, Catholics, or Jews)" (1974, pp. 172–73). I (1968, 1974) have said that the normal Democratic coalition was made up of southerners, westerners, urbanites, union members, and blacks.[11] In other words, the Democratic party is usually seen as a coalition of minorities. Why shouldn't we follow this line of analysis rather than seeking groups with distinctive attitudes in policy areas?

The most direct answer is that activists who fall into the traditional categories do not have shared attitudes from which we can infer probable behavior. Therefore it is much less useful to interpret parties this way. Two tests were used to try to find attitude groups that corresponded to the traditional classifications. In the first, a mean agreement score was calculated for all activists who fit into the category. (These agreement

---

11 I did classify the Republican groups on the basis of their attitudes on issues. Miller and Levitin's (1976) classification of voters as "Silent Minority," "Center," and "New Liberals" is also a move in this direction. For other analyses of the Democratic party on the basis of demographic groupings, see Rubin (1976), Ladd and Hadley (1978), and Nie, Verba, and Petrocik (1976, chapters 13–14). These are but examples. Many scholars have used demographic classifications of one kind or another.

TABLE 3–5
Agreement and Clusters Formed within Categoric Groupings

Category	Mean Agreement* Score	Number of Clusters	Percent Unclustered
	Republicans		
Blacks†	—	—	—
Roman Catholics	.25	2	42.2%
Urban	.27	2	47.3
East	.25	1	53.9
Midwest	.26	1	50.8
South	.34	2	31.4
Deep South	.45	1	33.3
Self-identified liberals	.14	0	100.0
Self-identified conservatives	.32	2	32.9
	Democrats		
Blacks	.31	0	100.0
Roman Catholics	.24	1	69.0
Urban	.27	3	26.7
East	.25	2	45.2
Midwest	.37	2	31.5
South	.24	3	34.5
Deep South†	—	—	—
Self-identified liberals	.34	4	23.1
Self-identified conservatives†	—	—	—

* The higher the agreement score, the greater the agreement between members of the category.
† Too few cases for analysis.
Data source: 1972 Hofstetter study.

scores, you will recall, represent the extent of agreement beyond that to be expected by chance.) The data are presented in Table 3–5. The extent of agreement among activists in the categoric groupings is much less than in the issue groups. The average scores for the groupings in Table 3–5 (grand means) are .29 for the Republicans and .29 for the Democrats. The average agreement scores for the issue groups are .48 for the Republicans and .50 for the Democrats. The average agreement scores among all activists are .29 for Republicans and .30 for the Democrats. In other words, the categoric groupings do not provide information that we don't have just by knowing whether the activists are Democrats or Republicans, but the issue groups are much more distinctive.

The second test was a cluster analysis of those who fell into the traditional categories to see whether each such set of activists, black Democrats, eastern Republicans, or whatever, would form groups. The same criteria were used as in the analysis that produced the issue groups. The data resulting from this test also appear in Table 3–5. In most cases, either multiple groups were formed—which means that the members of each group had different attitudes—or no groups were formed—which means the activists were isolates who didn't agree with anyone.

Three fifths of the time, multiple groups were formed. The most extreme cases were the urban Democrats, the southern Democrats, and the liberal Democrats. These categories all contain large numbers of Democratic activists. Their potential influence is limited, however, as they would have the Democratic party move in three or four *different* directions. In a couple of instances, liberal Republicans and black Democrats, no groups were formed. These categories were made up entirely of isolates. In three of the four cases in which a single group was formed, a majority of the members of the category remains outside the group. In only one instance, Republicans from the Deep South, is there a high agreement score and a group formed that includes a majority of the activists in the category. As we have already seen, southern Republicans also provide the *only* case in which a majority of the activists from a single region belong to one attitudinal group.[12]

There was a time when a demographic classification of party groups was reasonably exact. Not too long ago, Arthur Holcombe could write: "The Democratic party, since the great realignment of parties in the course of the struggle over slavery, has consisted of three principal factions: the cotton and tobacco planters and associated interests in the South, a substantial part of the grain growers and cattlemen and associated interests in the North and West, and a diversified group of urban interests in the same sections, in which since the Al Smith campaign of 1928 labor interests have been growing more important" (1950, p. 122). Any such classification rested, of course, on an assumption of regional (or occupational, or ethnic, or whatever) homogeneity. Southerners, for example, were assumed to have sufficiently similar attitudes so a group of southerners would act coherently within a political party. V. O. Key, prescient on this as on so many matters, pointed out that "[f]or 50 years changes in both the North and the South have been gradually undermining southern solidarity" (1964, p. 239). These changes have continued apace. National media, mobility from one section of the country to another, and many other forces have eroded sectional and ethnic homogeneity. For some years we have had a national culture. Southerners and westerners, Irish-Americans and Polish-Americans, and all the other once distinctive categories are best understood as having subcultures that incorporate most of the features of the national culture.

---

[12] This was the dominant group in the Republican party. Even in this case, it is not very useful to think of the issue group in regional terms. Fifty-four percent of the members of the dominant Republican group come from outside the South, and 80 percent come from outside the Deep South.

In a similar way, our national political culture may be thought of as having a moderate political tone. Democrats tend toward the liberal side; Republicans to the moderate side. Democrats and Republicans are best analyzed by finding groups in which this liberalism or moderation varies across particular policy areas. In this way, we achieve more precision than when we use demographic categories of fading utility.

This does not mean that we can afford to abandon all references to southern Democrats or eastern Republicans. While an analysis that uses the issue groups is more powerful, the data that allow us to do this come (so far) from a single year. Therefore we have no choice but to use the more general ideological and demographic references in other circumstances.

COALITIONS

REPUBLICAN ISSUE COALITIONS

We have seen that issues are important to activists, and that activists form groups with different sets of preferences in the policy areas. Now what kinds of coalitions can be formed by these groups? The fundamental answer is that the dominant group in both parties ends up in a key position in the dominant coalition formed in each policy area. This hardly sounds surprising, but the reason is that we have been calling these groups "dominant." So far, we haven't said why they should be so regarded.

Take the dominant Republican group. It is the largest Republican group, and this makes it easier for other groups joining with it to form a majority coalition. But one could construct a case to show why other groups would form coalitions among themselves rather than with the dominant group. The dominant group is the largest, but it includes fewer than three out of ten Republican activists. Moreover, the median positions of the dominant group are more conservative than the median positions taken by all Republicans in each policy area. Why shouldn't the Republican activists who prefer more liberal postures form coalitions to move the Republican party toward the center?

The reason for the strength of the dominant group lies in its ability to recruit allies whose policy preferences are closer to its own than to moderate opponents. The issue coalitions differ from one policy area to another, but the dominant group ends up as a member of each winning coalition. The Republican moderates take a more liberal position in international involvement, but the dominant group can form a coalition with the conservative libertarians and the economic managers. The economic managers prefer a more liberal posture with respect to the federal government's role in fiscal affairs, but the dominant group can coalesce with the Republican moderates and the conservative libertarians. The situation with regard to social benefits is the same as for international involvement. In civil liberties, the conservative libertarians would prefer a more moderate posture, but the dominant group can form a coalition with the Republican moderates and the economic managers. Thus, there are three different issue coalitions in the four policy areas, and each one tends in a conservative direction.

The strength of the dominant conservative group thus lies both in its relative size and in its ability to find allies. The weakness of the Republican moderates, conversely, lies not only in their minority status but in their difficulty in finding groups with whom they can combine.

DEMOCRATIC ISSUE COALITIONS

The internal structure in the Democratic party is somewhat more complex than the Republican, but the process of coalition formation is essentially a mirror image of the Republican process. There are more issue groups in the Democratic party; there is greater issue distance between the most liberal and most conservative Democratic groups; the liberal pacifists take relatively liberal positions in every policy area; and the coercive individualists take relatively conservative positions in every policy area. But the dominant Democratic group, as the dominant Republican group, is the largest and has the easiest time finding policy partners.

In international involvement, the dominant group faces opposition in one direction from the liberal pacifists, and in the other direction from the liberal internationalists and the coercive individualists. But they can form a moderate liberal coalition in company with the moderate Democrats, the cautious liberals, and the thrifty liberals. There is pronounced division among Democrats on economic matters; but a majority coalition can be formed by the dominant group, the cautious liberals, the liberal internationalists, and the liberal pacifists. In social benefits, a winning coalition can be formed by the dominant group, the cautious liberals, the thrifty liberals, and the liberal internationalists. On civil liberties, the views of the dominant group, the liberal pacifists, the liberal internationalists, and the thrifty liberals are so similar that the process of coalition formation is almost automatic.

There are differences between the parties in the degree of exclusion. In the Republican party, the conservative libertarians and the economic managers are members of the dominant coalitions in three of the four policy areas, and the Republican moderates are twice. In the Democratic party, the Democratic moderates are part of a winning coalition only on international questions, and the coercive individualists are never part of a winning coalition. In the Republican party, the more conservative groups are always members of the dominant coalition. In the Democratic party, the most liberal group (the liberal pacifists) is included only twice. But in both parties, the dominant group was a member of the dominant coalition in all four policy areas.

There are two ways these predictions about coalition formation can be checked. One is to take the between-group agreement scores (which may be found in Appendix A–3.5) that are calculated across all the policy areas, and assume that the two groups with the highest agreement scores will form an initial protocoalition. At that point, agreement scores are recalculated between that protocoalition and the remaining groups, and the process repeats itself until a winning coalition is formed. The second way to check the process of coalition formation is to use the cluster procedure by which the issue groups were isolated, and gradually lower the criteria for admission until the equivalent of a multi-group coalition is formed. There are variations in detail in what one observes, but essentially these procedures verify the existence of the issue coalitions that have been discussed in the preceding paragraphs.

ISSUE COALITION DIFFERENCES BETWEEN THE PARTIES

These processes of coalition formation have consequences. Some of the most important consequences may be seen in Table 3–6. In every policy area, the median policy preferences of the dominant Republican coalitions are more conservative than those of all Republican activists. In

TABLE 3–6
Comparison of Issue Coalitions with All Party Activists

	Position in Policy Area*			
Group	International Involvement	Economic Management	Social Benefits	Civil Liberties
Dominant Republican coalition	Moderate conservative (3.4)	Moderate (3.5)	Moderate conservative (3.2)	Moderate conservative (3.2)
All Republican activists	Moderate (4.0)	Moderate (3.8)	Moderate (3.6)	Moderate (3.5)
Dominant Democratic coalition	Moderate liberal (5.0)	Moderate liberal (4.6)	Liberal (6.0)	Liberal (6.5)
All Democratic activists	Moderate liberal (4.9)	Moderate (4.4)	Liberal (5.9)	Liberal (6.0)

* The figures in parentheses are median positions on scales that vary between 1 and 7. In general a high score (7) represents a dove position in international involvement, and a willingness to use government power and resources in the domestic policy areas. A low score (1) represents the opposite. For the convention followed in giving substantive interpretations to these scores, see the explanation at the bottom of Table 3–3.
   Data source: 1972 Hofstetter study.

every policy area, the median policy preferences of the dominant Democratic coalitions are more liberal than those of all Democratic activists. Thus, the process of coalition formation in the electoral parties has a tendency to polarize the alternatives presented to the voters rather than move them toward the center of the political spectrum.

The polarization is more pronounced in the dominant Republican coalitions for a couple of reasons. For one thing, the more conservative Republican groups are always members of the dominant Republican coalitions, while the most liberal Democratic group is not part of the dominant coalition in international involvement or social benefits. For another, the policy preferences of the dominant Republican group are all more conservative than the median preference of all Republican activists, whereas the policy preferences of the dominant Democratic group are distinctly more liberal than the Democratic median only in civil liberties. This is reflected in the differences between the policy preferences of the dominant coalitions and those of all party activists. The dominant Republican coalitions are noticeably more conservative in every instance, while the dominant Democratic coalition is equally far away only in the civil liberties policy area.[13]

The data in Table 3–6 also suggest the nature of the choice these electoral coalitions present to the citizen. The choice is most pronounced with respect to social benefits and civil liberties. In these areas, Democratic policies are liberal and Republican policies moderate conservative. In international involvement, the citizen's choice is between moderate liberal and moderate conservative policies. A tendency toward the center is most notable in economic management, where Democratic policies are moderate liberal and Republican policies are moderate.

In understanding the party differences, one should also consider consensus. The consensus scores for all Republican activists and all Democratic activists, respectively, in the four policy areas are: international involvement, .57, .31; economic management, .62, .48; social benefits, .44, .66; civil liberties, .61, .73. The consensus scores have a value of 1.0 when everyone takes the same position, and a value of 0 when agreement is no greater than would be expected with an equal distribution, so these consensus scores tell us where we can expect strains and disagreements to show up within the parties.[14] The Republicans are least agreed about social benefit programs, but the similar sizes of the four consensus

---

[13] This should remind us of the importance of a careful specification of how attitudes aggregate at each level of analysis. The often made assumption that the policy preferences in any complex institution will lie at the central tendency (that is, mean, median, or mode) of the preferences of the individual members is apt to be wrong because it neglects the manner in which the preferences are aggregated.

[14] See Appendix A–3.6 for an explanation of how these consensus scores are calculated.

scores imply that Republican disagreements are spread rather equally across the four policy areas. In the Democratic case, however, disagreements are concentrated on foreign policy and economic questions. Democrats are united in favor of liberal positions on social benefits and civil liberties.

As already noted, we don't know how much change took place between 1972 and 1980 because of new cohorts of activists drawn into politics by the 1976 and 1980 campaigns. It seems likely that most of the groups continue to exist. With four policy areas and five possible issue positions in each area, there are 625 sets of issue profiles that could appear. Since only 11 of the possible 625 existed in 1972, this would suggest something more than chance and some real possibility of structural continuity.[15] At the same time, because of the ways coalitions are formed, relatively small changes in the size or preferences of groups could effect the strategic advantages each enjoys in coalition formation. A best guess based on these considerations is that the 1980 structure is roughly similar, with the dominant coalitions taking slightly different positions in some policy areas.

The case for approximate similarity in internal party structure is strengthened if you think about the applicability of the 1972 structure to more recent fights within the parties. In 1972, the Democrats showed more disagreement over international involvement than anything else. Divisions over the extent of foreign aid, keeping American troops overseas, and the extent of defense spending were marked. These same divisions showed up in Senate debate in late 1979 over the then pending SALT II treaty. Democratic Senators Henry Jackson and Sam Nunn announced they could not support the treaty unless there was an increase in defense spending. At that point, Senator George McGovern and several other Democrats sent President Carter a letter saying they might not vote for ratification if there was such an increase. These conflicting demands on the level of the defense budget reflected the split between the liberal internationalists and the liberal pacifists. This division goes back some time, too. Democrats have produced national leaders who have expanded American commitments overseas, and they have produced some notable pacifists. This "dissensus" on international questions helps understand

---

15 Actually, there were only 10 issue profiles even though there were 11 groups. The issue positions (liberal, moderate liberal, moderate, moderate conservative, conservative) cover fairly broad bands on the ideological spectrum. Because of this, the dominant Republican group and the Republican moderates have the same issue profile in Table 3–3 even though there are real differences between these groups in international involvement and social benefits. The median position of the dominant group is at the lowest point in the "moderate" range in both these issue areas, while the median position of the Republican moderates is just above the middle of the "moderate" range in international involvement and close to the top of the "moderate" range in social benefits.

why the New Freedom, New Deal–Fair Deal, and Great Society coalitions held together as long as the focus was on domestic questions, but came apart under the strains of World War I, the Cold War, and Vietnam.

The positions taken by the Democrats on economics and social benefits suggest the nature of the conflict between Edward Kennedy and Jimmy Carter. Democrats are united in favor of various welfare and benefit programs, but they are quite divided on spending and the power of the federal government. This portends a clash between those Democrats who like social programs and are willing to spend what is required, and those Democrats who like social programs but also want balanced budgets. Edward Kennedy falls into the former category, Jimmy Carter into the latter. Take the matter of national health care. Senator Kennedy said that administration's proposals (a limited "first-phase" package) contained "built in self-destruct buttons to halt the program in its tracks if things go wrong," later adding, "I think the President is sincere in his desire for health insurance. But I don't think it can be accomplished in piecemeal fashion." Then Health, Education, and Welfare Secretary Joseph Califano, speaking for the Carter administration, argued that health care problems "are closely tied to two other major national priorities: the need to bring inflation in the economy as a whole under tight rein and the need to spend the federal dollar prudently." Domestic policy staff head Stuart Eizenstat added: "We simply cannot set in motion an entitlement program and allow it to roll along regardless of cost and administrative problems or changed economic circumstances." Senator Kennedy denied that there was any personal clash with President Carter. "Look, I've been here [in the Senate] for 17 years, for heaven's sake. These are not personal matters —these are *issues.*" To which he might have added that the differences between him and President Carter on health care reflected a continuing division in the Democratic party.

The nature of the Republican coalition suggests a fair amount of change over the last generation. In 1949, V. O. Key wrote: "The stakes in control of southern Republican organizations nearly all turn on their relations with the national party; no southern Republican leader entertains seriously the notion that his party will during his lifetime gain control of his state government. . . . Most of them are overwhelmed by the futility of it all, but they keep the faith in a quiet spirit of dedication not unlike that of the Britisher who, although living in the jungle surrounded by heathen, dresses for dinner" (1949, pp. 292–93). No longer. Southerners are now very much part of the dominant group in the Republican coalition. Whereas in 1960 Republican activists were more liberal than Democrats on civil rights matters (Nexon, 1971, p. 721), by 1972 the Republican electoral coalition was divided in this policy area and more conservative than the Democrats.

Change is also apparent in Republican attitudes on international involvement. Many Republicans took isolationist stands prior to World War II, and disputes over the extent of U.S. involvement continued in the immediate postwar years. This division was very much part of the fight between the Eisenhower and Taft coalitions in 1952, but the 1972 data suggest that this Republican argument has faded away.

CAMPAIGN IMPLICATIONS OF ISSUE COALITIONS

Earlier in this chapter, we said that the activists' interest in issues made it appropriate to think of the parties as advocacy parties, but that "advocacy" had to be understood in light of what the activists were free to do. In the midst of a presidential campaign, groups of activists are not free to devise campaign strategies of their own. If the presidential candidate is campaigning in favor of busing, for example, activists in his party, whatever their own attitudes, can hardly claim their candidate will oppose busing once he is in the White House. But they can choose which issues they are going to emphasize in their own localities. In some cases, the choice is forced on them. If they are printing their own campaign pamphlets, they must decide which material about the presidential candidate they are going to include. If they are embarking on a "doorbelling" campaign, they must decide what they are going to tell potential voters about the candidate. The other way they "advocate" policies is to report their own attitudes upwards to coalition leaders. The policy preferences of leaders in a single county are hardly going to determine national strategy, but as these reports are aggregated, they indicate the policy preferences of the coalition to the strategy group. These aggregated preferences are taken into account.

Available data make it possible to verify these campaign implications of group and coalition preferences. In the case of the issue groups, there are data on the intensity of their feelings (whether they feel strongly or not), the extent of consensus (whether the members agree with each other on the issue), and whether or not the issue was emphasized. As you might expect, intensity of group feelings is significantly related to the emphasis they place on an issue. That is, the more strongly they feel for or against a question, the more likely they are to stress that issue in their local campaigning. The Pearsonian correlation, r, is .32. (If you have not encountered bivariate correlation before, you might want to consult the box on that topic on page 186 in Chapter 7.) But in addition, consensus is related to the degree to which groups emphasize an issue ($r = .17$). This is perhaps a little more surprising until you reflect on the group dynamics of reinforcement and sharing. Consensus is a vital property of a group and is therefore related to group behavior.

There also appears to be a strong relationship between coalition emphases and candidate emphases. The coalition emphases can be determined from the data set we have been using, and we know the candidate emphases from a content analysis of their speeches (Kessel, 1977). The correlation (r) between Senator McGovern's emphases and those of the Democratic coalition is .36.[16] That between President Nixon and the Republican coalition is .57; and if one excludes natural resources, which Nixon barely mentioned, the correlation goes up to .84. Data on the candidate's policy preferences are not available for Senator McGovern, but good estimates of Nixon's preferences are available from members of the White House staff who were in frequent contact with him (Kessel, 1975). Here again there is a strong relationship ($r = .56$) between the mean policy preferences of the coalition and those of the candidate.

The linkage between coalition and candidate flows in both directions. He or she learns of coalition preferences through reports that are aggregated by the campaign organization. They learn of his positions from his many public statements as well as from communications that come through party channels. The coalition cannot prevent a candidate from taking a position about which he feels strongly. Nor can the candidate force the coalition to emphasize issues on which they think he is taking an unwise stand. But there are forces that work toward mutual accommodation. The candidate doesn't want to get too far away from his supporters, and the coalition members can work most effectively for their candidate through a faithful representation of his positions.

Summary

The electoral parties consist of activists who have been recruited during one or another of the presidential campaigns through which the party has passed. These activists are middle class, interested in issues, and are more likely to agree with fellow partisans than with residents of their own communities. Their attitudes on issues allow them to be combined into groups: four generally moderate groups in the Republican party, and seven generally liberal groups in the Democratic party. These nationwide issue groups tell us more about parties than traditional categories. When the groups were combined (at least in 1972), the resulting issue coalitions were more conservative in the Republican party and more liberal in the Democratic party. The policy preferences of the groups correspond to the issues they emphasize, and the issues emphasized by the

---

[16] One must be cautious in interpreting this relationship. The relevant data from the content analysis are the frequencies of reference to six policy areas (the four used in this chapter plus natural resources and agriculture). A correlation resting on six data points is hardly reliable.

coalitions correspond to the issues stressed by the presidential candidates. Thus the internal structure of the electoral parties does affect their campaign strategies.

The more general argument, however, is that the reasons *why* a coalition behaves as it does depend on its internal structure and its external structure, and the reasons for taking action *when* it does are to be found in the temporal pattern. In this chapter, we have reviewed only the temporal pattern and the internal structure of electoral politics. We have not yet covered those outward-looking activities which arise from the need of the electoral coalitions to reach the voters. So, we shall turn to this topic in the next chapter.

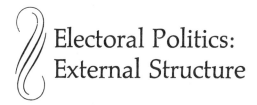

chapter 4

Electoral Politics:
External Structure

To a greater degree than is true of any other kind of politics, electoral politics is aimed at one primary audience: the voters.[1] Four

---

[1] A useful distinction can be made between primary and secondary audiences. Primary audiences are those whose support is essential for success in a given institutional domain. Secondary audiences are those whose political reactions are consequential, but come (often later) in other institutional domains. Thus voters whose ballots would be cast in the general election are a secondary audience for nomination politics, and become a primary audience for electoral politics.

There are some secondary audiences for electoral politics. If a candidate (or someone in his core group) is unusually reflective, or if he is running so far ahead as to be regarded as almost certain of election, there may be concerns for how his positions on issues are going to be regarded by the bureaucracy and Congress, and how this is going to affect the candidate's ability to accomplish things in executive politics or legislative politics if he is elected. Thus in 1960, Senator John Kennedy asked Clark Clifford, who had been special counsel to President Truman, and Professor Richard Neustadt, author of *Presidential Power*, to draft reports on what would have to be done. In 1972, Senator George McGovern asked Clark Clifford and Theodore Sorenson, special counsel to President Kennedy, for similar advice; and Harry MacPherson, special counsel to President Johnson, was asked to contribute his ideas for a possible McGovern administration. In 1976, Jimmy Carter set up a staff headed by Atlanta attorney Jack Watson that worked separately from the campaign staff to make plans for a possible transition. In these cases, a rudimentary external structure was created whose activities were focused on secondary audiences whose support would be needed in other institutional domains.

A related situation concerns an incumbent president who is a candidate for reelection. In this case, the president is simultaneously engaged in electoral politics and executive politics. The primary audiences for executive politics are likely to pay attention to the president's campaign statements, to see if they signal any switch in administration policy. In this case, the president is likely to be aware of both his executive and electoral audiences, and has, of course, extensive structures to link him to both audiences.

types of activities are necessary for a campaign to reach this audience. Hundreds of persons are engaged in *campaign operations, research, public relations,* and *finance.* In this chapter, we shall want to examine each of these four activities in some detail. Before doing so, though, we ought to review two general points about campaign organizations: their growth and development, and the division of authority.

DEVELOPMENT OF CAMPAIGN STAFFS

The staffs that carry on the functions of electoral parties are 20th-century developments, as is the staff that serves the institutionalized presidency. Until the 1920s, national parties largely disappeared between elections. The national chairperson of the incumbent party was frequently appointed postmaster general, a post from which he could conduct party affairs.[2] For example, Republican national chairman Will Hayes was appointed postmaster general in the Harding administration. One looked in vain, though, for any substantial party headquarters. Party activity was so sporadic that most of it could be taken care of from the personal offices of whomever happened to be the party leaders at the time.

For both parties, the beginnings of professional staffing came in the wake of major defeats. After the election of 1928, in which Herbert Hoover received 444 electoral votes to Al Smith's 87, Democratic national chairman John Raskob hired talented phrasemaker Charles Michelson.[3] Michelson's publicity helped to insure that Hoover's popularity was short-lived, and in the happier year of 1932 he was joined by (among others) Emil Hurja, a mining analyst who introduced Democrats to systematic analysis of voting data (Herring, 1940, pp. 208, 265; Michelson, 1944).

The beginnings of modern Republican organization came after the election of 1936, in which Franklin Roosevelt carried 46 states while Kansas Governor Alf Landon carried only Maine and Vermont. John D. M. Hamilton, Republican national chairman during the ensuing four years, appears to have been the first full-time salaried national chairman. He gave the GOP some staff to work with, and envisioned a corps of party civil servants with lifetime careers and a pension plan. Hamilton also took steps toward regular financing with a system of state quotas and sustaining memberships (Cotter and Hennessy, 1964; Lamb, 1966).

---

[2] The movement of party leaders from the postmaster generalship—Will Hayes, James Farley, Robert Hannegan—to the attorney generalship—Howard McGrath, Herbert Brownell, Robert Kennedy, John Mitchell—was a sign that patronage involving United States Attorneys and federal judgeships was becoming more important in running national campaigns than the appointment of postmasters and rural mail carriers. This change took place during the Truman administration.

[3] Charles Michelson was, incidentally, the brother of Nobel prize-winning physicist Albert A. Michelson.

From these beginnings, party headquarters grew from "two ladies occupying one room in a Washington office building," as Franklin Roosevelt described Democratic headquarters in the 1920s (Key, 1964, p. 322) to institutions that employ a hundred or so persons during noncampaign years, and hundreds more scattered through several floors of office space during the campaign proper (Bone, 1971, p. 170). Parallel growth has taken place on the state level, although there the development of headquarters staff is even more recent. About 90 percent of the state parties now have headquarters, and half of these have been opened since 1960. Huckshorn reports that during 1962–63, when he visited some 18 Republican state parties, 7 did not have a permanent headquarters. By the 1969–72 period, all but one of these states had headquarters (1976, pp. 254–55).

Another surge of Republican organizational activity took place after 1976. National chairperson Bill Brock was quite concerned about the future of the party, which, at the state level, was about as weak as it had been following the defeats of 1936 and 1964. Brock supplied organizational directors for all state parties in 1978 at a cost of $1 million, and put together a staff of 15 regional political directors to provide liaison between the national committee and the state committees. A local election campaign division, with 15 staff members working directly in local election campaigns, especially those for state legislatures, was particularly important. In the judgment of John Bibby, the "Brock program of assistance to party organizations has been unprecedented in the history of American political parties" (forthcoming).

DIVISION OF AUTHORITY

Division of authority in political organizations is hardly a recent development. History tells us of many struggles for the ears of ancient monarchs, and there are various bases of power in all forms of politics. Still, some organizational features fragment authority in electoral politics, and it would be well to know what they are. As we have just seen, in recent decades the national committees have developed staffs capable of conducting national campaigns. Many candidates, however, have chosen to work through their own organizations, such as the President Ford Committee. A candidate organization does the same things as a national committee staff, speechwriting, media contact, and the like. But the existence of a candidate organization separate from the national committee staff means that there are at least two campaign chairpersons and two rival sets of division heads. Furthermore, the candidate is not part of either organization. Most of the time, he is off campaigning, which means physically separate from both headquarters. And the candidate has some staff, often including some of his core group, traveling with him. This creates a third headquarters, or at the very least a third point at which many executive decisions about the campaign are made.

All of the arguments for responsibility, efficiency, and economy would seem to go against multiple centers of authority and duplicate senior staffs. Why do they exist? There are several factors that lead to the creation of a separate campaign organization. The most important is that the national committee staff is by tradition neutral in nomination politics. There are good reasons for this. The national committee is charged with making the arrangements for the national convention. Given at least two aspirants who think they ought to be the nominee, if the national committee were to facilitate the chances of Candidate A, Candidate B would have every reason to be angry. So the national committee staff is neutral. It doesn't take any action to harm Candidate A or Candidate B, but neither does it promote the candidacy of either at the expense of other aspirants.

As we have already seen, the staff needed for nomination politics is much smaller than the organization needed for a general election campaign. Still to be nominated, a candidate must have speeches written, press releases distributed, polls taken, funds raised, and so on. In the course of a quest for the nomination, close working relations develop between the senior members of this staff and the candidate. Many become members of the candidate's core group. At a minimum, the candidate knows what senior members of this staff can do, and how well they can do it.

Once the nomination is in hand, there are two prospective campaign staffs in being, the candidate's own organization that has taken him through the convention, and the national committee staff. There are also rivalries that separate these staffs. The national committee staff includes persons who have had experience in previous presidential campaigns, experience that is often in short supply on the candidate's own staff. They have been in touch with the state organizations. They know, for example, if there is a split in the state organization in Montana just who is on which side. They know which state organizations can get things done, and which states are going to need close supervision in order to accomplish essential tasks during the campaign. From the point of view of the candidate's staff members, they have the more essential knowledge: how to work with the candidate. They know how to do what he or she wants to have done. The national committee staff, which has been occupied with routine party activities while they have been out winning primary elections, seems stuffy and slow to react. And while others were skeptical early on, the candidate's staff has seen their leader triumph in nomination politics. They feel they have earned the right to conduct the fall campaign. In short, after the convention there are two rival staffs, and—especially if the convention has been held in late summer—there is little time to deal with this dilemma.

Multiple Headquarters

There have been a good many variations, but there have been two basic organizational patterns in electoral politics. The first is to merge the two staffs and conduct a unified campaign through the national committee staff. The second is to allow the existing candidate organization to conduct the campaign and have the national committee staff take care of "other party business." The advantage of the former is that you take advantage of an experienced staff, and you have established lines of communication into every state whether the candidate was involved there in the springtime or not. The advantage of the separate approach is that there is a working organization in being, and separateness allows the candidate to stress his independence from other politicians. Thus, when Adlai Stevenson wanted to underscore his independence from an unpopular Truman administration, he had his headquarters in Springfield, Illinois; and when Jimmy Carter wanted to accent the fact that he was not part of the Washington scene in 1976, Carter headquarters was kept in Atlanta.

Many proponents of a unified campaign point to that of Franklin Roosevelt in 1932 as an example of how a campaign should be run. Dwight Eisenhower in 1956, Adlai Stevenson the same year, John Kennedy in 1960, Barry Goldwater in 1964, Lyndon Johnson the same year, and Hubert Humphrey in 1968 all conducted their campaigns from national committee headquarters. Adlai Stevenson in 1952, Richard Nixon in 1960, 1968, and 1972, George McGovern in 1972, and Gerald Ford and Jimmy Carter in 1976 all maintained separate campaign headquarters (Ogden and Peterson, 1968, chap. 5; Cotter and Hennessy, 1964, pp. 122–27). A minimum requirement for a unified campaign is someone who can exercise unquestioned control over the merged staffs and who has the complete trust of the candidate. Robert Kennedy played this role at the Democratic National Committee in 1960. Even so, it was difficult to overcome some of the rivalries among other staff members.

The tendency to have the campaign conducted by a separate candidate organization was given a powerful push by the Federal Election Campaign Act of 1974. This act stipulates that federal funds will go to a separate candidate organization during the primaries. There is an option under which the candidate may designate the national committee as the agent to spend public funds in the general election campaign; but by the time this choice is made, all the accounting and reporting procedures have been set up in the candidate organization. Neither candidate used this option in 1976. Gerald Ford wrote in his memoirs that he wanted to run his 1976 campaign through the Republican National Committee, but apparently was told that he could not do so (Ford, 1979, p. 295).

Regardless of where the headquarters offices are located or how many of them there are, there is another campaign headquarters, and that is wherever the candidate happens to be. This used to be "the train"; now it is "the plane." Not only does the physical presence of the candidate signify the location of "the campaign" as far as most of the media representatives are concerned, but there are certain things that can be done from "the plane" (or sometimes from the motorcade en route to a campaign event) and nowhere else. The candidate is moved on jet aircraft, not only to respond to as many requests for candidate appearances as possible, but also to appear in as many media markets as can be done between sunrise and sunset and thus generate broader coverage in the local press. Speeches must be ready for each stop. And there are likely to be over a hundred reporters flying along, most of them in a press plane, whose needs must be borne in mind and whose questions require answers.

A reasonably large staff must accompany the candidate. His senior speech writers need to be close at hand to alter speeches to take account of late-breaking events, and to work with the candidate during the in-flight time. His press secretary needs to be along to handle the traveling press and those encountered along the way. Often persons close to the candidate travel along so there will be a few familiar faces among the blur he sees moving from airport to airport, and to help provide background for reporters. Usually there is a very senior staff person who goes along to organize all this. Governor Sherman Adams of New Hampshire rode Eisenhower's campaign train in 1952 to provide liaison between the train and other campaign leaders. H. R. Haldeman was in charge of Nixon's campaign plane in 1968. Both, of course, ended up as the principal assistants once the candidates were in the White House.

In theory, basic decisions are made when the candidate is available to meet with his strategy group, or the candidate delegates authority to others to act in his name. In practice, there are unexpected developments—a foreign crisis, a charge by the opposition—that require instant response from "the plane." This is frustrating to those in the headquarters offices. Although they are supposed to be in instant radio communication with "the plane," sometimes they must wait until the plane is on the ground and a telephone line is available, or until the traveling party returns from a campaign event somewhere. Gary Hart recalled the situation in the 1972 McGovern campaign:

> Generally, the communications between the traveling party and the headquarters were good. . . . But occasionally, some momentous decision would be made by the Senator which we would find out about only third-hand, hours after the fact. That sprang from a feeling which one gets traveling on the plane with the candidate, traveling staff, and reporters,

that the entire campaign is there and that everything else is at best secondary and will follow along, like the camel's body following its nose
wherever it is led. (1973, p. 300)

Frustrating though it is, this situation is likely to continue.

Multiple Chairpersons

Since a campaign is being led from at least three sources—the national
committee, the candidate's personal staff, and "the plane"—there is a
considerable fragmentation of authority. Nor is this all. It is not uncom-
mon for more than one person to believe that he or she has been promised
the leadership position in a campaign. In the 1960 Nixon campaign, former
Republican national chairman Leonard Hall was given the title of campaign chairman, and Robert Finch, a close friend of the candidate from
Los Angeles, was called campaign director. In the 1972 McGovern campaign, Gary Hart, Frank Mankiewicz, and Lawrence O'Brien, who had
been recruited in that order, all had titles suggesting they were in charge of
that campaign. (Of course, there were also Thruston B. Morton and Jean
Westwood, who were the Republican and Democratic national committee
chairpersons during these two campaigns.) Each of these persons was, in
fact, playing an important role in these campaigns, and that role varied
according to the background and skills of the particular individual. But
who was in charge? That question was deliberately left unresolved by the
candidate, who wanted to use all these people in the campaign.

Multiple Groups and Multiple Bases of Authority

On top of all this, there are different points of view that arise as one
person or another acts as a spokesperson for one of the groups in the candidate's supporting coalition. As we have seen, each group has a different
set of policy preferences, and its members attempt to persuade the candidate that he or she should move closer to their position. Finally, as we
are about to see, different kinds of expertise are needed in a campaign—
speech writing, fund raising, and so on—and these give rise to a functional
division of authority. The regional directors in campaign operations feel
that the speech writers don't understand how the campaign is moving out
across the country; the speech writers think that the regional directors
don't have a feel for issues; the finance people think that the other groups
are spending money faster than they can possibly raise it. Since each of
these actors has a base of expertise in his or her own area, each has a
basis on which to speak. The division of responsibility between the few
at the apex of the campaign and those with specific responsibilities is not

unlike that in Congress between the floor leaders and committee chairman. Nonetheless, this is a source of tension within a campaign organization. Thus, one of the reasons given by F. Clifton White for Barry Goldwater's defeat in 1964 was not that the senator was a candidate of the minority party who took policy positions at some remove from the majority of the American people. Rather:

> . . . the really important decisions of the campaign were . . . hammered out in the so-called "Think Tank" on the third floor of an office building at 1625 I Street in downtown Washington. There Denison Kitchell, Bill Baroody and their stable of speech writers and research experts held court. It was a court that was notably unreceptive to ideas from outside its own circle. (White, 1967, pp. 415–16)

Clif White happened to be the director of Citizens for Goldwater-Miller, and in this quote he was expressing his unhappiness with the research division. But the quote could have come just as easily from an ad agency person whose favored slogan has been rejected, or from a regional coordinator who felt that others just didn't understand New England.

Multiple headquarters. Multiple chairpersons. Multiple groups. Multiple bases of expertise. How seriously do these affect the progress of the campaign? Many things determine the answer to this, but one of the most important is the candidate's standing with the voters. If the candidate is popular, and running well ahead of his opponent, then organizational problems are not too serious. Staff members' morale is high, and visions of White House offices dance in their heads. If the contestants are in a tight race, there is anxiety; but along with the anxiety, there is some effort to put forth the extra effort that might make a difference in the election. But if the candidate is running behind, then organizational tensions are felt. Reluctant to believe that the candidate is unpopular, or that he or she is saying the wrong things about the issues, there is a tendency to think that improper tactics are being used, or that there is some organizational defect. It is easy to think it is someone else's fault that the party is running behind, and with responsibility so divided, there are many scapegoats close at hand.[4]

CAMPAIGN OPERATIONS

Whatever else it may be, a campaign staff is not a tidy structure. It does not retain the same institutional form from one campaign to another. In one campaign, the presidential campaign organization will be distinct from

---

[4] One could argue that a losing campaign is the best to study. There are likely to be just as many organizational problems in a winning campaign organization, but the euphoria that goes with victory tends to hide the problems from participants and observers.

the national committee staff. In another, the campaign may be run from the national committee. Division titles change from one campaign to another. Activities found in one organizational unit in a given campaign may have been assigned to another organizational unit four years earlier. Fortunately, we are not interested in who has which title or what an organization chart might look like. We are interested in what the campaign organization *does*. In this regard, it is safe to assume that there are four sets of activities: campaign operations, research, public relations, and finance. Each of these is needed to reach the voters, and each will be carried out by persons located somewhere within any campaign organization.

Where to Campaign?

Of all the decisions taken in a campaign, those with the most extensive implications for what the campaign organization does concern geographic concentration. Many things that will affect the outcome of an election—the attitudes the voters have at the outset of a campaign, the positions taken by the opposition candidate—are beyond the control of the campaign managers. They can make decisions, though, about how they will use the resources they control. Essentially this refers to where the candidate will campaign, where money will be spent, and what organizational efforts to put forth. Given finite time and finite resources, these cannot be expended everywhere, and there are obvious incentives to use them where there will be the greatest return in votes.

As long as we continue to elect our presidents through the Electoral College, and as long as the states cast all of their electoral votes for the candidate receiving a plurality in the state,[5] this decision is going to be geographic. There are 538 electoral votes in all, and since the number of votes cast is roughly proportional to the state's population, there is a premium on carrying large states. If they all voted for the same candidate, the 11 largest states—California, New York, Pennsylvania, Illinois, Texas, Ohio, Michigan, Florida, New Jersey, Massachusetts, and either Indiana or North Carolina—could elect a president regardless of what the other 39 did. If the Electoral College were to be abolished, then the emphasis would shift to ways and means of getting the largest majorities of popular votes. It is conceivable that such a decision might be made on a nongeographic basis, such as opting for a campaign directed at middle class voters, but for the present the decisions rest on the traditional criteria.

---

[5] Seemingly forgotten in the discussion about possible elimination of the Electoral College is the state's power to cast its electoral votes in some other way than by giving all of them to the candidate winning a plurality. Michigan cast its electoral votes by congressional district in 1892, and its right to do so was upheld by the Supreme Court in *Shoemaker* v. *United States* (Corwin, 1948, pp. 50, 418).

This decision is likely to be made at the highest levels of the campaign organization. The way it is made depends on the quality of information available to the decision-makers, and how systematic their analysis is. As long ago as 1932, James A. Farley was making decisions based on analyses of probable Democratic majorities in each state.

> Acting on the principle that success can do its own succeeding without any help from anyone, the Democratic National Committee merely adapted its campaign expenditures to Mr. Hurja's figures. Down to 1932 political parties had largely used the scatter-gun method. A campaign chairman, with the evenhanded justice of a blinded divinity, would spill his funds equitably and inefficiently over an entire map. Armed with the Hurja prognostication Mr. Farley . . . tempered the wind to the shorn lamb, turned the hose on the dry ground, and made his nickels last. (*Fortune*, April, 1935, p. 136, quoted in Herring, 1940)

In 1976, both parties were quite systematic in making their decisions about geographic concentration. Hamilton Jordan wrote a long memorandum for Jimmy Carter and Walter Mondale, in which he devoted no less than 31 pages to the development of formulas to determine the percent of effort to be devoted to each state. These formulas reflected three criteria: size, Democratic potential, and need. Points awarded for *size* were straightforward applications of Electoral College arithmetic. Each state was given one point for each electoral vote, and size was deemed to be as important as Democratic potential and need combined. States were divided into four categories according to *Democratic potential*, that is, their likelihood of voting Democratic if worked effectively. The assignment of states to these four categories was curious. California, which had gone Republican in three of the last four presidential elections, was put in the top category of Democratic potential along with Massachusetts, which had gone Democratic in all four of the elections. Oregon, with a voting history identical to California's, was assigned to the next to the top category in Democratic potential along with Pennsylvania, which had gone Democratic in three of the four elections. The estimates of *need* were based on four pieces of information: strategic premises, survey information, whether Carter had campaigned in a primary election in the state, and the results of that primary. States were again put into four categories. The "most needed" class included most of the critical large industrial states and two important border states. The "least needed" category included states that could be carried with a minimum of effort, such as Georgia, some small states, such as Arizona, and some states likely to go Republican, such as Kansas and Nebraska. Finally, the entire percent of effort computation (based on size, Democratic potential, and need) was matched against a "value of a day's campaigning estimate," in which Jimmy Carter, for example, was assigned 7 points and Chip Carter was assigned 2 points, to determine how often given spokespersons for the ticket ought to campaign in the state (Schram, 1977, pp. 239–50, 386–91).

The 1976 Republican plan, drawn up by their strategy group, was quite different. It was a long document (120 pages plus appendices) which took into account the position in which Ford found himself (far behind Carter) and the voters' perceptions of the two candidates. After contrasting the perceptions with what the strategy group took to be the actual strengths and weaknesses of the two candidates, the report set forth a strategy for changing these perceptions through actions Ford was to take, attacks to be made on Carter, use of media, and employment of available financial resources. A threefold classification of states—"Our Base," "Swing States," and "His Base"—was included in this more general strategy plan. In general, the classification of states by the Republican strategy group was similar to that in Jordan's analysis, except that the Republican group had a much longer list of swing states, and they saw Ford's base as being much smaller than Jordan had calculated Carter's base. Nine of the states presumed to be likely to vote for Carter for one reason or another by Jordan were seen as swing states by the Republicans[6] (Schram, 1977, pp. 253–68). Within the swing states, the Republicans further defined Ford's target constituency as "the upper blue-collar and white-collar workers, often from a family which has risen in mobility in the last generation . . . many of whom are Catholics" (Schram, 1977, p. 263). But the undeniable common element between the two plans reflected Electoral College arithmetic. Of the 11 largest states noted above, 8 made up Jordan's list of critical large industrial states, and all of them save Massachusetts appeared on the Republican list of swing states.

While a tendency toward systematic use of campaign resources undoubtedly has been growing in recent years, campaigners do not always make rational decisions. In 1960, Richard Nixon pledged to visit all 50 states, and in order to do so devoted most of the Sunday before the election to a long flight to Alaska, a state that cast barely 1 percent of the electoral votes needed. During the final week of the 1964 campaign, Barry Goldwater made appearances in four great metropolitan centers, but he also devoted time to the voters in Dover, Delaware; Cedar Rapids, Iowa; Cheyenne, Wyoming; and Las Vegas, Nevada. These were not locations where the election was going to be won or lost. But even if the campaign managers do nothing more than acquiesce to local pressures—schedule the candidate where state leaders want him to come, and keep him away

---

[6] All but one of these states ended up voting for Carter in the 1976 general election. For the Ford strategists to have accepted Jordan's estimate of the Carter base (if they had known about it) would have been virtually to concede the election to Carter. Jordan assumed that between the South and a few normally Democratic states elsewhere, Carter only had to carry a few more states elsewhere to win in the Electoral College.

from areas where he is unpopular—this acquiescence is a decision that controls much of what the campaign organization does.

The Plane

Wherever it is decided that the candidate shall go, there must be some means of moving him around, and this means "the plane."[7] The shift to aircraft as the primary means of moving the candidate around has been a gradual consequence of technological developments. The advent of jet aircraft meant that it was no longer possible to reject the plea of a West Coast politico for a presidential candidate's appearance on the grounds that he or she was campaigning in, say, Illinois that day. Now it became possible for him to get to the West Coast if the reason was sufficiently compelling. A second crucial step was the development of the Boeing 727; this made it possible to stay on the same plane and still get into smaller airports with shorter runways. Finally, the development of communication equipment (and having enough money to be able to put it onto the candidate's plane) meant reasonably constant communication between "the plane" and other campaign headquarters.

Campaign trains are still used, but as a means of evoking nostalgia for "traditional" politics, giving the television cameramen something different to shoot, and reaching groups of contiguous small- and medium-size cities that might affect important electoral votes. Thus, in 1976 Jimmy Carter took a whistlestop tour from Newark across New Jersey and Pennsylvania toward Chicago, hoping to invoke the spirit of Harry Truman's 1948 effort, and Gerald Ford campaigned across Illinois. And, of course, there is the motorcade that is used to move the candidate through suburban areas and back and forth from an airport to a rally site.

As we have already seen, moving the candidate around the country means more than just moving the candidate. A considerable retinue accompanies him or her, and this somewhat complicates the logistics. A plane, such as Peanut One used by Jimmy Carter in 1976, or Yai Bi Kin (Navajo for House in the Sky) used by Barry Goldwater in 1964, usually carries some senior advisors and friends, speech writers, press secretary and his aides, state dignitaries, Secret Service personnel, pool reporters, and the secretaries who help some of these people get their work done. The configuration of the plane must provide some privacy for the candidate, working space, an area for typewriters, mimeograph, Xerox, and the communications equipment. Since there isn't enough space aboard the candidate's aircraft for the press that travels with him or her, there is also a press plane that follows along.

---

[7] "The plane" appears in quotation marks because the phrase has a variety of meanings in conversations at campaign headquarters. It may refer to the "rival" headquarters, or the traveling party, or the present geographic location of the aircraft.

Scheduling

Responsibility for planning campaign trips is divided among four sets of persons: the strategy committee (or some ranking decision maker), regional and state coordinators and state party leaders, the tour committee, and advance men. The basic decisions about time allocations are made at the highest levels of the campaign in the manner already discussed. Questions about where the candidate should go within a state are talked out between regional and state coordinators, and party leaders in the state concerned. The candidate's general schedule (3:00 P.M., Press plane arrives Metropolitan Airport; 3:30 P.M., Candidate plane arrives Metropolitan Airport; 3:45 P.M., Candidate departs for Metro City Hotel; and so on) is worked out by a person on the tour committee.[8] Since the candidate will be making appearances in several localities on a typical day, all of these details have to be combined into a master schedule. Finally, responsibility for arrangements in the community where the candidate is to appear is in the hands of the advance man.

The Advance Man

The person who advances a candidate's appearance usually gets to the city about five days to a week before the appearance. Any number of things must be done. The route between the airport and the rally site must be checked out and timed exactly in traffic conditions similar to those the candidate's motorcade will encounter. The rally site, whether an auditorium, shopping center, or whatever, must be checked out so it will accord with the candidate's preferences, and so locations for photographers and the traveling and local press will be available but will not interfere with the voters who ought to be present. Large numbers of local politicos will want to be close to the candidate, or too small an audience may be in prospect. The advance man must cut the number of politicos down to a manageable number, and do what he can to increase the size of the crowd. If the candidate is staying overnight, hotel reservations must be made. Arrangements must be made with local police to insure the candidate's safety. If they are available, the Secret Service can be of great help in all this. They are familiar with the things that need to be done, and there is enough overlap between logistical needs and safety needs that many of the necessary arrangements fall into their province.

The advance man normally has the final say about all of the details of the appearance. There are certain to be things that will be disputed—

---

[8] The tour committee will typically have one person working on the presidential candidate's schedule; one on the vice presidential candidate's schedule; one handling party notables, such as ex-presidents; one handling celebrities, such as movie stars; and one or more coordinating the appearance of others appearing on behalf of the ticket.

who will have an opportunity to shake hands with the candidate, whose car will be how close to the candidate's in the motorcade, and so on— and it is up to the advance man to settle these matters.[9] Once the candidate shows up, the advance man is at his side and in charge of things as long as the candidate is in the city. Once the candidate's plane leaves for the next city, where another advance man will have been setting things up, the advance man says good-bye and leaves for another city to make arrangements for another appearance some days hence (Hoagland, 1960; Ogden and Peterson, 1968, chap. 9).

Organizational Groups

The rest of the persons involved in campaign operations are usually organized along interest group or regional lines. The nature of an interest group operation is suggested by the names of units that have been organized in one campaign or another: Senior Citizens for Kennedy, Viva Kennedy, Scientists and Engineers for Johnson-Humphrey, Educators for Johnson and Humphrey, Mothers for a Moral America, Pilots for Goldwater-Miller, Nationalities Division, Civil Rights Division, Agriculture Division, Labor Division, Minorities Division, Arts & Sciences Division, Funeral Directors Committee for the Reelection of the President, Motorcyclists Committee for the Reelection of the President, Democrats for Nixon, Heritage Groups, and National McGovern-Shriver Labor Committee. Each of these campaign units is set up to reach a particular segment of the population. One must know something more than the name of the unit, of course, to be certain that it is a functioning part of the campaign organization. It may be only a paper committee that has been set up to sponsor some campaign event, as was Mothers for a Moral America, or it may be essentially a fund-raising operation, in which one receives a membership card in return for the payment of dues.

Assuming that the campaign unit is more than a letterhead committee, it is likely to have certain characteristics. First, the target population must be large enough and have enough political importance for their support to be worth the expenditure of resources. Often attention will be devoted to areas where the party is weak. For some time, for instance, the Republican National Committee had a Labor Division, whereas the Democrats, who already had a lot of labor support, did not have a com-

---

[9] There are good reasons for this. The local party leaders have to work with each other after the rally, and the object of the whole campaign is to make the candidate more popular rather than less so. Consequently, if the local leaders are going to be angry at anyone, it is better that they be upset with the advance man rather than being angry at each other or with the candidate. Sometimes the advance man can avoid this altogether. If he has any experience, he will assure local leaders that his decisions are exactly in line with procedures followed in all the other campaign events being staged for the candidate.

parable unit. Second, the person in charge of the effort has some knowledge of the population in question. Thus, the Arts and Sciences Division of the Republican National Committee was headed by an academic on leave of absence, and the executive director of the Senior Citizens for Johnson and Humphrey was on leave from the United Automobile Workers' Department of Older and Retired Workers. Third, there needs to be some means of communicating with the population. A not unusual pattern includes a mailing list and a newsletter. The essential job of the staff members heading these units is to explain the candidate and the positions being taken in language that their groups understand. If they are sufficiently persuasive, they may also convey the wishes of the population segment back to the campaign leaders.

Regional Groups

The alternate form of campaign organization follows geographic lines. In this form, the head of the campaign division will be assisted by regional directors. The regions used vary a little from one campaign to another, but generally adhere to familiar areas, such as the Middle Atlantic states, the Middle West, or the West Coast. If resources permit, a pair of regional directors is used for each area. This allows one to remain at the headquarters while the other travels in the region. When this arrangement is used, the co-directors will change places every 10 days or so. This means that there is a familiar voice on the headquarters telephone when the state directors call in, and someone out in the field giving encouragement to campaign workers and gathering fresh information.

Establishing lines of communication through regional directors to state directors has the advantage of following the lines of the Electoral College, and the things that the regional directors do are directly related to producing electoral votes in their areas. As already noted, once the strategy group has decided that the candidate or other spokesmen for the ticket will spend time in a given state, the regional director and state chairmen negotiate on the particulars of the appearances. Which areas of the state are most likely to produce votes for the ticket without any special effort? Which areas may do so, but require some campaigning? These are questions that would be discussed in making a decision that the candidate ought to appear in, say, Rochester and Syracuse, but not in Buffalo.

Regional directors make similar judgments about states in their areas. This allows decisions to be made about allocations of resources. In 1960, for example, national campaign manager Robert Kennedy was told that Democratic prospects did not look good in Iowa, but there was a chance for his brother to carry Illinois. His response was simple: "We'll spend our money in Illinois."

A third activity of regional directors is coordination of straight-forward registration and get-out-the-vote drives. Since registration is a major factor holding down election day turnout (Rosenstone and Wolfinger, 1978; Kelley, Bowen, and Ayers, 1967), and since Democrats are less likely to register than Republicans, Democratic campaigners are somewhat more likely to emphasize registration drives than Republicans.[10] Both parties are concerned with maximizing their turnout. The election day efforts to do this were simple in the small towns of the 19th century. Each party had a poll watcher who knew the town's inhabitants. If supporters of his party had not showed up by midafternoon, someone would be sent round to remind them to come and vote. The technique is still essentially the same, but its application has been made more complex by changes in the population, and more efficient through the use of telephones and computers.

For election day activity to be effective, it must be preceded by planning and by identifying one's supporters. One begins with an estimate of the total vote needed to carry a state. A new figure is necessary for each election because, with population growth, the vote that carried the state in the preceding election is likely to be inadequate. The total vote for the state is then decomposed into county quotas, these likewise based on knowledge of party strength and the county populations. If each county meets its quota, then the state goal will be reached.

Next, the county leaders must locate the voters who will enable them to meet their quota. If there is registration by party, they have a pretty good idea where to start, but even if they have registration lists available, additional work must be done. Population mobility will have brought any number of new residents to the community, and the greater incidence of independent voting makes it necessary to ascertain whether each "loyal Democrat" in fact intends to vote for the Democratic candidate. This has been done traditionally by precinct workers calling on voters in their areas. If funds are available to set up phone banks, however, voters can be contacted much more speedily by bringing volunteers together in a "boiler shop" from which telephone calls are placed. The calls usually include a gentle sales pitch; but the crucial elements are to determine whether persons living in the household intend to vote, whether they need any aid in doing so, such as transportation or a baby-sitter, and whether they intend to support the party's candidate, are undecided, or intend to vote for the opposition candidate.

The immediate results of the telephone work provide information on how well the candidate is running. They are aggregated and forwarded up the line to state headquarters and national headquarters. But much of the information is fed into computers in order to provide useful lists

---

[10] The greater tendency among Democratic voters to remain unregistered accounts for the greater Democratic interest in schemes of automatic or permanent registration.

and sets of address labels. Those undecided about which candidate they should support are mailed literature about him or her. Depending on the quality of information elicited and the sophistication of the computer operation, voters may receive personal letters presenting specific arguments about the issues of concern to them. Those undecided about whether to vote receive extra calls shortly before the election encouraging them to do so. Names of persons who need transportation to the polls appear on special lists so this can be provided. And names of all those likely to vote for the candidate appear on lists that allow traditional election day contact to go forward.

This telephone and computer operation is simple enough to describe, but enormous amounts of effort are necessary to carry it out. During the 1972 Nixon campaign, nearly 16 million households were contacted in this way. More people were reached through this contact effort than had voted for Nixon in 1968. This undoubtedly represented the high point of this kind of campaigning. Some $12 million were poured into this contact operation (White, 1973, pp. 322–28), and money that would allow citizen contact on this lavish a scale is not available under the campaign finance laws that went into effect in 1974.

RESEARCH

The "research" that is needed in the middle of a campaign has very little to do with academic "research." The aim of campaign research is not the discovery of information that may be regarded as a contribution to knowledge. There is an element of discovery in polls taken to determine voters' perceptions, but much more campaign research involves processing already available information so it can be used for electoral purposes. When one speaks of research in a campaign headquarters, the usual reference is to the activities of those who work in a research division. This includes speech writers, "issue persons," pollsters, and individuals whose activities are similar to those of reference librarians.

The Art of Producing Campaign Speeches

The speech that is most often given during a campaign is not written at all. It evolves. The speech is a pastiche of applause lines the candidate has discovered in previous months of campaigning. It is a "theme song" made up of phrases the candidate likes, and which have demonstrated their ability to spark crowd reaction. It includes such lines as John Kennedy's "It's time to get America moving again," George Wallace's references to "pointy-headed bureaucrats who send us guidelines telling us when we can go to sleep at night and when we can get up in the morning," Richard Nixon's 1968 declaration that "It's time for new leadership," and Jimmy Carter's promise, "I'll never lie to you." Such a speech is used during the numerous brief stops when "remarks" are called for. There are too many of these for anything approaching an original statement to be developed for each, and neither a tired candidate nor a weary speech writer has any desire to depart from the familiar. The repetition is tedious to the candidate and to reporters who have heard the lines dozens of times, but repetition helps develop a candidate's image in the same way that endless exposure to Alka-Seltzer or Pepto-Bismol commercials fix the names of these products in the minds of television viewers.

Major addresses on foreign policy, economics, welfare, civil rights, or whatever, are quite different. When a candidate is making a major speech to, say, the Detroit Council on Foreign Relations, or giving an address on nationwide television, he or she is expected to state a position with some precision. Speeches for these occasions will be carefully considered, and often pass through several drafts. Just how the candidate and the speech writers work together in such circumstances varies enormously. Theodore Sorenson drafted most of John Kennedy's speeches in 1960, and those he did not write, he at least reviewed. Most speech topics Sorenson "discussed with the Senator only, and they were decided by him, in his plane or hotel and without reference to other materials, a day or two before the speech was given" (Sorenson, 1965, p. 208). In 1968, Richard Nixon worked with a number of speech writers, and set forth what he wanted in memoranda or oral instructions. For example, in late September he distributed a memorandum asking for excerpts running a page to a page and a half. The excerpts, he said, should be

> . . . meaty and quotable and . . . zero in primarily on the four major themes. If we scatter-gun too much we are not going to have an impact. . . . We must have at least two excerpts a week which hit some aspect of the law and order theme and one or two a week which hit some aspect of the spending theme and two or three a week which hit the foreign policy-respect for America theme. (Safire, 1975, pp. 71–72)

In a third pattern, members of the strategy group agree that certain material is called for, and set a speech writer to work on it. For example, late in the 1976 campaign, Jody Powell and Greg Schneiders agreed with speech writer Patrick Anderson that material was needed for a Pittsburgh dinner which would show that Carter knew about the difficulties caused by poor leadership but was optimistic about the future. Anderson wrote a speech including a number of "I see" lines—"I see a new spirit in America. I see a national pride restored. I see a revival of patriotism" (Schram, 1977, p. 344). A similar series of "I see" lines had been used in Carter's acceptance speech, but for that matter such lines had been written by William Safire for Richard Nixon in 1968, had been used by Barry

Goldwater in 1964, had been written by Samuel Rosenman and Robert E. Sherwood for Franklin Roosevelt, and had been used by Robert Ingersoll when he nominated James G. Blaine for president in 1876 (Safire, 1975, p. 54).

In the case of any major address, drafts flow back and forth between the candidate and the speech writers. This allows the candidate to continue making changes until he gets what he wants. For example, Patrick Anderson wrote, "When I started to run for president, there were those who said I would fail, because there was another governor who spoke for the South, a man who once stood in a schoolhouse door and cried out, 'segregation forever!' " Jimmy Carter, not wishing to insult George Wallace unnecessarily, changed the reason to ". . . there were those who said I would fail because I was from the South" (Schram, 1977, p. 180). Toward the end of the 1968 campaign, Richard Nixon wanted to make a statement concerning then-President Lyndon Johnson. As drafted by Bryce Harlow, it began, "Throughout this campaign the President has been even-handed and straightforward with the major presidential contenders about Vietnam. I know he has been under intense pressure to contrive a fake peace. . . ." Nixon altered this to read, "Throughout this campaign I have found the President impartial and candid with the major presidential contenders about Vietnam. I know he has been subjected— for many months, beginning long before the National Convention—to intense pressure to contrive what he has appropriately described as a 'fake peace' . . ." (Safire, 1975, p. 85). While the circumstances of a campaign hardly allow a candidate to write every word that he speaks or is released in his name, the speech writing process certainly allows him to place his personal tone on the text that is eventually used.

Insofar as the term "speech writer" suggests that a writer is in control of the process and the candidate simply reads his or her words, it distorts what goes on as a candidate presents his ideas to the electorate. Raymond Moley, who wrote Governor Franklin Roosevelt's speeches in 1932, distinguished between "the principal" who gives the addresses, "the collaborator" who has continuous access to the principal and provides him with drafts, and "the feeders" who route their ideas to the collaborator (1960). The collaborator needs to have a facility with words and some political experience; but more important, the collaborator should have the confidence of the principal, a knowledge of the phrasing the principal likes to use, and a willingness to set forth the ideas the principal wants to use regardless of whether the collaborator thinks the ideas are wise or not.

The feeders may be "issue persons" in the campaign organization proper, or they may be interested citizens who simply want to pass ideas along. Their existence does not imply that either the candidate or the speech writers are barren of ideas themselves, but rather that a great many ideas are needed in the course of a campaign and a rather large number of people think they have ideas that are going to win the election for the candidate. This combination of a need for good ideas, and a need for enough working time to develop substantive proposals so they will be helpful to the candidate, leads to a unique organizational imperative. There must be some kind of screen to protect the issues men and women and the speech writers from the large number of people who want to help but don't quite know how, yet at the same time have some provision so that good ideas do get through.

New Ideas and the Triple Test

While there are likely to be many good ideas, the number of usable ideas tends to be limited. This may come as a surprise to persons who have not been through a presidential campaign, but there are a number of tests any idea must pass before it is politically useful. If the candidate takes a position that gives offense to any group in the supporting coalition, they may not continue to work for him with continued fervor. If the candidate takes a position that is unappealing to some segment of a target constituency, this will reduce the number of votes he might otherwise receive. Furthermore, once a proposal is made, it is certain to be scrutinized by both the opposition and the reporters. If the program is inconsistent with some previously taken position, the candidate will be asked which of the policies he intends to pursue seriously. If he chooses the earlier policy, the just-announced program will be called frivolous. If he chooses the just-announced policy he will be accused of inconsistency. If he says he will implement both policies, opponents and reporters will say that he has not thought through the consequences of what he says. Finally, the proposal should be one that can be accomplished with the resources available to the government. Otherwise, it will be denounced as unworkable or as too expensive. It is this triple test—acceptable to coalition members and voters who are potential supporters, consistent with previously announced positions, and something that can be done with existing resources—that limits the number of ideas that are usable in a campaign.

In consequence of this, the chief qualification of a good issues person is that the individual be able to sense which ideas pass this triple test and should therefore be brought to the attention of the candidate and his or her speech writers. This is likely to be someone motivated by an interest in the substance of politics, and who has had enough previous campaign experience not to be a dogmatic advocate of any particular approach. Persons who have these skills—for example Bryce Harlow or Bill Prendergast in the Republican party or Ted Van Dyk or John Stewart in the Democratic party—are apt to be well known to those in the upper echelons of presidential politics and almost invisible to the general public. Because of their reputations with words and issues, they have been involved in the issues end of several campaigns.

In any particular campaign, there is likely to be a small in-house issues staff, and a larger number of outside consultants. The head of the in-house issues staff will be one who has worked with the candidate for some time. Outside consultants are active in many areas, but there are usually special groups dealing with the imperative policy areas of international involvement and economic management. Thus, Jimmy Carter's 1976 issues staff was headed by Stuart Eizenstat, a Harvard Law School graduate who had written speeches in the Johnson White House and had been active on Humphrey's 1968 issues staff. Zbigniew Brzezinski, who had taught at Harvard and Columbia, served as a principal advisor on international affairs, and Laurence R. Klein, who taught at the Wharton School and was then president-elect of the American Econometric Association, headed a team of economic consultants.

Polling's Changing Place

The importance of polling has been increasing for some time. This is evident both in the location of the principal pollster within the campaign staff and in the sophistication of the information about the voters that is provided. Private polls for candidates, of course, are not new, but as recently as the 1960s they were used in a rather rudimentary manner. Older politicians regarded surveys with some skepticism, and even proponents seemed to be fascinated by any similarity between survey estimates and election results. The usual pattern was to hire an outside polling firm, for the head of the firm to come in occasionally during the campaign to present results, and otherwise to stay in touch with a relatively low-ranking staff member. The reliability of the data was kept high through large numbers of interviews, and the presentation of results was restricted to marginals (that is, 57 percent for Candidate *A* and 43 percent for Candidate *B*) and very simple cross-tabulations. In the 1964 Goldwater campaign, for example, three national surveys of this kind were taken. The reports were kept by an intelligent young graduate of Stanford Law School (who had no training in survey analysis), and the last scheduled survey was cancelled because the surveys were bringing bad news.

This situation changed, not because of arguments about the importance of surveys but because successful politicians put great reliance on them. Ray Bliss was known to study his polls very closely, and knowledgeable analysts, especially Louis Harris among the Democrats and Walter deVries among the Republicans, spread the word about what could be done. By 1976, pollsters were principal members of the strategy groups in both parties. Robert Teeter of Market Opinion Research provided continuous information for the Republicans, and Pat Caddell did the same for the Democrats.

Not only were pollsters located where they could be much more active in charting campaign strategy, but the kind of information they provided was much more detailed. In 1968, David Derge based his analysis for the Nixon campaign on a panel study of voters in 13 states and on small daily cross-sections. The state-level data gave information on where campaign resources should be concentrated, and the daily information permitted him to pick up trends as they began to develop. Pat Caddell similarly had daily information that he could provide to the Carter campaign in 1976. He was able to tell them early on that Carter's support was soft; and as it eroded during the campaign, he was able to point to particular segments of the electorate as contributing disproportionately to the Democratic difficulties. (Caddell's credentials were further enhanced by his experience in the McGovern campaign. Since most Carter strategists were new to national politics, Caddell's possession of good fresh data and experience in interpreting it made it possible for him to establish himself as a knowledgeable advisor.) Robert Teeter added a number of useful analyses for the Republicans. Telephone polls allowed quick answers to questions of interest to the strategists; picked audiences watched the debates, indicating their agreement with the candidates by adjusting rheostats; spatial analyses summarized information on where candidates stood with respect to each other and the voters (Schram, 1977; Parry, 1977). The movement from simple cross-tabulations to nonmetric multidimensional scaling (the type of spatial analysis used to produce Figures 3–2 and 3–3)[11] in a decade's time is a measure of the progress made in using survey information; but having knowledgeable pollsters sitting in on strategy discussions is more important in making effective use of these data.

Information Retrieval in a Campaign

While pollsters and knowledgeable professionals were making use of survey data at the top levels of campaigns, the "reference librarians" of politics busied themselves storing information about issues so it could be made available when it was needed in a campaign and could be distributed throughout the campaign organization. Files are kept of statements made by one's own candidates, and by the opposition candidates. The purpose of this is to allow a quick check of what has been said when an opponent makes a charge during the campaign. If, for example, an opponent says, "Speaking in Houston last October, the President promised to reduce

---

[11] One wonders what the reaction of the politicos would be if they had any idea of the assumptions necessary to sustain nonmetric multidimensional scaling.

unemployment to 5 percent," and it is possible for the National Committee to reply, "The President said that he hoped to reduce unemployment as quickly as possible, but did not mention any specific target," and to release the exact quotation, this can be very helpful in rebutting the charge.

Another standard activity is the production of speaker's manuals and issue books. Stock speeches are written on various issues, and booklets summarize the stands being taken by both parties. These will be broken down by topic and will have facts and quotations showing the virtues of one party's stand juxtaposed with the limitations of what the opposition is doing. These are arranged so a speaker will be able to find an effective reply even as he or she listens to opposition statements.

A third headquarters project is an "answer desk" with a well-advertised telephone number. The persons who take the incoming calls are likely to be political veterans whose qualifications are similar to those who are working on the issues staff, and who provide quick replies to what the party's stand is on energy or agriculture or whatever the caller is concerned about. All of these activities are routine. A fair amount of work is necessary, though, to prepare for these tasks, and to keep the files up to date as the campaign develops.

PUBLIC RELATIONS

During 1976, the media efforts of the Carter campaign were directed by Gerald Rafshoon, and those of the Ford campaign by John Deardourff and Douglas Bailey. Both Rafshoon and the Deardourff-Bailey combination are typical of publicists who carry senior responsibility in presidential campaigns. Gerald Rafshoon Advertising, Inc., is a general advertising firm (that is, the bulk of its income comes from nonpolitical accounts) in Atlanta. Rafshoon's connection with Jimmy Carter went back to Carter's initial campaign for governor of Georgia in 1966. Deardourff and Bailey, on the other hand, have a firm that specializes in politics (Lelyveld, 1976a, 1976b; Witcover, 1977, p. 533). Both came from backgrounds in Republican politics, Deardourff in New York and Bailey in Massachusetts, and both learned enough about media campaigns so that they set up their own campaign management firm. Rafshoon and Deardourff were members of the respective strategy groups, and were thus able to have some say about the strategies as well as execute them.

Being at the center of the campaign organization is not new for publicists. Of all the things done by an electoral coalition to reach their primary audience, public relations is one of the most crucial and has been so recognized for a very long time. Presidents have had the aid of press agents since at least the time of Grover Cleveland. Public relations emerged as a distinct occupation in the early decades of the 20th century, and political applications were not too long in coming. Charles Michelson was a member of the Democratic strategy group in 1932, and in 1936 a Chicago advertising man, Hill Blackett, became the Republican's first public relations director (Kelley, 1956, chap. 1).

In developments since that time, the direction of public relations has been most commonly handled by a combination of an in-house public relations division and either a public relations or a campaign management firm. As television has become most important, so have the media specialists. This is *not* to say that public relations men have taken control of campaigns. Public relations is only one segment of a campaign, and the influence of a public relations firm ranges from a maximum, when one of their chiefs sits with other principals on the strategy group, to a minimum, when the agency is restricted to the technical functions of space and time acquisition. Still, the great days of party public relations directors probably came in the 1950s, with Jack Redding and Sam Brightman in the Democratic party and Robert Humphreys and Lou Guylay in the Republican party. With television so prominent in the 1970s, it was all but inevitable that more influence would flow to the Jerry Rafshoons, the John Deardourffs, and the Doug Baileys who knew how to work with that medium.

It may help to keep these things in perspective to remember that everything but the television material usually comes from the public relations division within the campaign organization. Even in Charles Michelson's time, this was not inconsiderable. Working in an era before electronic media began to rival newspapers, Michelson concentrated on getting stories and phrases into print. He sent statements to prominent Democrats whose names would assure them public attention. He sent news items and editorial suggestions directly to newspapers. His basic assumption was that he wanted to create anti-Hoover news, a task that became much easier once the depression began (Kelley, 1956, p. 31).

Newspaper Contact

This one-man operation evolved into what amounted to a small public relations firm within the national committee staff. This public relations division had a number of responsibilities. First of all, it worked directly with the Washington-based press. This meant the distribution of press releases. These included speeches and statements of the presidential candidate, which were made available in Washington at the same time that they were released on the campaign plane, but also statements by other party leaders as well. (If one wished to attack the opposition candidate directly, such a statement might come from a recognized partisan figure such as the national chairman. In this way, the presidential candidate could maintain a more statesmanlike manner.) Dealing with the press also meant answering newspersons' queries. This is less time consuming now that most of the major media have their political reporters traveling with the candidate, but still involves some effort.

An activity growing directly out of Michelson's distribution of materials is the press service. This is directed at the weekly newspapers published around the country. Most of them operate with much tighter resources than the dailies, and have no Washington contacts. They are quite willing to run material if it can be provided. Consequently, canned news articles, features, editorials, and photographs are sent out, often in mat form to make the reproduction as simple as possible.

Brochures, Bumper Stickers, and other Campaign Material

A third group of public relations personnel is concerned with art and production. Having an artist available means that pamphlets and brochures can be designed to say exactly what the party leaders want them to say. Once the pamphlets are ready to go, they are turned over to a commercial printer in the Washington area. Samples are sent out around the country, and anyone wanting them for distribution orders them from the printer. The production department also has a small offset press. Photoreproduction makes it possible to make copies of newspaper articles that appeared. Obviously, it is an advantage to have favorable comments come from neutral reporters since their source credibility is so much higher.

The production department is also much involved with party publications and campaign newsletters. These are, of course, frankly partisan since they are directed to an audience of committed activists. They vary all the way from one-page mimeographed newsletters to slickly produced small magazines. With the rise of sustaining memberships, these party publications fit into a useful dual relation. Supporters receive "subscriptions" when they make contributions. Hence these publications bring in money at the same time that they provide a channel for the distribution of party propaganda.

Campaign materials—bumper stickers, campaign buttons, balloons, hats, inflatable elephants and donkeys, and all the rest—are produced commercially. The public relations division may, to be sure, suggest the wording for a bumper sticker to a friendly supplier, but for the most part these initiatives come from those who want to make money from the campaign. The task for the public relations division is simply to catalog all these materials and send copies of the catalog out through party channels to persons who might buy them. From that point on, the transactions take place between the buyer and the manufacturer (Guylay, 1960; Cotter and Hennessy, 1964, pp. 129–33).

If any materials are prepared for the electronic media by the public relations division at campaign headquarters, they are likely to be for radio. There are two reasons for this. Radio spots do not require the elaborate technical facilities needed for television. And since radio time is so much less expensive than television time, it is more feasible for local committees to sponsor radio spots. When this is done, the local sponsors can obtain tapes through the campaign headquarters.

Television

Television materials come from the advertising agency or campaign management firm that has been hired for the campaign.[12] If there is an advertising section in the headquarters public relations staff, the chances are that its chief activity is liaison with the outside agency. The core of the agency responsibility—that is, the task to which it attends even if it does nothing else—is the purchase of advertising space (if any print media are being used) and television time. This is a technical task that a campaign headquarters is not equipped to undertake. A good advertising agency can immediately translate, by computer, a desired geographic concentration to a number of spots that must be purchased in given market areas. It also knows which programs to buy in order to attract either a large audience or one that has certain characteristics. Jimmy Carter commercials, for instance, appeared on "Hee-Haw" and the "Lawrence Welk Show" in 1976 because large numbers of potential Carter voters watched these programs (Lelyveld, 1976a). The television time itself is sold by station representatives to time buyers in the ad agencies. Given that much political time is purchased late, and that other advertisers are competing for the same desirable time spots (General Motors, General Foods, and all the others don't suspend their sales campaigns just because there is an election in the offing), it is in the interests of the politicos to have the time buying done by a professional who has been dealing with the station representatives for a long time. In other words, tell the agency what kind of audience is sought, and leave the decisions about how the audience shall be reached in its hands.

If there is a heavy concentration on a media campaign—and in 1976 the Ford campaign put some 55 percent of *all* funds available to them into media—then the agency is going to do much more than just buy time. The central task of those in charge of the media campaign is to devise some way of communicating the candidate's strengths to the voters. There is no single way of doing this; there are as many variations as there are advertising personnel and candidates. In 1968, Harry Treleaven built a

---

[12] There is a third possibility besides an advertising agency or a campaign management firm. This is the creation of an ad hoc "firm" composed of professional advertising personnel who take leaves of absence from their firms. This was the arrangement used in the 1960 and 1972 Nixon campaigns. In 1960, the "firm" was called Campaign Associates; in 1972, the November Group.

campaign for Nixon around two things. He used commercials made from montages of still photographs, with Nixon's voice on an accompanying sound track. This took advantage of Nixon's greater attractiveness on radio, where only his voice was heard. He also set up a series of studio question-and-answer sessions that allowed Nixon to answer relatively easy questions and thus exhibit his knowledge and experience (McGinnis, 1969). In 1972, the central theme of the campaign was "Re-elect the President," not a bad idea since "the President" was undoubtedly more popular than "Richard M. Nixon" (Greenstein, 1974, p. 137).

In the case of Jimmy Carter in 1976, Jerry Rafshoon departed from the general belief that a short commercial was better because of a limited viewer tolerance for politics. He produced five-minute and two-minute advertisements on the assumption that Carter was still credible after one had listened to him for a while, and that more time was needed to allow that credibility to come across to the viewer. Rafshoon constructed some of the Carter commercials around lines that Carter had delivered in stump speeches, taking advantage of the long time that Carter had been campaigning, and, of course, selecting the best deliveries of the lines from the many he had filmed. Rafshoon also filmed Carter against backgrounds that were familiar to Carter, such as his peanut fields, thus putting Carter at his ease and at the same time stressing that Carter was an outsider rather than a member of the Washington community (Lelyveld, 1976a).

The cameras of John Deardourff and Doug Bailey focused on a relaxed Jerry Ford in 1976. One of their commercials focused on his family life. He was shown talking with family members, daughter Susan was shown hugging him, son Michael, then a divinity student, spoke of his parents' religious feelings, and serenity blanketed the whole scene. "Sometimes a man's family can say a lot about a man," an announcer reminded the audience. Another commercial featured a discussion of Ford's non-imperial presidency. The president himself used this phrase while an announcer reminded the audience of the conditions under which Ford had taken office. The point to this, of course, was to emphasize restoration of trust in the presidency as one of the most important accomplishments of the short Ford administration (Lelyveld, 1976b; Witcover, 1977, pp. 538–39).

The themes that are selected to reach the voter are, of course, subject to change. October 25, 1968, and October 19, 1976, both found candidates in New York City. The importance of New York in the electoral college makes attention to that area almost standard in closing days of campaigns, but in these instances candidate Nixon and candidate Carter were both recording new commercials for use in the closing days of the campaigns. Both had started far ahead of their rivals, and both had seen their margins grow smaller and smaller with the passage of time. So now they were trying for themes that would keep them ahead. The aim of the Carter spots was to reassure women voters and to shore up support in the South, two audiences in whose favor Carter had been slipping (Witcover, 1977, pp. 622–23; Schram, 1977, pp. 330–32; McGinnis, 1969, chap. 1).

While the media specialists are important, it would be well to conclude this discussion with two caveats. First, they cannot erase a candidate's weaknesses. They can remind voters of a candidate's strengths, but advertising could not make Richard Nixon come across as a warm and open human being, or portray Gerald Ford as having a subtle mind, or convince reporters that Jimmy Carter was being precise on the issues. Second, advertisers do not create an entire campaign. As is evident from the other parts of this chapter, public relations is only one part of a campaign. The basic decisions are made by the candidates and the strategy groups on whom they rely. The media specialists may be represented in the strategy groups, and if they are skillful, they may be persuasive. But theirs are not the only voices.

RAISING THE MONEY

All the activity we have been discussing increases the ability of the electoral coalition to reach the voters. If a candidate can be moved at jet speed across the continent, he or she will be able to reach more widely dispersed audiences than a candidate could when campaigns moved along the rails from one town to another. If pollsters have daily telephone surveys going on, they can estimate public reaction to a campaign with vastly more precision than was possible when campaign managers had to rely on such cues as the size of crowds and how loudly they cheered. If the candidates can reach an audience of 100 million on television, they are in simultaneous contact with more people than were in the whole country when Woodrow Wilson was first elected president.[13] So a good case can be made that these developments help make the democratic process more effective. At the same time, many of the same developments have made campaigning much more expensive. Therefore, new methods of fund raising have been necessary.

The Increasing Cost of Campaigning

For some time, the costs of presidential campaigns were relatively stable, at least when compared with changes elsewhere in American society. In 1884, the campaigns of both Blaine and Cleveland cost some $2.7 million. Costs went up and down in ensuing years. The campaigns

---

[13] This is a very high figure. It is the estimated size of the audience for the first Ford-Carter debate in 1976, the largest television audience for a political event up to that time.

of 1920, 1928, and 1936 were more expensive than the just-preceding or the just-following contests. But as late as 1948, the costs of the Dewey and Truman campaigns together were estimated at $4,863,630. The costs of campaigning had increased some 80 percent, but over 64 years. In 1972, however, the costs of both the Nixon and McGovern campaigns were on the order of $76.5 million. In only 24 years, the cost of presidential campaigns had gone up an astronomic 1,573 percent (Alexander, 1972, 1976).

What led to this near 16-fold increase? Part of the cause was specific to 1972: the orgy of spending by the Nixon reelection campaign. They raised and spent some $58.4 million, just about the amount used by *all* parties for *all* candidates four years earlier. But an underlying reason is to be found in the costs of the items we have been discussing. The campaign train used by Democrat James Cox in 1920 cost that campaign $20,000; it cost the Republicans $3.9 million to move their candidates and battalions of surrogates and advance men in 1972. Polling was nonexistent in an earlier day. The 1968 Nixon campaign spent some $384,000 on surveys, and the Humphrey campaign put out $262,000 for theirs. The biggest factor in the constantly increasing costs, though, has been television. In 1948, the last year of principal reliance on radio, the Republicans spent about $500,000 and the Democrats over $600,000 on that medium. In 1952, however, the parties spent $6.1 million, split about equally between radio and television. From there the media costs went to $9.8 million, $14.2 million, $24.6 million, and $40.4 million in 1956, 1960, 1964, and 1968 respectively, with about twice as much being spent on television as on radio each year. Media costs actually dropped a bit in 1972, primarily because the Republicans put much more emphasis on the voter contact effort described earlier (Alexander, 1972, 1976).

Professional Fund Raising

While the amount of money needed for political campaigns is modest when compared to commercial advertising, campaign organizations need persons who know how to raise substantial amounts of cash. Professional fund raising came to national politics in 1937 in the person of Carlton G. Ketchum, a professional fund raiser from Pittsburgh. He convinced the Republicans to undertake systematic fund raising based on a number of principles that he had found effective in raising money for private causes. First, there was to be a single fund drive each year so donors would not be subject to repeated appeals. Second, national needs were to be divided into state quotas based on such factors as population and wealth. (The needs of states and counties where the money was being raised would be added to the national needs at the time of their annual fund drive.) Third, the money was to be raised by a separate finance committee. This reduced the problem of fund raisers who wanted to be political strategists, and placed a "fire wall" between the party and persons who expected an explicit quid pro quo for making a contribution. Fourth, the fund drives were to be in the hands of professionals, often hired by the finance committees from Ketchum, Inc., for the duration of the fund-raising effort. Many of these principles were neglected in practice. There were emergency fund drives for individual candidates; many states failed to meet the quotas assigned to them. Still, the basic structure was adopted, and continues to exist in the Republican party. The system places the Republican Finance Committee in the same posture as a United Fund. The Finance Committee must negotiate with the candidates and organizations about the amount of money they need, and they must negotiate with the states about the amount of money they are willing to raise (Heard, 1960, pp. 212–19; Ogden and Peterson, 1968, pp. 284–85).

In spite of this fundamental restructuring, a good deal of improvisation marked fund raising in both parties during the following decades. Both parties raised money in any way they could think of—fund-raising dinners, private meetings with leading party figures, personal appeals by candidates to their wealthy friends, and so on. Until the 1960s, a number of things held true. Large donors were much more important than small donors. Other things being equal, Republicans were able to raise more than Democrats, in part because of better access to possible donors, in part because of the Ketchum system just described. One of the things that was not equal was control of the White House. The party in power could raise money with relative ease, while the party out of power had great difficulty in doing so. Neither party began a campaign with enough cash on hand. This prevented budgeting, meant that cash was often required to acquire needed services, and also meant that campaign organizations often had to pay a premium to acquire things (e.g., television time) at the last moment. The net of all this is that both parties ran up debts to finance presidential campaigns, and both hoped that they would win in order to be able to pay off their debt with the help of an incumbent president. For example, at the end of the 1960 campaign the Democrats had a debt of $3.5 million, and the Republicans had a debt of $750,000. With John Kennedy in the White House, though, the Democrats had retired all but $500,000 of their debt by early 1963, and the Republicans had only got their much smaller original debt down to $225,000 by early 1964 (Cotter and Hennessy, 1964, p. 174). Two developments of the 60s and 70s changed this situation: mass fund appeals and federal financing.

Mass Fund Appeals

Mass fund appeals had been discussed for a long time. There were some obvious advantages to the idea. If the parties could develop a mass base, they would reduce their dependence on large givers and identify a cadre of party supporters. Solicitations for small contributions had been tried out on several occasions—for instance, by the Republicans in the late 30s and in a Dollars for Democrats drive in the late 50s—but without producing enough revenue to effect any real change in party financing. There were problems. One was the administrative cost to the parties of processing a small contribution. By the time proper records had been made, the donor thanked, and so on, the parties often lost money. Another element was time. It took less effort to ask one large donor than a host of small donors, and, in a campaign, money was needed in a hurry.

The first successful mass fund drive was sponsored by the Republicans in the early 60s under the stimulus of a real financial shortage. The Republican National Committee did not have enough money for its staff operation, since the Democrats were in the White House, and most Republican money was going to the congressional committees in anticipation of the upcoming election. After some discussion, the National Committee decided to solicit sustaining memberships at $10 by sending appeals to persons whose names appeared on various commercially available mailing lists. The program was first tried experimentally in three states, which were not contributing anything at the time, so as to minimize the danger of upsetting any going fund-raising operation. When the program proved successful in the test states, appeals were sent nationwide. The program brought in $700,000 in 1962, and slightly over $1 million in 1963, about two thirds of the national committee's operating funds that year. The contributors were sent a party newsletter, thus giving the party a self-sustaining publicity operation, and many of them provided the names of additional potential donors. Over time, the Republican direct mail campaign was built up to the point where it produced $7.9 million (over 80 percent of all Republican contributions) in 1978. The origin of this successful mass fund drive is usually attributed to the appeal of Barry Goldwater to conservative donors in 1964, but credit should be given to William S. Warner, then the executive director of the Republican National Committee, who originated the program two years before the Goldwater nomination.

The Democrats waited a decade for a direct mail campaign to tap large numbers of small contributors. The first real Democratic success with a mass appeal was part of the 1972 McGovern campaign. George McGovern had accumulated several lists, some from South Dakota, some from his activity in opposition to the war in Vietnam, and some from liberal appeals with which he had been associated. When the senator decided to run, he consulted with an Alabama direct mail expert, Morris Dees, and Dees brought in Thomas Collins from a New York City direct mail firm. Collins wrote a seven-page letter setting forth McGovern's positions and appealing for funds. (For some reason, contributors to direct mail campaigns are said to prefer long, detailed letters.) This was sent out at the time McGovern announced his candidacy. The returns were quite good, and a number of subsequent appeals followed. Previous donors were contacted repeatedly; Democratic National Committee lists were used once McGovern was the nominee; television appeals for funds were combined with direct mail appeals. The response to this was so substantial that special nighttime mail-opening sessions had to be used just to get the money into the bank. In consequence of these efforts, the McGovern campaign raised $3 million before he was nominated and $12 million during the general election campaign, at a total cost of $4.5 million (Alexander, 1976, pp. 299–304; Hart, 1973, pp. 42–44, 309–10). Morris Dees was later recruited into the 1976 Carter campaign but was reportedly unable to match his 1972 success.

The most successful Democratic fund-raising program in the late 70s was not sponsored by the then weak Democratic National Committee, but was organized by the Association of Democratic State Chairs under Morley Winograd. This program is called Dollars for Democrats (as was a campaign for small contributions sponsored by the National Committee in the late 1950s). Under it, a national fund-raising firm solicits small contributions and turns the revenues over to the state parties.

Federal Financing

Financing the 1976 campaign was quite different than any preceding election. The Federal Election Campaign Act of 1971 was amended in 1974 to provide for public financing of presidential (but not congressional) campaigns. Federal financing had been advocated for some time, in part to reduce the dependence of officeholders on financial supporters, and in part because of the rising cost of campaigning. In the aftermath of the Watergate revelations, it was possible to get such legislation through Congress. The law allowed $20 million plus an inflation allowance for the major presidential campaigns. The candidates were not required to accept these funds; but if they did so, they had to promise not to accept other funds.

This was a major change in the constraints affecting external activities. We have already seen the consequences of this, as they concerned much more organized fund raising in the Early Days of nomination politics and the centralization of authority in a national campaign organization. Now how did it affect the funds available for the general election campaign and the way they were spent? To begin, the federal funds were not a great deal of money as national media campaigns go. One way of putting this into perspective is to compare it with the advertising budgets of commercial firms. The largest advertising budget in 1976 was $357.1 million, spent by Procter and Gamble. The firms with the next largest budgets were

General Foods ($219.3 million), Bristol-Myers ($146.9 million), and General Motors ($145.1 million). Altogether, 76 American firms had 1976 advertising budgets that were larger than the $21.8 million allowed each major campaign that year (*Advertising Age*, May 16, 1977, p. 52).[14]

Both Ford and Carter accepted the public funds in 1976 and could not spend beyond this limit. The Ford strategy group foresaw the consequences of this a good deal better than the Carter strategists. The latter spent a lot of money during September moving the candidate and his entourage around the country. The Ford strategists held money back for a media campaign in the closing weeks of the campaign. Not only was this media effort intrinsically successful, but the Carter forces lacked money to counter it because of their earlier spending.

Prior to 1976, campaign treasurers had three prime functions: to raise money, to have resources available when they were needed to undertake critical activities, and to see to it that the laws were adhered to and that records could be produced on the required dates to demonstrate fidelity to the laws. With public financing, they have been relieved of the first obligation but will have to pay more attention to the others.

If candidates continue to accept federal funds, and the spending limits remain the same, the long-run effect will probably be to force some decisions about which electoral activities are cost effective. The 1972 Nixon voter contact operation alone cost some $12 million. The 1968 electronic media campaign conducted in Nixon's behalf cost $12.6 million. In other words, the 1972 Nixon voter contact program and the 1968 Nixon media campaign together would exceed present spending limits, and this without allowing anything for a campaign tour, polling, print advertising, headquarters salaries, or anything else. In the past, the strong tendency has been to carry on all possible campaign activities on an *implicit* assumption that whatever was done was going to increase a candidate's chances of winning elections. But is it really true, for instance, that a candidate wins votes by campaigning in a community? Or could he do better by staying home and working out just what he wanted to say together with his issues staff? Such questions have not been closely examined, but a fixed limit on spending may provide an impetus in that direction.

Summary

In this chapter, we have covered the four major types of activties that go into a presidential campaign: campaign operations, research, public relations, and finance. Much of this organizational effort goes unreported

---

[14] In making this comparison, remember that the campaign advertising is concentrated in the couple of months before the election while the commercial firms advertise throughout the year, but that the federal funds provided for the campaigns must cover *all* campaign expenses.

in media accounts of campaigns; but there must be some way of moving the presidential and vice presidential candidates around the country, figuring out what they are going to say and what the citizens will think of it, getting the campaign story out through the media, and obtaining funds to do all of this.

While the internal structure covered in the last chapter was largely ideological, the external activities that we have examined in this chapter could be said to be largely logistical. In other words, a structure of regional and state coordinators, survey research to determine voter attitudes, buying television time and producing spots, and raising money are not intrinsically liberal, moderate, or conservative. A campaign organization that could provide these services ought to be able to work for any candidate, regardless of his ideological bent.

While it is certainly true that a conservative or liberal ideologue who lacks organizational, research, communications, or fund-raising skills is next to useless around a campaign headquarters, this distinction between ideological positioning and logistical services should not be pressed too far. The personal contacts through which one sets up a campaign organization are different in the two parties. The phrases that ring true in a conservative speech would not fit into a liberal appeal. The sources of funds tend to be different. And so on. But the factor that brings issues most sharply into focus in these external activities is that their intent is to win the support of a particular set of voters, and the appeals that are directed to them must be consistent with their issue preferences. This points up the dual set of constraints that shape any campaign strategy. It must be consistent with the issue preferences of the supporting coalition, and at the same time win the votes of the citizens to whom the campaign appeals are directed.

part III

CAMPAIGN STRATEGIES

chapter 5

Campaign Strategies: The 1960s

"The President defended his economic policy in a speech in New York." Whether this was broadcast as part of a news summary, or was the lead sentence in a newspaper story, or was found in the middle of a paragraph in a history book, it is typical of the events that make up a campaign. By itself, it tells us very little. The sentence is much more interesting for the questions it calls to mind. Was the president running ahead of his opponent or was he behind? If ahead, was he maintaining his lead, or was his opponent catching up? Why was the president talking about economic management instead of international involvement or civil liberties? Was he addressing a business or a labor audience? Why was the president giving this speech in New York City rather than Chicago or Cheyenne? With answers to these and related questions in hand, we could give some meaning to the report. Without them, the fact that the president had given a speech on economics tells us no more than any other un-examined event.

Speeches, statements, television spots, and all the rest can be under-stood as part of a campaign strategy; but in order to do so, we need con-textual information. First of all, we need to know about *structural context*. What is the composition of the candidate's supporting coalition? What voters is the candidate trying to reach? And what kinds of things can he or she do and say that are going to win the approbation of the support-ing coalition and win votes at the same time? We have already noted the importance of these questions, and we shall continue to pay attention to them, but there is a larger sense in which structural context can be understood as well. This is the structure formed by the interplay of the two (or three in 1968) major strategies. Are both coalitions intent on winning swing votes in the large industrial states, as was the case in 1976? Does the strategy of one of the coalitions involve a vigorous exposition of what is a minority view nationwide? This happened in 1964 and 1972, and in both cases gave incumbent presidents a lot of maneuvering room in the middle ground of American politics. Is one of the normal party coalitions split? This happened in 1968, and reduced the strategic opportunities open to all three contenders for the presidency. In assessing the strategies to be discussed in this section of the book, you will want to keep these questions in mind.

Another important set of questions concerns the *temporal context*. In a narrow sense, these questions arise from the temporal pattern that we reviewed at the beginning of Chapter 3. Is the speech a trial balloon that is given during the Planning stage of the campaign? Is it a considered statement that is part of the Grand Opening? Is it a Strategic Adjustment that tries to respond to some particular problem? Or is it part of a last attempt that comes during the Time's Up stage? What might be termed a longer term temporal concern also leads to questions about the *historic context*. What did citizens regard as the leading problems in a given election year? How widely were looming problems, such as those implicit in baby booms or energy shortages, understood in the society? Was America involved in war, or was there a real threat of war? Was the economy prosperous or was inflation or unemployment, or both, a problem? These considerations are also important in understanding the opportunities open to campaign strategists, and you will want to keep them in mind when reading about specific campaigns.

THE 1964 CAMPAIGN

The events that set the stage for the 1964 campaign took place the preceding year. On Good Friday, 1963, Martin Luther King, Jr., was arrested and sent to a Birmingham jail because of his participation in a nonviolent black protest. In June, President Kennedy submitted a major civil rights bill, and thousands of blacks and whites came to Washington in August to lobby for the civil rights bill and hear King's "I have a dream" speech at the Lincoln Memorial. Then on Friday, November 22, an assassin's bullet tore out John Kennedy's brain. A mourning nation watching on television that weekend saw the late president's body lying in state and saw his funeral on Monday. President Lyndon B. Johnson set the tone of the initial months of his administration with the phrase, "Let us continue," and gave his full support to the civil rights bill, which was passed by a Republican–northern Democratic coalition. Vietnam was emerging as a problem in 1964. American troops were there, but the major commitment of American forces did not come until 1965. The economy was strong and was in the beginning of what was to be the longest un-interrupted expansion since World War II. The nation had been stunned by the assassination of President Kennedy, but otherwise 1964 was a high point in Americans' confidence in their ability to solve problems.

GOLDWATER'S CONSERVATIVE CAMPAIGN

"Let's grow up, conservatives! If we want to take this party back—and I think we can someday—let's go to work!" Thus spoke Senator Barry Goldwater to delegates to the 1960 Republican National Convention. His immediate goal was to spur their efforts on behalf of the 1960 nominee, Richard Nixon. His words expressed a long-range ambition of many Republican conservatives, though. For some time, they had wanted to give the Republican party a more conservative cast. Many did go to work—with the result that the senator himself was the party's nominee four years later. It is against the background of this ambition, and this accomplishment, that the internal structure of the Goldwater coalition must be understood.

Whereas other Republican coalitions fell somewhere toward the middle of the ideological spectrum, and could be interpreted in terms of tensions between conservative and moderate groups, the groups in the 1964 Republican coalition were largely conservative. First there was a group whose principal interests centered on economic questions. This included some persons who had been active in earlier Taft nomination coalitions, quite a few businessmen, and some younger Republicans who thought there was greater tactical advantage in a head-on confrontation with Democrats on economic questions. This group saw government regulation as socialistic, and viewed themselves as defenders of liberty. They certainly wished for less government management and reduced government spending.

The focus of the second group was on international involvement. Its view of the international scene was dominated by the cold war. The United States was seen as the leader of the free world, and was opposed by a monolithic Communist conspiracy directed from Moscow. Seeing the world in an "us" versus "them" perspective, it was also quite concerned with American security and favored increased defense spending. There was considerable overlap between the first two groups, but a potential tension lay here in the question of military hardware. The business-oriented economic conservatives wanted less spending and reduced taxes; those concerned about military security were willing to accept spending for defense purposes.

The third and fourth groups were characterized by more political goals, but were by no means unideological. The third group in the Goldwater coalition was made up largely of southerners. They tended to be younger, and were anxious for political power in their own states. They felt that this goal could be advanced by opposing Lyndon Johnson's Great

Society by raising questions of federalism. Regardless of policy area, they wanted less control from Washington and more control exercised from state capitals and county seats. Since the centerpiece of civil rights legislation had just been passed, the southerners tended to emphasize this, but their opposition to Washington-run programs was not limited to civil liberties.

The final group was made up of organizational loyalists—long-time Republican activists whose loyalty ran to the party rather than a particular candidate. This group was made up of such leaders as former national chairman Leonard Hall, Ohio state chairman Ray C. Bliss, and veteran public relations man Lou Guylay. This group was less ideological, more concerned about electoral victory and holding the party together. In 1964, however, this tended to give the professional politicians an ideological distinctiveness. Just because they were willing to listen to moderate ideas, and remembered that they had been successful during the Eisenhower years, they were the most liberal group in the Goldwater coalition. Among the four groups, the center of gravity tended to lie with the first two, with the latter two gaining some voice in unusual circumstances.

Goldwater Plans

The primary audience to whom the campaign was directed was made up of conservative voters. The strategy group paid great attention to a datum turned up by the Opinion Research Corporation in an August survey. This was that 41 percent of the public thought of themselves as conservative, while only 31 percent saw themselves as liberal and 28 percent somewhere in between. Members of the core group repeatedly pointed to this finding, rather than, for example, the 54 percent to 32 percent edge for President Johnson among favorable and strongly committed voters, and saw the conservative plurality as evidence that there would be response to an avowedly conservative campaign.

The geographic concentration was in the Midwest and the West. It was felt that little campaigning would be necessary in the South because of the region's conservatism. The question was how to expand beyond a southern base. It was further felt that no amount of campaigning would win votes in the East. These considerations dictated an emphasis on the Midwest and the West, and meant that the electoral votes of Ohio, Indiana, Illinois, California, and Texas were going to be particularly important.[1]

The first phase of the campaign was a tactical exercise intended to build party harmony, and it was a phase in which the organizational loyalists

---

[1] In spite of these plans, the Goldwater campaign has been repeatedly, and incorrectly, interpreted as having been based on a southern strategy or racist appeals, or both. In fact, Senator Goldwater spent relatively little time campaigning in the South. Many of the supporters opposed progress in civil rights, and many of his opponents attributed anticivil rights views to him, but the senator had pledged not to have a racist campaign and carefully avoided any racist appeals.

played a key role. Moderates could not understand why the senator was taking stands that were going to be costly to Republicans in November. Conservatives could not understand why the moderates were hesitant to support Goldwater in view of Goldwater's past efforts for them. Organizational loyalists could understand both of these attitudes, and set to work to try to bring moderates and conservatives together.

Richard Nixon and Dwight Eisenhower were especially active in this. Nixon and Goldwater released an exchange of correspondence, in which Nixon offered the senator a chance to explain his acceptance speech sentences, "Extremism in the defense of liberty is no vice. Moderation in the pursuit of justice is no virtue," and Goldwater did so by saying that "whole-hearted devotion to liberty is unassailable and half-hearted devotion to justice is indefensible." General Eisenhower invited both Goldwater coalition leaders and Republican governors and gubernatorial candidates to a unity meeting held at Hershey, Pennsylvania, on August 12. Here a statement putting a better face on Goldwater positions on foreign policy, civil rights, and extremism was released in the senator's name, moderates had a chance to question Goldwater at some length, and Eisenhower spoke about the importance of "an honest conciliation of views." The conciliation between the Goldwater coalition and the moderates, however, lasted only as long as the senator's first press conference question. He immediately claimed that his statement "was no conciliatory speech at all," and forthwith killed any real chance of gaining genuine support from Republican moderates.

Grand Opening for Goldwater

The second identifiable phase was the Grand Opening. The strategy group planned to emphasize ideas. It was thought that Goldwater would give a few major speeches, along with making a much larger number of campaign appearances. In the major speeches, the senator would set forth the details of the conservative position on the issue in question. It was assumed President Johnson would then state the liberal position on the same topic, and that a principled debate between the two sides would be joined.

The Labor Day speech inaugurating this strategy was given in Prescott, Arizona, where Goldwater had traditionally begun his campaigns. "The campaign we launch today," he said, "is dedicated to peace, to progress, and to purpose . . . [By this] we mean: peace through *preparedness*, progress through *freedom*, purpose through *Constitutional order* . . ." These three themes echoed the central concerns of the three conservative groups in his electoral coalition. Preparedness suggested a resolute foreign policy backed up by military strength. Freedom implied "withdrawing the central government from its many unwarranted interventions in our private economic lives." The reference to Constitutional order underscored the Constitutional basis of Goldwater's preference for state and local control of affairs. In the following weeks, these themes were developed in a number of speeches. In Los Angeles, he spoke about the need for a regular reduction in taxes. In Chicago, about the arrogation of power by the federal government generally, and the Supreme Court in particular. In Montgomery, Alabama, of a system of regular grants to the states that has since come to be called revenue sharing. In Fargo, North Dakota, of the need to allow market forces to work in place of federal price supports.

Goldwater's Adjustments

This Grand Opening lasted through much of September, but problems developed. For one thing, Lyndon Johnson showed no intention of playing the role assigned him by the Goldwater strategists. Either the Johnson coalition ignored the Goldwater challenges entirely or answers came from lower ranking "spokesmen." Certainly no principled debate took shape. Another problem was that certain Goldwater positions were causing difficulties. The most serious concerned the possibility of nuclear warfare and changes in social security. Polls taken by the Opinion Research Corporation showed even Republicans thought that President Johnson would do a better job than Senator Goldwater in keeping the peace and handling social security. Consequently, the core group decided on a Strategic Adjustment aimed at answering charges in these two areas, and the campaign entered a third phase.

The response to the nuclear question involved statements both by Senator Goldwater and other Republican spokesmen on the prudent approach that a Goldwater administration would follow, and the continuity between Goldwater statements and the positions taken by the Eisenhower, Kennedy, and Johnson administrations. In a "Conversation at Gettysburg" shown on nationwide television, for example, Dwight Eisenhower told Goldwater that allegations that Goldwater would start a nuclear war were "actual tommyrot." "You're not going to do any of these things— what do they call it—push the button? I can't imagine anything you would give more careful thought to than the President's responsibility as the Commander-in-Chief of all our armed forces, and as the man conducting our foreign relations." Less attention was given to dealing with social security, but an opportunity developed when a bill expanding social security died in conference committee. Then Goldwater pointed out that he had voted for the bill, just as he had voted to expand coverage on four previous occasions, and that while he had been a friend of social security, the Johnson administration was putting politics ahead of the needs of social security recipients.

Some three weeks were devoted to replying to these Democratic charges, and criticism of the campaign continued to come from sources within the Goldwater coalition. There was, of course, the basic difficulty that the election was approaching, and the gap between Johnson and Goldwater was remaining as wide as ever. A more specific concern, though, was that the defensive emphasis focused attention on issues that were producing Democratic votes. This led to another Strategic Adjustment. On October 11, the strategy group approved a plan drafted by public relations director Lou Guylay. Guylay's plan called for the development of Republican issues. This included an attack on the Johnson administration, stressing a decline in political morality, an increase in crime and violence, Communist gains, and a president who symbolized wheeling and dealing rather than world leadership. The Republican posture was to exhibit awareness of this situation and concern about it, to promise that these defects would be repaired in a Goldwater administration, and hold out hope for better days marked by a return of conscience and integrity to the White House.

This fourth phase continued many of the characteristics of the Grand Opening. There was television (Goldwater answering questions from "typical" citizens, and a program on which he was joined by Richard Nixon), emphasis on the Midwest and the West, and some major speeches on particular topics. Speaking in the Mormon Tabernacle, Goldwater tied his criticism about law and order to the Supreme Court decision banning prayers in the classroom. On October 16, in Chicago, Senator Goldwater spoke about civil rights. The speech had been some time in the writing. The senator wanted to give a statesmanlike address that no one could interpret as an appeal to white backlash. These requirements were more easily stated than met. Finally, a speech embodying ideas of political theorist Harry Jaffa and William Rehnquist, who was later appointed to the Supreme Court by President Nixon, was ready. The speech condemned both compulsory segregation and compulsory integration. "Our aim," Goldwater declared, "is neither to establish a segregated society nor to establish an integrated society. It is to preserve a *free* society."

At almost the same time, an event took place that tended to give some credence to the Republican attack on the Johnson administration. A ranking presidential assistant was arrested on a charge of homosexuality. While Republican strategists had no way of anticipating this when they approved a strategy emphasizing "a shocking decline in political morality," the event tended to support what they were saying. Yet this had no sooner happened than far more important foreign news appeared. Within a 48-hour period, Nikita Khrushchev fell from power in Russia, Harold Wilson became prime minister because of a Labour victory in British elections, and the Chinese exploded their first atomic device. These events, of course, dominated the headlines, and moved public attention right back to foreign affairs where Johnson was stronger.

A Tactical Adjustment the following week took advantage of the foreign events, with a speech interpreting them in accordance with the attitudes of the Goldwater group concerned with international involvement. The senator promised to call a conference to revitalize NATO, and said that we must recognize the whole of communism as our enemy and confront communism with a policy of firm resistance. But in spite of brave talk about what a Goldwater administration would do, it was now becoming quite obvious that Johnson was running too far ahead in the midwestern and western states that had been the geographic focus of the campaign for Goldwater to have any real hopes of victory.

Time's Up for Goldwater

The Time's Up phase of the campaign began with a rally in Madison Square Garden. Some fatigue and bitterness showed in Goldwater's speech that night. "Do you honestly think, after all these years in politics, that I don't *know* the easy way to get votes? The promises to make? The subjects to talk about—and the ones to avoid?" He went on to say that he didn't expect to get the votes of "lazy dole-happy people" or of "the socialist, ADA-type followers of Hubert Horatio Humphrey" because he would not make easy vote-getting promises. There were more speeches given that week, none of them memorable, and the senator ended up by speaking in Columbia, South Carolina, the Saturday night before the election. Seated on the stage with him were conservative Democrats who had turned Republican, such as Strom Thurmond, and conservative Democrats who had stayed with their party, such as former Secretary of State James F. Byrnes and Congressman John Bell Williams. His speech was carried on an 87-station television network throughout the South. By ending his campaign here, appearing with conservative southerners, and addressing himself to southern voters, Barry Goldwater was ending his campaign by fighting for those very southern votes his strategists had once taken for granted.

ALL THE WAY WITH LBJ!

In 1928, the Democratic party began a pattern of nominees that was to be used frequently during the middle third of the century. Governor Alfred E. Smith of New York won the presidential nomination, and Senator Joseph T. Robinson of Arkansas accepted the vice presidential nomination. These two leaders symbolized the internal structure of the Democratic electoral coalition. This coalition included liberal groups, which tended to come from the North, and relatively conservative groups, which usually came from the South. Just how these groups lined up varied from one policy area to another, but the major line of division in the Democratic party was a North-South distinction. Since the liberal groups were more numerous, the presidential nominee came from the North and the vice presidential nominee from the South or from the Border States. The presidential nominee was clearly left-of-center, but did not represent extreme views. The vice presidential nominee was less liberal, but sufficiently progressive so that his views were compatible with those of the head of the ticket. Usually the presidential nominee came from a large state, and usually the vice presidential nominee was a congressional leader. This was the pattern that was followed with Governor Franklin D. Roosevelt of New York and House Speaker John Nance Garner of Texas in 1932 and 1936, with Roosevelt and Senator Harry S Truman of Missouri in 1944, with Governor Adlai E. Stevenson of Illinois and Senator John Sparkman of Alabama in 1952, with Stevenson and Senator Estes Kefauver of Tennessee in 1956, and with Senator John F. Kennedy of Massachusetts and Senate Majority Leader Lyndon B. Johnson of Texas in 1960.[2]

LBJ's Plans

When Lyndon Johnson succeeded to the presidency after Kennedy's assassination in 1963, the roles were suddenly reversed. Johnson had liberal programs he wanted to see enacted into law, but was skeptical about whether either the country or the Democratic coalition would accept the leadership of a southerner. In part because he felt he had to hold the country and the coalition together to get his programs accepted, and in part because of his own style of leadership, he placed a great deal of emphasis on consensus. The broad outlines of this emerged in a speech at the University of Michigan on May 22, 1964, in which he first used the phrase "Great Society":

> In your time we have the opportunity to move not only toward the rich society and the powerful society, but upward to the Great Society. The Great Society rests on abundance and liberty for all. It demands an end to poverty and to racial injustice, to which we are totally committed in our time. But that is just the beginning. . . . most of all, the Great Society is not a safe harbor, a resting place, a final objective, a finished work. It is a challenge constantly renewed, beckoning us toward a destiny where the meaning of our lives matches the marvelous products of our labor.

---

[2] The departures from the pattern came in 1940 when President Roosevelt chose Secretary of Agriculture Henry A. Wallace of Iowa as his running mate, and in 1948 when President Truman agreed to the choice of the enormously popular Senate Majority Leader, Alben Barkley of Kentucky. Estes Kefauver was a partial exception to the pattern in 1956. Although he was from Tennessee, he had gained national visibility from televised hearings into organized crime and had sought the presidency in his own right.

Eight days later, President Johnson spoke more directly about the tasks of political leadership, in a speech at the University of Texas:

> I'm going to try to [make our people aware that they share a fundamental unity of interest, purpose and belief]. And on the basis of this unity, I intend to try and achieve a broad national consensus which can end obstruction and paralysis, and can liberate the energies of the nation for the work of the future.

Although there were some differences in emphasis between the two speeches, both emphasized consensus, a release of energies, and a striving to achieve vaguely described goals. There were real strategic advantages to this posture. It held groups together within the Democratic coalition by suggesting that all would share in great things soon to be attained. It helped soothe a nation still numb from the shock of his predecessor's assassination. And it left Johnson free to move in a variety of directions depending on whom the Republicans nominated.

The success of the Goldwater coalition in capturing the Republican nomination gave great freedom of choice to the Democrats. It meant that for the first time in at least two decades the great center ground of American politics would not be contested. It meant that there was only one group of voters who normally supported the Democrats, the southerners, who would be susceptible to Goldwater appeals. It meant that a substantial number of moderate or liberal Republicans would be open to potential Democratic appeals. It meant that Democratic leaders had the luxury of deciding whether they would rather accent issues that would define a Johnson program to be presented to the Congress in 1965, or whether they would try to attract as many voters as possible in order to give Johnson a record majority. For his part, Lyndon Johnson could see no conflict between trying to define issues and build a record majority. By pointing to a Great Society in which the foremost goals of many groups could be attained, he hoped to do both.

The selection of Senator Hubert Humphrey of Minnesota as the vice presidential nominee reversed the customary Democratic roles. With a progressive southerner as the presidential nominee, a liberal northerner was placed in the second spot. Even with this switch, the ticket still reflected the internal structure of the Democratic coalition. Humphrey was generally regarded as one of the ablest Democrats, and as a very active majority whip in the Senate, he had established good working relations with most groups in the Democratic party.

The Democrats' Grand Opening in '64

In a typical campaign pattern for an incumbent president, the Grand Opening plan called for the vice presidential nominee to shoulder a heavier campaign burden while the president spent more time in Washington. President Johnson sought to emphasize his use of time by maintaining that he wasn't committed to particular campaign trips. Thus, two days before the traditional opening of Democratic campaigns on Labor Day in Cadillac Square in Detroit, he told reporters:

> Our first obligation is to do this job that we are doing here, today, and I will be doing it all day today, and I will be doing it all day tomorrow, right in this house. But if I can get off a few hours Monday, I am going out there and speak to the folks at their Labor Day meeting like I would go to the Fourth of July, if I do, and then I am coming right back here to burn some midnight oil.

The president did go to Detroit. He identified himself with Democratic predecessors who had spoken in the same square on Labor Day. He spoke about the simple wants of the American people. But then he returned to Washington. Furthermore, most of Lyndon Johnson's early campaign efforts were limited to quick trips away from the Capital. For most of September, he devoted himself to visibly being the president.

The targets of the Democratic campaign plans could be put into three categories. First were those who ordinarily voted Democratic and who were unlikely to vote for Goldwater in any circumstances: liberals, labor, urban residents, and blacks. Second, there was a defensive strategy designed to protect Democratic strength in the South from the conservative appeals of Barry Goldwater. Third, there was an attempt to attract as many moderate Republicans as possible.

The campaign aimed at traditional Democratic supporters was easy. Goldwater statements were recalled on television. One remark, to the effect that the country would be better off if the East Coast could be sawed off and let float out to sea, was given visual form when the East Coast was sawed off from a wooden map of the country, and floated off in a body of water. A Goldwater comment that social security might be made voluntary was illustrated by tearing up a social security card. President Johnson stressed the prosperity of the country, telling machinists in Miami Beach, for example, "In the 42 months before January 1961, the workers' average weekly earnings, after taxes, rose only $1.25. But in the next 42 months, they rose $8.43—let me repeat, seven times as much." He told a Seattle audience of a number of steps that had been taken to guard against the danger of an accidental nuclear attack, and reminded steelworkers in Atlantic City that the nation would help the poor, the helpless, and the oppressed, adding: "We do these things because we love people instead of hate them; because we have faith in America, not fear of the future; [and] because you are strong men of vision . . ." Other examples could be given just as easily. The important point was that these were messages going to the already convinced. All that was necessary was to reinforce a decision to vote for Johnson.

The South was another matter. Many southerners found Barry Goldwater relatively attractive, and a four-part strategy was used to keep them from finding Goldwater so attractive that southern electoral votes would end up in the Republican column. The first part was a mobilization of newly registered black voters. Black leaders were convinced that Goldwater had the support of known antiblack leaders in community after community, and it was this, "the nature of the local leaders supporting Goldwater, that turned the [black] anti-Goldwater tide into a raging flood" (Lomax, 1964). The second part was to stress the Johnsons' own southern origins. For example, in North Carolina, Mrs. Johnson said that she was there to "say to you that to this Democratic candidate, and his wife, the South is a respected, valued, and beloved part of the country." The third element was a reminder to state and local Democratic leaders, hitherto complacent about presidential Republicanism, that it was in *their* interest to work for a Johnson victory. Goldwater success in their states, unlike previous Republican candidacies, could lead to Republican efforts to contest state and local offices. Finally, and most importantly, there was an economic appeal. President Johnson had been laying the basis for this for some time. In a May speech, he reminded an Atlanta audience of the difference between the 1960s and the 1930s.

> The average income in the South has increased six times since 19 and 30, rising much faster than the national average. Malaria and pellagra are going, and hunger is going. The acreage yield of our farms has doubled and the gross income per farm in your state has risen eight times. Nearly every home in Georgia has water and electricity and every child can go to school.

In New Orleans during the campaign, he attributed words to an unnamed southern senator.

> I would like to go back there and make them one more Democratic speech. I just feel like I've got one more in me. Poor old state, they haven't heard a Democratic speech in 30 years. All they ever hear at election time is Negro, Negro, Negro! The kind of speech they should have been hearing is about the economy and what a great future we could have in the South if we would just meet our economic problems, if we would just take a look at the resources of the South and develop them.

Over and over, President Johnson stressed that the South could progress by uniting with the rest of the country, by abandoning opposition to civil rights, and by developing the region's economy.

The goal of the strategy aimed at moderate Republicans was "to practice a politics of consensus that would make it as easy as possible for lifelong Republicans to switch their votes in November to the Democratic column" (Johnson, 1971, p. 104). So rather than attacking Senator Goldwater as typical of Republican conservatism, he was referred to as "the temporary Republican spokesman," and every opportunity was taken to distinguish Goldwater from moderate Republicans. For instance, when he went to Harrisburg to address a Democratic audience, the president told them he had not come to Pennsylvania as a partisan, and found kind words about former President Dwight Eisenhower and Governor William Scranton (who had been Goldwater's last major opponent for the nomination). At a speech at Johns Hopkins, Lyndon Johnson praised university president Milton Eisenhower and singled out Arthur Vandenberg and Henry Cabot Lodge as fine men who had supported a bipartisan foreign policy. In Indiana, Mr. Johnson said he knew that the state had usually voted Republican, but added, "I'm not sure whether there is a real Republican candidate this time." And a widely used television spot showed a man presumably walking away from the Republican convention in San Francisco. As he moved, he stepped directly on posters bearing pictures of Governors Rockefeller, Romney, and Scranton, and a voice told viewers that if they had doubts about Goldwater, they were in pretty good company.

LBJ's Adjustments

These appeals to normal Democratic voters, to southerners, and to moderate Republicans, continued throughout the campaign. There was, however, a Strategic Adjustment in the use of the president's time at the end of September. On the morning of September 28, Johnson left on a one-day six-state swing throughout New England. He drew crowds at every stop that were so large and so friendly as to impress veteran politicians and reporters. He was unable to maintain his schedule because of the time it took for his motorcade to move through the throngs; but by the time he headed back for Washington after two o'clock the following morning, it was clear that he was personally popular and that his own campaigning was quite effective. Consequently, a good many more campaign appearances were added to the president's schedule.

Lyndon Johnson left Washington for a week-long campaign trip on October 6. This took him to the Midwest, briefly to the South, and then on to the West. On this trip, he spoke in general terms of the things he hoped to accomplish. Thus in Denver, he promised:

> I intend to put education at the top of America's agenda. And if you do not quite understand the details of what I mean by the top of America's agenda, I will say this: That regardless of family financial status education should be open to every boy and girl born in America up to the highest level which he or she is able to master.

This was important, presaging historic action that was to be taken by the about-to-be-elected 89th Congress. What came through on the trip, though, was an off-the-cuff style that gave people a sense of Lyndon Johnson's drive and personality. For instance, on the way into Denver for his speech, he grabbed a bullhorn to speak to all those within hearing:

> Come on down to the Coliseum. . . . Get in your cars and come. You don't have to dress. Just bring your children and your dogs, anything you have, with you. It won't be long. You'll be back in time to put the kids to bed. Come on down to the speakin'. We're going to have a hot time in the old town tonight.

When he was in the South, he spoke as a southerner. When he was in the West, he spoke as a westerner. And he was no sooner back in Washington than he took off again to campaign across New York along with Robert Kennedy. The net of all this, in the carefully considered opinion of David S. Broder, was that Lyndon Johnson

> . . . has built a vast and enthusiastic personal following of his own. He is no longer just John Kennedy's successor. He is a towering political figure, with a constituency that is his, and his alone. (Broder, 1964)

In mid-October, there was a Tactical Adjustment to take advantage of the shift of attention to international involvement brought about by the Khrushchev ouster, Labour victory in Britain, and Chinese atomic explosion. Now the working president took the spotlight back from candidate Johnson. On successive days, President Johnson met with his senior foreign policy advisors, convened a meeting of the National Security Council, delivered a national television address on the meaning of the foreign events, held a briefing session for congressional leaders, met with his Cabinet, and discussed the implications of the developments with a group of elder statesmen that included a number of Republicans. Having now devoted six working days to these foreign events, not incidentally having created six straight days of media stories about his involvement with international affairs, he left for a campaign speech in St. Louis where he told his audience, "All those men I met with, men from both the Democratic and Republican parties, were in agreement about the broad course of American foreign policy."

LBJ's Triumphal Closing

The Time's Up phase of the Johnson campaign was a period of triumph. Far ahead in all of the polls, the president spent only one day in the South —in Florida, Georgia, South Carolina—where he tried to check Goldwater's strength by calling the Arizonan's proposals radical. The rest of the last week was devoted to large states with big electoral votes: Pennsylvania, California, Pennsylvania again, Illinois, New York, and Texas. There were set speeches, as in Mayor Richard Daley's Chicago, and before a giant rally in Madison Square Garden; but as heretofore Mr. Johnson was most effective in extemporaneous references to the atmosphere of fear and suspicion, which he ascribed to Senator Goldwater, and in his reminiscences about how he had conducted the presidency. In San Diego, for example, he spoke proudly about the bipartisan foreign policy that had been supported by presidents and opposition leaders in the Senate— Truman and Vandenberg, Eisenhower and himself, Kennedy and Dirksen —as one that was supported by the overwhelming majority of Americans and one that he would not abandon. Thoughtful observers were troubled by a lack of certainty about just where a Johnson presidency would go. A *Dallas Morning News* editorial complained that Johnson was supported by a confused bandwagon made up of "business tycoons, left-wing laborites, corporation lawyers, New Dealers, anti-New Dealers, etc." But Mr. Johnson himself was untroubled by these doubts. As he told fellow Texans the day before election, "I have spent my life getting ready for this moment." He had, after all, been in Washington for 33 years, and the editorial had been written 16 years earlier.

THE 1968 CAMPAIGN

The euphoria of 1964 was hard to find four years later. Under Lyndon Johnson's driving leadership, the 89th Congress passed most of the legislation that had been on the Democratic party's agenda for two decades, but this historic accomplishment had been obscured by more dramatic developments. The president who had spoken in 1964 of the need to handle foreign tests "with care, and coolness, and courage" had dispatched 500,000 troops to Vietnam, and 35,000 of them had been killed. A virulent inflation (which was to become more of a political issue in the 1970s) had begun with Johnson's decision not to ask for a tax increase to finance the war. The hope of peaceful progress in civil rights had been lost in urban riots, which had brought flames to cities across the country, and the most beloved black leader, Martin Luther King, Jr., had been slain in early April.

These events had undercut President Johnson's political base, and he had withdrawn from the contest for the Democratic nomination. The contenders were Senator Eugene McCarthy of Minnesota and Senator Robert F. Kennedy of New York, both of whom entered primaries, and Vice President Hubert Humphrey, who did not. But death was to be a participant in this contest, too. Moments after he had won the California primary, Robert Kennedy was assassinated. As things turned out, Vice President Humphrey had the strength to gain the nomination, but not before there had been a brutal confrontation between Chicago police and antiwar protestors. Even then, he had less than the support of the Democratic party because he faced opposition from antiwar groups, and from southern Democrats who were backing Alabama Governor George Wallace's third-party candidacy.

The Republicans had selected former Vice President Richard Nixon to face Humphrey and Wallace. Nixon had begun his quest of the nomination early, and had beaten New York Governor Nelson Rockefeller (who had not entered the race until after the King assassination) and California Governor Ronald Reagan (who had not made much of an effort before the convention itself).

GEORGE WALLACE'S THIRD PARTY

George C. Wallace was a governor of Alabama who had come to national attention by calling for "Segregation Forever" in his inaugural address, and by "standing in the schoolhouse door" as a symbol of resistance to federal desegregation of the University of Alabama. He had entered Democratic primaries in 1964 and had done well, in view of President Johnson's high popularity in his first year in office. In 1968, Wallace opted for a third-party effort. His hope was that, in a three-way race, no candidate would be able to get the required majority of electoral college votes and that the election would have to be decided in the House of Representatives.

There was precious little internal structure to the Wallace coalition. The core group was made up of men who had been close to Wallace in Alabama politics—Seymour Trammell, Bill Jones, and Cecil Jackson—and the state and local chairpersons were those who had been identified through mailings and other contacts from Montgomery. Every presidential coalition is held together by loyalty to the candidate, but with the Wallace coalition this was almost the only unifying characteristic. The American Independent party was created to put Governor Wallace on the ballot, but the identifiable structure and familiar activities of political parties were absent. Party conventions were held only where required by state law; and the party platform, issued in mid-October, was significant only as a statement of Wallace's personal views.

Wallace's Plan to Go National

The first order of business in the Planning phase was a need to master the arcane details of each state's electoral law in order to get on the ballot. This required considerable effort, since most of the laws benefit the major parties by making it difficult for any new party to qualify. It was eventually necessary to go to the U.S. Supreme Court to get on the ballot in Ohio, but when that was done the governor was duly qualified in all 50 states.

A more general strategic problem was how the Wallace forces were going to attract nonsouthern support, and do so without alienating the southerners already supporting Wallace. As Cecil Jackson explained the thinking of the core group:

At first the basic idea was to sweep from Maryland to Texas, including Oklahoma, Kentucky, and Delaware. Then, obviously, we would have to carry six or eight additional states. We planned to concentrate on key areas and big electoral votes. But we had so much trouble culling them down that we decided we're gonna hit the country. (Jenkins, 1968)

In other words, no decision had been made.

Grand Opening Third-Party Style

When Governor Wallace began speaking in the Grand Opening phase, he revealed a class-based strategy. His appeal was to blue-collar workers with high school educations and moderate incomes, and to small town and rural residents with strong beliefs in traditional values. This came across in both positive and negative references. The positive references were to "the barber, beautician, cab driver, and steelworker."

You'd better be thankful for the police and firemen, 'cause if it wasn't for them you couldn't walk in the streets. The wife of a working man can't go to the supermarket without the fear of being assaulted.

But Wallace's negative references were just as telling. He was opposed to the elite, and not just any elite, but to rule-makers and symbol manipulators. The opponents he chose were judges, bureaucrats, editors, intellectuals, and foundation officials.[3] These were the persons responsible for America's troubles, but all this would change when he took office. Over and over again, he promised to summon all the bureaucrats to Washington and have them throw their briefcases into the Potomac River. "We've had so much stuff jammed down our throats," Wallace told his listeners, "there's nothing left to jam. Everybody's going to get a chance for a good throat clearing on November 5."

Governor Wallace did not neglect his southern base. In fact, he used the same "they're looking down their noses at us" technique to appeal to Dixie audiences. When Richard Nixon said that George Wallace wasn't fit to be president, the governor replied: "Do you know what he was saying? He was saying no Southerner is fit to be president." And he attacked newspapers with the words: "Every one of the large newspapers are making fun of our movement. They're making fun of Southerners, that's what they're doing."

A Strategic Adjustment

The Wallace campaign went well as long as he stayed on the racial issue, which helped him in the South, and the law-and-order issue, which

---

[3] He also attacked hippies, militant revolutionary anarchists, and Communists, none of whom vote in very great numbers.

aided him throughout the country. But in October what amounted to a Strategic Adjustment was forced on him by the requirement that he have a vice presidential candidate. He chose Air Force General Curtis LeMay. At a Pittsburgh news conference announcing this choice, this exchange took place:

> Question: If you found it necessary to end the war, you would use nuclear weapons, wouldn't you?
> LeMay: If I found it necessary, I would use anything we could dream up—anything we could dream up—including nuclear weapons, if it was necessary.

Governor Wallace fairly sped to the microphone.

> All General LeMay has said—and I know you fellows better than he does because I've had to deal with you—he said that if the security of our country depended on the use of any weapon in the future he would use it. But he said he prefers not to use any sort of weapon. He prefers to negotiate. I believe we must defend our country, but I've always said we can win and defend in Vietnam without the use of nuclear weapons. But General LeMay hasn't said anything about the use of nuclear weapons.

Of course, General LeMay had talked about using nuclear weapons, and what he said produced a good many headlines. The general was promptly sent to Vietnam on an inspection tour, but the damage had been done.

A Fading Close

Wallace strength faded perceptibly after this point, and might have done so even without the LeMay remark. Richard Nixon, who was anxious to confine Wallace to the Deep South so he could pick up electoral votes in the Peripheral South, began to attack Wallace sharply. Labor union leaders, to whom Wallace's blue-collar appeal was a threat to their ability to lead their own members, organized a massive anti-Wallace, pro-Humphrey campaign. They gave wide circulation, for example, to a letter from an Alabama worker detailing unpleasant working conditions in Wallace's home state. What was happening was that themes from other policy areas—international involvement and economic management—were being used to counteract the governor's appeal on civil liberties questions, and voters were being told not to waste their votes on a third-party candidate.

When the Gallup Poll showed Wallace strength ebbing in late October, the governor attacked the poll, linking it with his opponents. "They lie when they poll. They are trying to rig an election. Eastern money runs everything. They are going to be pointed out as the liars they are." All in all, the Time's Up phase was not pleasant for George Wallace. He was tired, and he knew his hope of gaining electoral votes outside the South was forlorn. The day before the election, he was campaigning in front of the Georgia State House in the company of Georgia's segregationist governor, Lester Maddox. As Barry Goldwater before him, he ended up fighting to hold what once had been conceded to him.

HUBERT HUMPHREY, THE HAPPY WARRIOR OF 1968

Hubert H. Humphrey brought boundless enthusiasm, optimism, and energy to politics. It must have taken all of these qualities to sustain him in the opening stages of the 1968 campaign. He was finally at the head of the party whose leadership he had sought, but the coalition he hoped to lead was badly divided. On top of the defection to Wallace of many southern Democrats, those who opposed the Vietnam War were quite unwilling to work for Humphrey. They had suffered the double wound of defeat in a major platform battle, and seeing many of their fellows wounded from the tear gas and billy clubs of the Chicago police. Compounding this problem was the relation of Vice President Humphrey to President Johnson and his supporters. Any serious move to bring the Democratic doves back into the Humphrey coalition risked instant repudiation from the administration that was simultaneously fighting a war and trying to get peace talks started in Paris.

A Rushed Beginning

As if the problems with internal structure weren't bad enough, there was no time to organize a campaign or to plan how to handle this very difficult situation. The late-August convention, natural for a party in power on the assumption that the incumbent president would run and plans could be made on this basis, deprived the Humphrey core group of any time for the normal early phases of a campaign. Larry O'Brien was prevailed upon to stay as Democratic national chairman, and he had his fellow Springfield (Massachusetts) resident, Joseph Napolitan, draw up a campaign plan. Humphrey could also rely on such talented Minnesotans as Orville Freeman and Walter Mondale. Even so, there was only time for some hasty conferences at Humphrey's Waverly home to worry about lack of money, lack of support, lack of time, and lack of good ideas about how to heal the wounds in the party.

The Grand Opening was a mixture of improvization and hope. The senator inaugurated his campaign on September 9 with appearances in Philadelphia, Denver, and Los Angeles, and continued on the following days with appearances elsewhere. He spoke of pacific international programs, Food for Peace, the Peace Corps, and disarmament and arms control, in an effort to reach antiwar Democrats.[4] He pointed to administration accomplishments in social benefits—medicare, the Department of Housing and Urban Development, the Job Corps, education, and housing—and to progress in civil rights, policy areas on which Democrats were united. He attacked Richard Nixon, whom many Democrats detested. But none of this seemed to help. When he appeared on the hustings, he was confronted by demonstrators who chanted "Dump the Hump," "Chicago, Chicago," "Sieg Heil!" and the like. When he made a suggestion that some American troops could soon begin to be brought back from Vietnam, it was repudiated by both the president and the secretary of state. By the end of September, Humphrey was still trailing Richard Nixon 44 percent to 29 percent in the Gallup Poll. The hope for some event that would shift momentum—a Nixon mistake, a decision by Hanoi to begin serious negotiations, or something equally helpful—seemed more and more remote. The internal problems of the Humphrey coalition were going to have to be dealt with before any external strategy aimed at voters would be worthwhile. This meant that the nettle of Vietnam must be grasped by Humphrey himself.

The Salt Lake City Adjustment

Mr. Humphrey made this Strategic Adjustment in a nationally televised speech in the Mormon Tabernacle in Salt Lake City on September 30. In several ways—by removing the vice presidential seal from the rostrum, by notifying President Johnson only after copies of the speech had been given to newsmen, by explicit references in the speech itself—Vice President Humphrey emphasized that he was speaking for himself. His words were:

> As President, I would be willing to stop the bombing of North Vietnam as an acceptable risk for peace, because I believe that it could lead to success in negotiations and a shorter war. . . . In weighing that risk—and before taking action—I would place key importance on evidence, direct or indirect, by deed or word, of Communist willingness to restore the Demilitarized Zone between North and South Vietnam. If the Government of North Vietnam were to show bad faith, I would reserve the right to resume the bombing.

Lyndon Johnson was not pleased with this speech, but there were more hopeful reactions. A plea for funds had been added at the end, and the speech was no sooner over than pledges began to be phoned in. The

---

[4] As other vice presidents who have been nominated to run for president themselves, Humphrey found himself identified willy-nilly with both the successes and the failures of the Johnson administration. It was ironic that Humphrey, whose own record of policy initiatives has been matched by few in American political history, was so handicapped in 1968 by the Vietnam policy in which his own role was inconsequential.

demonstrators disappeared from Humphrey crowds and were replaced by friendlier faces. It was now possible to get about the business of appealing to voters, but time was very short.

A More Hopeful October

The outline of a viable strategy began to emerge on the basis of some private polls. While conceding that Humphrey was still far behind in national polls, state polls showed something different. Humphrey leaders claimed that it might be possible for the vice president to win by carrying some larger states—such as New York, New Jersey, Pennsylvania, Michigan, Minnesota, Missouri, and Texas—by quite small margins even though he lost other states by very large margins. They also claimed that their own polls showed Humphrey ahead, however narrowly, in these states. This claim rested on a very weak foundation. Some of the "polls" had been conducted by Joseph Napolitan himself. The results were aimed at journalists, potential donors, and Democratic workers, all of whom the Humphrey leaders wanted to convince of the plausibility of a Humphrey victory. Their plan worked (Chester, Hodgson, and Page, 1969, pp. 711–14; Frankel, 1968). The money and effort that was forthcoming certainly improved Humphrey's chances in fact. Even more important, the geographic concentration implied by these poll results was the one way that the vice president might get the electoral votes he needed.

In his campaigning, Humphrey continued to emphasize the issues that had served the Democrats well. In economic management, he did not emphasize the level of government spending, but rather Democratic support for employment. He favored making the federal government the employer of last resort, and while he stopped short of calling for income maintenance, he did favor increases in income supports. Fears of unemployment were summoned:

> Imagine what it'll be like if the unemployment rate is up to 7 percent. Who's to be unemployed? Which worker is to be laid off? Which family is to be without a check?

Memories of the depression were further stirred by a Democratic pamphlet that urged younger people to ask their fathers to tell them what things were like during the depression if they couldn't remember themselves. On social benefits, Vice President Humphrey called for a full 50 percent increase in social security benefits, sweeping aid to education coming directly from the federal government, and asked for comprehensive prenatal care for low-income women and medical care for all poor children during the first year of life. On civil liberties questions, Humphrey reiterated his support for the civil rights acts that had been passed, and generally endorsed Supreme Court decisions favoring rights of the accused.[5] The vice president did temper his outspoken enthusiasm for civil rights, matching the decrease in civil rights support among the electorate. He put civil rights in an employment context.

> I know what the opposition puts out to the blue-collar white worker. He says, "Watch out for that Humphrey. He is going to get a black man a job, and that means your job." I said, now listen here. I am for jobs. I am for an expanded economy in this country. I am for decent jobs and I am for jobs and I don't care whether the worker is black, white, green, or purple; fat, thin, tall, or short. I am for jobs.

He further argued that he was in the best position to assure racial harmony after the election as he was the only one of the three candidates who was trusted by both blacks and whites.[6]

All this almost worked. Between early October and late October, the Nixon-Humphrey margin in the national Gallup Poll closed from 43 percent–31 percent to 44 percent–36 percent, and the margin was even closer in the East. The Time's Up phase of the campaign was a good deal more pleasant for the Democratic coalition. The candidate campaigned across big states he hoped to carry, while the media campaign emphasized issues known to produce Democratic votes. One spot featured a man laughing for nearly a full minute, and closed with the message: "Agnew for Vice President? This would be funny if it weren't so serious. . . ." On October 29, Senator Eugene McCarthy finally endorsed Humphrey, and on October 31 President Johnson announced an immediate suspension to bombing North Vietnam, and said that serious peace talks would begin in Paris the following week. The McCarthy endorsement and the imminence of negotiations did not convert foreign policy into a Democratic advantage, but they were sufficient to allow pro-Democratic issues, such as social benefits and jobs, to have greater impact. The Gallup and Harris polls on the Sunday before the election showed Nixon with only a 42 percent–40

---

[5] Richard Nixon took positions "opposite" to those of Humphrey's on all the topics mentioned in this paragraph. (For instance, whereas Humphrey called for a 50 percent increase in social security benefits, Nixon endorsed a number of expansions in benefits that he said would be less costly.) Benjamin Page (1978, chaps. 3 and 4) has done an extensive analysis of the positions taken by the two major party candidates. The most frequent case was that Humphrey and Nixon took essentially the same stand. This happened on two thirds of all foreign issues and on many domestic issues. Where the candidates differed, they reflected traditional party divisions. When the party differences were low, as they were on 89 percent of foreign issues and 56 percent of domestic issues, candidate differences were low 66 percent of the time. On those topics where party divisions were high, candidate divisions were high 66 percent of the time. For obvious reasons, most attention is paid to points on which the candidates differ. It is worth remembering, though, that parties and candidates take essentially similar postures much of the time.

[6] Joe Napolitan took stronger measures to deemphasize civil rights in the Humphrey media campaign. He issued instructions that no black persons were to appear in any television spot.

percent lead over Humphrey. In the month since his Salt Lake City speech, Hubert Humphrey had almost led his coalition to victory.

THE POSSIBILITY OF A REPUBLICAN VICTORY

Just as Woodrow Wilson was given an opportunity in 1912 by the split in the then-majority Republican party, Richard Nixon was given an opportunity in 1968 by the fragmentation of the Democratic party. Ever since the 1930s, Republican candidates have had to take most of the independent vote and pick up at least a few Democratic votes to win. But with George Wallace attracting many Democratic and independent votes, and the antiwar Democratic activists sitting on their hands, Richard Nixon had an unusual opportunity to win with the normal Republican vote.

External Threats and Nixon's Plan from the Center

In spite of this happy augury, the Nixon coalition faced a difficult political situation. Hubert Humphrey was taking more liberal positions and George Wallace was taking more conservative positions. This didn't pose too much of an internal problem: Republican activists were unlikely to support Humphrey or Wallace. It did, however, pose quite an external problem. If Nixon took relatively liberal positions in order to woo voters away from Humphrey, he risked losing support to Wallace. If he took relatively conservative positions in order to woo voters away from Wallace, he risked losing support to Humphrey.

The problem can be seen in the geographic concentration planned for the campaign. There was a list of states selected by Nixon himself for extensive personal campaigning and for concentrated media campaigns. It included California in the West, South Carolina in the Deep South, Florida, North Carolina, Texas, and Virginia in the Peripheral South, Illinois, Ohio, Michigan, Wisconsin, and Missouri, all urban midwestern states,[7] and Pennsylvania, New Jersey, and New York in the East (Chester, Hodgson, and Page, 1969, p. 621). To the extent that Nixon took positions that would win support from Wallace in the southern states on the list, he would be vulnerable to Humphrey in the East and Midwest. To the extent that he took positions that would win support from Humphrey in the East and Midwest, he risked losing states in the South to Wallace.[8]

---

[7] The mean percentage living in urban areas in these five states was 73.6 percent. Illinois was the most urban (83 percent); Wisconsin the least (65.9 percent).

[8] Nixon was not seriously challenged in the West. He ultimately carried every state west of Iowa except for Texas, Washington, and Hawaii. This gave him a base on which to build, something Humphrey did not have. Nixon's western base did not help with the problem of getting enough electoral votes to keep the election out of the House, though. If California is excluded, all these states together cast only 70 electoral votes; 200 electoral votes had to come from somewhere else. Hence the importance of Nixon's own list.

If Richard Nixon was going to win the required majority of Electoral College votes, he needed to maintain a precarious balance between his two opponents. This meant that he had to sketch out his generally moderate conservative position, to create the impression of movement, to make statements, but to do all this without saying anything so definite that it would cause the majority of voters then leaning to Nixon to re-evaluate their positions.

A Symbolic Chicago Opening

The Grand Opening of the Nixon campaign began in Chicago on September 4. A parade through the downtown area was seen by hundreds of thousands of persons, seemingly relieved by the contrast between Nixon's peaceful arrival and the violence that had marked the Democratic convention a few weeks earlier. The centerpiece of the Chicago visit, though, was a telecast during which Nixon was interviewed by a panel of representative citizens. Since the panel members had been screened, this gave Mr. Nixon the opportunity to make statements without being pressed, as he might have been during a debate or by a determined news-man. In the opening exchange, for instance, he was asked:

> Would you comment on the accusation which was made from time to time that your views have shifted and that they are based on expediencies?

Nixon replied:

> I suppose what you are referring to is: Is there a new Nixon or an old Nixon? . . . My answer is, yes, there is a new Nixon, if you are talking in terms of new ideas for a new world and the America we live in. In terms of what I believe in the American view and the American dream, I think I am just where I was eight years ago.

Later a black panel member asked, "What do law and order mean to you?" This time the reply was:

> I am quite aware that the black community, when they hear it, think of power as being used in a way that is destructive to them, and yet I think we have to also remember that the black community as well as the white community has an interest in order and in law, providing that law is with justice. To me law and order must be combined with justice. Now that's what I want for America. I want the kind of law and order which deserves respect. (McGinnis, 1969, pp. 70–71)

This opportunity to appear responsive, and to associate himself with such popular symbols as the American dream and justice, was ideal for a candidate who had to maintain a delicate political balance. The television format was sharpened a bit, but was not basically altered, and was used in ten cities during the course of the campaign.

From Chicago, the campaign moved on to rallies on succeeding days in San Francisco, Houston, Pittsburgh, and White Plains (New York). Richard Nixon drew middle-class audiences, and made his appeal to those he termed "forgotten Americans":

> . . . those who did not indulge in violence, those who did not break the law, those who pay taxes and go to work, people who send their children to school, who go to their churches, people who are not haters, people who love this country. . . .

These were inclusive categories; most people do obey the law, pay their taxes, go to work, and so on. Certainly there was nothing in this language to disturb either moderate or conservative supporters.

As the campaign developed, Richard Nixon sent two types of messages. One was "the speech." This had a standard content. The tested applause lines were the same whether they came at a giant rally, after music and cascading balloons, or whether they were uttered at a prop-stop at a community airport.

> We need new leadership that will not only end the war in Vietnam but keep the nation out of other wars for eight years.
> I say that when crime has been going up nine times as fast as the population, when 43 percent of the people living in American cities are afraid to go out after dark, I say we need a complete housecleaning.
> The American flag is not going to be used as a doormat for anybody when we get in.
> Well, my friends, I say this, that when you are on the wrong road and you reach a dead end, the thing you do is to get off that road and onto a new road.

These statements were not unusual campaign oratory. Almost every candidate develops a standard speech, and certainly every out-party candidate tells his audience a new administration is needed.

Nixon's other type of message was more innovative. He used radio, a low-cost, low-salience medium for longer discussions directed to the more limited audience he thought might be interested in issues. In the course of the campaign, he gave such speeches on the presidency, order and justice, black capitalism, a new political coalition, training programs for the urban poor, revenue sharing, social security, NATO, the Alliance for Progress, the problems of youth, and defense policy. The combination of the set stump speech and the more thoughtful radio address afforded a contrast in style (Semple, 1968). One type of message was directed to a mass audience that wasn't sufficiently interested to think past slogans; the other type of message was directed to an attentive elite that was interested in public policy. And the two types of messages seemed to be directed to separate audiences whose policy preferences might differ. Consider these passages from two of his radio addresses. When calling for an open presidency, Mr. Nixon said:

> A president has to hear not only the clamorous voices of the organized, but also the quiet voices, the inner voices—the voices that speak from the heart and conscience. . . . A president must tell the people what cannot be done immediately, as well as what can. Hope is fragile, and too easily shattered by the disappointment that follows inevitably on promises unkept and unkeepable.

In another address entitled "Order and Justice under Law," he explained:

> It is true that law enforcement is primarily a local responsibility—but the public climate with regard to law is a function of national leadership. . . . A National Academy of Law Enforcement . . . would enable our law enforcement agencies to be equipped intellectually for the complex tasks they face in our modern world.

Nothing in these words disavowed positions taken in the stump speeches, but the tone was certainly different. Where "the speech" declared that the American flag wouldn't be used as a doormat, and suggested that a complete housecleaning would solve the problems of crime, the radio addresses spoke of fragile hope and complex tasks. It was as though the applause lines were addressed to conservatives who thought that problems could be solved if the government was just tough enough, and the radio speeches were addressed to moderates. Whether there was an explicit strategy of dual messages or not, we don't know. We do know that both sets of voters had to be reached, and that Nixon continued both types of speeches throughout the campaign.

Tactical Adjustments

The Nixon campaign was well enough planned that no Strategic Adjustments were necessary. There were some Tactical Adjustments from time to time. The first was a move to counter George Wallace as his strength peaked in late September and early October. In Atlanta on October 3, Nixon said that he and Wallace were both opposed to foreign policy failings and the rise in crime at home. But he challenged Wallace because of a statement that if any demonstrator laid down in front of his car it would be the last such occasion.

> We need politics at home that will go beyond simply saying that if somebody lies down in front of my presidential limousine it will be the last one he lies down in front of. Now look here. No president of the United States is going to do that, and anybody who says that shouldn't be president of the United States.

Campaigning later in Florida, he asked his audience: "Does Florida want to go off onto a third-party kick? Or does it want to play a role in the great decision of 1968?" It would be unwise to claim too much for the effects of these speeches; other anti-Wallace forces were active at the same time. Still, Wallace strength did subside during October, and this left Nixon in a much stronger position in the Peripheral South.

The Wallace challenge was not the serious one, though. By mid-October, the Nixon coalition was aware of growing Humphrey strength. Consequently, the core group met with the candidate at his Key Biscayne home on the weekend of October 13. Some previously taken decisions were reaffirmed. Nixon would continue to avoid debates with Humphrey, and continue to rely on radio speeches to delineate his positions. But there were some Tactical Adjustments as well. In order to counter Democratic success on social benefits questions, Nixon would stress his own support for social security, and he would begin to attack Vice President Humphrey more directly (White, 1969, pp. 370–71).

The Key Biscayne meeting was followed by stronger phrases. Vice President Humphrey became "the most expensive Senator in American history," and "a man who gives no indication he believes there's a bottom to the well of the U.S. Treasury." Nixon was particularly fond of the phrase "sock it to 'em" from the then-popular TV show "Laugh In." In Columbus, Ohio, for example, he said Ohio State played "rock 'em, sock 'em football, and that's just what we're going to do for the rest of the campaign. From now on we're going to sock it to 'em with everything we've got." In fact, though, Mr. Nixon continued to pursue very cautious, centrist politics. The number of appearances he made in any day was limited. He continued to take positions close to the known preferences of voters.[9]

No Room Left for Maneuver

Reporters traveling with Mr. Nixon in late October noticed any number of fluffs and misstatements. The Time's Up stage of the campaign had arrived, and the candidate was doubtless tired, but there was more to it than that. He was caught in the middle; and having positioned himself to take southern states from Wallace, it was next to impossible to prevent a resurgence of normal Democratic support for Humphrey in the East. Nixon's only new policy position was a call for clear-cut military superiority over the Soviet Union. Beyond this, he urged Humphrey to join him in a pledge to support the candidate who got the largest number of popular votes if no one won a majority in the Electoral College. Vice

---

[9] Page's study (1978, chap. 3) shows that Nixon took positions close to those of a plurality of the electorate on 79 percent of the issues, compared to 69 percent for Humphrey.

President Humphrey was no more likely to accept this proposal than Nixon had been to accept Humphrey's earlier challenge to debate. As things turned out, luck was with Nixon. By three o'clock of the morning after the election, it was apparent that Richard Nixon had carried Ohio, Illinois, and California, and had narrowly won the office that had eluded him eight years earlier.

Summary

There were contrasts aplenty between the 1964 and 1968 campaigns. The sense of mastery over international and economic matters, and the confidence that government could remove social inequities that had made it so difficult for Barry Goldwater to challenge the status quo in 1964 were missing in 1968. There were two coalitions in 1964, and three coalitions in 1968. But the principal strategic difference between the two campaigns was the greater freedom the 1964 nominees had to do what they chose. To be sure, nothing that Barry Goldwater tried worked very well, but he had time to try out four or five different strategies. Given a normal Democratic majority and Goldwater's position on the right, Lyndon Johnson had great freedom to defend his administration in a variety of ways.

In 1968, on the other hand, all three of the contestants had to fight from relatively fixed positions. George Wallace could not move very far from the civil liberties positions on which his national reputation was based. Hubert Humphrey was associated willy-nilly with the accomplishments and problems of the Johnson administration, and had to do something about the Vietnam question before he could make any progress with issues that normally united a Democratic coalition. And Richard Nixon was caught between the other two.

In addition, there were some other specific effects that could be traced to internal constraints, external constraints, and temporal constraints. We shall take a look at these at the end of Chapter 6. By that point, we shall have four campaigns among which comparisons can be made.

chapter 6

Campaign Strategies: The 1970s

THE 1972 CAMPAIGN

The 1972 campaign is often interpreted as a mirror image of the 1964 campaign. In important ways, this is true. In 1964, a Democratic incumbent faced a Republican challenge from the right, and in 1972, a Republican incumbent faced a Democratic challenge from the left. Both challengers proposed fairly drastic policy reorientations, and both had difficulty obtaining electoral support. Both incumbents had considerable freedom of action in selecting their strategies, and both won victories of historic proportions. But there were also features of the 1972 campaign quite unlike anything seen eight years earlier.

The issues were different in 1972. The nation was not confronted with serious international or economic problems in the mid-60s, but these were the major points of contention in 1972. In spite of four years of negotiations, and (by 1972) a total withdrawal of American ground combat troops, the war had not ended. Early in the year, President Nixon had traveled to China, with which diplomatic contacts had begun, and in the late spring, he went to Moscow to sign the first Strategic Arms Limitations Treaty. In domestic affairs, the inflation that had begun as a consequence of the Vietnam War had proven difficult to check, and wage and price controls had been instituted in 1971. The Consumer Price Index had risen 3.3 percent during 1972.

There were two events unique to 1972: the replacement of Democratic vice presidential candidate Thomas Eagleton, and a break-in at the Democratic National Committee headquarters by five men working for the

Committee to Re-elect the President. In early August, Senator Eagleton revealed that he had been hospitalized for nervous exhaustion and had received shock treatment. Senator McGovern stated that he was "1000 percent for Tom Eagleton" and had no intention of dropping him from the ticket, but within two weeks he had accepted his resignation. It is still not clear what the five men were looking for at the Democratic National Committee, but it is clear that they were acting on behalf of the Committee to Re-elect the President, and that committee officials, White House staff members, and President Nixon himself took action to prevent legal authorities from finding out what had happened. The departure of Senator Eagleton from the Democratic ticket had more serious political consequences (for reasons we shall see almost at once) in 1972. What became known as the Watergate affair had fewer consequences that year. The cover-up kept the public in the dark until after the election, and those who distrusted Richard Nixon enough to believe he was personally involved were likely to vote for George McGovern in any case. Ultimately, of course, the Watergate affair was to force Nixon from office.

GEORGE McGOVERN'S MORAL CHALLENGE

George McGovern's bid for the presidency was reminiscent of William Jennings Bryan's campaign in 1900. Both men came from the plains, and both spoke in terms of moral certainty. McGovern's views about the influence of business in the Nixon administration could be seen as a latter-day instance of Bryan's "Democracy against Plutocracy," and his attacks on Nixon's Vietnam policy showed the same fervor as Bryan's complaints about American imperialism. This analogy shouldn't be pressed too far. America in the 1970s was very different from the turn-of-the-century country just emerging as a world power. Still, the Bryan comparison sheds some light on the questions McGovern was trying to raise, and his political difficulties in doing so.

McGovern's Left-Center Plan and Organizational Difficulties

The organizational stage of the McGovern campaign would have been difficult in the best of circumstances. His nomination coalition had been built around the most liberal groups in the Democratic party: the antiwar movement and those favoring much expanded social programs and further busing. The idea behind this had been a left-centrist strategy: to co-opt the left as a base for a nomination drive, but to keep the organization open to centrist politicians so that McGovern could appeal to a normal Democratic spectrum in the general election. The Democratic left had been co-opted all right, but many of their views and personnel were unacceptable to veterans of past Democratic campaigns. One standard way of handling this situation is to work through those with good ties to the successful nomination coalition and to other party groups. Lawrence O'Brien and Senator Thomas Eagleton might have been very effective in this task. O'Brien had reassumed the chairmanship of the Democratic National Committee a couple of years earlier because he was the one person acceptable to all the leading Democrats, and Eagleton was a Roman Catholic with good ties to urban politicians and organized labor. But their organizational talents were not to be used. O'Brien became unhappy about the way the campaign was structured, and Eagleton was forced to resign as the vice presidential candidate after it was learned that he had been hospitalized for depression.

The Eagleton affair was costly to Senator McGovern's standing with the public. McGovern's swift move from "1000 percent support" for Eagleton to willingness to accept his resignation raised troublesome questions about McGovern's competence. But to appreciate the temporal impact of the Eagleton affair, one must remember that it came smack in the middle of what should have been the Organization stage of the campaign. In place of contributions and appointments, there were statements from Democratic leaders and the mass media, many to the effect that Senator Eagleton should leave the ticket. Contributors who had pledged large amounts to get the campaign started let the McGovern leaders know the money might not be forthcoming. Regional directors and state leaders reported no activity going on in the field. The reaction of the McGovern core group to all this was that Eagleton must go. There might be costs to dropping him from the ticket, but the campaign could not get under way with him.

August, the extra month available to the Democrats because of their early convention, was largely devoted to repair efforts of one kind and another. First came the selection of Sargent Shriver to replace Senator Eagleton. Some prominent Democrats had not been interested in running with McGovern, but Shriver accepted eagerly and his selection was ratified at a meeting of the Democratic National Committee. Organizational difficulties continued, notably over the management and budget for an urgent get-out-the-vote drive, but a campaign staff (regional and state coordinators) came into being, and some activity began throughout the country.

Senator McGovern did make two or three campaign trips during August to keep his name in the headlines. Perhaps the most important of these was a speech to the New York Society of Security Analysts on August 29. During the primaries, the senator had proposed giving $1,000 a month to every American, and had rather casually attached a cost figure of $21 in additional taxation for persons earning $20,000 or more.

Now, after some weeks of staff analysis, McGovern was ready to present a more carefully thought out proposal (White, 1973, pp. 126–28; Hart, 1973, p. 279). In his New York speech, he called for a $10 billion cut in defense spending over each of the next three years, and a "fair share tax reform" that would bring in an additional $22 billion by various changes in the tax laws. These funds would be used for two programs: $15 billion to local school systems, and a "National Income Insurance Program," consisting of public service jobs, an expansion of social security, and "approximately $4,000 in cash and food stamps for a family of four with no other income who are unable to work."

Multiple Plans and External Troubles

There did not appear to be an agreed-upon plan for the McGovern coalition by the time of the Grand Opening. Rather, there were a number of plans. None of these lasted long, and portions of each seemed to conflict with other plans that were presumably in effect. For example, Senator McGovern told Theodore White he thought he would carry California and New York, and that the geographic concentration of the campaign would be on Illinois, Michigan, Ohio, Pennsylvania, and New Jersey (White, 1973, p. 312). But the McGovern coalition had been responsible for expelling Chicago Mayor Richard Daley's delegation from the Democratic Convention, and in spite of a personal appeal, Mayor Daley had stated that each member of his organization was free to make his own judgment about supporting the McGovern-Shriver ticket. Labor would also be important in winning this band of states, but McGovern had only about half the labor support assembled for most Democrats and George Meany had announced that he was neutral between Nixon and McGovern.

Then there was the matter of the positions McGovern was taking. In international involvement, the senator wanted an immediate cessation of Vietnamese hostilities, as well as a rather deep cut in defense spending. His New York economic speech had called for higher taxes and further spending. Social benefits programs included income maintenance, more school aid, and national health insurance. On civil liberties, the senator supported busing, favored control of handguns, and said that crime was related to economic and racial discrimination. These liberal positions were quite consistent with the internal structure of the McGovern coalition, but they caused external trouble with the voters the senator was trying to reach. Pennsylvania steelworkers, for example, saw McGovern's position on the Vietnam War as equivalent to surrender, and felt that he wanted to give welfare recipients more than they were making in take-home pay (Sperling, 1972). It might be said that the lack of an overall campaign plan was the least of McGovern's difficulties. The McGovern coalition was short on many of the essentials of a successful campaign:

a smoothly working organization, external support, and positions that would attract large numbers of voters.

In part because of a lack of resources, in part to take advantage of the speed of jet travel, and in part because of a hope that the senator could arouse American voters, the McGovern campaign scheduled appearances in two to four different media markets each day. On September 6, for example, he was in San Diego, Dallas, and Houston. On September 12, he campaigned in Chicago, Cleveland, and Detroit. The idea was to generate local stories in addition to those filed by the traveling press for the national media. The underlying theme of these stories, regardless of the policy area being discussed, was one of opposition to the Nixon administration. In fact, a controversy over how this opposition should be conveyed was taking place within the McGovern core group. Frank Mankiewicz, Larry O'Brien, and Ted Van Dyk favored a negative accent on Nixon and the Republicans. Charles Guggenheim, Liz Stevens, and Gary Hart wanted more positive material used. A key factor in this dispute was the senator's own sense of moral fervor. He didn't need a plan to tell him that Richard Nixon and all of his works were evil, and as September wore on he became more and more negative.[1] Speaking in the inner-city Hill district of Pittsburgh, for example, he explicitly blamed poverty conditions on the war in Vietnam:

> . . . as much as any village bombed into rubble, the Hill district is a victim of the war in Vietnam—the longest, the cruelist, and the stupidest war in American history. Why aren't there any better schools here? Because your money has been used to blow up schools in Vietnam. Why aren't there more clinics to protect your health? Because your money has been used to bomb the life out of innocent civilians in Indochina. Every bomb that is dropped and every bullet that is fired in Southeast Asia has an echo that is heard in the Hill district. We have paid for the devastation of another land with the devastation, not just of our conscience, but of our own country.

Such language conveyed the depth of Senator McGovern's feelings, but it was not adding much support to his coalition. Nor were the efforts of campaigners who were working in McGovern's behalf. The polls, public and private, continued to show President Nixon far ahead. This disheartening situation produced anxiety among the coalition leaders. As campaign director Gary Hart put it, "there was nothing tangible, nothing concrete, nothing to show movement and progress. At the headquarters, the staff and volunteers grasped at straws for encouragement, cheering each appearance of one of the candidates on the evening news, savoring each favorable editorial or report of new administrative mal-

---

[1] This conclusion about McGovern's negativism, and those to follow about a positive or negative tone to the campaign or policy areas being emphasized, are based on a content analysis of the McGovern and Nixon speeches.

feasance, longing for some proof that victory lay ahead" (1973, pp. 299–300).

A Strategic Turn to a More Positive Approach

The manifest lack of progress dictated a Strategic Adjustment. Senator McGovern decided to make a series of nationally televised addresses during October, and reduced the number of negative references in his own public statements. The first televised speech on October 10 dealt with McGovern's public plan to end the Vietnam War by withdrawing all American forces within 90 days.

> ... when all is said and done, our purpose in Vietnam now comes down to this—our policy makers want to save face and they want to save the Saigon regime of General Thieu. Now that is a fundamental difference between President Nixon and me . . . It is a choice between four more years of war, or four years of peace. . . . On the night when the last American soldier from Vietnam has landed in San Francisco, there will be a new birth of confidence and hope for all of us.

The senator's second speech on October 20 dealt with economic management, the policy area to which he devoted the most attention during the fall campaign. McGovern criticized Nixon administration policies concerning interest, employment, wage and price controls, and taxes, and linked all of these to the administration's economic philosophy.

> Every single time this administration has faced an important economic choice, they have picked a policy that was right for the few and wrong for you. . . . This election is more than a contest between George McGovern and Richard Nixon. It is a fundamental struggle between the little people of America and the big, rich of America, between the average working man or woman and a powerful elite. . . . I want to be the kind of President who will see to it that America is good to every one of her people. I want us to claim that promise of Isaiah, "The people shall be righteous and they shall inherit the land."

These October efforts did produce some financial results. An appeal for funds at the end of the Vietnam speech brought in more than a million dollars, and by the end of the month so much money was coming in that there was difficulty in opening the mail. This was a happy contrast to the desperate lack of financial support in August, but there was still no evidence that the voters were changing their minds.

A Final Bitterness

By the time of the third speech, on October 25, a good deal of negativism was creeping back into Senator McGovern's rhetoric. The theme for this speech was corruption in the Nixon administration. Favors extended to campaign contributors, Watergate, and extensions of executive power were all discussed.

> The men who have collected millions in secret money, who have passed out special favors, who have ordered political sabotage, who have invaded our offices in the dead of the night—all these men work for Mr. Nixon. Most of them he hired himself. And their power comes from him alone. They act on his behalf, and they accept his orders.

This speech, a direct attack on Nixon's integrity, was symptomatic of McGovern's mood as the campaign moved into the Time's Up stage. It was now clear that he was not going to win, and the senator became increasingly bitter in his public comments. In late October, statements from both Hanoi and Washington indicated the probability of success in peace negotiations. Senator McGovern's reaction was to say that "when Dr. Kissinger came out and said 'peace is at hand' he was misleading the American people. He knew what he said was false." McGovern told questioners in Los Angeles that Richard Nixon had "conducted an evil administration. . . . I think the exploiting of racial fears is an evil practice. I think the aerial bombardment of Southeast Asia by Richard Nixon is the most evil thing ever done by any American President." And in Chicago on the Saturday before the election, George McGovern said:

> It's all right for people to be fooled once as they were in 1968. If they do it again, if they let this man lead them down the false hopes of peace once again in 1972, then the people have nobody to blame but themselves. . . . I'm going to give one more warning. If Mr. Nixon is elected on Tuesday, we may very well have four more years of war in Southeast Asia. Our prisoners will sit in their cells for another four years. Don't let this man trick you into believing that he stands for peace, when he's a man who makes war.

It was almost as though Senator McGovern was angry with the voters for refusing to listen to him. Whether or no, he was in the same position as Senator Goldwater eight years earlier. He had tried to raise some fundamental questions, and by election eve he knew that this would not lead to electoral success.

REELECT THE PRESIDENT: NIXON 1972

A Positive, Ethnic, Centrist Approach

"I ask everyone listening to me tonight—Democrats, Republicans, and Independents—to join our new majority; not on the basis of the party label you wear on your lapel but what you believe in your hearts." This appeal for a new majority was an important part of Richard Nixon's acceptance speech in 1972. Internally, the Nixon coalition was composed of groups supporting American involvement overseas and a strong defense posture, conservative economics, few new social programs, increased police authority, and opposition to busing. The new majority Nixon sought referred to his coalition's need for additional external support. Many moves had been made by his administration to win favor from three traditionally Democratic groupings: Catholics, labor, and southerners. The nomination of a Democrat unpopular with these constituencies gave Nixon a chance to capitalize on the moves he had already made. This was the major focus of the 1972 Republican campaign.

Perhaps the most important move to gain Catholic support was Nixon's consistent championship of aid to parochial schools. He urged this on a number of occasions, such as in a 1971 speech to the Knights of Columbus. Nixon had also made known his opposition to abortion in a letter to Terence Cardinal Cooke of New York. During the election campaign an unusual amount of effort went into Heritage (that is, white ethnic) groups, and three ethnic groups selected for inclusion in this massive mailing campaign were Irish, Polish, and Italian. Among other things, the president visited an immigration museum at the Statue of Liberty; stopped his motorcade in Wilkes-Barre, Pennsylvania, in order to pose with members of an Italian wedding party that happened to be emerging from a church as he drove by; turned up at an Italian-American celebration in Maryland, explaining that his daughter Julie couldn't make it and he was substituting for her; and spoke at a Columbus Day dinner. In this speech, he said:

> When we honor [labor leader] Peter Fosco, we see [an important attribute] very clearly, and that is, putting it quite bluntly, hard work. Italian Americans came to this country by the hundreds of thousands, and then by the millions. They came here not asking for something, asking only for the opportunity to work. They have worked and they have built. There is a second feature which is represented by this head table tonight. Those of Italian background bring with them a very deep religious faith . . .

This prose was typical of the 1972 Nixon.campaign in two respects. First, Nixon spoke positively of the virtues of whatever group he was addressing. This was not unusual for a politician, but in 1972 it provided a contrast with McGovern's negativism. Second, his constant references to the importance of hard work were an integral part of his appeal to blue-collar voters.

Relations between organized labor and the Nixon administration had been cool, and were to become so again, but in 1972 there was a tactical truce that presented an unusual opportunity for Republicans to get labor votes. Labor was by no means pro-Nixon. Rather, McGovern positions reduced the amount of labor support that would normally flow to a Democratic candidate.[2] As one labor leader put it, "Most of our members get the creeps when they think about Nixon, but McGovern worries them." The AFL-CIO was neutral and the Nixon coalition worked hard to take advantage of this posture. A well-advertised golf game was played by Richard Nixon and George Meany, and a plank supporting Section 14–B of the Taft-Hartley Act (permitting state right-to-work laws that were anathema to organized labor) was dropped from the Republican platform. Secretary of Labor James Hodgson addressed the Steelworkers, who did not endorse either candidate, but cancelled a speech before the Machinists, who endorsed McGovern.

In his Labor Day speech, which had been reviewed with AFL-CIO leaders before delivery (Safire, 1975, p. 595), President Nixon drew a contrast between the work ethic and the welfare ethic. "Above all," he argued, "the work ethic puts responsibility in the hands of the individual, in the belief that self-reliance and willingness to work make a person a better human being . . . [whereas] the welfare ethic destroys character and leads to a vicious cycle of dependency." Richard Nixon cited the importance of work over and over again during the campaign. He believed hard work to be responsible for his own success, and it was a natural link with the labor vote he hoped to win.

Southern support for Republican presidential candidates was not unusual. Herbert Hoover had carried five states in the "Solid South" as long ago as 1928, and Republicans had been making real efforts to increase their strength there since the 1950s. Still, southern voters were another large group of Democrats who disliked George McGovern and to whom the center-right policies of the Nixon administration were acceptable. Some seven former Democratic governors, and scores of lesser Democratic officials in the South, endorsed Richard Nixon rather than George McGovern. When President Nixon visited John Connally's Texas ranch in September, he was welcomed by some 200 Democrats, mostly southern, whom Connally had recruited to the Democrats for Nixon organization he headed. And when Nixon campaigned in Atlanta, he argued that southerners were not racist, any more than Michiganders were racist, because they opposed busing. "It simply means . . . parents in Georgia and parents all over the country want better education for their children, and that better education is going to come in the schools that are closer to home and not those clear across town." He went on to assert that the issues that were important in the South— peace, jobs, safety, local control—were the same issues that were important all over the country.

---

[2] Twenty individual unions endorsed McGovern; only the Teamsters endorsed Nixon.

A Triumphal March for the Incumbent

There were few temporal effects in the 1972 Nixon campaign. All the appeals to give added external support to his coalition—those to Catholics, labor, and the South—were in place by the Grand Opening, and the campaign went well enough that there was no need for either Strategic or Tactical Adjustments. Nixon used the traditional techniques of the incumbent: the ability to schedule headline-making events when his opponent was trying to make news, conferences with foreign leaders, a fiscal policy designed to stimulate the economy at election time, and spent his time visibly being president while surrogates spoke around the country in his name.

One technique resurrected from 1968 was the use of radio for more thoughtful addresses. Several of these were delivered. One devoted to his philosophy picked up the theme of a new majority, and gave an exposition of his values that echoed something of his earlier defense of the work ethic.

> The new American majority believes that each person should have more of the say in how he lives his own life . . . in taking care of those persons who cannot take care of themselves . . . in taking whatever action is needed to hold down the cost of living . . . and in a national defense second to none. . . . These are not the beliefs of a selfish people. On the contrary, they are the beliefs of a generous and self-reliant people, a people of intellect and character, whose values deserve respect in every segment of our population.

Richard Nixon's greatest asset in 1972, of course, was not a capacity to give an articulate presentation of moderate conservative values, but the success of his foreign policy. He had made his trips to Peking and Moscow earlier in the year, and the announcement of a breakthrough in the negotiations on Vietnam more or less coincided with the Time's Up phase when the president began campaigning full time. He had devoted much more attention to international involvement than to any other policy area throughout the campaign, and concluded his campaign in Ontario, California, on election eve with further references to his foreign policy record and his hopes for a "Generation Of Peace."

> Finally we have had a breakthrough in the negotiations, and I can tell you today that the significant point of that breakthrough is that the three principles that I laid down on May 8 . . . have been agreed to. . . . The trip to Peking . . . has great meaning . . . to [the] younger generation . . . Imagine how dangerous the world would be if one-fourth of all the people of the world who live in the People's Republic of China, ten, fifteen years from now had gathered enormous nuclear capability and had no communication with the United States . . . We could not allow that danger

. . . The trip to Moscow had a similar purpose . . . Imagine what we would leave to the younger generation had we . . . gone down the road to an inevitable confrontation and a nuclear explosion that possibly would have destroyed civilization as we know it.

In common with many winning campaigns, the 1972 Nixon triumph went too smoothly. There was domestic political success based on appeals to many Democrats alienated by the McGovern candidacy, and a foreign policy record that was appreciated by many voters. But as was all too soon to become apparent, there was also political sabotage, vast overspending, and a cover-up involving the president himself. This was tragic for Nixon and his hopes for future accomplishment. In 1960, he had shown a high order of statesmanship on at least two occasions: in forbidding any discussion of his opponent's religion, and in refusing to bring on a constitutional crisis by challenging the very close election results. Had a hint of these values been reflected in the actions of Richard Nixon and his appointees in 1972, he would have been able to govern on the basis of the record majority he had won, and to have led the nation in its bicentennial in 1976.

THE 1976 CAMPAIGN

The 1976 campaign was normal, and it was anything but normal. For the first time since 1960, most Democrats were in the Democratic coalition and most Republicans were in the Republican coalition. But the Democratic coalition was organized in support of a one-term governor from the Deep South, and the Republican coalition was led by a former congressman from Grand Rapids who had become the first unelected president in American history. Neither candidate could count on full support from *all* his nominal partisans, and therein lay the interesting strategic challenges of the 1976 campaign.

Gerald Ford had begun his short administration with the reassuring statement that "our long national nightmare is over." But his initial popularity dropped sharply after he pardoned Richard Nixon, and by the fall of 1974 America was in the deepest recession since the depression of the 1930s. The unemployment rate was up to 8.4 percent in 1975, and inflation, led by sharp increases in the costs of food, fuel, housing, and medical care, was worse than ever. By 1976, a 1972 dollar was worth only 73 cents![3] Against this background of Watergate and economic problems, questions of which candidate could be trusted and who could manage the economy loomed large in 1976.

---

[3] As of 1976, this was the worst four-year record on inflation since World War II. The 1976–80 record was to be even worse, but 1976 voters had no way of knowing that.

AN OUTSIDER LEADS THE MAJORITY PARTY

In midsummer, there were certainly some favorable omens for the Carter coalition. Internally, the coalition had been expanded in the classic manner by the selection of a vice presidential candidate, Walter Mondale, who was highly respected by liberals. Externally, the Gallup Poll showed Jimmy Carter running ahead of Gerald Ford by a remarkable 62 percent to 29 percent margin.

But for those who looked a bit more closely, there were signs of possible trouble. The campaign organization made minimal use of the Democratic talent now available to Carter. Walter Mondale and his ranking aide, Richard Moe, were admitted to the strategy group, but that was the only expansion. Campaign headquarters were kept in Atlanta and staff responsibilities remained essentially as they had been. Following a Kennedy pattern, Carter designees from out of state were put in charge of each state's presidential campaign. And while the external support available for Carter was widespread, it was very soft. Jimmy Carter might be the majority party's nominee, but many Democrats and independents were unenthusiastic about him.

A Southern-Based Strategy

Planning for the campaign, summarized in two memos written by campaign director Hamilton Jordan in June and August, did not assume that the early support would hold up. Quite the opposite. "We will probably not know until mid-October if the election is going to be close or if there is potential for a big victory." Therefore, Jordan asserted, the Carter coalition must "always maintain a high degree of flexibility in the allocation of our resources and the objectives of strategy." But the main key to the Carter strategy was an assumption that it had not been possible for a Democratic candidate to make since 1944: a sweep of the southern and border states. The South is the largest of the four sections of the country, and when Jordan added the District of Columbia, Massachusetts, Minnesota, and Wisconsin to this base, there was a total of 199 electoral votes. This would not be enough electoral votes to win; others would have to come from eight large industrial states, such as New York and Pennsylvania, and these critical states were in fact scheduled for more intensive campaign efforts. If the 199-vote base held, though, the additional necessary votes could be obtained by winning any of several combinations of states. Therefore, Jordan claimed, "the only way we can lose in November is to have this base fragmented" (Schram, 1977, pp. 239–50; Witcover, 1977, chap. 35).

The Jordan plan was quite specific about where the campaign was to be waged, but not about how it was to be done. The plan was silent about the issues that were to be used to appeal to voters in large industrial states while retaining support in the essential southern base. Indeed, it was not until nearly time for the Grand Opening that Carter himself asked his strategy group, "What are our themes going to be?" The absence of a clear answer to this question was to hobble the Carter campaign throughout the fall.

A Downhill Slide

The implicit statement made by the Grand Opening was that the Roosevelt coalition had been reassembled. The formal opening took place at FDR's "Little White House" in Warm Springs, Georgia, with two Roosevelt sons present, and the late president's favorite black accordionist playing "Happy Days Are Here Again." This was followed by a couple of other southern stops, presumably sufficient to reinforce regional pride, and then the Carter entourage moved north, where the additional electoral votes had to be won. In the following days, Governor Carter met voters at a New York subway stop and at a suburban rally in Columbus, Ohio; put on a "Polish Hill" T-shirt in Pittsburgh; addressed the AFL-CIO convention in Dearborn, Michigan; took part in Mayor Daley's torchlight parade in Chicago; and rode across Pennsylvania on a campaign train in emulation of Harry Truman's whistle-stop campaign of 1948.

A lot of little things seemed to go wrong as Carter sought support from blue-collar, ethnic voters. There was difficulty in dealing with questions about abortion, a fluff in which he said he would shift the tax burden to those over the median income, and publicity about an interview in *Playboy* in which he admitted lust in his heart and made some adverse comments about Lyndon Johnson. The difficulty with Carter's Grand Opening, though, was not small things going wrong. It was the lack of big things going right. On the one hand, he identified with liberal Democratic predecessors, and invoked their names whenever possible. But he was also making conservative statements, such as "Whenever there's a choice between government performing a function and the private sector performing a function, I believe in the private sector," and undecided voters did not know what to make of this contrast.

On September 23, the campaign was punctuated by the first of a series of televised debates. If any advantage was to be gained, it would likely come in the first debate "because of the large audience, and the mild 'openness' encouraged in the uncommitted by the debate format." The advantage went to President Ford, in part because of the candidates' performances, but much more because of the postdebate media focus on the question of who won (Sears, 1977; Sears and Chaffee, 1978). By this point, the race between Carter and Ford had become even outside the South.

Tactical Adjustments

At this juncture, there was a Tactical Adjustment. Jimmy Carter became much more negative in his comments about Gerald Ford. A number of explanations were given for this: that Carter was frustrated by the difficulty of running against the incumbent, that Carter hoped to go for a kill, and so on. Whatever the reason, President Ford was now likened to a car with four flat tires. His vetoes were said to be designed to keep people out of work. "Gerald Ford," Carter charged in Cleveland, "has hidden himself from the public even more than Richard Nixon at the depths of Watergate." After the president's second debate gaffe denying Soviet domination of Eastern Europe, Carter continued his attack, calling Ford's comment "a disgrace to the country." This gambit did not work. By mid-October, Harris showed Carter with a 4 percent lead, Gallup showed a 6 percent lead, and Pat Caddell's state-by-state polls for Carter showed a decline "in the West, in the Border States, and even in the South" (Schram, 1977, p. 329).

Bad news, of course, increases tension among campaign leaders, and when Elizabeth Drew was interviewing at this time, she found that the Carter leaders, "for all their confident talk, seemed tense and skittish. . . . It is clear that a decision has been made among Carter's top aides in Atlanta that he must cut out the strident tone that his campaign has taken on recently . . ." (1977, p. 471). Another Tactical Adjustment was in order. This time a decision was made to spend money on media in the South to protect the essential base, and to prepare new television ads for voters elsewhere, especially women, who preferred Carter on issues but thought Ford to be a lesser risk in the White House. An announcer on a commercial for the South claimed that "the South was being readmitted to the Union on November 2," and in a commercial aimed at wavering northerners Carter stated that mismanagement affected the quality of lives. These ads were taped on October 19. Efforts were also made to present a reassuring Carter during the third debate (in place of the aggressive Carter of the second debate), but essentially the last Tactical Adjustment of the campaign had been made (Schram, 1977, pp. 329–36; Witcover, 1977, pp. 622–23).

Hang-on-and-Hope

The principal activity of the Time's Up phase could be described as hang-on-and-hope. Hope that the southern base would hold. Hope that enough wavering voters would finally come down on Carter's side. There were no more resources to be committed, so the Carter strategy could only operate at the margins. The candidate's time was devoted to crucial states: New York, New Jersey, Pennsylvania, Ohio, Illinois, Texas (to protect the southern base) and California. Appeals were made to Democrats to turn out on election day. The local Democratic parties could provide some help here (although spending limits meant that the presidential campaign could not encourage them by providing "walking around money"), and the AFL-CIO could supply more substantial assistance. Political director Al Barkan pledged to have 100,000 workers on telephones and in the streets to turn out the labor vote. And finally, Governor Carter seemed to be reaching for the moderate independent vote when he modified liberal pledges already made by stating that a tax cut was a possibility in a Carter administration. Still, the principal ingredient of the Time's Up stage was hope. The final polls showed a virtual tie.

THE 1976 FORD REELECTION FIGHT

A Bold Plan to Obtain External Support

As is frequently the case, there was not a single plan for the Ford campaign. Rather, there were plans. There was a long basic document (120 pages plus appendices) written by several planners under the general direction of White House chief of staff Richard Cheney. There were plans emerging from the polls conducted by Robert Teeter. And there was a media plan developed by Doug Bailey and John Deardourff. What was unusual about these plans was the extent to which they coincided, the directness with which they dealt with Gerald Ford's weaknesses, and the extent to which they were oriented to the external need to reach the voters rather than the internal need to hold the supporting coalition together. All of these unusual aspects could be traced to the professional backgrounds (political science, polling, campaigning) of the planners.

The one major violation of the plans was the selection of Robert Dole as the vice presidential nominee. The campaign plan had called for a nominee "who is perceived as an Independent, or at least as a moderate Republican, without strong party identification [and with] . . . a strong image of freshness and non-Washington establishment." These were not the characteristics of Senator Dole. Dole's selection served an internal need to satisfy conservative groups that had supported Ronald Reagan's drive for the nomination.

The campaign plans dealt with the voters' perception of the candidates as individuals, their perception of issue stands, geographic concentration, timing, and the use of available funds. Discussion of the candidates as individuals stressed differences between their actual strengths and weaknesses, and public perceptions of them. Ford was perceived as an honest and decent person, but there were questions as to whether he was intelligent enough to be president and decisive enough as a leader. Carter had the advantage of supporting traditional American values and being a member of the majority party, but lacked a record of accomplishment and was vague on issues. The obvious implication of this was a campaign that would lay to rest questions about President Ford's intelligence and leadership capacity, and attack Governor Carter's inexperience and wavering stands on issues.

The plans dealing with issues grew out of the first use in a presidential campaign of nonmetric multidimensional scaling (the type of spatial analysis used to produce Figures 3–2 and 3–3). A two-dimensional solution was used, in which the horizontal dimension represented partisanship and economic management, and the vertical dimension reflected a social issue (that is, civil liberties questions about life-style, and defense spending). Not surprisingly, Carter was slightly to the left and Ford slightly to the right on the partisan-economic dimension. But to Robert Teeter's considerable astonishment, Jimmy Carter was seen as relatively conservative and Gerald Ford as relatively liberal on the social question. This implied an attack on Governor Carter's positions to try to alter the very advantageous posture he enjoyed, and a campaign that would stress Gerald Ford's support of traditional positions on the social issue.

The audience to whom the campaign should be directed was described in some detail. The electoral college was divided into "Our Base" (83 votes principally from Plains States and Mountain States), "His Base" (87 votes principally from the South), and the balance of 368 votes designated as "Swing States," including most of the large industrial states. How did the Ford strategists hope to carry these states, considering that Carter was far ahead in the polls in midsummer when these plans were drawn? The report pointed to a specific swing constituency:

> The target constituency in the suburbs for the President is the upper blue-collar and white-collar workers, often from a family which has risen in mobility in the last generation. . . . The upwardly mobile Catholics are a group becoming more independent and conservative, and they represent the key to victory in the northern industrial states where they are from 25–48 % of the voters. (Schram, 1977, p. 263.)

So far as timing was concerned, the president was told to hold off campaigning as long as possible. He should stay in the White House, appear "presidential" in every possible way, and husband resources for a final blitz. The financial recommendations carried the same message. Of the $21.8 million, only $500,000 was allocated for presidential travel, compared to $800,000 for polling. The largest allocation was $10 million for a media campaign. The plan had said that perceptions of both Ford and Carter must be altered. "In order to win, we must persuade over 15 % (or about 10 million people) to change their opinions. *This will require very aggressive—media oriented efforts . . .*" Finally, another $2.8 million was to be set aside as a reserve to be used as necessary in the final days of the campaign.

This was a bold, intelligent plan that gave President Ford some chance of catching up with his rival.[4] As already noted, it was unusual in the amount of attention it paid to the external needs of the Ford coalition, and in the bluntness with which it addressed Ford's own liabilities. Gerald Ford had spent a decade as a Republican leader in Congress, as vice president, and president; the report told him he was not seen as an effective leader. Ford had spent as many as 200 days a year on the road and loved to campaign; the document stated flatly that he was a terrible campaigner. The president's reaction was that it was pretty strong stuff, but after thinking about it overnight, he told his strategy group to go ahead (Schram, 1977, pp. 251–71; Witcover, 1977, chap. 36; Naughton, 1976; Perry, 1977).

A Quiet Opening

Since the plans were in effect during the Grand Opening, there was little visible campaign effort on the president's part. Senator Dole traveled around making speeches, but President Ford stuck close to the White House. During September, he held cabinet meetings, signed bills passed by Congress, talked about tax reform while strolling around the Rose Garden, and said that he was dismayed by Hanoi's failure to do more about American servicemen missing from action in the Vietnam War. Not forgetting who his primary audience was, Ford also met with six Roman Catholic bishops to discuss abortion, and posed for pictures with Polish Americans. When he did go to the University of Michigan for a campaign speech, and newsmen asked press secretary Ron Nessen if this was the formal beginning of the campaign, Nessen replied that this was the first campaign speech since the last one. All this made Ford look presidential, husbanded resources, and kept the focus of attention on Jimmy Carter, about whom many voters were undecided. Combined with Ford's success in the first debate, this strategy had turned a wide Carter margin into a very tight race by the end of September.

Gerald Ford made one brief campaign swing through the Deep South after the first debate, then headed back to Washington to prepare for the second. Since this was to deal with foreign affairs, the Ford strategy group was optimistic and laid on a campaign swing through southern California, Texas, and Oklahoma to capitalize on what it expected to be Ford's continued success. It was in the second debate, however, that President Ford made a serious gaffe about the autonomy of Eastern European governments.[5] Further, it took some time for Ford to concede that he had

---

[4] The one bit of bad advice contained in the plan was that Carter, a native of the Deep South (which had *never* seen one of its citizens elected to the White House), would be vulnerable in the South.

[5] In the course of an answer to a question about relations with the Soviet Union, President Ford said "There is no Soviet domination of Eastern Europe, and there never will be under a Ford administration."

made a mistake. The beginning of a Tactical Adjustment came the following afternoon in a hastily called news conference. But it was not until five days later, after a meeting with ethnic leaders, that Ford said unequivocally, "I made a mistake." The original statement was not all that unusual a form of verbal reversal, but it was given considerable coverage by the media after the debate, and it concerned precisely the constituency that was the focus of the Ford strategy. "The Poles hadn't made up their minds," said Andrew Greeley, "but they have now and there's nothing Ford can do to change it" (Apple, 1976). This judgment was later confirmed in a study of ethnic voters. Eighty percent had heard of this comment, and these respondents were very likely to cite it as a reason for their vote (Sears and Chaffee, 1978, p. 14).

A Final Media Blitz

Mid-October was not the best of times for the Ford campaign. Agriculture Secretary Earl Butz was forced to resign because of a widely reported racial slur, and there were some charges about Ford's personal and political finances. But soon it was late October, and the resources that had been carefully set aside for the Time's Up phase could be used. A new series of commercials had been prepared by the Deardourff-Bailey firm, and these were widely used during the closing days of the campaign. One raised questions about Governor Carter's ability, through the use of films of Atlanta residents saying that they did not want Carter to become president. Others portrayed Gerald Ford as a man who inspired confidence. In one, an announcer praised Ford's quiet style of leadership, and the president pointed out that "We've certainly created in the Ford Administration a nonimperial Presidency." Still another sketched warm relationships within the Ford family. Michael Ford, a divinity student, spoke of his father as very devout; Steven and Jack Ford had kind things to say about their father; Susan Ford was shown hugging her father from the back. "Sometimes," the announcer said, "a man's family can say a lot about a man." Together, the Deardourff-Bailey commercials presented Ford rather than Carter as the man to be trusted by wavering voters (Lelyveld, 1976b).

Another element of the television strategy was a series of conversations between President Ford, Edith Green, an Oregon Democrat Ford had known when both were in the House of Representatives, and sportscaster Joe Garagiola, whose political preferences were unknown but whose sports background was in keeping with the Jocks-for-Jerry tone of the campaign, and whose visible Italian-Americanism was perfect. Garagiola proved to be an effective interlocutor for the president. For example, he asked about the difference between the Nixon and Ford administrations, allowing Ford to reply, "Joe, there's one very, very fundamental difference. Under President Ford, there's not an imperial White House, which means there's no pomp, there's no ceremony, there's no dictatorial authority."

A final element to the Time's Up drive was intensive personal campaigning by the president himself, quite the opposite of the September seclusion in the Rose Garden. Much was said that was not memorable. For instance, in Columbus, Ford told a crowd, "Let's make it a home run and a touchdown for the winning team of Jerry Ford and Bob Dole." (Even in his favorite field, sports, Ford managed to mix his metaphors.) More generally, though, he spoke for a strong policy in international involvement and moderate conservatism in economic management. "Give me your mandate," he implored. "I stand on your side, for limited government, for fiscal responsibility, for rising prosperity, for lower taxes, for military strength and for peace in the world."

What Mr. Ford said was perhaps less important than where he said it, and to whom he said it. His trip included some stops in middle-sized states thought to be close (Virginia, the Carolinas, Missouri, Oregon, and Washington), but the bulk of the time was devoted to California, Illinois, Ohio, Pennsylvania, New Jersey, and New York. In Columbus, Ohio, and Syracuse, New York, he appeared with football coaches Woody Hayes and Ben Schwartzwalder, but also with Frank Lausche, a former five-time governor of Ohio who had come out of the "nationality" politics of Cleveland, with Cardinal Krol in Philadelphia, and with Cardinal Cooke in New York. Ford was reaching as best he could for those last few needed votes, and he poured all of his energy into it. By the time he reached Grand Rapids on election eve, his voice was gone, and his wife, Betty, had to read his concession statement the day after the election. The Carter coalition had prevailed, but Gerald Ford and his strategy group had the satisfaction of knowing that their plan had almost provided the basis of a come-from-far-behind victory.

CONSTRAINTS

As we have seen, the selection of a campaign strategy is subject to very real constraints. A candidate is not free to express all of his or her inner yearnings. A strategy group is not free to come up with any approach it thinks might win votes. Instead, there are *internal constraints, external constraints,* and *temporal constraints.*

INTERNAL CONSTRAINTS

The internal constraints arise from the attitudes of the groups that are members of the coalition. As we saw in Chapter 3, there was a substantial correlation in 1972 between the attitudes of the Nixon and McGovern coalitions and the positions emphasized by these candidates. In a similar way, one could argue that all of the strategies surveyed in this section of the book were acceptable to members of the supporting coalitions. Thus we saw Barry Goldwater promising to reduce government expenditures, Lyndon Johnson defending southern support by stressing Democratic loyalties and economic progress, Richard Nixon carefully charting a course between moderate and conservative wings of the Republican party, Hubert Humphrey relying on traditional New Deal–Fair Deal appeals, Jimmy Carter supporting a number of social programs favored by Democratic groups, and Gerald Ford favoring moderately conservative economic policies.

But what is more important—at least to understand internal constraints —is what was *not* done. Barry Goldwater and George McGovern could have moderated their springtime appeals, and made real efforts to win middle-of-the-road voters, but this would have cost Goldwater support of conservative ideologues and would have disappointed the young militants supporting McGovern. Or Senator Goldwater could have, in fact, pursued a southern strategy, and Senator McGovern could have proposed more radical redistributions of wealth. Either strategy would have made it more difficult for them to retain support of their organizational loyalists. In 1968, Richard Nixon could have told the electorate that better relations with China were needed, and Hubert Humphrey could have stated that the glut of social legislation passed by the 89th Congress meant that there were few resources available for any social programs. Neutral observers were making both points. But many conservatives were dismayed when Richard Nixon went to Peking, and frank talk about the fiscal consequences of Great Society programs was not what the urban/labor/black wing of the Democratic party wanted to hear. Elizabeth Drew pointed out that both President Ford and Governor Carter were committed to expensive programs in 1976. Shortly after the Republican convention, Ford had called for further progress in housing, health, recreation, and education; Carter was pledged to support job programs, health insurance, child care, federalization of welfare, housing, aid to cities, and aid to education (Drew, 1977, p. 438). Both Ford and Carter could have consistently argued that, to accomplish the goals to which their parties were pledged, some increase in taxes would be necessary. But to assert this would offend economic conservatives who were to be found in both the Ford and Carter coalitions. President Ford certainly could have found a vice presidential candidate who would have had greater appeal to independent voters in large industrial states than Robert Dole, but selection of a moderate running mate would have put off Reagan supporters. Doubtless you can think of more examples of plausible campaign strategies consistent with some campaign goal or with a fair reading of public policy. But the central point is that none of the strategies we listed was used. Each was avoided simply because it would have given offense to some group in the candidate's coalition, and was therefore unavailable.

EXTERNAL CONSTRAINTS

External constraints result from some inadequacy in the structure needed to obtain citizen support, from the need to reach some particular set of voters, or from lack of freedom to maneuver because of positions taken by the opposing coalition. The most common defects with respect to campaign operations, research, or public relations activities result from inexperience. Unless an incumbent president has been renominated, an electoral coalition is based on the preceding nomination coalition. Especially in the out-party, key decision-makers may be taking part in their first presidential campaigns. This was true, for example, of Denison Kitchell and Dean Burch in the 1964 Goldwater campaign, John Mitchell in the 1968 Nixon effort, Gary Hart in the 1972 McGovern campaign, and Hamilton Jordan and Jody Powell with Carter in 1976. There are usually some persons around with campaign experience, but there have been campaigns—Goldwater in 1964 and Carter in 1976—run almost entirely by novices. Newspaper articles are written about the "political geniuses" who are managing the campaign, but the simple fact is that they are in a situation they do not understand. Frequently they will try to repeat tactics to which they attribute success in nomination politics, and these tactics are often inappropriate.

Financial inadequacies have hobbled campaigns in two ways. Prior to federal funding, it was a simple lack of cash for candidates thought to be running far behind. Among the campaigns we've reviewed, this constraint was probably most serious for the Humphrey campaign in 1968. The federal funding limit, on the other hand, has brought the need for much more careful planning for the use of available, but finite, resources. Such planning gave the Ford coalition a real strategic advantage in the closing days of the 1976 campaign.

The need—real or perceived—to reach a certain set of voters often excludes certain campaign gambits. For example, in 1964 President Johnson could have attacked the Republican party quite directly by telling voters: "For years, we've been telling you that the Republicans were hidebound reactionaries and you wouldn't listen. Now you have proof! They've nominated Barry Goldwater!" President Nixon could have made a similar attack on the Democrats in 1972, citing the McGovern nomination as proof that the Democrats were indeed wild radicals. These attacks could have had long-term payoffs by weakening identification with the opposite party, but they would also have hampered Lyndon Johnson's 1964 appeal to moderate Republicans and Richard Nixon's 1972 efforts to get urban Democrats to cast Republican votes. Hence these plausible strategies were not used.

The activities of the rival coalition (or coalitions) create an external constraint similar to that resulting from the structure of competition in nomination politics. A candidate frequently lacks maneuvering room because of positions taken by a rival, or because of positions the candidate has already taken in response to a rival's gambit. For example, when Jimmy Carter spoke about a tax cut in a last-minute appeal to independent voters who were worried about the cost of living, he was moving into a position that Gerald Ford had occupied by a highly advertised tax cut plan. And in 1968, when Richard Nixon took relatively conservative positions to counter George Wallace's attractiveness to the Peripheral South, he was ill positioned to respond to Hubert Humphrey when the vice president began to make headway in the East with more liberal appeals.

A further difficulty, of course, is that internal and external constraints often have different consequences. Few of the groups within the 1972 Nixon coalition would have been offended by an attack on Democrats, but that was ruled out by external constraints. The 1976 Ford coalition would certainly have been strengthened externally by the selection of a moderate vice presidential candidate, but this was not done because of internal constraints. The trick is to find a strategy that will be acceptable in view of both internal and external constraints.

TEMPORAL CONSTRAINTS

The temporal constraints have already been discussed rather explicitly, so there is no need to do more than summarize them here. An electoral coalition has relatively little time for organization and planning. Plans adopted and launched during the Grand Opening are difficult to modify. It takes time to learn that a strategy is inappropriate, and still more time to hit on a politically viable alternative. Hence one seldom sees more than one or two Strategic Adjustments, even though it may be apparent to outside observers that a strategy is unsuccessful. Temporal constraints are more apparent, of course, during the Time's Up stage. Both candidates are likely to be bone-tired by this point; but both know that one will soon begin the slow transition from titular leader of the party to the "where-are-they-now" category, while the other will soon experience the exhilarations and the frustrations of the White House.

part IV

THE CITIZEN IN PRESIDENTIAL ELECTIONS

chapter 7

The Structure of Citizen Knowledge

The difference is dramatic. Throughout the campaign, thousands of persons are engaged in the joint enterprise of trying to persuade the electorate to support one party or the other. On election day, the solitary citizen is alone in the voting booth. To be sure, the outcome of the election is the result of decisions made by millions of voters across the country, but each citizen makes his or her own choice.

To this point, the acting unit has been the coalition-in-institution. In order to analyze this acting unit in electoral politics, we considered the individuals aggregated into groups that made up the internal structure of the coalition, the institutionally patterned activities that constituted the external structure, and observed these as they moved through the four stages of the temporal pattern. Now our acting unit becomes the individual.

The link between campaign strategy and citizen response is information. Broadly speaking, the aim of the entire campaign is to transmit persuasive information to the electorate. The citizen's response is similarly based on knowledge. If very little is known, the citizen may not bother to vote. If the bulk of what is known favors one party, the citizen is likely to vote for that party's candidate. If the citizen is aware of information favoring both sides, there must be some means of resolving this conflict. It follows that to analyze this individual activity, *the internal structure is the citizen's cognitive structure*, specifically what she or he knows about politics.[1]

---

[1] There are, of course, other internal structures that could be used for individual

There are several elements to cognitive structure. Perhaps the most basic is *information level,* how much the citizen knows. However much information a citizen possesses, it is organized into *attitudes,* valenced cognitions about political objects. The valence may be positive, negative, or neutral. In other words, there are some political objects (Jimmy Carter, Ted Kennedy, Ronald Reagan, the Republican party, Congress, a particular economic policy, and so on) about which the citizen feels positively, some political objects about which he or she feels negatively, and some political objects about which she or he doesn't care one way or the other.

Since attitudes may be positive, negative, or neutral, one is led to theories of *cognitive consistency.* For example, if a person was a Democrat, and had positive views about the Democratic candidate, about the record of the last Democratic president, favored a high level of government spending, and wanted more welfare programs, we would say that this person's views were consistent when judged against a partisan criterion. If, on the other hand, a Democrat preferred the Republican candidate and the Democratic party's position on issues, we would say that there was an attitude conflict.

Not all of the attitude objects are of equal importance. At one time, whether the candidates seem trustworthy may get more attention; at another, foreign policy may be dominant. Politics itself may be quite visible in one person's cognitive landscape, and be remote from the concerns of another who is more interested in art. These variations in the relative prominence of attitude objects are referred to as *salience* and *centrality.* If the situation calls attention to the attitude object, for example, if some dramatic foreign development leads to greater news coverage, we say international involvement is more salient. If the attitude object is of more enduring concern, as with a person who is more interested in politics than art or business affairs, we say that politics is central to this person. If an attitude object is more salient, or central, or both, then attitudes about that topic will be more important in the citizen's cognitive structure.

The *external structure* for the citizen *consists of the informational environment and the citizen's opportunities for political participation.* The notion of an informational environment is that an individual is surrounded at all times by a number of information sources. These include television, radio, newspapers, magazines, books, and all of the persons and things that an individual can see or listen to. As the citizen is in contact with these sources, whether sitting at home reading a newspaper or walk-

---

level analysis. *Personality* is often used, as is *motivation.* In common with *cognitive structure,* these cannot be directly observed, but must be inferred from some other evidence. Cognitive structure is the concept that is most appropriate for analysis of this subject matter.

ing into a campaign rally, information is absorbed from them. The citizen's opportunities for participation range all the way from such effortless things as simply absorbing information or voting to quite demanding activities, such as making a financial contribution or actually campaigning on behalf of a candidate. The citizen may take part in any of these activities as she or he sees fit. As far as the election outcome is concerned, the citizen's decision about whether or not to vote and choice of presidential candidate are of prime concern.

Internal and external structure are intimately dependent on one another. As Daniel Levinson puts it, "An essential feature of human life is the *interpenetration* of self and world. Each is inside the other. Our thinking about the one must take account of the other" (1977, p. 47). This is clearly true for individual political activity. The citizen's cognitive structure is the result of all the information he or she has absorbed and organized, whether from a forgotten civics book read 30 years earlier or a television newscast seen that very day. The citizen's attitudes, in turn, are linked to votes and other forms of political participation. To the extent that the citizen cares about politics and is involved in it, further information is acquired and so the cycle continues. Thus the question as to *why* a citizen takes a particular action depends on both internal structure and external structure, on both the citizen's attitudes and on the opportunities for participation.

There are also temporal patterns that deal with the citizen. An individual's attitudes or behavior, or both, may remain stable or fluctuate. The resulting *temporal patterns may be observed within a campaign, between elections, or over one's lifetime.* In general, a person who is concerned about politics and who strongly identifies with one political party is more likely to exhibit stable attitudes and stable behavior. A person with little political information and little interest may show quite irregular behavior—not bothering to vote in many instances and swinging unpredictably between parties when he or she does cast a ballot. Also speaking generally, the longer the time period, the greater the likelihood of a change in attitudes or a variation in behavior. In this section of the book, we shall be concerned with all these matters as they affect the citizen's response to campaign strategies.

In this chapter, we shall ask first how much citizens know—what the distribution of political information is across the electorate. Then we shall turn to the content of political information in the mass media— the relationship between the information in the media and the citizen's political knowledge, and the degree to which that knowledge depends on the citizen's involvement with the informational environment. We shall conclude with a look at the temporal patterns that can be discerned within a campaign. Chapter 8 will deal with the relationships between citizen attitudes and presidential choice. Chapter 9 will look at one particularly important attitude, party identification, at cognitive consistency, and at the stability of attitudes between elections.

HOW MUCH DO CITIZENS KNOW ABOUT PRESIDENTIAL POLITICS?

At 6:25 p.m. on Monday September 27, 1976—some four days after the first Carter-Ford debate—an interviewer from the Center for Political Studies at the University of Michigan began questioning a 34-year-old airline ramp attendant who lived on Long Island. After some initial items, the interviewer came to a series of questions that the Center for Political Studies has used in every election survey since 1952.

Interviewer: *Now, back to national politics. I'd like to ask you what you think are the good and bad points about both parties. Is there anything in particular that you like about the Democratic party?*
Respondent: They will spend more domestically than out of the country.
Interviewer: *Is there anything in particular that you don't like about the Democratic party?*
Respondent: No.
Interviewer: *Is there anything in particular that you like about the Republican party?*
Respondent: Ford's firm stand in Korea, and getting people out of Lebanon.
Interviewer: *Is there anything in particular that you don't like about the Republican party?*
Respondent: Lack of domestic spending.
Interviewer: *Now I'd like to ask you about the good and bad points of the two major candidates for president. Is there anything in particular about Mr. Carter that might make you want to vote for him?*
Respondent: Just a change.
Interviewer: *Is there anything in particular about Mr. Carter that might make you want to vote against him?*
Respondent: No.
Interviewer: *Is there anything in particular about Mr. Ford that might make you want to vote for him?*
Respondent: I like his foreign policy.
Interviewer: *Is there anything in particular about Mr. Ford that might make you want to vote against him?*
Respondent: Cutting domestic spending.

This voter was close to the middle of several social and political spectra. He was in his mid-30s, a high school graduate, regarded himself as average middle class, and was an independent. He liked Republican foreign policy, and Democratic domestic spending. As a Catholic who lived in New York, he was also the type of voter regarded as crucial by both parties. Balanced between the attractions of Republican foreign policy and Democratic domestic policy, he resolved his own dilemma with the belief that it was time for a change. He had decided to vote for Jimmy Carter during the Democratic Convention, and did so in November. What is most important to our present purpose, though, is the amount of information the airline ramp attendant showed in his responses. He was as close to the average level of information as it was possible to be.

However typical this airline employee may have been, it is hazardous to rest our analysis on any single case. We can develop a better sense of how much Americans know about presidential politics by looking at several responses to this series of questions. Let's begin with a woman from Philadelphia. She was 30 years old, single, and a free-lance photographer who was working as an artist. Politically, she was an independent, and she had a good deal to say about the parties and candidates.

Interviewer: *Like about the Democratic party?*[2]
Respondent: I think in general that Democrats have more interest in the average person. The social reform and work with the underprivileged is stronger.
Interviewer: *Anything else?*
Respondent: Their economic policies are usually different than the Republicans; there is usually larger government spending and more concern about unemployment.
Interviewer: *Dislike about the Democratic party?*
Respondent: I don't like the close identification with the labor movement—an inordinate amount of influence.
Interviewer: *Anything else?*
Respondent: There is corruption in all the parties, especially at the local level.
Interviewer: *Like about the Republican party?*
Respondent: To me financially the usual tax shelters and financial policies are better due to my income.
Interviewer: *Anything else?*
Respondent: At times there is not a great deal of difference. The liberal part of the Republican party is much more applicable to me. I don't like to see the two party system die.
Interviewer: *Dislike about the Republican party?*
Respondent: I don't like the increased military spending. The ultra-conservative factions. The often large influence by the very powerful large companies.
Interviewer: *Anything else?*
Respondent: That's all.
Interviewer: *Like about Carter?*
Respondent: He seems very sincere; that's possibly cosmetically done. I prefer his stands on abortion and I admire him for standing up for that—not being snowed under by the Catholic Church.
Interviewer: *Dislike about Carter?*

---

[2] Since the full wording of the basic question sequence was given for the airline ramp attendant, an abbreviated form will be used with this and subsequent examples.

Respondent: The main thing is not knowing enough about him. I think he's naive in international affairs.

Interviewer: *Anything else?*

Respondent: At times the whole Southern Mafia type of feeling upsets me. He could be a Southern Nixon. I'm also concerned about how his tax changes would affect my bracket.

Interviewer: *Like about Ford?*

Respondent: "Old Jer's too dumb to be crooked." That's facetious. I think he's very honest.

Interviewer: *Anything else?*

Respondent: He's certainly had enough practice so that the country won't have to sit around and wait another 1½ years to figure out what's going on the way Carter will I'm afraid.

Interviewer: *Dislike about Ford?*

Respondent: His increased military spending. His stand on abortion.

Interviewer: *Anything else?*

Respondent: That's all I can think of right now. Lackluster. Neither of them are terribly attractive.

In comparison with many other respondents, this photographer was quite articulate—enough so that it would be risky to assert which of her many attitudes was most important in her voting decision. She delayed making her choice until mid-October, and then concluded that she would vote for "Old Jer."

An interviewer in St. Louis talked with a 67-year-old woman who had been born in Central Europe and had lived there until World War I. Her husband had been a tool and die maker until his retirement. She impressed the interviewer with her warmth and expansiveness.

Interviewer: *Like about the Democratic party?*

Respondent: They are more progressive; do more for the workers. They believe in the unions. Of course, the Teamsters are overdoing it. They are for socialized medicine to curb doctors' abuses; they charge too much.

Interviewer: *Anything else?*

Respondent: More for the people. I'd like to see Mondale for President and Carter V.P. It's not true they're war mongers. It's not true they're big spenders. The Republicans are big spenders too. The Democrats gave us social security and medicare. It's not like we paid for it.

Interviewer: *Dislike about the Democratic party?*

Respondent: A few individuals I don't care for: Hays, Wilbur Mills. I wish they would vote some old fogies out and vote some new young ones in.

Interviewer: *Like about the Republican party?*

Respondent: There are some good progressive ones: Javits, Brooke, Percy.

Interviewer: *Dislike about the Republican party?*

Respondent: Too conservative. They should help the cities, not give money to foreign countries. That nutty Kissinger; they depend too much on him.

Interviewer: *Anything else?*

Respondent: Why do we have a foreign-born Secretary of State? Of course, I'm foreign born.

Interviewer: *Like about Carter?*

Respondent: He promises to do something about unemployment and inflation. Government should do something about unemployment—teach a trade rather than food stamps and welfare. He promises to pass socialized medicine; cut out bureaucrats, expensive do-nothing bureaucrats in Washington. He says he never told a lie. He shouldn't have interviewed *Playboy*. Carter's and Ford's stands are the same on abortion. He's not connected with the Washington establishment. He'll work with Congress.

Interviewer: *Dislike about Carter?*

Respondent: No.

Interviewer: *Like about Ford?*

Respondent: No.

Interviewer: *Dislike about Ford?*

Respondent: I don't like his vetoes, his pardon of Nixon, so many things. He's a do-nothing President. He's for unemployment to curb the inflation. Always against progressiveness.

Interviewer: *Anything else?*

Respondent: He was the biggest hawk in Congress. Now he's talking about peace. He's picking on Carter on the Yugoslav issue; that means he *would* send troops to Yugoslavia. We're from Yugoslavia. Why should we support one Communist against another? That makes no sense! We were there five years ago. No freedom. Americans are good politicians, but bad statesmen. Europeans outwit us all the time.

In contrast with the relatively balanced comments of the airline ramp attendant and the photographer, almost everything this woman said favored the Democrats. Not surprisingly, she had decided to vote for Jimmy Carter during the primaries.

Our next example is a 40-year-old housewife who lived in a frame house in Bellingham, Washington. A staunch Lutheran, she had been in the middle of a conversation about church affairs when the interviewer arrived.

Interviewer: *Like about the Democratic party?*

Respondent: One thing that has been good: tax loopholes are going to have to be checked a lot more they are saying.

Interviewer: *Dislike about the Democratic party?*

Respondent: I feel that their platform at the convention just wanted to do too much and it worries me. Too expensive.

Interviewer: *Like about the Republican party?*

Respondent: The fact that they didn't want to do quite as much. They didn't want to get quite as many new projects going.

Interviewer: *Anything else?*

Respondent: They feel that private enterprise should be encouraged more to solve the problems of inflation. It's a matter of degree with the two parties.

They are not as much for price control either. Things would have to be pretty bad before I'd go for price controls. Republicans wouldn't be as hasty as Democrats on this.

Interviewer: *Dislike about the Republican party?*

Respondent: No.

Interviewer: *Like about Carter?*

Respondent: Certainly a personable guy. He seems so very human. The fact that he's a Christian—not that Ford isn't. He seems to be very honest.

Interviewer: *Dislike about Carter?*

Respondent: I think he hasn't had anywhere near the experience dealing with national problems that President Ford has had. And he seems to want to start a lot of programs that would cost a lot of money.

Interviewer: *Like about Ford?*

Respondent: I think his experience above all. He was in Congress before. He has had to deal with international and national issues, and his record has been good.

Interviewer: *Dislike about Ford?*

Respondent: I wasn't happy about his having Dole. That's about all.

Things that she liked about the Republicans came as easily to the mind of this middle-class westerner as attractive aspects of the Democratic party came to the St. Louis immigrant. Both could list things they liked about the opposition, but both had made their own voting decisions very early. The St. Louis resident voted for Carter; the Washingtonian voted for Ford.

A 32-year-old Arkansan had grown up in a family of 10 children. She now had 2 of her own, and juggled a busy schedule so as to care for them and work as a counselor in a Little Rock high school.

Interviewer: *Like about the Democratic party?*

Respondent: As a party concerned with the small person. The average person tends to see them as a party with strength.

Interviewer: *Anything else?*

Respondent: No. I'm not much for following politicians.

Interviewer: *Dislike about the Democratic party?*

Respondent: Even though it seems they're working for poor excluded urban groups and ethnic groups, I still think they have a lot of work to be done on involvement on the part of women.

Interviewer: *Like about the Republican party?*

Respondent: No.

Interviewer: *Dislike about the Republican party?*

Respondent: Favoritism toward big business. It shows up in the way they like to run government.

Interviewer: *Anything else?*

Respondent: Just their feeling that money is power.

Interviewer: *Like about Carter?*

Respondent: He hasn't been President before. Therefore he hasn't had a chance to make errors. I'll give him a chance.

Interviewer: *Anything else?*

Respondent: Basic cut of honesty.

Interviewer: *Dislike about Carter?*

Respondent: I'm skeptical as most blacks of his being a Southern white. I know that's prejudiced, but I just can't help it.

Interviewer: *Like about Ford?*

Respondent: I think his experience gives him the potential to do . . . A good job could be done if he'd use his experience.

Interviewer: *Anything else?*

Respondent: That's his only asset.

Interviewer: *Dislike about Ford?*

Respondent: He's a Richard Nixon appointee.

Interviewer: *Anything else?*

Respondent: I could go on and scream about failure to act on positive social legislation and his general unconcern for the working class.

In spite of her generally pro-Democratic attitudes, her skepticism about Carter and positive view of President Ford's experience were enough to delay her decision until election day. Then she voted for Jimmy Carter.

Then there was a high school graduate from Findlay, Ohio. He was also in his early 30s, and spent his working hours making pull tabs for the tops of beer cans.

Interviewer: *Like about the Democratic party?*

Respondent: No.

Interviewer: *Dislike about the Democratic party?*

Respondent: Just somewhat of the talk I've heard about Carter's opinions.

Interviewer: *What did you hear?*

Respondent: How he won't let the money get back to the people.

Interviewer: *What money?*

Respondent: The government money.

Interviewer: *Anything else?*

Respondent: No.

Interviewer: *Like about the Republican party?*

Respondent: I like what Ford has already done in office. Nothing in particular.

Interviewer: *Dislike about the Republican party?*

Respondent: No.

Interviewer: *Like about Carter?*

Respondent: When I first saw him on TV and such, he gave me the impression of a real go-getter—one who wanted to do everything.

Interviewer: *Dislike about Carter?*

Respondent: Just the talk I've heard.

Interviewer: *What?*

Respondent: All about taking money from people, the programs, cutting the budget.

Interviewer: *Like about Ford?*

Respondent: His past experience. And I think he shows his power more than Carter.

Interviewer: *Dislike about Ford?*
Respondent: No.

There is no way to know from the interview what this Findlay worker had heard about Jimmy Carter's spending plans, but he was disturbed about it. In any case, he was pro-Ford because of his positive, if amorphous, attitude about Ford's experience. He had decided to vote for President Ford before either convention.

Finally, there was a white-haired 72-year-old lady who lived with her daughter's family in a small frame house outside Richmond, Virginia. Her education had stopped with the tenth grade, and her level of political information was meager indeed.

Interviewer: *Like about the Democratic party?*
Respondent: No.
Interviewer: *Dislike about the Democratic party?*
Respondent: They're different from the Republicans.
Interviewer: *Like about the Republican party?*
Respondent: No.
Interviewer: *Dislike about the Republican party?*
Respondent: No.
Interviewer: *Like about Carter?*
Respondent: No.
Interviewer: *Dislike about Carter?*
Respondent: No.
Interviewer: *Like about Ford?*
Respondent: No.
Interviewer: *Dislike about Ford?*
Respondent: No.

How this woman might have decided between the candidates knowing only that there was some kind of difference between the parties makes for interesting speculation, but only that. Along with many other uninformed persons, she didn't vote.

With seven examples, we are in a little better position to understand citizens' perceptions than when we had only one.[3] We have the views of two easterners, two midwesterners, two southerners, and one westerner. In a very close election, three respondents reported voting for Carter, three for Ford, and one did not vote. We certainly saw some common attitudes: that the Democratic party takes more interest in the underprivileged, that Republican fiscal policies are more advantageous for the middle class, admiration for Jimmy Carter's sincerity, and trust in

---

[3] This subsample of seven respondents also illustrates why it is risky to generalize on the basis of a small number of cases. For instance, our seven respondents included no one in their 20s or their 50s, no one from any of the Sun Belt states, and only two men.

Gerald Ford's experience. But what these seven interviews best illustrate are the various information levels among the electorate. The Long Island airline ramp attendant had an average level of information, and the succeeding half-dozen examples exhibited—in decreasing order—the various levels of knowledge about politics.

FIGURE 7–1
Distribution of Information Levels, 1976

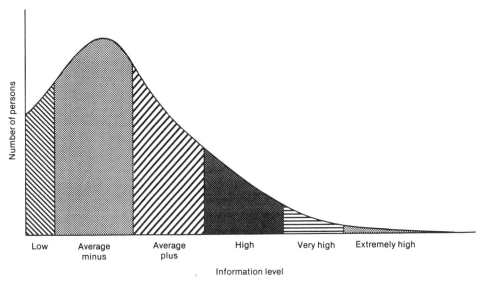

Figure 7–1 portrays the distribution of the information levels these examples typify. The free-lance photographer from Philadelphia is in the middle of the *extremely high* category.[4] The Yugoslav immigrant living in St. Louis comes from the *very high* category. The housewife from Bellingham, Washington, displayed *high* knowledge. The school counselor in Little Rock was closer to typical, and is in the middle of the *average plus* category. The airline ramp attendant from Long Island falls right between the *average plus* and the *average minus* ranges. The worker from the Findlay, Ohio, beer-can factory knows a little less than most American citizens, and thus represents the *average minus* category. The elderly lady living outside Richmond, Virginia, showed a *low* level of information.[5]

---

[4] While the language that follows will be varied to avoid six identically worded sentences, each of the examples comes from the middle of the range that it typifies. For a discussion of how the information level categories were constructed, see Appendix A–7.1.

[5] There are three high categories and only one low category because the names

The proportions of citizens falling into each of the information categories are shown in Table 7–1. Fully two thirds of all citizens fall into the average minus or average plus categories. The low and high categories account for another 29 percent. The very high and extremely high categories are quite rare; together they constitute only 4 percent of all the

TABLE 7–1
Distribution of Information Levels within Electorate

Information Level	Percent of Electorate
Low	17.5%
Average minus	41.2
Average plus	25.5
High	11.7
Very high	3.2
Extremely high	0.9

Data source: 1976 CPS Election Study.

responses. Put another way, there were four times as many persons as uninformed as the elderly Virginia woman as there were individuals as knowledgeable as the St. Louis immigrant and the Philadelphia photographer. If you want a sense of Americans' political knowledge, think of the Ohio beer-can worker, the Long Island airline ramp attendant, and the Little Rock high school counselor. Two out of three Americans know this much about politics.

SOURCES OF INFORMATION ABOUT POLITICS

CONTACT WITH ELECTRONIC AND PRINT SOURCES

Why do citizens have the amount of information they do? Why are there more persons in the average minus category than any other? What allows the St. Louis immigrant and the Philadelphia photographer to know so much more about politics than most of their fellow citizens? There are two basic answers to these questions. One deals with the amount of information that is available, the other with the extent to which each citizen seeks knowledge from the informational environment. We shall look at both of these considerations.

Most citizens acquire their information about politics through the mass media. Table 7–2 presents information about the extent of use of the major media, and about each medium's impact on information level.

---

were chosen to indicate how far away from the mean the category is. Since the mean information level itself is close to zero, there is room for only the average minus and zero categories between the mean and zero points.

TABLE 7–2
Information Level by Medium Used

	Information Level						
Medium Used	*Low*	*Average Minus*	*Average Plus*	*High*	*Very High*	*Extremely High*	*Total*
Magazines							
Not used	78.6%	59.5%	42.3%	23.8%	17.3%	13.3%	51.8%
Used	21.4	40.5	57.7	76.2	82.7	86.7	48.2
Kendall's Tau–c = .39							
Newspapers							
Not used	44.3	33.0	21.8	10.3	14.5	11.1	28.3
Used	55.7	67.0	78.2	89.7	85.5	88.9	71.7
Kendall's Tau–c = .23							
Television							
Not used	27.4	11.7	4.8	4.3	2.9	0	11.2
Used	72.6	88.3	95.2	95.7	97.1	100.0	88.8
Kendall's Tau–c = .16							

Data source: 1976 CPS Election Study.

Television is the most widely used, as has been the case for some time. Eighty-nine percent report using television as a news source, in contrast to 72 percent who say they read newspapers and to slightly less than half who report reading magazines. When one looks at the association between use of a news source and information level, however, the ordering is reversed. Television, which is readily available even to those in the low information category, has the least impact on information level. Newspapers and especially magazines, used by fewer persons and requiring more effort, have a much stronger association with a respondent's level of information.

Why should print media have greater impact on what people know about politics than television? One possible explanation is that people are making different uses of the media. It might be that people are being entertained by watching situation comedies and cops-and-robbers shows on television while they are reading articles about politics in newspapers and magazines. This is a perfectly plausible explanation, but it can be rejected. When the analysis is limited to prime information sources in both print and electronic media, the print advantage emerges even more strongly. Table 7–3 presents data on the relation between information level and the frequency with which persons read newspaper articles about national politics and watch the evening network news shows on television. Again, nearly twice as many persons say they frequently watch network news as report frequently reading about national politics. But watching television news has relatively little impact on one's political knowledge, while reading about national politics has a substantial impact. Why so?

Bivariate Correlation = Association Between Two Things

Bivariate correlation may be understood simply as an association between two things that can take on different values. The prefix *bi* means two, and a variable is any other mathematical term than a constant. The fundamental idea in correlation is association as opposed to independence. Hence, bivariate correlation just means an association between two variables.

The underlying ideas go back some time. The central notion of constant conjunction came from the 18th-century Scotch philosopher, David Hume. John Stuart Mill, the 19th-century British philosopher, extended this idea in his Method of Concomitant Variation. Essentially, if an increase in variable *A* tends to produce an increase in variable *B*, it may be taken as evidence that the two are associated.

In the accompanying table, information level is associated with reading newspapers, but information level is independent of the hypothetical variable. There are two ways to see this. The first is to inspect the pattern

	Information Level						
	Low	Average Minus	Average Plus	High	Very High	Extremely High	Total
Newspapers read?							
No	44.3%	33.0%	21.8%	10.3%	14.5%	11.1%	28.3%
Yes	55.7	67.0	78.2	89.7	85.5	88.9	71.7
Kendall's Tau–c = .23							
Hypothetical variable							
Present ...	56.1	59.9	59.1	58.0	62.1	60.9	58.9
Absent ...	43.9	40.1	40.9	42.0	37.9	39.1	41.1
Kendall's Tau–c = 0							

of the cell entries (which in this case are column percentages), and compare these to the characteristics of the total sample. Let's take the newspaper example first. Of those in the low information column, only 55.7 percent read newspapers as compared to 71.7 percent in the total sample. This percentage increases to 67.0 in the average minus column. By the time we get to the average plus column, more people are reading newspapers (78.2 percent) than is the case in the total sample. In the high column, 89.7 percent read newspapers, as compared to 71.7 overall. The percentage drops just slightly in the very high column, but then comes back up in the extremely high column. As you move across all six magnitudes in the information level scale, the percentage of those reading newspapers increases from 55.7 to 88.9, as compared to 71.7 for the total sample. The opposite is true for those who do not read newspapers. Therefore you conclude that there is an association between reading newspapers and having a higher information level.

If you read across the rows for the hypothetical variable and compare the entries with the figures for the total sample, you see that the percentages in both rows are virtually the same as those for the total sample. Since it doesn't make any difference which column a given case falls into, we say that information level is independent of this hypothetical variable.

The second way to tell whether there is an association is to look at the summary measure of correlation (in this case Kendall's Tau–c) that appears underneath the data. It is called a summary measure because it summarizes the strength of the correlation (you can see at a glance that .23 is greater than 0 in the example), but doesn't tell you anything else. If it has a value of 0, it means the two variables are independent of each other. If it has a value of 1.0 (almost never seen with real world political data), it means there is complete association between the variables. Generally, you judge the strength of the association by seeing how far away it is from 0. You show that two variables are associated by showing that they are *not* independent of each other.

Different measures of correlation are used depending on the nature of the data. For instance, Kendall's Tau–c was used in this example, but Pearson's r was used in Chapter 3. There are differences between various measures, but the fundamental idea is covariation.

Measures of correlation are often used to infer cause and effect. Before one concludes that there is causation, though, one must show both a statistical association and a logical reason for the relationship between the variables. There may be accidental statistical association. For example, the divorce rate in Manhattan might increase at the same time as wheat production in Kansas rises. Clearly, Kansas wheat does not cause New York divorces. In the instance of newspaper reading, however, it is plausible to assume that one picks up information from reading newspapers, and since there is a statistical association, we may say that we have shown cause and effect in this particular sense.

TELEVISION

The first reason why television conveys comparatively little information is that there is simply less political news on television. The evening network shows have only 22 minutes of news time to fill. They usually carry between 15 and 25 news items, which means about 2 minutes for the lead story at the beginning of the newscast and no more than a few seconds for "other items" mentioned toward the end. From 5 to 9 of these stories are carried by all three commercial networks, and there is substantial overlap among the networks on the remaining stories (Levin, 1977). With so little time per item, and a standard package of news to present, this format is essentially a headline service.[6] It scarcely goes be-

---

[6] The format referred to here is that commonly followed by the early evening net-

TABLE 7–3
Information Level by Use of Specific Sources

| Frequency of Use | Information Level | | | | | | |
---	Low	Average Minus	Average Plus	High	Very High	Extremely High	Total
Newspapers to read about national politics							
Never	35.4%	16.8%	6.7%	2.7%	0%	0%	14.8%
Rarely	32.9	24.9	12.6	7.7	6.9	0	20.0
Sometimes	27.4	42.1	40.0	28.6	36.4	33.3	37.2
Frequently	4.3	16.1	40.7	60.9	56.6	66.7	28.0
Kendall's Tau–c = .40							
Television to watch evening network news							
Never	15.2	9.6	6.7	4.8	10.4	11.1	9.2
Rarely	19.1	12.9	12.0	13.7	9.2	8.9	13.6
Sometimes	28.4	24.3	22.1	18.8	18.5	28.9	23.6
Frequently	37.2	53.2	59.2	62.7	61.8	51.1	53.6
Kendall's Tau–c = .12							

Data source: 1976 CPS Election Study.

yond the topics on the front page of a newspaper, and because of the time constraints, even these front-page items are covered in very abbreviated form.

Then there is the kind of news on which television chooses to focus. In an exhaustive study of all network newscasts between July 10 and election day, 1972, Richard Hofstetter distinguished between "political bias," a tendency to favor one candidate or the other, and "structural bias," a tendency to use a particular kind of story thought to be more appropriate for television. There was very little political bias, but a lot of structural bias (Hofstetter, 1976). The producers of television news had a preference for pictures over explanation. The consequences of this were pointed out by two other students of television news, Thomas Patterson and Robert McClure. "One dimension of the election," they wrote, "fits perfectly the networks' demand for good pictures. It is the 'horse race' aspect of the run for the White House. For a presidential election is surely a super contest with all the elements that are associated with spectacular sports events: huge crowds, rabid followers, dramatic

work news shows in the late 1970s, in which the amount of time devoted to any story depends on the news organization's judgment of the importance of the story. There are other formats that are possible, such as giving extra time or time on succeeding evenings to a story that needs to be explored in depth, or such as public television's very effective "MacNeil–Lehrer Report," which devotes the entire half hour to a presentation of different points of view on a single story.

do-or-die battles, winners and losers. It is this part of the election that the networks emphasize" (Patterson and McClure, 1976, pp. 40–41). Their analyses showed that horse-race topics dominated political television in both 1972 and 1976. In 1976, 60 percent of television coverage was devoted to horse-race topics, 28 percent to substantive topics, and 12 percent fell into a miscellaneous category (Patterson, 1978, p. 184).

A Comparison of Television and Newspaper Coverage

Doris Graber has been studying television and newspaper coverage of presidential campaigns since 1968. During the last 30 days of each campaign, she has obtained and analyzed 20 newspapers published in various parts of the country. For 1972, a similar content analysis was done of videotapes of the network newscasts; and for 1968 and 1976, story logs (which contain the same information in more abbreviated form) were analyzed.

The first cut in her coding procedure separated issue coverage from discussion of the qualities of the presidential candidates. For the press in 1968, the ratio of issues to personal qualities was 44 to 56, a somewhat greater attention to the candidates, but still an approximate balance. In 1972, however, she found that press attention to issues had slipped, and was approximately the same as that for television. The ratio of issues to qualities was 36 to 64 for the press, and 37 to 63 for television. In the press in 1976, the ratio of issues to qualities was 39 to 61. Both newspapers and television were carrying about three issue stories for every five dealing with the candidates.

The issue coverage was further analyzed into five categories. Three of these were roughly the same as issue areas we have been discussing. The fourth dealt with what might be called general politics: the institutions of government, the incumbent's and the challenger's policies, ethics, opinion polls, and so on. The last dealt with campaign stories. The proportions of television and newspaper coverage in each of these five categories are shown in Table 7–4.

Professor Graber's research supports several generalizations. First, relatively little journalistic attention is being paid to the policy areas. Since 36 percent and 37 percent of all 1972 press and television coverage, respectively, went to issues, the figures in Table 7–4 mean that, for example, only 7.5 percent of all press coverage and only 4.9 percent of all television coverage was devoted to international involvement in 1972. Second, as between the policy areas (except for television in 1968), international involvement has gotten the most coverage, then economics, then social benefits and civil liberties. Third, the bulk of television coverage has gone to campaign topics. (Graber's estimate of 57 percent of 1976 coverage going to campaign topics is remarkably similar to the McClure-

TABLE 7–4
Issue Coverage in Television and Newspapers

Issue	1968	1972	1976
		Television	
International involvement	11.5%	13.1%	15.8%
Economic management	3.2	6.1	8.8
Social benefits and civil liberties	4.6	4.6	5.9
General politics	23.9	17.0	12.2
Campaign	56.9	59.2	57.2
		Newspapers	
International involvement	26.3%	20.9%	16.9%
Economic management	16.4	12.4	11.9
Social benefits and civil liberties	13.9	7.5	6.4
General politics	23.7	23.7	20.0
Campaign	19.6	35.4	44.9

Source: Doris Graber, *The Mass Media and Politics* (Washington: Congressional Quarterly Press, 1980).

Patterson estimate of 60 percent devoted to horse-race topics that year.) Fourth, perhaps most surprising in view of the different needs and capacities of the two media, newspapers have moved in the direction of television concentration on campaign stories during these three election years. Newspapers still devoted more attention to the policy areas in 1976 than television, but the difference between the two media was much narrower than it had been in 1968.

The televised debates between Gerald Ford and Jimmy Carter in 1976 provided an important exception to the media tendency to avoid issues. The first debate stressed economic issues, the second foreign policy, and the third a mix of issues. The postdebate coverage did not maintain this focus. Instead, more attention was paid to the familiar questions of personality, performance, and who the media felt had "won" the debate.[7] Even so, issue coverage was estimated at 37 percent for both television and newspapers, a figure substantially higher than that for normal campaign content (Sears and Chaffee, 1978).

PRINT MEDIA

If television has the advantage of vivid pictures, writers have the advantage of being able to discuss topics at sufficient length to convey de-

---

[7] The media concentration on the identity of the "winners" had a decided effect on citizens' judgments about who had done better in the debate. The longer the time between the debate itself and a survey about the "winner," the greater the proportion of respondents who named the media-identified "winner" as the candidate who had done better.

tailed information. The best of them worry about what to write. Thus, David Broder, the *Washington Post*'s thoughtful political analyst:

> Where do the candidates come from? What motivates them to want to be president? . . . When they have to make a decision do they pull in a big group of people or go with whatever seems to be the consensus or do they go off by themselves and meditate on what they should do? . . . Are they really open for questioning, or do they go into a debate or press conference to defend their own views? (Barber, 1978, p. 134)

Theodore White, author of The Making of the President series, has been skillfully depicted by James David Barber as "our age's most influential artist of pointillistic journalism: microscopic fact-dots blended by the mind's eye to compose a meaningful conglomerate." One example of this is White's description of the Rockefeller estate at Pocantico Hills:

> Behind a low fieldstone wall stretches some of the loveliest land anywhere in America . . . From the terrace on the far side one looks out over the Hudson River . . . As one gazes down in enchantment on the broad-flowing river, it is difficult to imagine sorrow or anger or any ordinary human concern penetrating this paradise. (Barber, 1978, pp. 126–27)

One would not want to argue that all wordsmiths compose their phrases with the skill of a Theodore White, but newspapers, magazines, and books do provide more "microscopic fact-dots" than the electronic media. This is reflected in the stronger relationship between the use of print media and information level.

Another reason for the greater impact of print is the degree of attention it requires. Television is regularly reported to be the most used medium, but what does "watching television" mean? In one careful study of network newscasts, viewers filled out diaries indicating whether they gave the program full attention, partial attention, or were out of the room. During the two-week period of the study, 59 percent of adult Americans did not give full attention to a single evening network news program, and only 14 percent gave full attention to more than four newscasts.[8] In contrast, 73 percent reported reading two or more newspapers over any two *days* in the same two-week period (Stevenson, 1978, p. 12; Tables 1–3).

Robert Stevenson explains this difference between wide apparent use of television and the rather casual actual use, on the basis of the contrasting skills required by television and print media:

> Television, of course, is ideally suited for . . . passive surveillance. It requires (or allows) no personal selection of content like a newspaper

---

[8] Those who watched the network newscasts most frequently tended to be over 60 and to have grade school educations. (There *is* a reason for all those false teeth, laxative, and sedative commercials you see while watching network newscasts.)

does, no active cognitive processing of content as reading does, and no imagination to create in the mind a picture of the event. For people who lack the mental skills to read a newspaper or magazine efficiently or the physical acuity to read easily or the knowledge or interest to profit from selective reading, for these people, television is a psychologically gratifying experience. (Stevenson, 1978, p. 21)

Doris Graber echoes this, as a result of her comparison of newspapers and television. "The reader who finds press coverage confusing as well as depressing can . . . turn to television for a simpler, clearer, and more encouraging image of the unfolding electoral scene" (Graber, 1976, p. 302).

Thus the content of newspapers and television, and the cognitive processes engaged by the print and electronic media, provide explanations for the greater impact of print media. The print sources contain somewhat more stories about complex topics, have sufficient space to develop more in the way of analysis, and make use of higher cognitive processes if the readers are to comprehend the information.

COGNITIVE INTERACTION WITH THE INFORMATIONAL ENVIRONMENT

If the content of the informational environment provides one reason why individuals know as much as they do, a second is to be found in the extent of cognitive interaction with the informational environment. A person's cognitive structure is intimately related to the informational environment in at least two ways. First, an individual continuously monitors the environment to pick up cues. His or her attention is directed to particular parts of the environment by a perceptual schema. This is the aspect of cognitive structure that guides one's perception, and makes it more likely (but not certain) that some things will be noticed and others neglected. The information that is picked up as a result of this scanning in turn has the capacity to modify the perceptual schema that will guide further monitoring of the environment (Neisser, 1976). Because of this continual monitoring, the informational environment provides a medium that supports a cognitive structure, because an individual interacts with it much as air supports an aircraft as it moves through that medium. If the environment is rich in information, the individual has an opportunity to acquire as many facts as she or he can absorb.

The ability to absorb information is the second way in which cognitive structure and informational environment are interrelated. The more developed one's cognitive structure is, the easier it is to understand new information as it is acquired. An incoming cue takes on meaning to the individual only as it is related to an existing cognitive category with contextual information that allows the person to interpret the cue. As a consequence, the relationship between cognitive structure is not additive, but multiplicative. Not only will a person with a well-developed cognitive structure be more likely to pick up information, but he or she will be better able to understand the meaning of the newly acquired information.

Table 7–5 shows the relation between information level and three measures of the extent to which one is engaged in the informational environment. The more education a person has, the more likely it is that he will have the cognitive skills to pick up cues from the environment. The more frequently a person is accustomed to follow public affairs, the more likely it is that he or she will monitor campaign information. And the more interested a person is in a specific campaign, the more likely it is that she or he will follow it. We can see from Table 7–5 that each of these factors is related to information level. We can also see that the two factors that directly measure a tendency to be involved with the informational environment, following public affairs and interest in the presidential campaign, have stronger relationships with information level than does education. Therefore, we can infer that each of these three factors serves as an indicator of a generalized tendency to

TABLE 7–5
Information Level by Involvement with Informational Environment

	Information Level						
	Low	Average Minus	Average Plus	High	Very High	Extremely High	Total
Education							
Grade school	27.6%	19.6%	11.9%	6.7%	7.6%	5.9%	17.0%
Some high school	20.4	17.5	12.2	7.3	0	5.9	14.8
High school graduate	41.5	39.0	34.8	28.6	13.5	9.8	36.1
Some college	6.0	15.1	20.4	22.1	28.1	37.3	16.3
College graduate	4.5	8.9	20.6	35.3	50.8	41.2	15.8
Kendall's Tau–c = .28							
Frequency with which *respondent follows* *public affairs*							
Hardly at all	32.3	13.3	4.0	1.2	2.3	4.4	12.0
Only now and then	30.8	23.2	11.1	6.8	5.2	0	18.4
Some of the time	27.2	34.6	33.9	24.7	28.3	17.8	31.6
Most of the time	9.7	28.9	50.9	67.3	64.2	77.8	38.0
Kendall's Tau–c = .37							
Respondent's interest *in political campaign*							
Not much interested	52.6	21.5	8.5	6.4	7.7	0	21.2
Somewhat interested	39.1	49.7	40.4	29.6	30.1	23.5	42.3
Very much interested	8.3	28.8	51.1	64.0	62.3	76.5	36.5
Kendall's Tau–c = .40							

Data source: 1976 CPS Election Study.

monitor the informational environment, and that the more closely a citizen follows politics, the more likely it is that he or she will be among the better informed.

Now we have two explanations of why some citizens are well informed and others are poorly informed. The first has to do with how much information a given news source contains and the types of cognitive processes that are activated by use of that news source. The second has to do with how actively a person monitors whatever news sources are available to him or her. Which of these is the stronger explanation? This is hard to answer. To some degree, the processes operate jointly. One's knowledge is increased both by an information-rich environment, *and* by more closely monitoring whatever information is available. A further complication is that one news source, television, seems to transmit information best to those least able to pay attention. Still, there are a couple of clues. For one thing, the relationships between information level and being engaged in the informational environment are generally stronger than those for use of specific news sources. For another, when one controls the relation between information level and reliance on a good news source for whether or not the respondent is paying attention, the relation drops sharply.[9] The opposite does not occur. Therefore, how closely a citizen monitors his or her informational environment appears to be more important than how rich a given information source is.

TIME AND POLITICAL KNOWLEDGE

Internal structure—at least the amount of information arrayed within a cognitive pattern—is dependent on external structure. Are citizens' cognitions also subject to temporal effects? The answer is yes, but under some special circumstances. The first of these is some dramatic event in the campaign itself. For example, when Senator Thomas Eagleton was dropped as the Democratic vice presidential candidate in 1972, this made some difference in how presidential candidate George McGovern was perceived. The special circumstances in this case were quite obvious. Not only was the resignation of a vice presidential candidate unprecedented, but the event took place so early in the campaign that there were still a good many persons who did not know much about Senator McGovern. For these persons, Eagleton's resignation and the context in which it occurred created a vivid first impression.

Another instance of altered cognitive content comes from the 1964

---

[9] For example, the relation for the total sample between information level and reading about politics in newspapers (Tau–*c*) is .40. For those who said they were not much interested in the campaign, this relation drops to .19, and for those who said they hardly ever followed public affairs, the same relation is .10. No matter how good the news source, if a person doesn't pay attention, he or she isn't going to pick up much information.

campaign. During October of that contest between Johnson and Goldwater, certain domestic issues (law and order, alleged corruption, social security, unemployment) were gaining in salience while references to war and peace were declining. The increasingly salient domestic issues were among those being discussed by the candidates, and there hadn't been much consequential foreign news for a while. Then within 48 hours, Nikita Khrushchev was deposed as premier of the Soviet Union, the Labour party won an unexpected election victory in Great Britain, and China exploded an atomic device. This caused foreign affairs to gain in salience at the expense of the domestic campaign topics. In this case, the unusual circumstance was represented by an explosion of information on a topic (foreign developments bearing on the chances of war or peace) that was important to voters and about which they knew relatively little. Ordinarily, citizens would already have a fair amount of information about topics important to them, and would not care about other matters. Both these normal circumstances tend to inhibit communication. In this instance, new information bearing on the chances of war and peace suddenly became available. Again, communication took place because of special circumstances.

Perhaps the most important temporal effect takes place over the course of the campaign. For the electorate as a whole, there is no relation between citizens' information level and time. Well-informed persons are likely to be as knowledgeable in early September as on the day before election, and uninformed persons are not likely to be knowledgeable at any particular time. There is one category of citizens, however, whose information level does tend to increase as the campaign progresses. Here the special circumstances are that these are persons who have attended high school, who say they are somewhat interested in the campaign, and who follow public affairs some of the time—persons, in other words, who fall into the *middle* of the scales related to monitoring the informational environment. If one looks at those who have attended college, who say they are very much interested in the campaign, and who follow public affairs most of the time, there is no relation between time and information level. This grouping is constantly monitoring the informational environment, is likely to have picked up a good many cues before the campaign began, and hence is unlikely to learn much new information during the campaign. Nor is there any relation between information level and time for those who didn't go beyond grade school, who say they are not much interested in the campaign, and who follow public affairs only now and then if they do so at all. Politics is so remote from the lives of these people that the campaigners face insurmountable communication thresholds in trying to reach them. But a temporal effect can be found for those who are "average" in their receptivity to political communications, who are neither avid followers of politics, nor among those who ignore public affairs altogether. For those who fall into the middle of all three scales, there is at least a moderate relationship ($r = .19$) between the passage of time in the campaign and information level.[10]

It would be a mistake to regard this temporal effect as either strong or negligible. Essentially what is happening is that as the campaign progresses, there are fewer persons with a "low" information level and more with an "average plus" information level. This does not mean that a great deal of information is being communicated, but it does mean that a campaign is more than a hollow ritual. When we reviewed the stages of a campaign in Chapter 3, we saw that proposals to shorten presidential campaigns did not take account of the planning and organization necessary to conduct a campaign on a subcontinental scale. To this we can now add that if campaigns were to end a month earlier, there would be a larger number of uninformed citizens, and this would mean they would be less at ease with the electoral choice they are asked to make.

Summary

In this chapter, we have seen that internal cognitive structure was dependent on external informational environment. Most citizens know relatively little about politics, but there are some who are quite well informed. The well informed are more likely to use print sources. The print sources contain more information to begin with, and require more involved cognitive processes for its comprehension. The well informed are also likely to be those who monitor the informational environment most closely because of education or their interest in politics. The degree to which one is engaged in the informational environment is a stronger explanation of information level than the use of print sources. Finally, time does matter. Neither the very interested, nor the quite uninterested, learn much as a campaign progresses; but the citizen with a middling involvement tends to increase his or her understanding a bit as a result of the campaign.

---

[10] It is necessary to isolate those in the middle of all three scales in order to find this relationship. The correlations between time and information level for those in the middle categories of the individual scales are all significant, but lower. For those who attended high school but did not go on to college, $r = .05$. For those who said they were somewhat interested in the campaign, $r = .06$. For those who said they followed public affairs some of the time, $r = .10$. There were no significant correlations for those on the high or low ends of any of the three scales.

chapter 8

Presidential Choice

In this chapter, we shall deal directly with the use of the citizen's knowledge about politics to choose between presidential candidates. Whereas the last chapter dealt with how much the citizen knew about politics, now our concern shifts to how this information is organized into attitudes about various political objects, and the relation of these attitudes to voting choice. There are many areas of life in which attitudes are weak predictors of action, but voting is not one of them. Especially when there are well-developed attitudes, one can predict how citizens will vote with considerable confidence. Consequently, if you understand attitudes you will be able to understand the citizen response to campaign strategies.

SALIENCE, PARTISAN VALENCE, AND IMPORTANCE

There are three attitudinal properties that are especially helpful in understanding voting. The first of these is *salience*, the prominence of an attitudinal object. The more publicized a topic, the more likely that it will be salient for the citizen. The more salient it is, the more likely the citizen is to have an attitude about it. For example, an American would be much more likely to have an attitude about Southeast Asia during the Vietnam War when the media were filled with information about it than before or after the war when the topic was much less salient.

The second relevant attitudinal property is *valence*. One's feelings about an attitudinal object may be positive, neutral, or negative. For ex-

197

ample, a citizen may have a very positive attitude about one candidate and a slightly negative attitude about another, or a positive attitude about a candidate's trustworthiness and a negative attitude about the same candidate's intelligence. The citizen reacts positively or negatively to a candidate according to the valence of his or her attitudes about that candidate. (Remember that chemical ions combine depending on the valence of each ion. The word "valence" is used with attitudes because of this rough analogy between citizen reaction and chemical reaction.) Where vote choice is concerned, we are not concerned with positive or negative attitudes per se, but with how the attitudes about specific political objects sum to form a *partisan valence*. If one person had positive attitudes about the Republican candidate and negative attitudes about the Democratic candidate, we would say that this person's attitudes were pro-Republican. If another had negative attitudes about the Republican candidate's position on economic management and positive attitudes about the Democratic candidate's position about international involvement, we would say that her or his attitudes were pro-Democratic. If a third person had positive attitudes about the Republican candidate as a person and positive attitudes about the Democratic candidate's stands on issues, we would say that in this case partisan valence was mixed.

Finally, we are interested in *importance*, the extent to which vote depends on a given attitude. Strictly speaking, this is not an attitudinal property, but the link between the citizen's attitude and the vote that is cast. An attitude that is salient and quite favorable to one party is usually important, though this need not be the case. Voters may base their decisions on other attitudes, or they may believe that a given issue is not one over which a president will have much influence. In either situation, the attitude would not be important in vote choice.

We want to separate these three properties because salience and partisan valence and importance may vary independently of each other. As we shall see, general attitudes about candidates and issues were salient in 1976, as were attitudes about candidate personality and party affect in 1968, but neither party enjoyed anything more than the barest advantage in any of these categories. Attitudes about persons in the parties (other than the candidates) were decidedly pro-Republican in 1972 and decidedly pro-Democratic in 1976, but were not salient in either campaign. Attitudes about the public records of the candidates were important in 1976 voting decisions, although they were not too salient and only slightly favored Gerald Ford over Jimmy Carter. Attitudes about agricultural policy have never been salient in modern times, have strongly favored the Democrats in every election save 1968, and have been important only to the small proportion of voters engaged in farming. So when someone says that a given attitude is consequential in an election, one must ask whether it is

Maximum Likelihood Estimate = Best Guess

A literal reduction of the phrase "Maximum Likelihood Estimate" is "Best Guess." For our purposes in this chapter, it is the best guess about the importance of an attitude in determining a citizen's vote.

The details of the Maximum Likelihood Estimate (or MLE) are a little technical, but three ideas are all that are necessary to understand its meaning. First, in common with all statistics derived from surveys, it is an *estimate*. When you read of a survey that finds, for instance, that 40 percent intend to vote for Ronald Reagan if Edward Kennedy is his opponent, this 40 percent figure rests on a "confidence limit," say $\pm$ 3 percent, and a "level of significance," usually 19 chances out of 20. Therefore the full meaning of "40 percent" is "we estimate that in 19 cases out of 20 the proportion of all population members intending to vote for Reagan will fall between 37 percent and 43 percent." In a similar way, the figure given for the MLE is the best statistical guess about the relative importance of the attitude in determining the vote. The higher the MLE, the more important the attitude.

The second basic idea is that this is a *multivariate* procedure. The bivariate correlation explained in the box in Chapter 7 was an association between two variables, presumably one cause and one effect. A multivariate study permits analysis of multiple variables at the same time. Controls are exercised over other possible causes. For example, in a three-variable solution, we shall be looking at the effects of attitudes about candidates, parties, and issues on vote. The multivariate analysis allows us to isolate the effect of candidate attitudes while controlling for the effects of party and issue attitudes, to isolate the effect of party attitudes while controlling for the effect of candidate and issue attitudes, and to isolate the effect of issue attitudes while controlling for the effects of candidate and party attitudes.

The third basic idea is that probit analysis, from which the MLEs are derived, is a *curvilinear* rather than a linear procedure. This just means that the data points representing vote are assumed to fit a curve rather than a straight line. Linear regression, the form of multivariate analysis most commonly used in political science, assumes that the data points will lie on a straight line. Identical solutions were calculated with 1976 data using linear regression and probit analysis. The linear regression explained 47 percent of the variance in vote; the probit analysis explained 73 percent of the variance in vote. Since the probit prediction was half again more powerful than the linear regression, the curvilinear assumption is clearly more appropriate for voting data.

For additional discussion, and the method used to standardize the probit estimates, see Appendix A–8.1.

consequential because it is salient, because it favors one party rather than the other, because it is related to the voting decision, or some combination of the three.[1]

The same responses that we used to analyze information level in Chapter 7 provide data to analyze these attitudinal properties. The responses are classified by the category of attitude object—at first the broad categories of candidates, parties, and issues, then more detailed categories that allow more specific analysis. The *salience* of a category of attitude objects is measured by the proportion of all comments falling into the category. The larger the proportion of comments, the more salient the category. *Partisan valence* is measured by the proportion of comments in the category that is favorable to the Democrats. The proportion of comments in the category favoring the Republicans is, of course, the complement of the pro-Democratic percentage, so this single figure tells us which party has how much of an advantage. The higher the figure, the better things are for the Democrats; the lower the figure, the better things are for the Republicans. The *importance* of the category in the voting decision is measured by maximum likelihood estimates obtained through probit analysis. (See box on p. 199.) The probit model gives us a very powerful explanation of presidential choice. Between 85 and 90 percent of the individual cases are correctly predicted in the solution for each election year.

CANDIDATES, PARTIES, AND ISSUES

As a first broad approximation, let's look at the pattern formed by the mean figures for attitudes about candidates, parties, and issues. These data are presented in Figure 8–1. The ordering of the three categories is the same for both salience and importance. Issues come first, then candidates, and then parties. Moreover, attitudes about parties are a long way back of attitudes about either issues or candidates. Partisan valence is rather different. The strongest advantage over time goes to the Republicans because of the relative attractiveness of their candidates. Issues, on the other hand, tend to help the Democrats, and the Democrats derive a slight advantage from the less-important attitudes about parties.

---

[1] There are a number of well-known explanations of voting that are based on summary measures of the effects of attitude components. Frequently these summary measures are products of a measure of partisan valence multiplied by a measure of importance (Stokes et al., 1958; Comparative State Election Project, 1973). These provide good explanations, but, as all summary measures, they contain less information. One cannot tell whether partisan valence or importance is causing the summary measure to go up or down.

FIGURE 8–1

Broad Attitudes and Presidential Choice, Mean Figures 1952–1976

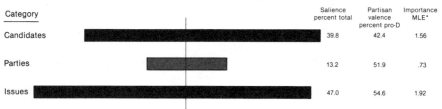

Category	Salience percent total	Partisan valence percent pro-D	Importance MLE*
Candidates	39.8	42.4	1.56
Parties	13.2	51.9	.73
Issues	47.0	54.6	1.92

Explanation of figure: *Salience* is measured by the proportion of the total comments dealing with the attitude object. It is indicated by the total length of the bar. The longer the bar, the more salient the category. *Partisan valence* is measured by the proportion of comments favorable to the Democrats. The farther the bar is to the left, the more favorable to the Democrats. The farther to the right, the more favorable to the Republicans. *Importance*, the relation of the attitude category to vote choice, is measured by a standardized maximum likelihood estimate. (See box on p. 199.) This is indicated in the figure by shade. If a bar is black, the attitude category is very important. If a bar is dark gray, the attitude category is important. If a bar is light gray, the attitude category is somewhat important. If a bar is hollow, the attitude category is not significantly related to vote choice.

Data source: 1952 through 1976 SRC/CPS Election Studies.

When we look at these three broad categories over time, whose data are presented in Figure 8–2, it appears that the general pattern is reasonably stable. There is, to be sure, election-to-election variation. The most marked variation is to be found in partisan valence. Democrats had advantages in all three attitude categories in 1964, and the Republicans did in 1968 (when analysis is confined to Nixon and Humphrey voters only) and in 1972. (Indeed, it would be remarkable if we did not find something of this kind since there was a Democratic landslide in 1964 and a Republican landslide in 1972.) There is also some variation in the salience and importance of the attitude categories. For example, attitudes about candidates were least important in 1952[2] and most important in 1976. But the general pattern is sufficiently stable that individual elections can be explained on the basis of how they depart from the normal pattern, rather than discovering a new pattern in each election. It appears that the interests of the electorate set some bounds to election-to-election variation, and all fluctuation takes place within this range.

The one clear case of change over this time period is a decline in both salience and importance of attitudes about the parties. These attitudes were not that consequential at the beginning of the time period. They were never more than 16.5 percent of all attitudes, and they have not been very important since the 1950s. It is somewhat risky to talk about

---

[2] This finding is itself worth noting. The 1952 election is usually dismissed as a deviating election, resulting in large part from General Eisenhower's considerable personal popularity. The probit analysis indicates that attitudes about parties and issues were both more important that year.

FIGURE 8–2
Broad Attitudes and Presidential Choice

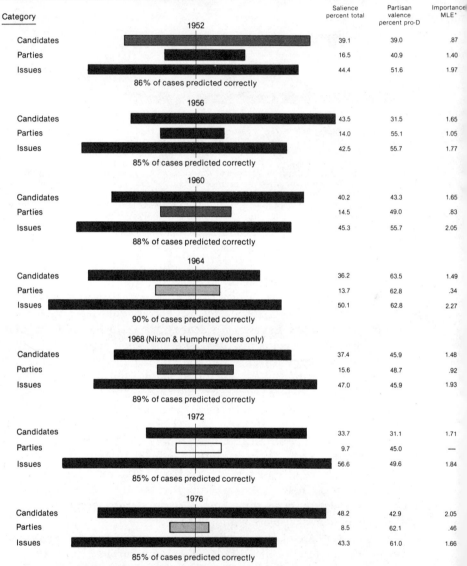

Category		Salience percent total	Partisan valence percent pro-D	Importance MLE*
1952				
Candidates		39.1	39.0	.87
Parties		16.5	40.9	1.40
Issues		44.4	51.6	1.97
86% of cases predicted correctly				
1956				
Candidates		43.5	31.5	1.65
Parties		14.0	55.1	1.05
Issues		42.5	55.7	1.77
85% of cases predicted correctly				
1960				
Candidates		40.2	43.3	1.65
Parties		14.5	49.0	.83
Issues		45.3	55.7	2.05
88% of cases predicted correctly				
1964				
Candidates		36.2	63.5	1.49
Parties		13.7	62.8	.34
Issues		50.1	62.8	2.27
90% of cases predicted correctly				
1968 (Nixon & Humphrey voters only)				
Candidates		37.4	45.9	1.48
Parties		15.6	48.7	.92
Issues		47.0	45.9	1.93
89% of cases predicted correctly				
1972				
Candidates		33.7	31.1	1.71
Parties		9.7	45.0	—
Issues		56.6	49.6	1.84
85% of cases predicted correctly				
1976				
Candidates		48.2	42.9	2.05
Parties		8.5	62.1	.46
Issues		43.3	61.0	1.66
85% of cases predicted correctly				

— denotes insignificant figure

Explanation of figure: *Salience* is measured by the proportion of the total comments dealing with the attitude object. It is indicated by the total length of the bar. The longer the bar, the more salient the category. *Partisan valence* is measured by the proportion of comments favorable to the Democrats. The farther the bar is to the left, the more favorable to the Democrats. The farther to the right, the more favorable to the Republicans. *Importance,* the relation of the attitude category to vote choice is measured by a standardized maximum likelihood estimate. (See box on p. 199.) This is indicated in the figure by shade. If a bar is black, the attitude category is very important. If a bar is dark gray, the attitude category is important. If a bar is light gray, the attitude category is somewhat important. If a bar is hollow, the attitude category is not significantly related to vote choice.
Data source: 1952 through 1976 SRC/CPS Election Studies.

long-term change when there are only seven data points, but it would appear that attitudes about parties are marked by both election-to-election variation and long-term decline.

By far the most noteworthy finding in this analysis is the relative salience and importance of issues.[3] This is remarkable on several grounds. First of all, the questions (quoted early in Chapter 7) do not ask about issues. They ask for the respondents' views about parties and candidates, but the largest part of their answers concern issues. Second, the mass media give much less attention to issues than they do to "horse-race" topics. Therefore, issues are more important within the citizens' cognitive structures than they are in the informational environment from which the citizens pick up their cues. Third, many political scientists argue that the '50s were relatively placid. For example, one notable analysis states:

> By the fifties [New Deal] issues had faded. The times were prosperous and the candidates in 1952 and 1956 were not perceived as polarized on those issues. Nor were there other issues to take their place. The result was that citizens did not take coherent issue positions, nor did they vote on the basis of issues. (Nie, Verba, and Petrocik, 1976, p. 192)

Proponents of this position argue that issues did not become important until 1964, when President Johnson and Senator Goldwater offered the voters a clear choice, and again in 1972, when President Nixon and Senator McGovern took distinctive issue stands. There is no support in the present analysis for the argument that voters were unconcerned with issues in the 1950s. Issues were more salient in 1964 and 1972 than in other years, but the change is on the order of a few percentage points on an already substantial base. This does not represent any sea change in the nature of American politics. Issues were also more important in vote choice in 1964 than in any other year in this time series, but issues were more important in 1960, 1952, and 1968 than they were in 1972. The evidence here points to the continuing consequence of issues in presidential choice, not to their emergence in special circumstances.

Of the three broad categories, candidate attitudes have been salient, usually favorable to the Republicans, and very important in voting choices. Party attitudes have been much less salient, have sometimes favored Democrats and sometimes favored the Republicans, and were much less

---

[3] The salience of issues reflects some coding decisions. References to liberal or conservative policies are regarded as issue comments. Similarly, when a person mentions business or labor, it is assumed he or she is talking about economic management; when she or he mentions blacks, it is assumed that the reference is to civil liberties; when he or she mentions farmers, agriculture. The six-component solution devised by Donald E. Stokes assigns references to liberal or conservative postures to "parties as managers of government," and all references to groups to a separate "group-related" component. When choosing between candidates, parties, and issues, and in view of the vocabulary a respondent might be expected to use, I think it is appropriate to code these as issue references.

important in the 1970s than they were in the 1950s. Issue attitudes have been salient, usually favorable to the Democrats, and very important in voting choices.

REACTION AND CHOICE IN SPECIFIC ELECTIONS

Useful as these generalizations are, they do not take us very far toward an understanding of any specific election. The categories are too broad to allow us to trace much of the linkage between coalition strategies and citizen response. What is needed for this purpose are categories that are specific enough to permit concrete statements about the individual election, yet inclusive enough so that statements falling into each will occur over a series of elections. Therefore, we will decompose the three broad categories into 16 more specific categories.

Candidate references will be divided into seven classes. Two deal with attitudes about the candidates' experience. *Record and incumbency* concerns perception of the candidates' record in public offices they have held previously, and—much more frequently—comments about an incumbent when he is running for reelection. *Experience* is a shortened name for nonpublic office experience; military experience, diplomatic background, campaign ability, and so forth would all be included here. Two more categories are also office related. *Management* deals with executive capacity and statements about how the candidate would be likely to run the government if elected. *Intelligence* is given a broad enough definition to include comments about the candidate's education and practical capacity as well as wisdom as such. The other specific categories do not deal as directly with potential executive ability. *Trust* touches upon confidence, honesty, and any specific incidents reflecting on the candidate's integrity. *Personality* includes any comments about image and mannerisms, such as warmth, aloofness, dignity, and so forth. The *general* category is composed principally of comments that are too general to be assigned to one of the specific categories ("He's a good man" or "I like him"), but also includes some statements on such topics as the candidate's age or wealth or family that did not occur frequently enough to justify the creation of separate attitudinal categories.

The relatively infrequent party comments were divided into two classes. Attitudes about *people in the party* concern all other party members besides the candidates: incumbent presidents not running for reelection, prominent senators and governors, party workers, and so on. All other party comments were categorized as *party affect*. This included trust of one party or the other, references to party factions, and the importance of achieving or preventing a party victory.

There were seven categories of issue attitudes. Four of these dealt with the same policy areas we considered in Chapter 3 in connection with the issue groups that made up the electoral coalitions: *international involvement, economic management, social benefits,* and *civil liberties.* Two more are minor policy areas. *Natural resources* may be thought of as a special case of economic management, in which regulatory policy is used in the areas of the environment and energy. *Agriculture* policy has been a special case of social benefits, in which the beneficiaries were the farmers, although this may be changing as the farmers become a smaller proportion of the population and food costs rise. As with the candidate comments, there was a *general* issue category composed of comments too broad to fit into any specific class. This included such items as the policy stands of the parties, liberalism or conservatism, or comments about "domestic policy" without any indication which domestic policy was meant.

Decomposition of the 3 broad attitude categories into 16 relatively specific categories permits a number of things. The essential difference is that we are trading the simple generalizations derived from the three-component solution for a more detailed understanding of the role of attitudes in presidential choice that can be obtained from inspection of the 16 categories. The detailed solution will not support statements that candidate attitudes usually favor the Republicans and that issue attitudes usually favor the Democrats. Instead, we see that some candidate attributes favor the Democrats in some elections and others favor the Republicans, and that some issues have usually favored the Democrats while others have usually favored the Republicans.

The average pattern formed by these 16 categories over the series of elections from 1952 through 1976 is shown in Figure 8–3. The general comments are the most salient and most important of all the candidate attitudes, perhaps reflecting the generally low level of information among the voters.[4] Views about the candidates' personalities are next most salient, but rank third in mean importance. Trust in the candidates is somewhat less salient than personality on the average, but tends to be a little more important in voting choice. The next pair of candidate attitudes are those concerning record and experience. Both are about equally related to vote choice. It appears that nonoffice experience is more salient than the candidate's political record, but record tends to be more visible when there is an incumbent running for reelection. The least salient and least important pair of attitudes are those concerning management capacity and intelligence. It is dismaying to reflect on the finding that in voting for the most

---

[4] There is a strong association between salience and importance if one looks at the mean figures from the whole series of elections. The association is much weaker in particular elections. In specific elections, there appears to be more chance for an issue to be salient but not important, and vice versa.

FIGURE 8–3

Specific Attitudes and Presidential Choice, Mean Figures 1952–1976

Category	Salience percent total	Partisan valence percent pro-D	Importance MLE*
Candidates			
General	13.8		.71
Record-incumbency	2.5		.37
Experience	5.3		.40
Management	3.2		.23
Intelligence	2.3		.16
Trust	5.4		.50
Personality	7.1		.43
Parties			
People in party	4.4	46.7	.25
Party affect	8.8	53.7	.80
Issues			
General	14.3	48.7	1.01
International involvement	9.1	31.7	.57
Economic management	14.1	65.3	.76
Social benefits	4.8	70.1	.27
Civil liberties	3.6	50.4	.31
National resources	0.2	77.3	.04
Agriculture	1.8	68.5	.18

Explanation of figure: *Salience* is measured by the proportion of the total comments dealing with the attitude object. It is indicated by the total length of the bar. The longer the bar, the more salient the category. *Partisan valence* is measured by the proportion of comments favorable to the Democrats. The farther the bar is to the left, the more favorable to the Democrats. The farther to the right, the more favorable to the Republicans. *No partisan valence is reported for the candidate categories. There is so much variation between candidate pairs that mean figures have no significance. Importance,* the relation of the attitude category to vote choice, is measured by a standardized maximum likelihood estimate. (See box on p. 199.) It is indicated by the shade of the bar. The darker the bar, the more important the category. The bar is hollow to denote nonsignificance if the category was not significant in the majority of elections.
Data source: 1952 through 1976 SRC/CPS Election Studies.

demanding office in the Western world, intelligence is the last thing Americans consider.

The display in Figure 8–3 has the candidate attitudes at the far left side, reflecting only salience and importance. Mean partisan valence figures have not been calculated; there is too much variation between the pairs of candidates who run in succeeding elections for the average figures to have any meaning. The Carter-Ford comparison in 1976, for example, engendered quite different candidate attitudes from the McGovern-Nixon comparison four years earlier. Consequently, unlike the specific issue attitudes, there is no typical partisan advantage among the specific candidate attitudes.

Over time party affect has tended to be more salient than all but one of the candidate attitudes, and to be more important than any of the candidate attitudes in vote choice. Attitudes about other party leaders have only been half as salient, and not nearly as important. The Democrats have had a slight advantage in party affect, and Republican party leaders were slightly more attractive.

The general attitudes about issues are the most salient and most important of all the 16 categories. Moreover, it turns out that these general issue attitudes have been favorable to the winning party in each of the seven elections. It is as though there was a group of persons who have stable interests in each of the specific policy areas, so that the subtraction of the specific comments results in a general issue category that is a rather sensitive indicator of partisan advantage in any specific election.

Among the policy area attitudes, those about economics are most salient and most important, ranking second overall only to the general issue attitudes. The economic attitudes typically give a strong edge to the Democrats. Views on international involvement are next most salient, and have been rather important. International attitudes are the one set of policy views that normally give the Republicans a substantial advantage. Attitudes about social benefits and civil liberties are about equally salient. Both are visible, but both are another step down from international involvement. Social benefits is usually of some importance, and provides a substantial advantage to the Democrats. Civil liberties has been important in certain elections, sometimes favoring the Democrats and sometimes the Republicans. Agriculture and natural resources have a strong Democratic valence, but neither policy area is normally salient or important.

These mean figures, especially the measures of importance, do not have any particular statistical standing, but they do provide a baseline against which specific elections can be compared. They enable us to see something of the citizens' reaction to campaign strategies, and to know what attitudes determined their choices.[5] Since we know about the campaign strategies from Chapters 5 and 6, we can see there are departures from the normal pattern that correspond with the campaign emphases. Specifically, we shall look for citizen *reaction* in *departures from the normal pattern in salience and partisan valence* (and in the absolute pattern of partisan valence for the candidate attitudes where no baseline exists). Then we shall explain *choice* in terms of the *absolute pattern of impor-*

---

[5] I say that we can only see *something* of the citizens' reaction, because of the limits of what can be discerned from a single cross-sectional survey of the national electorate. To understand the impact of the campaign in detail, one would need longitudinal data to see what changes had taken place in voters' attitudes as the campaign progressed, and studies that focus on particular sets of voters (southern independents, Catholics from industrial states, and so forth) to whom the campaign was being directed.

tance and partisan valence in the election in question. We shall begin with the election of 1964.[6]

JOHNSON VANQUISHES GOLDWATER, 1964

Reaction "This will not be an engagement of personalities," Senator Barry Goldwater promised his supporters when he announced his candidacy. "It will be an engagement of principles." This was certainly a proper forecast of the voters' reaction. As you can see by comparing Figure 8–4 with Figure 8–3, the most striking departures from the normal pattern of attitudes concerned issues. With a whole range of social programs being challenged for the first time since the New Deal, attitudes about social benefits were twice as salient as usual, and moved from a Democratic advantage of 70 percent to one of 89 percent. With a southern president urging civil rights progress in North and South, and the senator (however careful about campaign statements in this area) having voted against the centerpiece of civil rights legislation, civil liberties attitudes were salient, and decidedly more Democratic. On international matters, the Goldwater strategy emphasized preparedness, military strength, and confronting communism with a policy of firmness. The Democratic strategy portrayed Lyndon Johnson as a man of peace who would not take precipitate action

---

[6] The detailed solutions for the 1952, 1956, and 1960 campaigns are:

	1952		
Category	Total	Pro-D	MLE*
Candidates			
General	11.1%	35.3%	0.26
Record-incumbency	1.0	86.3	—
Experience	9.1	61.1	0.29
Management	2.2	21.3	0.29
Intelligence	1.9	58.5	—
Trust	8.7	21.8	0.63
Personality	5.1	26.7	0.26
Parties			
People in party	5.9	33.6	—
Party affect	10.7	45.0	1.36
Issues			
General	8.3	45.8	0.77
International involvement	8.8	20.1	0.76
Economic management ...	22.8	62.5	1.25
Social benefits	1.8	80.9	—
Civil liberties	1.4	40.7	—
National resources	0.2	82.1	—
Agriculture	1.1	80.1	0.34
	87% predicted right		

— denotes insignificant figure

when faced with a dangerous situation. The contrast was all in Johnson's favor. International attitudes were no more salient than usual, but shifted from 32 percent pro-Democratic to 54 percent pro-Democratic. In fact, this was the only election in which every issue attitude favored the Democrats.

The pro-Democratic reaction was not limited to issues. Party affect was salient in 1964 and shifted in a Democratic direction. The initial stimulus for this had been an adverse public reaction to the Republican Convention in San Francisco. These attitudes were successfully reinforced, though, by the Democratic strategy that emphasized the unusual nature of the 1964 Republican challenge. All of the statements about "the temporary Republican spokesman," and the efforts to distinguish between "good" moderate Republicans, such as Dwight Eisenhower, and "bad" conservative Republicans around Goldwater paid off handsomely for the Democrats.

In the comparison between Johnson and Goldwater as individuals, the office-related attitudes (record, experience, management, intelligence) all had a decidedly Democratic valence. Johnson had the good fortune to run for reelection when he had been in office for less than a year. Attitudes about presidents become less positive with the passage of time (Mueller, 1973; Stimson, 1976). As Ford in 1976, Lyndon Johnson had the chance to run while he still enjoyed the favorable reputation of a man newly

	1956			1960	
Total	Pro-D	MLE*	Total	Pro-D	MLE*
19.6%	33.2%	0.44	17.3%	41.7%	0.82
3.5	13.1	0.38	0.9	35.3	0.22
3.7	36.6	0.40	9.1	30.9	1.02
2.1	41.5	0.44	1.8	34.6	0.24
2.6	65.9	—	3.6	63.0	0.26
5.9	18.8	—	1.4	46.5	—
6.2	28.3	0.51	6.0	58.2	—
5.2	55.6	0.29	4.9	39.4	—
8.8	54.8	1.10	9.6	53.9	0.76
10.0	45.7	0.71	19.2	64.3	1.38
8.8	16.9	0.58	9.4	32.3	0.80
13.1	74.1	0.71	10.9	56.1	0.32
5.0	83.5	0.51	1.5	53.4	—
2.0	46.2	—	2.2	64.6	—
0.4	67.4	—	0.2	76.2	—
3.1	79.7	0.47	1.9	70.8	—
86% predicted right			88% predicted right		

FIGURE 8–4
Specific Attitudes and 1964 Presidential Choice

Category	Salience percent total	Partisan valence percent pro-D	Importance MLE*
Candidates			
General	10.6	66.5	.86
Record-incumbency	2.3	93.1	—
Experience	6.3	76.4	—
Management	2.7	64.7	—
Intelligence	1.6	75.5	—
Trust	2.1	18.2	.38
Personality	10.4	52.9	.53
Parties			
People in party	3.0	49.0	—
Party affect	10.7	66.7	1.12
Issues			
General	17.6	54.5	1.59
International involvement	8.0	54.4	.65
Economic management	7.5	59.5	.55
Social benefits	10.5	88.7	.38
Civil liberties	5.5	67.3	.64
National resources	.2	77.3	—
Agriculture	.7	64.9	—

90% of cases predicted correctly
— denotes insignificant figure

Explanation of figure: *Salience* is measured by the proportion of the total comments dealing with the attitude object. It is indicated by the total length of the bar. The longer the bar, the more salient the category. *Partisan valence* is measured by the proportion of comments favorable to the Democrats. The farther the bar is to the left, the more favorable to the Democrats. The farther to the right, the more favorable to the Republicans. *Importance*, the relation of the attitude category to vote choice, is measured by a standardized maximum likelihood estimate. (See box on p. 199.) This is indicated in the figure by shade. If a bar is black, the attitude category is very important. If a bar is dark gray, the attitude category is important. If a bar is light gray, the attitude category is somewhat important. If a bar is hollow, the attitude category is not significantly related to vote choice.
Data source: 1964 SRC Election Study.

come to office. But unlike Ford, Johnson was seen as the heir of a popular predecessor and benefited from positive feelings about John Kennedy.

Attitudes about the candidates' personalities were more salient than usual, and much more evenly balanced. What was happening here was that Johnson began with a marked edge, but Barry Goldwater became better liked as he became better known during the campaign. The only positive reaction to the Republican campaign was found in trust. Barry Goldwater was far more widely trusted than Lyndon Johnson. Here there was some resonance for the Republican strategy of attacking the moral standards of the White House and calling for a return to conscience and integrity.

Choice   The strongest forces producing the Democratic landslide were positive feelings about the status quo. The attitudes most tightly associated with vote were general feelings about issues, affect toward the Democratic party, and general feelings about the candidates, in that order, with fairly large steps between the three. The liberal issue/Democratic party combination was a little less favorable than the Democratic party/ Lyndon Johnson combination, but the former was more important in determining votes.

On specific issues, attitudes on international involvement and civil liberties—the two policy areas where Republicans normally do best, but which had shifted in a Democratic direction in 1964—were the most important. Then came economics and attitudes about the candidates' personalities. Both of these tended in a Democratic direction. Least important were attitudes about social benefits, with a lopsided Democratic margin, and trust, which produced the sole Republican advantage. "In your heart," the Goldwater slogan asserted, "you know he's right." In their hearts, the voters were convinced Barry Goldwater was honest—but this was hardly enough to win when every other attitude was producing Democratic votes.

A STRUGGLE BETWEEN PARTY REGULARS, 1968

Reaction   There was one quite atypical feature to the 1968 campaign. The Wallace effort was the most formidable third-party challenge since 1924. But when one restricts the analysis to those voting for Nixon or Humphrey, as in Figure 8–5, the result is a rather typical party pattern.[7] This should not be too surprising. Both Nixon and Humphrey had been prominent party leaders for about two decades. Both had been vice president, and therefore associated willy-nilly with the records made by administrations over which they had little influence. And Page (1978, chaps. 3–4) has shown that both Nixon and Humphrey took similar positions on the majority of issues. Consequently, we should expect to find a typical partisan reaction to a contest between them.

The one category that was sharply more salient and somewhat more Republican than usual was general attitudes on issues. This probably reflected Richard Nixon's purposefully vague statements on issues. Nixon had, after all, identified himself with "new ideas," and "the American Dream," and called for "new leadership," "a new road," and "a complete housecleaning." These phrases hardly committed Mr. Nixon to any spe-

---

[7] Restricting the analysis to Nixon and Humphrey voters retains comparability between the 1968 solution and those for other elections. And while the Wallace effort elicited unusual support, 86 percent of the voters still chose one of the major-party candidates. For a full analysis of the Wallace vote, as well as the Nixon and Humphrey votes, see Comparative State Election Project, 1973.

FIGURE 8–5

Specific Attitudes and 1968 Presidential Choice (Nixon and Humphrey voters only)

Category	Salience percent total	Partisan valence percent pro-D	Importance MLE*
Candidates			
General	13.8	43.3	.64
Record-incumbency	1.7	61.6	.49
Experience	3.0	39.8	.33
Management	2.6	34.0	—
Intelligence	2.2	50.0	—
Trust	4.3	52.1	.39
Personality	9.9	48.2	.44
Parties			
People in party	5.4	40.9	.44
Party affect	10.2	52.8	.76
Issues			
General	19.7	44.4	1.23
International involvement	8.4	27.2	—
Economic management	9.4	55.0	.61
Social benefits	4.0	67.6	—
Civil liberties	5.1	50.1	—
National resources	—	—	—
Agriculture	0.5	35.7	—

88% of cases predicted correctly

— denotes insignificant figure

Explanation of figure: *Salience* is measured by the proportion of the total comments dealing with the attitude object. It is indicated by the total length of the bar. The longer the bar, the more salient the category. *Partisan valence* is measured by the proportion of comments favorable to the Democrats. The farther the bar is to the left, the more favorable to the Democrats. The farther the bar to the right, the more favorable to the Republicans. *Importance*, the relation of the attitude category to vote choice, is measured by a standardized maximum likelihood estimate. (See box on p. 199.) This is indicated in the figure by shade. If a bar is black, the attitude category is very important. If a bar is dark gray, the attitude category is important. If a bar is light gray, the attitude category is somewhat important. If a bar is hollow, the attitude category is not significantly related to vote choice.

Data source: 1968 SRC Election Study.

cific course of action, but they sounded positive and seemed to produce a Republican advantage in this attitude category.

Economic management was less salient than usual, but also less helpful to the Democrats than ordinarily the case. What happened here was that while Hubert Humphrey stressed traditional Democratic economic themes (reminding his audiences of the specter of unemployment under Republicans, and so forth), the incumbent Democratic administration was vulnerable because of inflation that had begun during the Vietnam War. It was this nerve that Nixon touched when he attacked Humphrey as "the most expensive senator in U.S. history." The net of pro-Democratic attitudes on jobs and pro-Republican attitudes on inflation was a less-than-customary Democratic advantage in this policy area. International attitudes were about as salient as usual, and gave the Republicans slightly more than their normal advantage, doubtless a reflection of the Vietnam War.

Confronted with an essentially partisan choice between Humphrey and Nixon, attitudes about parties were a little more visible than usual. The "people in the party" category was more pro-Republican than normal, due to the unpopularity (by 1968) of Lyndon Johnson.

There was nothing unusual about the salience of the candidate attitudes. Humphrey's record in office was more favorably perceived, as was Nixon's nonoffice experience and management capacity. Nixon derived more benefit from the general attitudes about candidates (which again could be seen as reaction to his nonspecific campaigning) because this category, as usual, was the most salient of those concerning candidates.

Choice The narrow electoral decision in 1968 was a consequence of the offsetting character of some pro-Republican attitudes balanced by an almost equal number of pro-Democratic attitudes. Four attitudes were important in determining the vote.[8] The general attitudes on issues were very important, and the general attitudes on candidates were important, and both of these favored Nixon. Party affect and attitudes about economic management were both important, and these two categories favored Humphrey. Attitudes about experience, personality, and people in the party were all somewhat important, and all favored Nixon. Attitudes about the administration's record and trust were also somewhat important, and favored Humphrey. In sum, there was a slight Republican advantage in the number of favorable attitudes (five to four), and a slight Republican edge in importance. These slight attitudinal advantages produced an echo in the 43.4 percent of the vote cast for Richard Nixon and the 42.7 percent cast for Hubert Humphrey.

UNUSUAL CANDIDATE POSTURES, 1972

Reaction 1972 was a year when an incumbent following policies at variance with those he had long espoused was challenged by an opponent calling for even sharper departures from established policies. Richard Nixon, long known as an opponent of communism and government regulation of the economy, had traveled to Peking and Moscow in pursuit of

---

[8] In view of the attention paid to Vietnam in 1968, it is noteworthy that international attitudes were *not* significantly related to vote. One reason for this is that Nixon and Humphrey were perceived to be taking very similar stands, and their policies gave the voters little choice (Page and Brody, 1972). But if the analysis is restricted to those who were making up their minds late in the campaign, or if the dependent variable is shifted from vote choice to political activity, then attitudes on Vietnam become significant.

his hope for a "Generation of Peace," and wage and price controls were in place in an attempt to deal with an intractable inflation. George McGovern was calling for a reduction of American involvement overseas, especially in Vietnam, and another quantum increase in the level of domestic spending and social benefit programs. This confrontation produced a high level of comments on issues, particularly in the three policy areas concerned: international involvement, economic management, and social benefits. If one adds civil liberties, on which there was also substantial disagreement between the candidates and which was a little more salient than usual, there were as many comments in these four policy areas as there were in all the candidate and party categories put together.

Economics might well have been salient because of unarrested inflation even if the candidates had ignored it. Senator McGovern did not. He spoke more about economics than any other policy area, calling for more spending and portraying himself as being on the side of the average person in contrast to the powerful elite interests that had the ear of Richard Nixon. President Nixon took a conservative posture, campaigning against big spenders in the Democratic Congress. The consequence of all this was that economic management was 10 percent more favorable to the Democrats than it usually was.

Both candidates also devoted a good deal of attention to international questions. Richard Nixon constantly referred to his international travels; the SALT treaty was signed in White House ceremonies during October; the "peace is at hand" announcement came shortly before the election. George McGovern stressed his public plan for peace in Vietnam. The result was that international involvement was more salient than in any other election, and had its normal (pro-Republican) partisan valence.

The most decided shift away from normal partisan valence was in social benefits. Senator McGovern had announced his intention to increase school funding, expand social security, provide public service jobs, and give a person unable to work approximately $1,000 a month in cash and food stamps. Mr. Nixon contrasted a work ethic built on self-reliance with a welfare that he claimed destroyed character. As you can see by comparing Figures 8–3 and 8–6, attitudes on social benefits shifted 22 percent away from normal, and actually produced a slight Republican advantage.

The most prominent civil liberties question in 1972 concerned the use of busing to achieve school integration. Senator McGovern said that he had fought all his political life for integration and would not change regardless of political cost. Nixon opposed busing on the ground that parents wanted better educations for their children, and that meant neighborhood schools. In this policy area, too, there was a marked shift in partisan valence, producing another Republican advantage. At the same time, an equal shift was taking place with respect to general attitudes. These were a little less salient than usual, but also favored the GOP.

FIGURE 8–6
Specific Attitudes and 1972 Vote

Category	Salience percent total	Partisan valence percent pro-D	Importance MLE*
Candidates			
General	10.9	32.4	.75
Record-incumbency	2.7	5.5	.58
Experience	1.9	22.0	—
Management	4.5	22.1	.28
Intelligence	2.0	11.1	.37
Trust	6.9	60.6	.85
Personality	4.6	20.2	.62
Parties			
People in party	2.9	39.0	—
Party affect	7.1	47.2	—
Issues			
General	12.3	36.2	.94
International involvement	15.2	32.8	.61
Economic management	18.4	75.0	.80
Social benefits	6.2	47.7	.35
Civil liberties	4.2	38.8	.44
National resources	.1	—	—
Agriculture	.3	66.7	—

86% of cases predicted correctly

— denotes insignificant figure

Explanation of figure: *Salience* is measured by the proportion of the total comments dealing with the attitude object. It is indicated by the total length of the bar. The longer the bar, the more salient the category. *Partisan valence* is measured by the proportion of comments favorable to the Democrats. The farther the bar is to the left, the more favorable to the Democrats. The farther to the right, the more favorable to the Republicans. *Importance,* the relation of the attitude category to vote choice, is measured by a standardized maximum likelihood estimate. (See box on p. 199.) This is indicated in the figure by shade. If a bar is black, the attitude category is very important. If a bar is dark gray, the attitude category is important. If a bar is light gray, the attitude category is somewhat important. If a bar is hollow, the attitude category is not significantly related to vote choice.

Data source: 1972 CPS Election Study.

Candidate attitudes were less salient than usual with two exceptions. One was management that reflected a public belief that Richard Nixon was better able to cope with the presidency than George McGovern. The other was trust—and while all the other candidate attitudes favored Richard Nixon by rather substantial margins, the voters trusted George McGovern. All the time that the senator spent reminding the electorate that the "men who . . . have passed out special favors, who have ordered political sabotage . . . work for Mr. Nixon" yielded a substantial partisan advantage.[9]

[9] That Johnson was distrusted in 1964 and Nixon was distrusted in 1972 were probably important preludes to the later public reactions to Vietnam and Watergate.

Choice   Senator McGovern was twice as well off in the attitude-vote relationship as Senator Goldwater had been eight years earlier. Whereas the Arizona senator had only the single attitude of trust, which was only somewhat important, the South Dakota senator enjoyed a partisan advantage on two attitudes, economic management and trust, both of which were important in the voting decisions of 1972. The trouble with that, of course, was that being twice as well off as Senator Goldwater still spelled political defeat.

All the other attitudes predisposed voters to support the incumbent president. General attitudes on issues, general attitudes about the candidates, attitudes about the candidates personalities, Nixon's record in office, and international involvement were all important, and all had Republican valence. Attitudes about the candidates' intelligence, management capacity, social benefits, and civil liberties were all somewhat important, and all of these also favored Richard Nixon. President Nixon's 60.7 percent of the vote did not quite match President Johnson's percentage in 1964, but fortune allowed both of these veteran politicians to achieve substantial victories in their reelection campaigns.

AN OUTSIDER BARELY WINS, 1976

Reaction   A principal assumption of the Carter strategy was that 1976 would be a year in which candidates were more important than issues. "There aren't many people, including me, who really understand all the issues," claimed campaign manager Hamilton Jordan. "They're so damned complex, the average fellow out there is looking beyond them to what sort of person the candidate is" (Wooten, 1976). The reaction to the campaign strategies that can be seen by comparing Figures 8–3 and 8–7 shows that the assumption was only partly correct. There were some candidate attributes that were unusually salient in 1976. But the reaction also shows that Carter's quick rise to prominence would have been followed by an even speedier fall if it had not been for economic issues.

The data in Figure 8–7 suggest that the Ford strategy was much more successful. There were three candidate attributes that were unusually salient—management capacity, record in office, and trust—and there were Ford advantages in all of these areas. Recall that Gerald Ford spent most of September in the Rose Garden looking presidential, that Jimmy Carter responded with a personal attack on Ford, that Ford commercials at the end of the campaign had featured Georgians questioning the quality of Carter's gubernatorial record, and that other commercials praised Ford's quiet style of leadership. It is therefore significant that there was a decided Republican advantage in management, a reasonably strong edge for Ford in trust, and at least a slight advantage when record in office was mentioned. (Nearly a quarter of all comments about Ford's record

FIGURE 8–7
Specific Attitudes and 1976 Vote

Category		Salience percent total	Partisan valence percent pro-D	Importance MLE*
Candidates				
General		13.1	49.8	.68
Record-incumbency		5.7	48.1	.73
Experience		4.7	28.9	.44
Management		6.7	29.6	.64
Intelligence		2.0	48.4	.27
Trust		8.3	40.8	.80
Personality		7.6	48.0	.47
Parties				
People in party		3.8	69.6	.25
Party affect		4.7	56.0	.39
Issues				
General		12.8	50.3	.48
International involvement		5.0	38.4	.31
Economic management		17.2	74.9	1.10
Social benefits		4.4	69.1	.23
Civil liberties		2.8	45.3	.28
National resources		.5	83.5	—
Agriculture		.5	81.4	.25

85% of cases predicted correctly

— denotes insignificant figure

Explanation of figure: *Salience* is measured by the proportion of the total comments dealing with the attitude object. It is indicated by the total length of the bar. The longer the bar, the more salient the category. *Partisan valence* is measured by the proportion of comments favorable to the Democrats. The farther the bar is to the left, the more favorable to the Democrats. The farther to the right, the more favorable to the Republicans. *Importance*, the relation of the attitude category to vote choice, is measured by a standardized maximum likelihood estimate. (See box on p. 199.) This is indicated in the figure by shade. If a bar is black, the attitude category is very important. If a bar is dark gray, the attitude category is important. If a bar is light gray, the attitude category is somewhat important. If a bar is hollow, the attitude category is not significantly related to vote choice.

Data source: 1976 CPS Election Study.

concerned his pardon of former President Nixon, and these were quite unfavorable. Since he still had a slight advantage in all comments, this means that the voters had quite favorable perceptions of Ford's actions, with the important exception of the Nixon pardon.) Since the campaign lasted only two months, while Gerald Ford had been in the White House for nearly two years, it is likely that the campaign effect was primarily one of reinforcement, but it should not be regarded as less successful for that reason.[10]

---

[10] 1976 was the only year in which *all* of the candidate attitudes favored one of the contenders.

The issue attitudes were clearly dominated by economic concerns. In common with most Democratic candidates, Governor Carter pledged to continue a number of expensive programs, although he did admit the possibility of a tax cut in the last week of the campaign. In common with most Republican candidates, President Ford was critical of government spending. He made a tax cut a central feature of his campaign. But more important than the stands being taken by either candidate, the nation had just passed through the most serious recession since the 1930s. Evaluations of President Ford were very much affected by whether the respondent had suffered any personal hardship because of the recession, and by the respondent's evaluation of government economic performance (Miller and Miller, 1977). The voter reaction to all this was that the economic management was even more salient than usual, and even more pro-Democratic than usual.

All the attention paid to Gerald Ford's misstatement about Poland in the second presidential debate may have hurt him a bit. The partisan valence in international involvement was not quite as Republican as usual. It is more likely, though, that Ford was handicapped by the relative international tranquility. Even though Ford's edge was less than that enjoyed by Eisenhower or Nixon, there was a Republican advantage in this policy area. But with no visible international threat in 1976, international involvement was much less salient.[11]

Choice   The reasons for presidential votes were spread in 1976 as never before. Virtually every attitude category was significantly related to presidential choice. Only natural resources missed, and that by the barest of margins.[12] With so many attitudes involved, one cannot say that any single attitude provided the key to the election. What can be said is that economic management was the only very important attitude category, and the lopsided Democratic margin in this policy area probably sustained Jimmy Carter in the face of a well-executed Republican strategy.

There were 4 important attitudes. All these dealt with the candidates —trust, record in office, management capacity, and general attitudes— and by varying margins, all favored Gerald Ford. The remaining 10 attitudes were only somewhat important, and they were split 5 to 5. Ford was helped by views on personality, experience, and intelligence, and by the issue areas of international involvement and civil liberties.

---

[11] Also noteworthy was that after all the environmental activity of the late '60s and early '70s, an OPEC oil embargo (which had car owners lining up at gas stations in 1973–74), and major congressional attention to rival energy plans, comments about natural resources reached a "peak" of one half of 1 percent of all comments in 1976. It will be worth watching to see if this policy area remains as remote from public view in the face of environmental and energy problems in the 1980s.

[12] To be considered statistically significant, a maximum likelihood estimate must be twice its standard error. The MLE for natural resources was 1.98 times its standard error.

Carter was aided by both party categories, general issue attitudes, social benefits, and agriculture.

The dominant impression is that Carter was elected because of economic circumstances, and in spite of his being less favorably perceived as a person. If so, this might also explain the collapse of his popularity during his first term. No other president had been elected without some characteristics that were favorably perceived by the electorate. When the Carter administration was unable to cope with inflation, the major problem in the policy area responsible for his election, there was nothing else to sustain the president's reputation.

Summary

By asking how the citizen's political knowledge was organized into attitudes, we have been able to see the relation between what was known and the citizen's choice of presidential candidates. As between the broad categories of candidates, parties, and issues, issues and candidates are much more important. Issues have typically helped the Democrats and candidates have helped the Republicans. Attitudes about parties have not been as consequential and seem to have become even less so during the 1970s.

By decomposing the 3 broad categories into 16 specific attitudinal categories, we could see more, but we lost our easy generalizations about issues and candidates helping one party or the other. Many citizens are able to discriminate among various facets of politics. For example, even in the face of the victorious campaigns that led to the Johnson and Nixon landslides of 1964 and 1972, voters continued to distrust these presidents while regarding them as qualified in all other respects. A consequence of this ability to discriminate is that it is rare for all the candidate or issue attitudes to be on one side or the other. Only in 1964 were all the issue attitudes on the Democratic side, and only in 1976 were all the candidate attitudes on the Republican side.

The salience of all candidate attitudes has fluctuated between 34 and 48 percent (of the total), and the salience of all issue attitudes has fluctuated between 43 and 57 percent.[13] Since the attention devoted to both seems to be bounded, it follows that in both cases the number of general (usually vague) comments goes down when citizens have specific things to say, and up when they do not.

---

[13] All of these statements about normal ranges and departures from the mean need to be treated with a good deal of caution. Remember that these average figures rest on only seven data points, and that the seven data points are spread over a quarter of a century. We have a baseline against which comparisons can be made, but an exceedingly fragile one. The same caveat applies to the interpretation of *reaction* as departures from the mean.

The principal covariation has been between general issue attitudes and attitudes about economics. When economic management was salient, as it was during the '50s and again during the '70s, there are fewer general comments. During the more prosperous '60s, there were more general comments. It is as though economics reaches enough lives so that, in times of adversity, those suffering from inflation or unemployment have something concrete to talk about. During better times, at least some of these people retreat to much more diffuse impressions. The partisan valence of economic attitudes has also varied over a 20-point range. Fifty-six percent of the comments were pro-Democratic in 1960 and 55 percent in 1968, as against 74 percent in 1956, 75 percent in 1972, and 75 percent in 1976. In four out of five cases, this variation (from the 65 percent mean) went against an administration that did not seem to be coping well with economic problems.

In contrast, the salience of the other major policy area, international involvement, has been rather stable. It was more salient in 1972 and less so in 1976, but otherwise didn't budge from 8 or 9 percent. The proportion of citizens interested in foreign affairs appears to be relatively constant.

Among candidate attitudes, the only noteworthy variation in salience was found in trust. It was salient in 1952, then dropped until 1960, then became more visible from 1964 through 1976. Trust disappeared from the forefront of our national consciousness during the Eisenhower years, then returned as a problem demanding attention during the Johnson and Nixon years. Management capacity has also become a little more visible during the 1970s, but with only two elections it's hard to say if this represents increased concern with what a president can do once he is elected or is just an accidental shift.

While we can be quite certain which attitudes were related to vote choice in any given election, it's very difficult to make any general statements about importance over time. Indeed, only three attitude categories—general attitudes about candidates, general attitudes about issues, and economic management—have been significantly related to vote choice in each of the seven elections, and only one attitude category—natural resources—has not been significantly related to vote in at least one election. There does appear to be a modest relation between the number of important categories and an incumbent president running for reelection. There was an average of 12 attitudes significantly related to vote when a president was trying for another term, and an average of 9 when this was not the case. This supports the view that when citizens have the opportunity to acquire further information, as by watching what a president does during his term in office, they will be able to make use of that knowledge.

As is usually the case, there are further questions that grow out of these findings. If citizens can discriminate between different facets of politics so that some attitudes favor Republicans and other attitudes favor Democrats, how do they resolve the attitude conflicts that result? And if attitudes can be related to vote choice in a given election, but may not be important in the following election, what does this imply about the stability of attitudes from one election to the next? These are among the questions we shall explore in the following chapter.

chapter 9

℘ Party Identification

Another series of questions put to thousands of respondents by interviewers from the Center for Political Studies begins: "Generally speaking, do you usually think of yourself as a Republican, a Democrat, an independent, or what?" If the respondent says "Republican," the next question is: "Would you call yourself a strong Republican or a not very strong Republican?" If the respondent says "Democrat," the same follow-up question is asked with respect to the Democratic party. If the answer to the first question is "independent," then the respondent is asked: "Do you think of yourself as closer to the Republican or Democratic party?"

Party identification, the concept measured by these questions, is thought of as having a *strength component* and a *direction component*. Each individual is categorized on the strength component according to the answers to the follow-up questions. If the respondent says "strong" to the partisan follow-up question, then he or she is treated as a Strong Partisan. If the answer is "not very strong," then the respondent is called a Weak Partisan. If the answer to the independent follow-up question is that the respondent is closer to one party or the other, he or she is regarded as an Independent Partisan or Leaner. Only if the respondent twice asserts her or his independence is the respondent called an Independent. The direction component is simply Republican versus Democrat. When the strength component and the direction component are combined, the result is a seven-magnitude scale: Strong Democrat, Weak Democrat, Independent Democrat, Independent, Independent Republican, Weak Republican, Strong Republican. An eighth category, Apolitical, is often added, not as a magnitude that belongs at any point on the party identification scale, but as a category to include those few persons who are unable to answer the questions.

The basic idea here is that each individual has an attachment to, or repulsion from, a political party. Persons attracted to the Republican party are not supposed to be attracted to the Democratic party, and vice versa. As the formal statement in *The American Voter* put it, party identification is "the individual's affective orientation to an important group-object in the environment. . . . the political party serves as the group toward which the individual may develop an identification, positive or negative, of some degree or intensity" (Campbell, Converse, Miller and Stokes, 1960, pp. 121–22). Party identification is the individual's standing decision to support one party or the other.

It is important to note that the party identification questions invoke two types of attitude objects. The first is the self in the part of the question that asks "Do you think of yourself . . .?" The second set of attitude objects is comprised of Republicans, Democrats, and independents in the subsequent phrases of the questions. What this implies is that the respondent is in fact being asked: What is your self-perception? What are your perceptions of Republicans and Democrats and independents? And given your self-perception and your perceptions of each of these political groups, how do you relate to them? Since an individual's self-image is likely to be both relatively stable and relatively central in the individual's cognitive structure, and since an individual will be receiving a constant stream of cues about Republicans, Democrats, and independents, this more complex form of the question has important implications for the measurement of party identification. This is a point to which we shall want to return.

AGGREGATE STABILITY OF PARTY IDENTIFICATION

Until 1964, the distribution of party identification was remarkably stable. As you can see from the data in Table 9–1, the proportion of Democrats varied between 44 percent and 47 percent, and the proportion of Republicans varied between 27 percent and 29 percent. This much variation can be accounted for by sampling error alone. The Democrats' advantage of roughly 7-to-4 seemed relatively fixed.

A similar point could be made about the strength component alone. The proportions of Strong Partisans (disregarding whether they were Democrats or Republicans) were 35 percent, 36 percent, and 35 percent in 1952, 1956, and 1960 respectively. Then the proportion of Strong Republicans dropped in 1964, and the proportion of Strong Democrats declined soon thereafter. Moreover, the loss of Strong Partisans by both

TABLE 9–1
Distribution of Party Identification by Year

Category	1952	1956	1960	1964	1968	1972	1976	1978
Strong Democrat	22%	21%	21%	26%	20%	15%	15%	15%
Weak Democrat	25	23	25	25	25	25	25	24
Independent Democrat	10	7	8	9	10	11	12	14
Independent	5	9	8	8	11	13	14	14
Independent Republican	7	8	7	6	9	11	10	· 10
Weak Republican	14	14	13	13	14	13	14	13
Strong Republican	13	15	14	11	10	10	9	8
Apolitical	4	3	4	2	1	2	1	3

Data source: 1952 through 1978 SRC/CPS Election Studies.

parties continued so that by 1978 (the most recent data available at this writing) the proportion of Strong Partisans had dropped from 35 percent to 23 percent.

Another way of looking at the same change is the increase in the number of Independents. If one looks only at the true Independents (those in the middle category), the proportion of citizens not identifying with either party rises from 5 percent in 1952 to 14 percent in 1978. If the Leaners are included along with the Independents, then the increase is from 22 percent of the electorate in 1952 to 38 percent in the late 1970s. Either way, the greater number of Independents and the smaller number of Strong Partisans open the possibility of much wider swings from one election to the next.

A good deal has been written about how the smaller number of persons identifying with the parties spells party weakness, if not the demise of the party system itself. Consequently it is worth paying some attention to evidence of stability in Table 9–1. For one thing, while there are fewer Strong Partisans than once was the case, nothing has happened to the Democrats' advantage over the Republicans. This has varied a bit from one election to the next. Republicans were best off in 1956, and Democrats were in 1964. But if one calculates a ratio of all Strong Democrats, Weak Democrats, and Independent Democrats to all Strong Republicans, Weak Republicans, and Independent Republicans, the figures are 1.67, 1.37, 1.58, 2.0, 1.61, 1.50, and 1.57 for the presidential election years from 1952 through 1976. The ratios for 1956 (1.37) and 1964 (2.0) are visible in this series, but otherwise the balance between the parties has been remarkably stable.

It is also the case that most of the change in the distribution of party identification took place between 1962 and 1972. There was very little change during the first decade in which party identification was measured, and as already noted, this was followed by a rapid erosion in the proportion of Strong Partisans. The 1972–78 data, however, seem to be nearly as stable as were the 1952–62 data. There is no way of knowing how long this will last, but for at least half a dozen years, the rate of change abated.

ASSOCIATION BETWEEN PARTY IDENTIFICATION AND PRESIDENTIAL CHOICE

Another striking fact about party identification has been the strong association between that attitude and presidential choice. The authors of *The Voter Decides* and *The American Voter* were very careful not to say that party identification caused citizens to vote one way or the other; there were other attitudes involved. (The authors of introductory textbooks were not always as meticulous about this point.) It was clear, however, that there was a very strong bivariate correlation between party identification and vote choice. If one could know only one thing about each voter, and had to predict the voter's presidential choice on the basis of this fact, party identification would be the best information to have.

Table 9–2 presents the bivariate associations between party identification and vote choice for each presidential election. Several things are evident from these data. For example, except for 1964, Strong Republicans have been more likely to support their candidate than Strong Democrats. The dominant finding, though, is the close association between party identification and presidential vote. The relationship was a little weaker in 1964, when a fair number of Republicans voted for Lyndon Johnson, and in 1972, when a larger number of Democrats voted for Richard Nixon. But a "weaker" association between party identification and presidential choice means that Kendall's Tau–c correlation drops to "only" .62 in 1964 and .54 in 1972. Even including these figures, the series of correlations is .72, .75, .77, .62, .77, .54, and .70 for the presidential elections from 1952 through 1976. The association has been quite strong and remarkably stable in view of the variety of candidates and circumstances that have characterized these elections.

Some Questions about Party Identification

Satisfying as these data are in demonstrating the importance of party identification, they also raise some questions. As you run your eye across the percentages in the party identification categories and compare them to the row totals, you can see the patterns of vote by identification category that lead to the very high measures of association. But notice the votes cast by the Weak Partisans. In 1956, 1960, 1964, 1972, and 1976, more Weak Democrats defected to the Republican candidate than Independent Democrats. And in 1960, 1964, 1968, and 1976, more Weak

TABLE 9–2

Association between Party Identification and Presidential Choice

				Party Identification				
Candidate	Strong Democrat	Weak Democrat	Independent Democrat	Independent	Independent Republican	Weak Republican	Strong Republican	Total
1952								
Stevenson ..	84%	62%	61%	20%	7%	7%	2%	42%
Eisenhower .	16	38	39	80	93	93	98	58
Tau–c = .72								
1956								
Stevenson ..	85	63	67	17	7	7	1	40
Eisenhower .	15	37	33	83	93	93	99	60
Tau–c = .75								
1960								
Kennedy ...	89	72	89	47	13	18	1	50
Nixon	11	28	11	53	87	82	99	50
Tau–c = .77								
1964								
Johnson ...	95	82	90	77	25	43	10	68
Goldwater..	5	18	10	23	75	57	90	32
Tau–c = .62								
1968								
Humphrey..	92	68	64	30	5	11	3	46
Nixon	8	32	36	70	95	89	97	54
Tau–c = .77								
1972								
McGovern..	73	49	61	30	13	9	3	36
Nixon	27	51	39	70	87	91	97	64
Tau–c = .54								
1976								
Carter	92	75	76	43	14	22	3	51
Ford	8	25	24	57	86	78	97	49
Tau–c = .70								

Data source: 1952 through 1976 SRC/CPS Election Studies.

Republicans defected than Independent Republicans. Remember that the Weak Partisans identify with a party rather than independents when answering the first party identification question. What is going on here? In particular, *what are the party identification questions measuring* that would account for this behavior?

A second paradox arises out of the strong bivariate correlations between party identification and vote. It is nice to know that the correlation has dropped below .7 only twice, and even then has shown a very strong relationship between attitude and vote. Standing alone, this doesn't raise any question. But remember what we learned about party attitudes in Chapter 8. The data in Figure 8–2 (and elsewhere) showed that attitudes about parties were steadily declining in their importance in the vote decision. How can party identification be of continuing importance while attitudes about parties are becoming less consequential? Specifically, *how does party identification interact with other attitudes in vote choice,* and how can this interaction explain this paradox?

Third, we saw in Table 9–1 that during the 1950s, and again during the 1970s, the aggregate distribution of party identification was rather stable. Aggregate stability, however, may result *either* from individual level stability *or* from an equilibrium condition. Let's assume that there is a population of 500 made up of 300 Democrats and 200 Republicans. If no Democrats switch to the Republican party, and if no Republicans switch to the Democratic party, the party balance in the population remains 300 Democrats and 200 Republicans. Here aggregate level stability results from individual level stability. Alternatively, if 25 Democrats switch to the Republican party, and if 25 Republicans switch to the Democratic party, the party balance still remains the same. In this case, aggregate level stability results from an equilibrium condition in which movements in opposite directions cancel each other out.

Now let's say that over a given time period, 35 Republicans switch to the Democratic party and only 25 Democrats switch to the Republican party. There is a considerable difference in the rate of change among those switching parties: 58 percent moving in a Democratic direction and only 42 percent moving in a Republican direction. This would result in a population of 310 Democrats and 190 Republicans. In terms of overall balance between the parties, there would be only a 2 percent shift. The nature of equilibrium processes is such that it takes a very great difference in the rate of change at the individual level before you notice much change at the aggregate level. Consequently, aggregate level stability (especially when it is as approximate as that in Table 9–1) tells you very little about individual level stability. To say anything more, we must ask: *How stable is party identification at the individual level?*

We shall address these three questions—What is party identification measuring? How does party identification interact with other attitudes in vote choice? How stable is party identification at the individual level?—in the balance of this chapter.

THE TWO DIMENSIONS OF PARTY IDENTIFICATION

When the concept of party identification was first introduced in 1954, the emphasis was placed on the idea of psychological attachment to a party. The idea that groups exercised influence over their members was familiar enough to social psychologists, but at that time most political scientists thought of belonging to a political party either in terms of voting for that party or as being registered as a Republican or a Democrat.

Consequently, the originators of the concept, Angus Campbell, Gerald Gurin, and Warren Miller, went out of their way to point to parties as groups that were sources of influence.

> The sense of personal attachment which the individual feels toward the group of his choice is referred to . . . as identification, and, with respect to parties as groups, as *party identification*. Strong identification is equated with high significance of the group as an influential standard. . . . [It is assumed] that most Americans identify themselves with one or the other of the two major political parties, and that this sense of attachment and belonging is predictably associated with their political behavior. (Campbell, Gurin, and Miller, 1954, pp. 88–89, 111)

This theory (which was no more developed than the quote would suggest) was accompanied by empirical material showing that most Americans did identify with a party, and that citizens' party identification was associated with their political behavior.

While the concept of party identification led to some elegant theories in other areas, the question of how members of specific party identification categories should be expected to behave was treated largely as an empirical question. The original investigators were well aware, for example, that Weak Partisans were sometimes more likely to defect than Independent Partisans; they published data showing this; this made their data available so other scholars could conduct independent investigations; but they did not offer any explanations of why this should or should not occur. By the 1970s, though, with literally hundreds of scholars sifting through the party identification data, a number of persons became uncomfortable with the accumulating findings, and a lively exchange took place in the literature (Petrocik, 1974; Brody, 1977; Wolfinger and others, 1977; Miller and Miller, 1977; Fiorina, 1977; Shively, 1977, 1979; Van Wingen and Valentine, 1978; Weisberg, 1979). The principal questions concerning the categories of party identification were: Why do Weak Partisans sometimes defect at rates greater than Independent Partisans? What does being an Independent mean? Are the Independent Partisans more like the Weak Partisans or the Independents?

The most interesting suggestion made in this exchange was the possibility that party identification had two dimensions rather than a single dimension. The traditional seven-category scale implied that Independent was a neutral category halfway between Strong Republican and Strong Democrat. But if party identification was conceptualized as having two dimensions instead of just one, then one dimension could reflect the respondent's attitude toward parties, and the other dimension could reflect the respondent's attitude toward independents (Van Wingen and Valentine, 1978; Weisberg, 1979). Furthermore, these two attitudes—one about parties, the other about independents—might not be related to one another. If the two dimensions are not related, then several combinations are possible. In one combination, respondents might have positive attitudes toward one party and negative attitudes about independents. In another combination, respondents might have positive views toward both a party *and* independents. In still another combination, respondents might not think much of independents, but might think that *both* parties were doing a good job.

This multidimensional view of party identification is consistent with the way in which the party identification question has always been asked. Remember that the basic question is: "Generally speaking, do you usually think of yourself as a Republican, a Democrat, an independent, or what?" This invokes the respondent's self-image and perceptions of Republicans, Democrats, and independents. The traditional conception was that *one* of the political groups would serve as a reference group (that is, a positively valued group that was a source of cues); but if you admit the possibility of multiple reference groups, or the possibility that none of the political groups was evaluated positively, then how the respondent sees herself or himself with respect to Republicans, Democrats, and independents becomes a much more complex matter.

Some very strong evidence supporting the two-dimensional interpretation emerged from a 1979 pilot study designed to lay plans for the 1980 Election Study. (The evidence has to be regarded as preliminary since there were only 280 respondents rather than a full national sample.) This pilot study asked about party identification in several different ways, and an analysis of the answers showed clearly that two dimensions were involved. One dimension concerned positive and negative views about parties; the other positive and negative views about political independence.

Two of the questions in the study asked separately about support for parties and independence. The party item asked: "Do you think of yourself as a supporter of one of the political parties or not?" The independence item asked, "Do you ever think of yourself as a political independent or not?"[1] Table 9–3A shows a cross-tabulation of the answers to these questions. If the traditional interpretation that being an Independent is the opposite of being a Strong Partisan is correct, then all the cases ought to be either in the upper right-hand cell (as party supporters who are not independents) or the lower left-hand cell (as independents who are not party supporters). The data suggest that this traditional interpretation applies to a majority of the respondents, but the others are split between those who relate to both a political party *and* independence, and those who do not relate to either a political party *or* independence. Clearly, partisanship and independence are not mutually exclusive.

---

[1] The interpretation of two dimensions rests on much more than this pair of questions. Among other things, Professor Weisberg found two dimensions (one pro-party versus antiparty, the other proindependence versus antiindependence) in a factor analysis of 19 different items.

TABLE 9–3
The Two Dimensions of Party Identification

A. Party Support by Independence

Party Supporter?	Ever Independent?	
	Yes	*No*
Yes	19.2%*	24.4%
No	36.2	20.1

B. What Is Traditional Identification Question Measuring?

Party Supporter or Independent	Traditional Strength Component				
	Strong Partisan	*Weak Partisan*	*Inde-pendent Partisan*	*Inde-pendent*	*Total*
Party supporter .... (upper right-hand cell)	59.3%†	25.0%	3.6%	2.7%	25.1%
Supports party and independent .... (upper left-hand cell)	28.8	19.7	21.8	2.7	19.8
Neither .... (lower right-hand cell)	8.5	26.3	12.7	29.7	18.9
Only independent .... (lower left-hand cell)	3.4	28.9	61.8	64.9	36.1
Tau–b = .52					

* The cell entries are percentages of the total.
† The cell entries are column percentages.
Source: Data presented by Herbert F. Weisberg at 1979 Annual Meeting of the American Political Science Association at a Roundtable on Theory and Measurement in the CPS Election Surveys. The 1979 Pilot to the 1980 Survey.

Now if there are two dimensions, what is the traditional party identification series measuring? Data to answer this question are shown in Table 9–3B, where the traditional strength component is cross-tabulated against the four categories from Table 9–3A. Most of the Strong Partisans are, in fact, party supporters, although there is a sizable number of Strong Partisans who also think of themselves as independents. The Weak Partisan category is a mishmash; it contains a little bit of everything. The jumble of types who are categorized as Weak Partisans undoubtedly accounts for their less predictable behavior. The Independent Partisans and Independents are more similar to each other than either is to the Weak Partisans. Majorities of both categories do think of themselves as independents. They can be distinguished because a sizable number of Independent Partisans respond to both partisan and independent cues, while a sizable number of Independents are responding to neither.

The other thing that should be noted from Table 9–3B is the strong association between the traditional party identification categories and the two-dimensional classification. The strong correlation means that the one-dimensional classification is picking up a lot, but not all, of the information contained in the two dimensions. It also happens that of the several one-dimensional classification schemes tried in the pilot study, the traditional party identification series produced the best scale. Consequently, we can continue to use the traditional classification with the caveat that it is an imperfect reflection of more complex attitudes about partisanship and independence.

INTERACTION BETWEEN PARTY IDENTIFICATION AND OTHER ATTITUDES

THE EXTENT OF COGNITIVE CONSISTENCY

The extent to which citizens' political cognitions are consistent with one another has been a matter of considerable controversy among political scientists. This is not the place to review all the positions taken by various protagonists (for some of the leading arguments, see Lane, 1973; Nie and Andersen, 1974; Converse, 1975; Bennett, 1977; Sullivan, Pierson, and Marcus, 1978; and Bishop, Tuchfarber, and Oldendick, 1978), but one of the problems concerns how cognitive consistency should be measured.

Any measure of cognitive consistency has two aspects. One is the criterion by which consistency is judged. This criterion may be liberalism-conservatism, partisanship, rules of logic that imply a necessary connection between elements, or something else. If the criterion is, let's say, liberalism-conservatism, and all of a person's attitudes are what we have agreed to call "liberal," then we would say that, by this criterion, the person has consistent attitudes. If some of the person's attitudes are "liberal," and some are "conservative," then we would say that the person's attitudes are inconsistent.

It is important to know just what criterion for consistency is being used. Attitudes that are consistent by one criterion may be inconsistent by another criterion. For example, if Republicans take a more liberal position than Democrats on foreign policy, and a more conservative position on economics, then an individual Republican who held the same attitudes would be consistent by a partisan criterion, but inconsistent by a liberal-conservative criterion. The criterion for consistency must be explicit so we know how to judge in each case.

The second aspect of measurement is whether the data concern a population of individuals, or whether there is sufficient information about each individual to know if each person's own attitudes are consistent. This is essentially a level of analysis problem comparable to our movement in this book between the coalition and the individual, except that here the two levels are individual and within-individual. The type of data you have determines what inferences can be properly drawn.

If the data concern a population of individuals, then the proper meaning of consistency is that attitudes are consistent across individuals. For example, if attitudes on civil rights and attitudes on jobs are correlated, then person *A*, who favors government action to protect civil rights, is also likely to favor government action to provide jobs. Person *B*, who opposes government activity in the civil rights area, is also likely to think that persons should find their own jobs without government help. The essential variation here is between *A* and *B* (and other members of the population studied). These data do not demonstrate (although they do not rule out) any necessary relationship between civil rights and jobs in the thinking of either *A* or *B*.

On the other hand, if one can "get inside" each person's cognitive structure, one can make inferences about consistency within the individual. If, for example, one has depth interviews with a person, and the person has explained the relationships she or he sees between civil rights and jobs, then the investigator can assert that the attitudes are consistent to that person. Or if one has survey data that provide some criterion that can be applied to each individual a similar conclusion can be reached. If a person had said that he or she is a conservative, and if the same person gives a conservative answer to questions about civil rights and jobs, then that person's attitudes may be said to be consistent. Since the concept of consistency is that there are links between the elements of an individual's thought, within-individual data are the proper ones to use.

Table 9–4 gives the distributions for two measures of cognitive consistency that have been constructed using partisan criteria and within-individual data. The index of partisan issue consistency is based on proximity measures on issues. To measure proximity, one question asks a respondent where he or she stands on an issue. A second asks what her or his perception is of the candidate's stand on the same issue. With this information, one can determine the distance (proximity) between the respondent's preference and perception of the candidate's position. The index of partisan attitude consistency is based on the same series of questions we used in Chapter 7 to measure information level and in Chapter 8 for the probit model of presidential vote choice. Partisan criteria were used for assessing consistency with both indexes. If respondents were Republicans, they were regarded as consistent if they perceived the Republican candidate's position to be closer to their own when answering the proximity questions, or if they expressed pro-Republican or anti-Democratic attitudes when answering the series of questions quoted at the outset of Chapter 7. If the respondents were Democrats, they were regarded as consistent if they perceived the Democratic candidate's posi-

TABLE 9–4
Distribution of Cognitive Consistency by Two Indexes

Cognitive Consistency Score	Percent of Electorate Falling within Range	
	Partisan Issue Consistency, 1972	Partisan Attitude Consistency, 1972
1.0	16.3%	5.8%
.81–.90	13.4	4.1
.71–.80	13.2	10.7
.61–.70	11.4	17.2
.51–.60	7.3	17.4
.5	15.3	18.3
.40–.49	4.1	12.9
.30–.39	3.4	8.5
.20–.29	8.1	2.8
.10–.19	1.8	0.8
0	5.7	1.5

A higher consistency score indicates more consistent attitudes. For details on the construction of these indexes, see Appendix A–9.1.
Data sources: Partisan Issue Consistency Index; 1972 Hofstetter Survey of General Public.
Partisan Attitude Consistency Index; 1972 CPS Election Study.

tion to be closer to their own when answering the proximity questions, or if they expressed pro-Democratic or anti-Republican views when answering the longer series of questions. Details about the construction of the two indexes may be found in Appendix A–9.1, but the essential point to bear in mind when examining Table 9–4 is that a high score on either index means greater cognitive consistency.

The cognitive consistency indexes show that most people experience a moderate degree of partisan inconsistency.[2] The distributions on the two indexes are not identical (nor would they be expected to be since the two indexes were differently constructed), but they are in agreement on three basic points. First, only a relatively small proportion of the total population has completely consistent attitudes. Second, both of the distributions have bulges at the .5 mark, meaning that there are citizens whose attitudes are equally balanced between the parties.[3] Third, and by far the most important, the largest proportion of respondents (45 percent on the Partisan Issue Consistency Index and 49 percent on the Partisan Attitude Consistency Index) have scores between .6 and .9. This means that the majority of their attitudes favor their own party, but they can see some favorable aspects about the opposing party.

---

[2] See Figure 10–2 for the distributions of the Partisan Attitude Consistency Index for two other years.

[3] This is of interest because all Independents were excluded from these indexes. Hence some Strong Partisans, Weak Partisans, or Leaners must be equally divided in their attitudes.

Think back to the St. Louis immigrant and the woman living in Bellingham, Washington, whose interviews you read at the beginning of Chapter
7. These two respondents were very high and high, respectively, in terms
of their information levels, but reasonably typical as far as partisan consistency was concerned. The St. Louis woman certainly favored the Democrats, but did say that there were some good progressive Republicans. The
Washington housewife leaned toward the Republicans, but liked Democratic plans to check tax loopholes and approved of Jimmy Carter's
Christianity. To understand how such persons make their vote choices,
we need a theory that will explain decisions made in the face of a moderate
amount of inconsistent information.

PARTY IDENTIFICATION AS ARBITER

Attitude conflict is one of the most familiar findings in the voting field.
Paul Lazarsfeld and his colleagues (1944) devised a theory of cross-
pressures to deal with such conflict after analyzing the data gathered in
the first important voting survey. Cross-pressures simply refers to the
extent of forces (the citizen's own attitudes, peer influences, or whatever)
pulling a person in opposite directions in an election situation. The more
cross-pressured a person is, the more likely the person is to delay his or her
voting decision, or try in some similar way to avoid the cross-pressures.
More recently, Peter Sperlich has introduced some qualifications to this
straightforward theory.

> First . . . attitudinal conflicts which are not at least of a certain minimum
> importance to the person are not likely to produce cross-pressure effects.
> Second . . . the more important the attitudinal conflict, the stronger will
> be the behavioral effect. (1971, p. 90)

When he speaks of "importance," Sperlich is referring to centrality (about
which more shortly), but his propositions hold if we understand "importance" to refer to the extent of partisan inconsistency, and the behavioral effect resulting from this inconsistency to be defection to the
opposite party in voting.

Figure 9–1 shows a plot of voting defection by partisan issue consistency. Both of the effects predicted by Sperlich's adaptation of cross-
pressure theory are present. The data points for consistency scores above
.6 are depicted by dots, and the relationship between these consistency
scores and the likelihood of defection by the solid line. Both the dots and
the solid line appear in the lower left part of the figure. The consistency
scores from .6 down to 0 are depicted by x's, and the relationship between these scores and the likelihood of defection by the dashed line. The
x's and the dashed line begin in the lower part slightly to the left of
center and proceed to the upper right part of the figure.

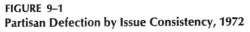

FIGURE 9–1
Partisan Defection by Issue Consistency, 1972

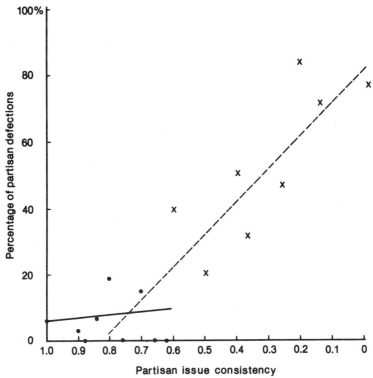

The dots represent defection rates for partisan consistency scores of .6 or higher. The x's represent defection rates for consistency scores of .6 or lower. The regression lines, the lines that represent the prediction one makes about the dependent variable (partisan defection) from knowledge of the independent variable (cognitive consistency) have been calculated by weighting the data points in this figure for the number of cases they represent. For consistency scores higher than .6, represented by the solid line, there is little relation between consistency scores and defection rate; $r = .17$. For consistency scores of .6 or lower, represented by the dashed line, there is a very strong relation; $r = .83$.

Now notice that the solid line is nearly parallel to the bottom of the figure. This means that as one increases inconsistency (that is, as the consistency scores decrease), there is very little effect on the probability of defection. Voters, only two thirds of whose attitudes favor their party, are just as likely to support their party, as voters whose attitudes are completely consistent. In Sperlich's words, "attitudinal conflicts which are not at least of a certain minimum importance to the person are not likely to produce cross-pressure effects." In 1972, the magnitude of inconsistency which was necessary before much defection took place was a score of about .6.

In contrast, the dashed line representing the relation between inconsistency and defection for low consistency scores moves upward and to the right. This means that after one reaches a certain threshold (the .6 score in this instance), the more a voter agrees with the opposition, the greater the likelihood the voter will defect. After the threshold is reached, there is a strong relationship between inconsistency and defection.

This relationship appears to be quite robust. That is, one can vary the strength of party identification, interest in the campaign, concern with the outcome of the election, education, newspaper usage, and national television usage—all variables that affect information level and political activity—and obtain roughly the same relationships. Until one reaches a given threshold, there is little relation between partisan inconsistency and vote defection. After that threshold is reached, there is a strong relationship.[4]

All this implies that party identification interacts with other attitudes to affect presidential vote choice in two ways.[5] First, as we saw in the proportion of high consistency scores in Table 9–4, most of an identifier's perceptions favor his or her party. Second, as we saw in Figure 9–1, party identification appears to act as if it were an arbiter in the presence of the moderate cognitive inconsistency that most people experience. Attitude conflicts tend to be resolved in favor of one's own party.[6] Therefore, most identifiers vote for their own party's candidate.

PARTY IDENTIFICATION AS CENTRAL

Party identification, acting through the more specific attitudes, appears to exercise a strong effect on presidential vote choice. It continues to do so at a time when attitudes about parties seem to be much less consequential. In 1972, the year from which the data for this analysis of cognitive consistency came, party attitudes made up less than 10 percent of the total and were not significantly related to vote choice. How can this paradox of inconsequential party attitudes and very consequential party identification be reconciled?

---

[4] For a demonstration of similar results with 1968 data, see Fogel, 1974.

[5] Party identification has a different effect on votes for other offices. Among other reasons for this, once you shift from the presidency to subpresidential offices, the voters know much less about the candidates and so are less likely to need an arbiter to resolve attitude conflicts. See Hinckley, Hofstetter, and Kessel, 1974, pp. 143–45.

[6] I would see this explanation as compatible with Shively's argument that party identification has a "decisional function," a "function of providing political cues to voters who feel themselves in need of guidance because they must make political decisions under confusing circumstances" (1979). In this case, the confusion results from the moderate inconsistency.

One answer is that party identification is much more likely to be a central attitude. Attitude objects are said to possess centrality when they are of enduring concern to the individual, and such attitudes are more important than others in the individual's cognitive structure. Whatever the degree of a person's interest in politics, the attitude objects in the party identification question are more likely to be of "enduring concern" (and hence central), than other political objects. If the individual was very interested in politics, and regarded more than one of the political groups (that is, Republicans, Democrats, or independents) as reference groups, then the question would focus on both the self and multiple reference groups. This would produce a complex attitude, but certainly a central one. If only one political group was a positive reference group for the person, then the likelihood would be that there would be a strong affective tie between the person and the party with which she or he identified. If the person was relatively unconcerned with politics, at least the self-image would be important, though whether he or she would say she or he thought of himself or herself as a Republican or a Democrat or an independent would be less predictable. Even so, of the person's political attitudes, party identification would be most likely to be central and so exercise some influence over other attitudes.

Questions that simply ask about political parties, on the other hand, do not have any special standing. They tap attitudes about objects that are wholly external to the individual. Even if you assume that political parties are important to a person, it follows that the link between the self and the party (or parties) is going to be more important. Hence party identification, rather than an attitude about some aspect of parties, will occupy a more central position in the person's cognitive structure. The centrality of party identification thus resolves our paradox of the declining importance of party attitudes and the continued importance of party identification. Even if attitudes about parties as such were to disappear entirely, party identification could continue to act as an arbiter in the face of conflicting attitudes about candidates and issues.

INDIVIDUAL LEVEL STABILITY OF PARTY IDENTIFICATION

HOW STABLE IS PARTY IDENTIFICATION?

If party identification is a central attitude, it ought to be a stable attitude. The argument from centrality is that, since other attitudes are arrayed around the central attitude, there are greater psychological costs to changing a central attitude (with consequences for a whole cluster of associated attitudes) than simply altering one of the peripheral attitudes. We have already seen that party identification has been relatively stable on the aggregate level, especially in the 1950s and again in the mid-1970s. Now how stable is party identification on the individual level?

In what has been recognized as a classic analysis, Philip Converse (1964) demonstrated that party identification was more stable on the individual level than other attitudes. Table 9–5 presents data on this same point from 1972 respondents who were reinterviewed in 1976. Three measures of stability are given: Kendall's Tau–*b* correlations for 1972 and 1976, the proportion of respondents who change positions between the two time points, and the mean extent of change along the party identification scale.

TABLE 9–5
Stability of Political Attitudes, 1972–1976

Attitude	Tau–b Correlation	Percent of Respondents Changing Position*	Mean Change*
Party identification	.69	50.2%	−.10
Neo-isolationism	.31		
Foreign aid	.27		
Cut military spending	.36		
Govt. handling of economy	.27		
Tax rate	.26	67.8	.14
Federal power	.28		
Standard of living	.36	67.5	.17
Health insurance	.42	66.2	.15
Civil rights too fast?	.44		
Aid minority groups	.38	67.3	.23
School integration	.41		
Busing	.42	35.4	−.15

* The percent of respondents changing positions and the extent of the mean change is reported only for those attitudes measured on seven category scales, because a respondent is more likely to select a different answer whenever she or he is given more to choose among. The mean percent of persons reporting changes on seven category scales is 60.4; on three category scales, 40.7; on two category scales, 30.4. The seven category scales provide the appropriate comparison for party identification.

Data source: 1972–1976 CPS Panel Study. (No 1974 data were used. This analysis was based on only the two time points.)

Table 9–5 compares the stability of party identification with specific attitudes from four policy areas. From top to bottom, they are international involvement, economic management, social benefits, and civil liberties. The attitudes about civil liberties appear to be the most stable of the policy attitudes, but the correlation for party identification between the two time points is far higher.

Both of the other measures confirm this impression of stability. In all but one case, busing,[7] fewer respondents shifted position on party identi-

---

[7] Busing was a special case. Both the 1972 and 1976 distributions were skewed because of strong opposition to busing. Of the 64.6 percent with stable attitudes on this topic, 90 percent were persons who were strongly opposed to busing in both 1972 and 1976.

fication than did so on other attitudes. The average extent of change on party identification was also less than it was for any of the specific attitudes.

When changes did take place on party identification, two thirds of the changers moved only one category along the party identification scale. The largest number of changers consisted of 1972 Weak Democrats who said they were Strong Democrats in 1976; the second largest number was made up of 1972 Strong Republicans who said they were Weak Republicans in 1976. Given what we know (from Table 9–3B) about the jumbled nature of the Weak Partisan category, this does not represent much of a change.

INFORMATION LEVEL, COGNITIVE CONSISTENCY, AND PARTY IDENTIFICATION

While party identification as a central attitude exercises some influence on the more specific attitudes, the specific attitudes also are able to alter party identification (Jackson, 1975; Fiorina, forthcoming, chap. 5). The specific attitudes can influence the stability of party identification in two ways. First, the specific attitudes provide informational support. The more citizens know about politics, the more likely they are to know why they are Republicans or Democrats. Because of this, their party identifications are better anchored in a bed of related attitudes. Second, the other attitudes support party identification if they are consistent with it. We have already seen that one can tolerate a certain amount of cognitive inconsistency without defecting in voting. It is probable that the same thing applies to the stability of party identification. The specific attitudes change rather easily. As long as only a few of the attitudes in the cluster associated with party identification are inconsistent, this can be tolerated. When a substantial number of other attitudes become inconsistent with one's party identification, though, then the probability of changing party identification becomes much greater.

In Table 9–6, we see what happens to the stability of party identifica-

TABLE 9–6
Stability of Party Identification by Cognitive Properties*

Cognitive Property in 1972	Level			
	Low	Average Minus	Average Plus	High
Information level	.49	.67	.70	.59
Partisan attitude consistency	.56	.60	.73	.63

* Entries are Kendall's Tau–b correlations between party identification in 1972 and 1976 for respondents in the category. The correlation for all respondents was .69.
Data source: 1972–1976 CPS Election Study.

consistency. In general, the data support the argument in the preceding paragraph. When either information level or cognitive consistency is low, then the correlations (.49 and .56, respectively) are lower. This tells us that party identification is less stable when information or partisan consistency is low. As we move into the average minus and the average plus categories, the correlations rise. This tells us that party identification becomes more stable as information increases and as the other attitudes become more consistent. So far, so good. But notice what happens as we move from the average plus category to the high category. The correlations decline, meaning that in the high categories, party identification is less stable. Why should this be so?

The reason why party identification becomes less stable when either information level or cognitive consistency is high is to be found in the lack of association between information level and partisan consistency.[8] The best-informed citizens are likely to have attitudes that are inconsistent with their party identifications. Recall the free-lance photographer from Philadelphia. She was the best informed of the seven respondents, and she could certainly see good points about both the Republicans and the Democrats. Persons who know this much are open to change because of conflicting attitudes. Citizens with the most consistent attitudes, on the other hand, are likely not to know very much. Recall the beer-can worker from Findlay, Ohio. His attitudes were almost completely pro-Republican, but he was not very well informed. Persons of this kind are open to the persuasion of the opposite party—if anyone can get their attention—because they don't have enough information for their attitudes to be very well anchored.

The apparently anomalous results can be reconciled with the general argument about the stabilizing effects of greater information and attitudinal consistency. When examined closely, the expected effects of more information and more consistency can be found. It is just that there are very few people who are both well informed and completely consistent in their attitudes. This fact, however, places an important limit on the stability of party identification.

Summary

In this chapter, we have seen something of the complexity of party identification, its relation to presidential vote choice, and its stability. As to complexity, there is persuasive preliminary evidence that party identi-

---

[8] The relation varies a bit depending on the year and the measure of partisan consistency used. I have plotted information level against partisan attitude consistency for 1952, 1972, and 1976. I have also plotted information level against partisan issue consistency for 1972. In every case, the slope was very close to 0, meaning that information level and partisan consistency were independent of each other.

fication probably reflects two attitudes—one about political parties, one about independence. The traditional measure of party identification picks up some of this complexity, but not quite all of it. As to presidential vote choice, we saw a strong association at the bivariate level, and later examined this in light of the centrality of party identification when it interacts with more specific attitudes. On stability, party identification was relatively stable at the aggregate level during the 1950s and again during the mid-1970s, much more stable at the individual level than other attitudes, and its stability could be increased with enhanced information and greater cognitive consistency.

In this section of the book, we covered the concepts of internal structure, external structure, and time as they applied to citizen activity in presidential elections. Internal cognitive structure was analyzed with respect to information level, and the salience, partisan valence, consistency, and centrality of attitudes. Internal structure was very much dependent on external structure because of the content of the informational environment as affected by media characteristics and campaign strategies, and because of the citizen's involvement with the informational environment. The citizen's activity in the political environment, specifically presidential vote choice, was shown to be highly predictable from the nature of the citizen's attitudes. Temporal effects were shown, both the modest increase in the "average" citizen's information level in the course of a campaign, and in the variation of both specific attitudes and party identification from one campaign to another.

As we saw in earlier sections of the book, campaign strategists are not free to choose just any strategy. They are limited by the internal composition of their supporting coalition and by the external support they are trying to obtain. So, too, citizens are unlikely to respond in just any way. They are limited by the matrix of attitudes that exists at the beginning of the campaign. But, just as we have seen a variety of strategies followed by different coalitions with different goals, the response of the electorate also varies from one election to the next. For if the matrix of attitudes is relatively inflexible in the very short term, it is rather more flexible in the longer term. And the reaction of the electorate in the next election will be determined by a modification of those attitudes as a result of what the administration does in office over the next four years, by the strategy its opposition chooses to challenge it, and by the strategy with which it chooses to defend its record.

part V

CONCLUSION

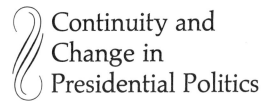

chapter 10

Continuity and Change in Presidential Politics

Introduction

Presidential parties are alive and playing a dynamic role in American politics. After all the material reviewed in the preceding chapters, this might not seem to be a very surprising statement. Yet there are scholars who claim this is not the case. Walter Dean Burnham asserts that "The American electorate is now deep into the most sweeping transformation it has experienced since the Civil War. . . . This critical realignment . . . is cutting across older partisan linkages between the rulers and the ruled. The consequence is an astonishingly rapid dissolution of the political party as an effective intervenor between the voter and the objects of his vote at the polls" (1975, p. 308). Everett Carll Ladd claims that the "series of strange electoral performances [in the 1960s and 1970s] is chiefly the result of the pronounced weakening of American political parties that has taken place in recent decades—a process that by now has brought them to the point of virtual death as organizations" (1978, p. 51). One does not have to look far to find visions of crape; current writings about political parties are filled with "decomposition," "dealignment," "disarray," "decay," and other mournful nouns.

The Eye of the Beholder You might wonder how political scientists could watch events such as national conventions where thousands of delegates and alternates meet to transact business, and then turn to their typewriters to write these obituary notices. This is a complex question, but at least three things seem to be involved. First, there is a matter of gaining attention. If one were to write, "The Democratic party, whose activities can be traced back to the days of Thomas Jefferson, continues to exist," the world would yawn. Second, among those who study political parties, there has long been a group that thinks that parties *ought* to be stronger than they are. "England and France," Woodrow Wilson wrote nearly a century ago, "recognize and support simple, straightforward, in-artificial party government . . . whilst we . . . permit only a less direct government by party majorities . . . The English take their parties straight, —we take ours mixed" (1884, pp. 97–98). Wilson's intellectual heirs continue to champion stronger parties, but their normative preoccupations lead them to lament party weakness rather than undertaking patient studies to determine how much strength parties have. Third, those who do gather data often fasten their gaze on some one aspect—a reduction in the number of strong partisans in the electorate or a change in party rules—and then generalize from those data to "political parties" as a whole. Those who grieve over the imminent disappearance of political parties have something in mind, but the something differs from one observer to another (Ranney, 1978, p. 215).

The Availability of Evidence   Collection of data concerning political parties has been quite uneven. As you could tell from the section on citizen activity, richly detailed surveys of the electorate have been conducted regularly for a considerable time period. We also have good time series data on legislative parties because of the roll call votes recorded for all members of the House and the Senate. In part because of the availability of these data, there has been a good deal more work on voting behavior and legislative politics, and theories of these forms of politics are much better articulated. On the other hand, the 1972 Hofstetter data set is the only national study of electoral activists, and good data about the presidency are very hard to come by. Partly because of the unevenness of data collections, and partly because many scholars specialize in only one or two subjects, it has not been generally understood that one cannot collect data on only one institutional domain and then make generalizations about "political parties."

Table 10–1 presents the most complete simultaneously collected data that are available about Democrats and Republicans in several different institutional domains. We do not have measures on those involved in nomination politics that year; but we do have identical questions that were addressed to citizens, electoral activists, and members of the White House staff, and votes of members of the House of Representatives in the same policy areas.

There is considerable variation as one moves across the several sets of actors. In the case of economic management, the variation goes across the full ideological spectrum from liberal to conservative. In general, citizens take moderate positions while Democratic activists take more

TABLE 10–1
Positions of Various Party Groupings by Policy Area, 1972

Party Grouping	Policy Area			
	International Involvement	Economic Management	Social Benefits	Civil Liberties
Democratic representatives	Moderate	Liberal	Liberal	Moderate
Democratic electoral activists	Moderate liberal	Moderate	Liberal	Liberal
Democratic citizens	Moderate	Moderate	Moderate liberal	Moderate conservative
Republican citizens	Moderate	Moderate	Moderate	Moderate conservative
Republican electoral activists	Moderate	Moderate	Moderate	Moderate conservative
Republican White House staff	Moderate conservative	Moderate conservative	Moderate conservative	Moderate conservative
Republican representatives	Conservative	Conservative	Moderate conservative	Moderate conservative

Data sources: Electoral activists and citizens, 1972 Hofstetter study; White House staff, interviews with Domestic Council staff members; congressional data courtesy of Aage R. Clausen.
For discussion of the scores that determine the positions in the policy areas, see Appendix A–10.1.

liberal positions and Republican activists take more conservative positions. In general, the more involved the activists are with policy questions, the farther out they are along the ideological spectrum. There are a couple of exceptions to the liberal-to-conservative ordering. Representatives tend to take more conservative positions in international involvement, and Democratic electoral activists were more liberal on civil liberties (especially on busing) than representatives who had to run for reelection. Since these data come only from a single year, we ought to be cautious in interpreting this pattern. What is quite clear, however, is that *moving from one institutional setting to another does make a difference.* Most scholars have been careful to recognize that *findings are time specific.* (In other words, one does not assume that the attitudes that were important in 1976 voting decisions are also important in 1980 voting decisions until one has a chance to test this by looking at 1980 data.) What needs to be recognized is that *findings are also institution specific.*

One major message of this book is that one cannot make verifiable statements about political parties as a whole. No one can observe the entire Democratic party or the entire Republican party. What can be observed is a particular coalition in a particular institution or sets of citizens who think of themselves as Democrats or Republicans. Therefore, we cannot describe "the Democratic party" or "the Republican party" except as an abstraction; but we can say what the Carter coalition has been doing at the Democratic National Convention, or what a group of strong Republicans think about Ronald Reagan, and independent observers can inspect the evidence to determine whether or not our assertions are true. It follows that such questions as "Whither political parties?" are inherently unanswerable as long as the question refers to entire political parties. In order to ask about continuity and change, the general question must be decomposed into answerable segments.

Some Answerable Questions   In this chapter, we want to examine evidence on change in the topics that have been covered in this book. What about coalition formation? What about the structure and temporal pattern of nomination politics? What about the structure and temporal pattern of electoral politics? What about the information level and consistency of citizens' perceptions? What about the relation of attitudes to citizens' voting choices? What about the informational environment?

We shall restrict our attention to the time period covered in the book, 1952 to the present. To the extent that evidence is available, we want to ask whether the most recent data show a pattern that is new, or significantly broadened in scope, since 1952. We want to distinguish between election-to-election variations, and those which suggest longer run change. And we want to ask whether any changes that have occurred have tended to weaken or strengthen national political coalitions.

COALITION COMPOSITION

Coalition building, of course, has been going on for a very long time. One can analyze the election of John Quincy Adams in 1824 as a result of the maneuvering of the four protocoalitions supporting Adams, Andrew Jackson, William H. Crawford, and Henry Clay (Riker, 1962, chap. 7). For that matter, coalition building among the English barons preceded the issuance of the Magna Carta, so coalition formation is hardly unique to American politics or a development in recent decades.

Some Differences in Convention Delegates

One change that has taken place concerns the identity of the actors involved in nomination coalitions. Calls for party reform go back a long way (Ranney, 1975); but since 1968 both parties have adopted procedures whose goal was to open nomination politics to hitherto under-represented population categories: women, blacks, and young persons. The McGovern-Fraser Commission adopted quotas for the 1972 Democratic Convention. The Mikulski Commission softened this to an affirmative action program for the 1976 convention, and the Winograd Commission recommended that each state's delegation to the 1980 Democratic Convention be increased by 10 percent and that these seats be filled by party leaders and elected state officials. Republican committees (the DO Committee, the Rule 29 Committee, and the Rules Review Committee) have limited themselves to encouraging state parties to send more female, black, and youthful delegates. These party reforms and recommendations have led to an increase in the proportion of minority delegates, especially female Democrats. Women made up 13 percent of Democratic delegates in 1968, 40 percent in 1972, and 33 percent in 1976 (Ranney, 1978, p. 232).

What has not changed, however, is the tendency for delegates to come from the upper socioeconomic strata. Twenty-six percent of the Democratic delegates and 46 percent of the Republican delegates had incomes over $30,000 in 1972; 64 percent of the Democrats and 72 percent of the Republicans came from professional or managerial backgrounds; 28 percent of the Democrats and 32 percent of the Republicans had postgraduate degrees. "Domination of the presidential elite by a skill-based middle class was even more complete in 1972 than in 1948–1952" (Kirkpatrick, 1976, p. 65).

The views of Democratic delegates in 1972 and 1976 were unrepresentative of citizens who thought of themselves as Democrats (Kirkpatrick, 1976, chap. 10; Ladd, 1978, p. 65). These attitudes, of course, have consequences in the type of platform adopted and the type of candidate nominated by the convention. But differences between activists and citizens are not new. In 1956 and 1964, Republican activists had attitudes that were different from those of Republican citizens (McClosky, Hoffman, and O'Hara, 1960; Jennings, 1966). The only variation here is which party's nomination coalition has views that are more similar to citizens' attitudes.

A Continuing Interest in Issues

What about the activists' interest in issues? We saw in Chapter 2 that members of nomination coalitions had a strong interest in issues, and in Chapter 3 that the same thing was true of electoral activists. But is this new? In the absence of hard evidence, this question cannot be answered with complete certainty. What we do know is that as soon as political scientists began asking activists if they were interested in issues, the answer was yes. This question was not asked directly in the first survey of convention delegates in 1956, but Democratic delegates agreed at levels that "suggested unanimity within the sample" on taxes on small and middle income, slum clearance, social security, and minimum wages, as did Republicans on government regulation of business, business taxes, regulation of trade unions, and minimum wages. Members of both parties' coalitions agreed on issues important to their constituents (McClosky, Hoffman, and O'Hara, 1960, pp. 424–25). There is no evidence that nomination or electoral activists were uninterested in issues at any point during the time period under consideration, and instances of earlier issue-oriented behavior—for example, the positions on civil rights taken by then-Minneapolis Mayor Hubert Humphrey and the Dixiecrats at the 1948 Democratic Convention—can be cited.

As between the two parties' nomination coalitions, there appears to have been one reversal of characteristic attitudes. There had been an historic split in the Republican party between internationalist and isolationist wings. Democrats were consequently more willing to favor military alliances and defense spending in 1956 (McClosky, Hoffman, and O'Hara, p. 415). By the '70s, Republicans were more likely than Democrats to favor reliance on military means when necessary (Kirkpatrick, 1976, pp. 181–85). Otherwise, the parties' relative postures have remained the same.

Costain reports an increase in ideological voting in contests between winning and losing coalitions at Democratic conventions. The "balance of left factional and nonleft factional voting noted in the Humphrey, McGovern, and Carter votes is less likely to indicate the emergence of a new consensus . . . than a continuing struggle between a vital left bloc in the convention and all the other groups in the convention which must join together in order to defeat the left" (Costain, 1978, p. 110). This would be parallel to Republican contests throughout this period, in which all the nonright groups have had to coalesce to defeat a continuingly active right coalition.

Continuing Nationalization

There are some hints that both nomination and electoral coalitions are more national in character. The most conservative groups in earlier Republican coalitions were all southern, with the exception of Ohio (which was simply being loyal to Senator Taft) and Illinois. The most liberal groups in earlier Democratic coalitions were all from the West and Midwest (Munger and Blackhurst, 1965). Now the conservative Republican coalition includes groups from every region except the East, and the liberal Democratic coalition includes groups from every region except the South (Costain, 1978). In Chapter 3, we saw that the attitude groups making up the Republican and Democratic electoral coalitions were drawn from every region. Without earlier comparable data, we must be cautious in interpretation but we do know that earlier authorities, such as Key and Holcombe, placed great stress on sectionalism. Therefore, it would seem that the current compositibn of nomination and electoral coalitions reflects the continuing nationalization of American politics.

In short, coalition-building goes on apace. More women are involved; the majority of actors still come from the skill-based middle class. Because of the activists' interest in issues, the coalitions are formed around groups that take similar issue positions, with the principal ideological thrust coming from conservatives in the Republican party and from liberals in the Democratic party. These coalitions are increasingly nation-wide in scope.

NOMINATION POLITICS

The pattern of first-ballot nominations was well established by the 1950s. There have only been three conventions since 1936[1] that did not have first-ballot nominations. The Republicans picked Wendell Willkie on the sixth ballot in 1940 and Thomas E. Dewey on the third ballot in 1948, and the Democrats nominated Adlai Stevenson on the third ballot in 1952. The typical pattern since 1936, though, has been that of first-ballot ratification of a decision made in preconvention activity.

A Longer Nomination Process

The nomination process lasts a bit longer now than it did in the 1950s. The most important factors contributing to this were the victories of George McGovern in 1972 and Jimmy Carter in 1976. Unlike earlier aspirants who were well known before the primaries (such as Eisenhower, Kennedy, or Goldwater), both McGovern and Carter had been discounted as serious contenders. But both began very early, both captured the nomination, and together they established a pattern of earlier activity that others have followed.

There are other considerations that have worked in the same direction. The Federal Election Campaign Act of 1974 makes it necessary to set up a committee to raise early money in order to qualify for federal matching funds. Party reforms stipulating that more delegates are to be elected at the district (rather than state) level require more organization. And the heavy press coverage of the first glimmerings of strength in the Initial Contests—polls reflecting strength in New Hampshire, surveys of dele-gates likely to attend Iowa caucuses, straw votes in Florida—have placed

---

[1] Until 1936, the Democrats had a rule that a two-thirds majority was necessary for nomination. Woodrow Wilson was nominated on the 46th ballot in 1912, James M. Cox on the 44th ballot in 1920, John W. Davis on the 104th ballot in 1924, and Frank-lin D. Roosevelt on the 6th ballot in 1932. Other factors besides the two-thirds rule were involved in these long contests. The relative strength of urban and rural groups in the Democratic party was changing, and poorer preconvention communication made multiple ballots more valuable as signals of the probable success of various coalitions.

a premium on a good initial showing. This, of course, requires a lot of early effort in the states where the Initial Contests are being held. For all these reasons, the nomination process has been pushed back into the third year of the incumbent's term.

The Consequences of an Increasing Number of Primaries

The proportion of delegates chosen in primaries increased very sharply in the 1970s. In 1952, 39 percent of both Republican and Democratic delegates had been so selected,[2] and the proportion remained fairly stable through 1968. But the Democratic percentage jumped to 65 percent in 1972 and 76 percent in 1976, while the Republican proportion rose to 57 percent in 1972 and 71 percent in 1976 (Arterton, 1978, p. 7). This had some major consequences.

The first clear implication of a high proportion of primaries rather than conventions was to further handicap late entrants. With many delegates chosen before their entrances into the race, their hope of building a winning coalition depended on groups of uncommitted delegates having been picked. An uninstructed delegation is more likely to come from a state convention. Political activists attending a convention are more likely than citizens to think of the strategic advantages of joining a coalition at an opportune moment, while citizens voting in primaries tend to opt for the most attractive candidate in preference to "none of the above."

A second consequence of more primaries is to strengthen aspirants—as long as they are equipped to come into a state and run an effective primary campaign—at the expense of state party leaders. This is not new. In California in 1952, for example, "many Democrats, dissatisfied with [the state party] leadership, rallied behind [Senator Estes] Kefauver, whose slate of delegates soundly trounced the so-called 'uninstructed' slate to the National Convention" that was made up of party officials. Increasing the number of primaries simply increases the number of opportunities for coalition leaders to act independently of state party leaders. In turn, this increases the likelihood that an outsider can capture the party's nomination, but this is not new either. The authors of a comprehensive review of the nomination process from the 1830s through 1956 concluded: "It is in the nature of presidential nominating contests that new men are always under consideration and must sometimes be nominated. The Republican choice in 1940, for example, lay mainly between three men whose fame had not yet matured: Dewey, a defeated first-time candidate for governor; Taft, a junior senator of two years' standing; and Willkie, a

---

[2] Fifty-nine percent of Republican delegates, and 54 percent of Democratic delegates had been elected by primaries in 1916. From that point the popularity of primaries declined until only 36 percent of both parties' delegates were so chosen in 1948.

public utility magnate who had never held public office" (David, Goldman, and Bain, 1956, p. 161). So, presidential aspirants—some of whom are outsiders—gain power at the expense of state and local party leaders. And since one of these aspirants is ultimately elected president, this means that the process tends to produce a president who is less beholden to state and local leaders.

A third concomitant of the growing number of primaries has been the establishment of party rules as clearly superior to state law. The McGovern-Fraser guidelines gave states a choice between conventions that adhered to certain criteria or primaries, and many states opted for primaries. These rules were tested in a case growing out of the seating of a reform delegation from Illinois at the 1972 Democratic National Convention in place of an elected delegation led by Chicago Mayor Richard J. Daley. When the case reached the U.S. Supreme Court, Mr. Justice Brennen held for the Court: "The Convention serves the pervasive national interest in the selection of candidates for national office, and this national interest is greater than any interest of an individual state." This led the leading scholar of party reform to conclude that "the national party organs' power to make rules governing presidential nominating processes is, in both political reality and legal principle, at its highest peak by far since the early 1820s" (Ranney, 1978, p. 230).

Challenging Incumbent Presidents

Yet another change in nomination politics has been the increasing number of challenges to incumbent presidents. Perhaps the most significant were George Wallace's 1964 campaign in the primaries and the 1972 challenges of liberal Republican Representative Pete McClosky of California and conservative Republican Representative John Ashbrook of Ohio. These were significant because Lyndon Johnson was certain to be renominated in 1964 and Richard Nixon was certain to be renominated in 1972, but both these sitting presidents were challenged from within their own parties. Dwight Eisenhower did not face this in 1956. More recently, politically vulnerable presidents—Johnson in 1968, Ford in 1976, Carter in 1980—have faced very serious challenges, and strong presidents may be tested as well. Lively nomination politics is no longer confined to the party out of power.

To sum up, the pattern of modern nomination politics was well established by the beginning of our time period. What we have seen is an expansion of the pattern. There are now more primaries; nomination politics lasts a bit longer; real contests have moved to the in-party. The national parties and the leaders of the nomination coalitions have been strengthened at the expense of state political leaders by the spread of this modern pattern.

ELECTORAL POLITICS

Professionalization of Campaigns

As we saw in Chapter 4, the origins of professional campaign staffs came a generation earlier than the 1950s. Expertise was brought to the Democratic National Committee when national chairman John Raskob hired Charles Michelson to handle publicity in the late 1920s, and Republican national chairman John D. M. Hamilton began a tradition of party civil service in the 1936–1940 period. One could argue that professionalization has continued since 1952, but the case should not be pressed too far. There are certain slots on a campaign staff that are now usually filled by those with appropriate professional background. "Professionalization," Arterton reminds us, "has succeeded to a greater degree in precisely those areas of campaign behavior that demand a level of expertise: management, polling, computer services, media production, media purchasing, and financial reporting" (forthcoming). Even more important in terms of their impact on campaign strategy has been the professionals' incorporation in strategy groups that make basic campaign decisions. This reached a high point in 1976 with professional campaign managers John Deardourff and Stuart Spencer and pollster Robert Teeter sitting in when the Ford strategy was being determined.

The reason for not wanting to make too much of the spreading professionalism is that its antecedents are so clear. Campaign management firms had been organized well before the 1950s, especially in California. Persons coming from public relations or newspaper backgrounds involved in the 1952 Eisenhower campaign included Robert Humphreys, James C. Hagerty, Murray Chotiner, and Robert Mullen. Batten, Barton, Durstein, and Osborn, as well as the Kudner, Ted Bates, and Whitaker and Baxter firms were all working on this campaign (Kelley, 1956, chaps. 5, 6). The 1952 Republican campaign plan "outlined basic strategy, organization, appeals, types of speeches, literature, advertising, television and radio programs, the relative weight to be given to various media, the kinds, places, and times of campaign trips and rallies, and the areas in which efforts were to be concentrated" (Kelley, 1956, p. 1). This makes it hard to argue that expertise and experience were lacking at the beginning of our time period.

The National Committees

The Republican National Committee has taken on a number of new activities. Credit for this belongs to Mary Louise Smith, RNC chairperson during the Ford administration, and particularly to her successor, Bill Brock. One important Brock innovation was national committee agreement during 1977–78 to pay the salary for an organizational director for each state party. This was subject to some conditions. For instance, the organizational director had to be acceptable to the national committee, but the program meant that every state committee had a trained staff director. In addition, there were 15 field directors, who maintained liaison with state party organizations in two- to six-state areas, such as Michigan and Pennsylvania; Indiana, Kansas, Kentucky, and Missouri; or Arkansas, Louisiana, Mississippi, and Texas. A Local Election Campaign Division of equal size focused in state legislative elections across the country in 1978. Their efforts included some 75 campaign seminars, $1 million in direct cash grants to GOP candidates, and help with surveys, radio and TV spots, and scheduling. A Computer Services Division conducted analyses for state parties that installed terminals and paid telephone line charges. In 1978, all this cost some $3 million in direct contributions and the salaries of organizers and consultants, and was in addition to the normal operations of the National Committee that were carried forward at the same time (Republican National Committee Chairman's Report, 1979).

For a number of reasons, there was not even a pale reflection of this new strength at the Democratic National Committee. One reason was that the Republicans had established a much stronger financial base. The Democrats took great pride in providing $102,000 to their candidates in 1978 while the Republicans were spending $3 million to help their candidates. An even more important reason, though, was a lack of concern with the National Committee during the presidencies of Lyndon Johnson and Jimmy Carter.

John Bibby (forthcoming) argues that there has been a difference between the parties in the ways they have moved toward nationalization. The Democrats have stressed rules with the activities of the McGovern-Fraser Commission, the Mikulski Commission, and the Winograd Commission. The Republicans have stressed organization. While it could be said that the Republican activity strengthens both state and national parties, the ability of the national party to provide cash and campaign services to the states certainly gives the National Committee more leverage than hitherto in state affairs.

There has been a move away from a "unified" campaign structure at the national level, in which presidential campaigns are conducted through the National Committee. At least one of the campaigns was run by the National Committee staff from 1952 through 1968, and both were organized this way in 1956 and 1964. During the 1970s, though, the campaign headquarters have been located in separate presidential campaign committees, and the Federal Election Campaign Act of 1974 makes it likely that this will continue to be the case. Gerald Ford had given a speech as vice president in which he said that campaigns should be run through the National Committee, and wanted to run his own campaign that way in 1976, but was told that the new campaign finance law required a separate committee (Ford, 1979, p. 295). (President Ford was misinformed about this. There is a provision that allows a candidate to designate the National Committee as the agent to spend public funds.) The effective location of power to make decisions about national campaign strategy will reside among those persons authorized to act by the presidential candidate in any case. The effect of the 1974 statute is to reduce the candidate's opportunity to concentrate that authority in the National Committee if he wishes to do so.

Increasing Technology and Escalating Costs

There have been several changes in the technology through which a campaign is conducted. One has been the move from the campaign train to the campaign plane. The train is now used for nostalgia, and the special circumstance of several medium-size cities that are more conveniently accessible by rail. Otherwise the campaign moves by jet in order to appear in a number of different media markets the same day. This moves the candidate about more rapidly, of course, but hasn't affected the relative power of national and state parties very much.

Changes have taken place in the communications used to reach the voters and to find out what they are thinking. Nineteen fifty-two was the first year in which extensive use was made of television, but it was only one of several media that were employed. By the late 1970s, television almost completely dominated the media campaign. In the 1950s polling was employed, but it was intermittent and focused on high reliability estimates of candidate standing. By the 1970s, the information flow was continuous and there were at least some instances of very sophisticated analysis. These shifts have moved influence from the state level to the national level. Heretofore, state leaders could claim special knowledge of the situation in their states. Now national leaders armed with computer printouts may have better data on both the views of citizens in a given state and the media outlets that should be used to reach them.[3] The changes in communication techniques have also shifted power on the national level away from generalists and into the hands of specialists. It is sometimes said that these technological changes have diminished the influence of politicians. A better interpretation would be that power has shifted to different types of politicians—those who have mastered the use of media and polling.[4]

---

[3] Remember our finding in Chapter 3 that the county campaign leaders' perception of views in their communities was no more accurate than one would expect by chance. This means that use of polls is improving the politicians' understanding of citizens' thinking.

[4] If we go back to the 1950s, we find Joseph Napolitan active in Springfield, Massachusetts, politics, and we find John Deardourff on the staff of Representative Jessica McC. Weis of New York. Napolitan came into national politics when his Springfield friend, Lawrence O'Brien, was a leader in the Kennedy campaign, and Deardourff was on Nelson Rockefeller's campaign staff. Today, Napolitan is a leading Democratic campaign consultant and Deardourff a leading Republican consultant.

The use of jets, polls, and particularly television has made presidential campaigning much more expensive. Even ignoring the Nixon orgy of spending in 1972, the cost of the major party general election campaigns rose 335 percent from 1952 through 1968. In terms of cost per vote cast, expenditures rose from 19 cents to 60 cents over the same time period (Alexander, 1972, pp. 6–7).

There were also two important developments in campaign funding during this time period. One was the Republican sustaining membership campaign begun in 1962. By 1978, the Republicans had over 500,000 individual contributors. Fifty-eight percent of their contributions were in amounts of $25 or less, and another 28 percent were in the $25 to $50 range.

The second development was federal funding of general election campaigns at a level of $20 million in 1974 dollars. This direct federal funding will have at least three effects. First, it will enable both parties to put on campaigns by preventing destitution, such as the Humphrey campaign experienced in September 1968. Second, the act guarantees the national committees a minor role (they are authorized to spend about $3 million), but makes it less likely the campaigns will be run through them. Third, the tight limits—in constant dollars, about 70 percent of the amount spent in 1968—will compel some hard decisions about the best use of the funds.

Taken together, the conflicting effects of the several developments in electoral politics are not easy to summarize. They certainly tend to favor national party leaders rather than state leaders because they point toward centralized decision-making. One of the national committees, the Republican, is providing a range of services to the party throughout the country and has developed a mass financial base, but the authority of both national committees has been reduced by provisions of the Federal Election Campaign Act of 1974. Modern modes of transportation and communication have made presidential campaigns much more expensive, and have shifted influence toward politicians who understand these techniques. But in spite of the shifts brought on by technology, the presidential candidate and his advisors still face the central problem of deciding which voters they wish to appeal to, and how they are going to do so successfully.

CITIZEN ATTITUDES AND ACTIONS

Levels of Information

There is no evidence that American citizens knew substantially more or substantially less about politics in 1976 than they did a quarter of a century earlier. Figure 10–1 shows the 1976 distribution of information levels that was portrayed in Figure 7–1. To this has been added the same information for 1952. By comparing the solid line for 1976 with the dashed

FIGURE 10–1
Distributions of Information Levels, 1952 and 1976

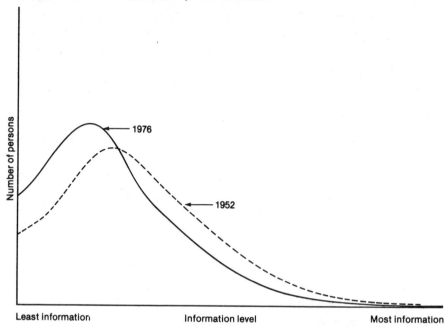

line for 1952, it can be seen that the information levels were somewhat lower in 1976. That is, there were a few more people falling into the higher information categories in 1952, and a few more in the lower information categories in 1976. But the difference between the means for the two years is not significant, and the shapes of the 1952 and 1976 curves are very similar.

Using the Media

There have been a few changes in the composition of the media since 1952. That was the first year in which wide use was made of television for campaign purposes. In 1952, television sets were in 34 percent of U.S. homes, but by 1976 television was available in 97 percent of the homes. The average number of hours per day spent watching TV also increased from 4:51 in 1955 to 6:26 in 1975. Total circulation of magazines and newspapers increased, but when adjusted for population growth magazine circulation went up and newspaper circulation dropped. Daily newspaper circulation moved from 48.2 per 100 adults to 38.2 per 100 adults during our time period, while magazine circulation rose from 142.4 per 100 adults to 157.3 over the same years (Sterling and Haight, 1979).

When asked about their sources of information about the campaign, the respondents' answers showed the same pattern. Only half said they learned about politics through television in 1952, but this figure rose to 89 percent in 1976. Newspapers dropped slightly from 79 percent to 72 percent, while magazines rose from 41 percent to 48 percent. By the 1970s, the pattern was of nearly universal television use, continued wide use of newspapers, and use of magazines by the more literate half of the population.

Media and Information Levels

When we turn from the use of various media to their impact on citizen's information levels, we see something different. Table 10–2 gives measures of association between use of a given medium and the level of information a respondent has. In 1952, when there was a mixed pattern of media use, magazines, newspapers, and television all had the same effect on how much a respondent knew. By 1976, however, we have the pattern that we already saw in Table 7–2. The higher measure of association between magazines and information level, and the lower measure of association between television and information level, means that use of the more demanding print medium produces more information whereas use of television conveys less information.

TABLE 10–2
Association between Information Level and Informational Environment, 1952 and 1976

	Measure of Association (Kendall's Tau–c)	
	1952	1976
Medium used		
Magazines	.28	.39
Newspapers	.27	.23
Television	.30	.16
Involvement with informational environment		
Education	.28	.28
Political interest	.43	.40

Data source: 1952 and 1976 SRC/CPS Election Studies.

While the effects of obtaining information through one medium or another seem to have changed, the effect of simply being involved with the informational environment has not altered at all. Two of the three questions related to citizens' seeking out information (which were reported in Table 7–5) were also asked in 1952. As you can see from Table 10–2, the association between seeking out information and knowing about politics is exactly the same in 1976 as it was in the early 1950s.

Issues and Candidates

As we saw in Chapter 8, there have been very few long-term changes in citizens' attitudes about issues and candidates. In spite of repeated assertions in the literature that the 1950s were relatively issueless, and that issues did not emerge until the Goldwater challenge to the status quo in 1964, attitudes about issues have been quite salient in every single election. They were somewhat more prominent in 1964 and 1972, but this change was an increase on a base that was already substantial. Attitudes about political parties have become less salient in the 1970s, but parties have been by far the least visible attitude objects throughout the whole period.[5]

The partisan favorability of attitudes, of course, varies from election to election. When considering only the three broad categories, attitudes about candidates have usually favored the Republicans and attitudes about issues have usually favored the Democrats. There are many exceptions to this when the more detailed set of attitudes is considered, but overall the Republicans have had the more attractive candidate every year except 1964, and Democrats have profited more from attitudes about issues except in 1968 and 1972.

When citizens' attitudes are related to their voting decisions, there has been a decline in the importance of parties, but no long-term change in the importance of attitudes about candidates and issues. Attitudes about parties were very important in the 1950s, but have not been so since that decade and played no role in the 1972 election. Candidate attitudes have been very important in every election save for 1952, and attitudes about issues have been the most important category except in 1976. The probit analysis relating all the attitudes to presidential choice predicted 86 percent of the cases in 1952 and 85 percent of the cases in 1976.

Party Identification

As we saw in Chapter 9, there have been two related changes in the distribution of party identification. The first was the sharp decline in the mid-'60s in the proportion of persons who think of themselves as Strong Partisans. Thirty-eight percent were either Strong Democrats or Strong Republicans in 1952; only 24 percent were by 1976. The second has been the gradual growth in the proportion of true Independents. Only 5 percent fell into this category nationwide in 1952; 14 percent did so in 1976.

It is important that the effects of these changes in the distribution of

---

[5] Whether there ever was a time when attitudes about parties were as salient as attitudes about candidates or issues cannot be determined with these data. Without pre-1952 evidence, we don't know one way or the other.

party identification neither be underestimated nor overestimated. The decline in the number of Strong Partisans and the increase in the number of Independents open the possibility of wider fluctuation from one election to the next. Hence, the 1976 election results are not as reliable a guide to the 1980 election outcome as the 1952 results were to the 1956 outcome. At the same time, citizens have not been departing from the political parties in very massive proportions. Ninety-one percent of citizens could be classified as Strong, Weak, or Independent Democrats or Republicans in 1952; 85 percent could be so classified in 1976 (Miller and Miller, 1977, pp. 8–20). The advantage enjoyed by the Democrats over the Republicans as a consequence of these party identifications was 57 percent to 34 percent in 1952; the Democratic advantage was 52 percent to 33 percent in 1976. So if we can expect wider fluctuations, we can also expect those fluctuations to be on either side of the same center of electoral gravity.

It is also important that this relative stability on the aggregate level not be confused with stability on the individual level. The relative stability of party identification types in the population results from an equilibrium condition, in which individual changes in one direction are cancelled out by individual changes in the opposite direction. When we move to the individual level, it turns out that attitudes are neither more nor less stable in the 1970s than they were in the 1950s. There have been two panel studies that provide data on individual level stability and change. One was from 1956 through 1960. The second, which provided the data we reviewed in Chapter 9, was from 1972 through 1976. When results of the two studies were compared, party identification was just as stable in the 1970s as it had been in the 1950s. And "where more specific issues can be directly matched, continuity values seem amazingly stationary across the two panels" (Converse and Markus, 1979, p. 43).

Cognitive Consistency

The extent of cognitive consistency does not seem to have changed over our time period, at least when consistency is measured against a partisan criterion on the individual level. Figure 10–2 shows the distributions for partisan attitude consistency for 1952 and 1976. Partisan attitude consistency does show some variation from election to election. In 1972, probably because George McGovern was perceived to be taking stands that were inconsistent with the preferences of many Democrats, the proportion of completely consistent attitudes was much lower. But as a comparison of the dashed line for 1952 with the solid line for 1976 shows clearly, the proportions of consistent and inconsistent attitudes at the beginning and end of this time period are virtually the same. There is no evidence of long-term change.

FIGURE 10–2
Distribution of Cognitive Consistency, 1952 and 1976

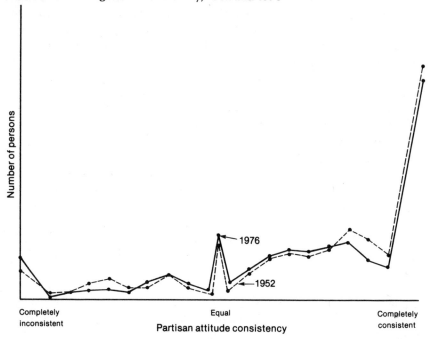

In sum, there have been changes in the media that are available and the use that is made of them. There has been a decline in the salience and importance of attitudes about political parties, and in the proportion of citizens who think of themselves as Strong Partisans. However, there have not been any changes in citizens' information level, in the relation between information level and involvement with the informational environment, in the temporal stability of attitudes, in cognitive consistency, in the partisan advantage resulting from the distribution of party identification, in the salience or importance of attitudes about candidates or issues, and —most important of all—in the relation between these attitudes and the presidential choice made by the citizens.

CONCLUSION

Continuity and Change

There is, as always, an amalgam of continuity and change.[6] Let's take the elements of continuity first. The actors who are recruited to nomina-

---

[6] It ought to be said that this review of continuity and change has been restricted to the topics covered in the body of this book. Thus, there are aspects of political parties (for example, congressional parties and what citizens know about Congress) that have not been taken into consideration. Obviously, I think the topics that have

tion and electoral politics continue to be, in Kirkpatrick's nice phrase, the "skill-based middle class." As far back as we have reliable data, these activists have been interested in issues. The underlying purposes of coalition building persist. The coalition must recruit delegates to win the nomination, and must persuade voters to win an election. This means there must be a national campaign organization, some means of scheduling the candidate and moving the candidate and entourage around the country, speeches that explain the candidate's positions, material released in a form the media can use, funds raised, and so forth. Many of these activities are carried on by professionals, and have been during the time period under review.

Most of the cognitive elements underlying the citizen response have been quite stable. The amount of information known by the electorate, the partisan consistency of their attitudes, the salience and importance of attitudes about both candidates and issues, and the relation of these attitudes to presidential choice have shown little variation.

What elements have changed? There are now more women and minorities among convention delegates. The coalitions formed in nomination and electoral politics are more national in character. Nomination politics now lasts longer; national party rules are now recognized as superior to state law; there has been a considerable increase in the proportion of delegates selected in primaries; incumbent presidents have been challenged for renomination with some regularity. There have been a number of essentially technological innovations in the conduct of election campaigns. Jet aircraft, television, continual opinion surveys, and computers have become part of campaigns just as they have become part of much of American life in the late 20th century. Professionals who know how to unite this technology with politics now play a larger role in strategy decisions, and the Republican party has deployed persons who know how to conduct such campaigns in order to strengthen party units throughout the country. All of this is expensive, and campaigns now cost many times what they did. The Republican party has developed a very successful mass finance drive, and federal funding for presidential campaigns was inaugurated in 1976. At the same time that there has been this increased organizational activity, fewer citizens think of themselves as Strong Partisans, and attitudes about the parties have become even less salient and have declined as factors in determining presidential choice.

Are National Coalitions Weaker or Stronger?

Whether any organizational entity is becoming weaker or stronger depends, of course, on one's point of view. What strengthens one entity

---

been covered are central to an understanding of political parties, but the coverage is not comprehensive.

may weaken another. Since our concern in this book is with presidential politics, we want to know whether the nomination and electoral coalitions —and the institutions in which they transact their essential business— are being weakened or strengthened.

To answer this question, we want to focus on the changes just listed. The nonchanges neither weaken nor strengthen. The continuity of organization and continuity in citizens' cognitions do mean that parties are not dying or dissolving, but that is a slightly different point. So, which changes have weakened and which have strengthened?

I think there are three changes that have weakened national political parties. The first is the frequency with which presidents are now challenged for their own party's nomination. Strictly speaking, this does not affect nomination or electoral politics as much as it does the politics of the executive branch. It does mean, though, that a president and his immediate assistants have to divert time and resources from executive leadership to protect the president's political base, and this makes it more difficult for the administration to make the kind of record on which it would want to be judged.

Second, I do not think the Federal Election Campaign Act of 1974 has helped national parties. It does free the parties from dependence on interest groups, and it means that the national parties do not have to wait for state parties to meet their quotas in national fund drives. But the act largely removes the national committees from financial decisions about presidential campaigns, and inhibits presidential candidates who might wish to do so from conducting their campaigns through the national committee.

Third, there is the decline in importance of attitudes about the parties in citizens' presidential choices and, more particularly, the reduced number of Strong Partisans among the electorate. To be sure, how one sees this depends on whether it is viewed from the perspective of the majority or minority party. From a minority perspective, the increased independence could be seen as giving the minority party a more frequent chance to appeal successfully to enough majority party voters to win. But from the perspective of either party, the smaller number of Strong Partisans means that there is a smaller deliverable vote.

At the same time, there have been several changes that have strengthened national parties. The increased number of primaries means that an effectively organized nomination coalition can go into states and win delegates without being beholden to state leaders. The coalitions that are being formed in both nomination and electoral contexts are moving steadily from a regional to a national character. National party rules have been held to be superior to state law. The Republican party has achieved an independent base of small contributors and now offers a wide range of services. Professionals now have better information about citizens' views and are taking part more frequently in basic strategy decisions. All of these changes have tended to produce more nationalized, more professionalized parties.

When I was a very small boy, I could watch airplanes from nearby Wright Field as they maneuvered overhead. Usually they were biplanes, but now and again I saw a triplane. When I was slightly older, one of the events that marked late morning was the arrival of the horse-drawn bakery truck. It was full of good smells, and a source of curiosity as to how the horse knew where to stop even though the deliveryman was sometimes away from the truck giving some housewife the goods she had ordered. I haven't seen many triplanes or horse-drawn bakery trucks lately, but I do not believe this means the end of the aviation or baking industries. Similarly, I have not read much lately about party bosses, such as E. H. Crump of Memphis, Edward J. Flynn of the Bronx, Tom Prendergast of Kansas City, Frank Hague of Jersey City, or others who were in power in the 1930s, but I do not take this as evidence of the disappearance of political parties. Today we have presidential parties.

appendix

Indexes and Measures

A–3.1 DIFFERENCE SCORES

The statement in the interview schedule preceding the six party norms was: "Now let's consider party work. Would you say you feel a *strong* obligation or *some* obligation *to do* each of the following— or to *avoid* doing each of the following, in the conduct of political affairs?" Then each respondent was read statements, such as "Hold strong personal beliefs about a number of different issues" and "Weigh prior service to the party very heavily in selecting candidates for nomination." The answers to these items formed a five-magnitude scale: Strong Obligation to Do, Some Obligation to Do, No Obligation to Do or Avoid, Some Obligation to Avoid, Strong Obligation to Avoid. For Republican activists, for example, the responses to the two items quoted formed these distributions:

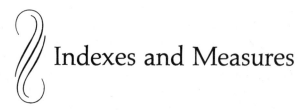

	Obligation to Do		No Obligation	Obligation to Avoid	
	Strong	Some		Some	Strong
Have personal beliefs	56.5	28.8	12.0	0.5	2.1
Weigh party service	28.8	33.2	30.5	5.7	3.8

The difference scores are simply the difference between the proportion who report a strong obligation to do whatever action is mentioned and the proportion who say they have a strong obligation to avoid that action. This provides a summary measure that can be used in place of the full

266

distribution. In the example, the difference score for the Republican activists was 54.4 for holding strong personal issue beliefs, and 23.0 for weighing prior party service in selecting nominees. Having single numbers facilitates camparisons between parties and between norms. Difference scores of this kind were used by Arthur Miller (1974).

A–3.2 AGREEMENT SCORES

The agreement scores between activists and citizens were based on responses to ten attitude items that were given to both. The items were printed on cards, and each respondent placed the card containing the statement on a Sort Board that was divided into seven categories: Strongly Agree, Agree, Slightly Agree, Not Sure, Slightly Disagree, Agree, Strongly Disagree. The items, classified by policy area, were:

International Involvement
We should bring all American troops back from foreign countries.
We must have peace in Vietnam.

Economic Management
Wages and prices should not be controlled by the government.
Government spending should be cut.

Social Benefits
Welfare payments ought to be increased.
Social security benefits ought to be increased.

Civil Liberties
Busing should not be used to desegregate schools.
The police ought to be given more authority.

Natural Resources
The government should act to stop pollution.

Agriculture
Farmers should be guaranteed a good income.

Each of these items reflected a central dimension in the policy area in question, and some were worded negatively to guard against response-set bias. Each answer was given a score ranging from 7 for Strongly Agree to 1 for Strongly Disagree. Each person's set of responses thus comprised a row vector with ten components. For example, the vector $(7,7,7,4,4,4,4,1,1,1)$ would correspond to "Strongly Agree" answers to the first three items, "Not Sure" to the next four items, and "Strongly Disagree" answers to the last three items.

Vector subtraction (taking absolute differences) is used to begin to calculate an observed attitude distance between any two persons. If a person had "Not Sure" responses (that is, scores of 4) to every item, the attitude distance between this person and the example given in the preceding paragraph would be:

$$(7,7,7,4,4,4,4,1,1,1)$$
$$(4,4,4,4,4,4,4,4,4,4)$$
$$(3,3,3,0,0,0,0,3,3,3)$$

One then takes the sum of the components in the vector of absolute differences to obtain an observed attitude distance. In this example, the observed attitude distance would be 18. This assumes that the measurement is accurate enough to permit the operation of subtraction, a very strong assumption in view of the measurement method used, but avoids any other assumptions about the relative importance of the components or their spatial location with respect to each other.

The formula for an agreement score is:

$$\text{Agreement Score} = \left(1 - \frac{\text{Observed Attitude Distance}}{\text{Maximum Attitude Distance}}\right)$$

Since the Maximum Attitude Distance in this case is 60 (6 units along each of 10 scales), the Agreement Score in the example would be $(1 - 18/60)$ or .7. The raw Agreement Scores have the property of varying between a value of 1.0 when both persons give identical responses to every item, and 0 when both persons are located at the opposite ends of every single scale. The Agreement Scores reported in Chapter 3 have been corrected so the 0 point is set at a level corresponding to the agreement to be expected with randomly distributed responses. This follows a suggestion by Weisberg (1978) that a measure should represent percentage improvement over chance. A value of 1.0 represents complete agreement with both the raw Agreement Scores and the corrected Agreement Scores.

For the Agreement Scores denoting attitudinal similarity, the responses of each activist were matched against the mean responses of citizens interviewed in the activist's county.

In the case of Agreement Scores for perceptual accuracy, the stimulus items given the activists were adapted so as to begin with the phrase, "Voters in this area favor. . . ." (For example, "Voters in this area favor cutting government spending.") The Agreement Scores were then calculated between each activist's responses to these perceptual items and the mean responses for the corresponding attitude items for citizens interviewed in the activist's county.

A–3.3   USE OF CLUSTER PROCEDURE TO ISOLATE ISSUE GROUPS

A total of 15 issue items were given to each activist interviewed. These included the 10 items mentioned in A–3.2, plus 5 more:

The government should help countries all over the world. (International Involvement)

America should spend whatever is necessary to have a strong military force. (International Involvement)

The federal government is getting too powerful. (Economic Management)

The government ought to help pay everyone's medical bills. (Social Benefits)

I favor letting Negroes move into white neighborhoods. (Civil Liberties)

On the basis of the activists' responses to these 15 items, Agreement Scores were calculated between each pair of Republican activists and each pair of Democratic activists. After deleting those activists with missing data, we had a 181-by-181 matrix of Agreement Scores for Republican activists, and a 182-by-182 matrix of Agreement Scores for Democratic activists. These matrices were used as input to an OSIRIS CLUSTER program that had been modified to handle matrices this large.

The OSIRIS CLUSTER program accepts similarities data (for example, correlations, or in this case, Agreement Scores), and groups the cases with the closest relations to each other in the same cluster. There are three parameters that must be set in the program: STARTMIN, ENDMIN, and STAYMIN. All of these stipulate minimum cutoff values that stop the clustering procedure. STARTMIN denotes a minimum score to start a cluster. The clustering procedure begins with the pair of cases having the highest score with respect to each other. As long as there is a pair of cases whose score is higher than STARTMIN when the previous cluster has been assembled, another cluster is begun with the two unclustered cases having the highest score with respect to each other. If there is no pair with a score higher than the stipulated STARTMIN, the clustering procedure terminates. (This is the operational meaning of being an isolate with respect to the issue groups. In addition to being excluded from other groups by the ENDMIN and STAYMIN parameters, there exists no other activist for whom the isolate has an Agreement Score above the stipulated STARTMIN.)

Once a cluster is begun, the case with the highest average score with respect to the two clustered cases is added to form a three-case cluster. Then the case with the highest average score with respect to the three clustered cases is added to form a four-case cluster. This process continues until there is no unclustered case whose average score with the cases already in the cluster is above ENDMIN. The STAYMIN parameter causes any case whose average score has fallen below the STAYMIN level (because of the addition of other cases after it was already in the cluster) to be deleted.

Since the procedure considers only unclustered cases when forming new clusters, it has a tendency to inflate earlier clusters at the expense of those formed later. (A later cluster might provide a better fit for a case than the cluster to which it was already assigned, but the case would not be considered for the second cluster.) Therefore the standard OSIRIS CLUSTER program was modified to check the average score of each case with every existing cluster after all the clusters had been formed. Each case with a higher score with another cluster would be moved to it. These moves would, of course, change all the average scores somewhat, so another check would be made, and cases would again be reassigned. The modified program will go through as many iterations of this kind as the user chooses. This is controlled by stipulating an ITER parameter. By selecting an appropriately high number, the user can insure that each case ends up in the cluster with which it has the highest average score.

In the analysis runs that isolated the issue groups, the STARTMIN, ENDMIN, and STAYMIN parameters were set at .9, .7, and .7, respectively, for raw Agreement Scores. The ITER parameter was set at 30. This produced the 4 Republican issue groups and 65 isolates, and the 7 Democratic issue groups and 22 isolates.

To this point, the procedure had been entirely blind. We had not made any assumptions about the probable character of the groups beyond the definitional stipulation that members of the same group should share attitudes, and the operational assumption that these clustering procedures would lead to groups with common attitudes. (We had avoided any assumption that all liberals, or all Catholics, or all southerners, or all of any category would belong to the same group.) Once group membership (or the lack of it in the case of isolates) had been determined, a new variable was created denoting which group each member belonged to, and added to each activist's data set.

The addition of this information as an attribute of each activist made possible the determination of the attitudinal and demographic characteristics of the groups. The median scores, the textual discussion of group attitudes on individual issues, the demographic characteristics, and other findings were based on this procedure.

The integrity of the issue groups was tested in two ways. First, random numbers were generated (and tested for sequential dependency), and were used as data for a hypothetical population of activists. Agreement Scores were calculated on the basis of these "attitudes," and the matrix of Agreement Scores thus derived was used as input to the CLUSTER program. The STARTMIN, ENDMIN, and STAYMIN parameters were again set at .9, .7, and .7. No clusters were formed. This meant two things. The level of agreement within our issue groups was above random chance, and the issue groups were not just artifacts created by use of the software.

Second, we looked at the within-group and between-group Agreement Scores of the four Republican and seven Democratic issue groups. (These data are shown in Appendix A–3.5.) The average corrected within-group score was .49 for Republican groups, and .51 for Democratic groups. The average corrected between–group score was .35 for Republican groups, and .30 for Democratic groups. The average corrected Agreement Score for all Republicans was .29, and for all Democrats .30. Thus we could be sure that we had a higher degree of agreement within the groups than among other possible combinations.

While the CLUSTER program was used in this instance to isolate issue groups from larger populations of activists, it can also be used to observe how the groups combine into coalitions. This is done by gradually lowering the parameters, and by determining which cases (and by inference, groups) move together. If done in small steps, one can see the stages of coalition formation in something of the same manner that time-lapse photography allows one to observe the opening of a flower. Although no more than a brief reference was made to this in the text, the processes of coalition formation in the Republican and Democratic parties were studied in this way. Essentially, the results substantiate the analysis presented in the text.

A–3.4   MULTIDIMENSIONAL SCALING

Multidimensional scaling is an analytical technique that accepts similarities data (such as correlations or Agreement Scores) and provides a geometric plot of the data points, such that the most similar cases are located closest together and the most dissimilar cases are located farthest apart. Imagine three data points, a, b, and c. Assume that the ab correlation is .9, that the bc correlation is .1, and that the ac correlation is also .1. If these correlations were analyzed by multidimensional scaling, a and b should be located quite close together in the resulting plot (because of the high correlation between them), while c should be located equidistant from a and b (because c has the same correlation with both) and much farther away (because the correlation between c and a or b is so low). Achieving such a plot becomes much more difficult as the number of data points goes up; but the goal remains that the more closely associated the data, the closer the data points should be to each other. The degree to which this goal has been achieved is determined by a measure of goodness of fit called Stress. A Stress value of 0 means that the goal has been achieved with every pair of data points; a Stress value of 1 means that you have the worst possible configuration.

Multidimensional scaling is a data reduction technique similar to factor analysis or cluster analysis in that it assumes there is some simpler underlying pattern to the multiple relationships in a large data matrix. If this assumption is correct in a given case, then one should be able to achieve a solution with low stress and low dimensionality. In such a case, the resulting geometric plot can be studied, and the observer's knowledge of the cases may permit an intuitive interpretation of the meaning of the dimensions. For example, if there was a two-dimensional plot in which liberal Democrats appeared in the upper left quadrant, liberal Republicans in the upper right quadrant, conservative Democrats in the lower left quadrant, and conservative Republicans in the lower right quadrant, then the horizontal axis could be interpreted as a Democrat-Republican dimension, and the vertical axis could be interpreted as a liberal-conservative dimension. (For further discussion of the technique itself, see Kruskal and Wish [1978] and Rabinowitz [1975].)

Multidimensional scaling could not be used for direct identification of the issue groups. For one thing, the plot is of individual cases, and with 181 Republican activists and 182 Democratic activists, the resulting plot would be so dense that it would be difficult to read, and almost impossible to tell where one group ended and another began. Since the identity of the issue group members had been determined in a cluster analysis, however, multidimensional scaling could be used to help develop a spatial representation that might suggest the relationships of the issue groups to each other.

Figures 3–2 and 3–3 were developed with the aid of multidimensional scaling, but are not based exclusively on that technique. Rather than trying to analyze all of the cases, 5 cases were chosen from each of the 7 Democratic issue groups, and 6 cases were chosen from each of the 4 Republican issue groups. The cases selected from each group were those with the highest average Agreement Scores with other members of their groups. After this selection, a 35-by-35 matrix of Agreement Scores was constructed for the Democrats, and a 24-by-24 matrix for the Republicans. These were used as input to the OSIRIS MDSCAL Program (the Shepard-Kruskal Multidimensional Scaling Program).

Two analysis runs were made with the data for each party. The first began with 3 dimensions; the second with 6. The Stress associated with the number of dimensions in each solution is shown in Table A–1. These results suggested several things. The similarity of pattern between the parties (leaving aside the single instance of very high Stress for Democrats) strongly substantiated the argument in the book that the internal structures of the Republican and Democratic parties are quite similar. The number of dimensions and high Stress values meant that the structures in both parties were multidimensional, and the best MDSCAL solution would have five dimensions. And the lack of a solution two-dimension solution with a low Stress value meant that no two-dimensional plot would provide more than an approximate guide to the location of the groups with respect to each other in an issue space.

The plot that provided the basis for Figure 3–2 came from the four-

TABLE A–1

Number of Dimensions	Stress	
	Republicans	Democrats
1	.63	.65
2	.50	.49
3	.41	.38
1	.63	.85
2	.52	.55
3	.38	.36
4	.31	.26
5	.24	.20
6	.25	.21

dimensional Republican solution with dimension 2 as the horizontal axis and dimension 3 as the vertical axis. The plot that provided the basis for Figure 3.3 came from the two-dimensional Democratic solution (in the 3 dimension analysis run). Dimension 1 is the horizontal axis and dimension 2 is the vertical axis. The circles in Figures 3–2 and 3–3 have nothing to do with multidimensional scaling at all. The MDSCAL plot gave locations for the individual group members. I simply assumed that the center of the space defined by the 5 Democratic or 6 Republican cases could be taken as the central location of the group in an issue space, and then drew circles proportionate to the size of the groups. The cases belonging to different groups did plot separately in all but one instance. The Dominant Democratic group was located more or less on top of the Thrifty Liberals. Consequently I moved the Thrifty Liberals a short distance to an unoccupied area that was consistent with the Thrifty Liberals' issue proximity to the other Democratic groups.

Considerable emphasis is put on the *approximate* utility of Figures 3–2 and 3–3 for two reasons. First, the Stress values tell us that the Republican plot gives us only part of a fair solution, and the Democratic plot was a poor solution (even before I moved the Thrifty Liberals). Second, the size of the circles is a useful device to convey an impression of the relative size of the groups, but it is certain that some individual group members would be located outside the area suggested by the circle. Tables 3–3 and 3–4 contain more accurate information. Figures 3–2 and 3–3 are visual devices that convey some of this information.

A–3.5 WITHIN- AND BETWEEN-GROUP AGREEMENT SCORES

The Agreement Scores in Table A–2 have been corrected so that 0 corresponds to the degree of agreement expected by chance, and 1.0 corresponds to complete agreement. The figures may therefore be interpreted as the percentage improvement over chance.

TABLE A–2

A.

Republicans	Dominant Group	Conservative Libertarians	Economic Managers	Republican Moderates	Isolates
Dominant group	.51	.43	.32	.40	.24
Conservative libertarians		.46	.31	.33	.18
Economic managers			.45	.30	.20
Republican moderates				.49	.19
Isolates					.12

B.

Democrats	Dominant Group	Liberal Pacifists	Liberal Internationalists	Cautious Liberals	Thrifty Liberals	Democratic Moderates	Coercive Individualists	Isolates
Dominant group	.53	.43	.41	.35	.36	.38	.19	.17
Liberal pacifists		.52	.28	.31	.33	.29	—.01	.12
Liberal internationalists			.51	.40	.35	.23	.19	.15
Cautious liberals				.49	.36	.32	.29	.21
Thrifty liberals					.52	.32	.22	.17
Democratic moderates						.47	.27	.17
Coercive individualists							.44	.14
Isolates								.04

A–3.6 CONSENSUS SCORES

The Consensus Score is another measure of agreement. Whereas the Agreement Score is derived from a comparison of individual responses, the Consensus Score is based on an analysis of the distribution of responses for the group in question. It is based on two assumptions. The first is that if consensus does exist in a group, responses should tend to fall into a modal category. The second is an assumption that measurement error will lead to some consensual responses falling into one category on either side of the "true" modal category. Therefore one is justified in comparing the number of responses actually falling into the mode and two adjacent categories with the number that would be expected to do so if there was an equal distribution of answers in each magnitude of the scale. This leads to the formula:

$$\text{Consensus} = \left(\frac{\text{Frequency observed} - \text{Frequency expected}}{\text{N} - \text{Frequency expected}} \right)$$

The Consensus Score takes on values bounded by $+ 1.0$ and

$$\left(\frac{n - f_e}{N - f_e} \right)$$

where n is the minimum number of responses that could be in a modal category. A value of $+ 1.0$ occurs when there is complete consensus—that is, when all the responses fall into the mode and two adjacent categories. A value of 0 occurs when the number of cases in the mode and two adjacent categories is just that expected if the answers were equally distributed among all categories. Negative values occur when there is disagreement. In this case the largest number of answers would not fall into adjacent categories, in other words, when one subgroup would agree with a statement and another would disagree.

A–7.1   INFORMATION LEVEL MEASURE

The measure of information level is a simple count of the number of responses given to the series of open-ended questions about parties and candidates. The Center for Political Studies coded up to 10 responses (that is, 5 likes and 5 dislikes) for each party and candidate. This gave the measure of theoretical range from 0 to 40. The actual range was from 0 to 31.

The distribution of the measure is portrayed in Figure 7–1, and the data are presented in Table A–3. The mean value is 7.1, and the standard deviation is 5. In constructing the categories for Table 7–1 (and the subsequent cross-tabulations), the categories start at the mean value, and a new category begins at each standard deviation (except for the highest where there were very few cases).

This measure makes the same assumption that is made for open-ended questions: that the better informed person will have more to say about a topic than a less informed person. It is open to the same challenge: that a garrulous person will respond at greater length than one who is taciturn, even though the latter may know more. In order to check the validity of this information level measure, correlations were run between it and a

TABLE A–3

Information Level Category	Number of Responses	Percent of Electorate
Low	0–1–2	17.5%
Average minus	3–4–5–6–7	41.2
Average plus	8–9–10–11–12	25.5
High	13–14–15–16–17	11.7
Very high	18–19–20–21–22	3.2
Extremely high	23 through 31	0.9

host of other variables with which it might be related. The highest correlation (Tau–c = .44) was with the interviewer's own estimate of the respondent's level of political information. Other high correlations are shown in Table A–4.

TABLE A–4

Related Variable	Kendall's Tau–c
Interest in the campaign	.40
Reads about national politics in newspapers	.40
Reads magazines	.39
Follows public affairs	.37
Tries to influence another person's vote	.35
Reads about international affairs in newspapers	.35
Interviewer's estimate of respondent's intelligence	.34

Since all of these variables should be correlated with a true measure of political information, we may regard this measure as valid.

A–8.1   PROBIT ANALYSIS

Probit analysis was a technique first developed in biology, then extended to economics, and that has begun to be applied in political science (McKelvey and Zavonia, 1969; Rosenstone and Wolfinger, 1978) in recent years. It was developed to handle the problem of a dichotomous dependent variable. It has since been extended to other applications, but it is the dichotomous dependent variable that makes it particularly appropriate for voting analyses.

The problem can be visualized with a single independent and single dependent variable. If both are free to vary, then a relationship is shown by drawing a regression line that minimizes the distance of any data point from the line. If the relationship is as shown in the figure at the top of p. 277 ($y = bx + u$ where $b = 1$), then one would say that the two variables are related because a unit change in x would be associated with a unit change in $y \pm$ an error term, u. Now consider what happens if y, the

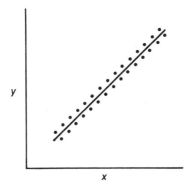

dependent variable, can take on just two values. No matter what kind of straight line one draws, as in (A) or (B), many of the data points are going to be far from the line. The line also "predicts" that many data points should fall in the middle of the two values or outside of the values. Since the dependent variable is restricted to the two values, this is impossible. If, however, one draws an S-curve as in (C), then a great many of the data points are going to be located close to the curve, and very few "impossible" predictions will be made.

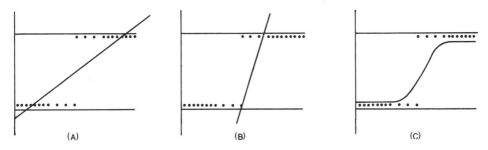

There are several functions in the mathematical literature that produce an S-curve of the desired form. All of these rely on some assumed underlying distribution. If the two values are 1 and 0, then the basic model is

$$P = \mathrm{Prob}(Y_i = 1) = F(\beta' X_i) \quad \text{and} \quad P = \mathrm{Prob}(Y_i = 0) = 1 - F(\beta' X_i)$$

One of the functions that can be used to estimate these probabilities is to assume that $F(\beta' X_i)$ has a cumulative normal distribution. In this case, a change in one unit of the independent variable will produce a change in the probability that $Y_i = 1$ by an amount that is directly proportional to $\beta' F(\beta' X_i)$. Unlike simple linear regression, these equations cannot be solved. They can only be estimated. Hence one is moving from a statement that a unit change in x produces a known change of so many units in y, to a Maximum Likelihood Estimate that a unit change in X_i will produce a change in *probability* that Y_i will take on one value rather than the other. (The word "probit" in probit analysis is an abbreviation for "probability unit." It is also sometimes called "normit" by way of reference to the cumulative normal distribution.) It is obviously more complex than regression analysis, but its assumptions make it a superior form of analysis for voting data. Its increased power is indicated by the comparison using identical 1976 data. The regression solution explained 47 percent of the variance in the vote. The probit solution explained 73 percent of the variance in the vote. For further information about probit analysis, see Hanushek and Jackson (1977, chap. 7); Aldrich and Cnudde (1975); Nelson (1976); and Nelson and Olson (1978).

The Maximum Likelihood Estimates in Chapter 8 were reported as "MLE*" to denote the fact that they had been standardized. The computer program written by (and kindly made available by) Richard McKelvey does not contain any standardization. Indeed, it is questionable whether one should do this at all. The computer program does supply the sample variance for the independent and dependent variables. This made it possible to standardize by multiplying by the ratio of the square roots of the sample variances. In other words, the Maximum Likelihood Estimate is standardized by multiplying it by the standard deviation of the independent variable divided by the standard deviation of the dependent variable.

The reason for standardizing can be seen from an example. The Maximum Likelihood Estimates for economic management and agriculture in 1976 were .29 and .52, respectively. This suggests that attitudes about agriculture were more important in the 1976 election than attitudes about economics. Now recall that a unit change in any independent variable produces a change in the probability that the dependent variable will take on one value rather than the other. This is important because the variance for economic management was 3.52 and the variance for agriculture was .05. This means that attitudes on economics vary across many more units than attitudes on agriculture, and therefore have a greater opportunity to affect vote. It is this consideration that one takes into account when standardizing. In this example, standardization increases the Maximum Likelihood Estimate for economics from .29 to 1.10, and decreases the MLE for agriculture from .52 to .25, thereby reflecting the much greater range through which economic attitudes vary, and the restricted range for attitudes on agriculture.

There is another reason for standardizing in this particular way that is related to a goal of the analysis. By controlling for the effects of variance, standardization allows a better comparison between the effects of the attitude components in a given election. But we also want to be able to make comparisons across elections. Now it happens that the variance for vote has been remarkably stable (see Table A–5).

TABLE A–5

Year	Sample Variance for Vote
1952	.244
1956	.241
1960	.250
1964	.219
1968	.248
1972	.230
1976	.250

The variance was slightly depressed in the one-sided elections of 1964 and 1972, but even including these years the variance in the dependent variable (i.e., vote) has been quite similar. This means that when one uses this method of standardization for any one election, the denominator of the ratio is virtually the same for any year, and this allows us to make comparisons between the effects of attitude components across elections.

A–8.2 ATTITUDE CATEGORIES FOR VOTING ANALYSES

The Center for Political Studies Master Code categories included in the specific attitude categories in 1976 are shown in Table A–6 (page 280).

For the three broad attitude categories, the master codes in the seven-candidate categories, the two-party categories, and the seven-issue categories were simply combined.

Parallel coding decisions were made in the other years.

A–9.1 INDEXES OF PARTISAN ISSUE CONSISTENCY AND PARTISAN ATTITUDE CONSISTENCY

Both of the indexes were based on the assumption that partisans would have more favorable perceptions of their own party than of the opposition. Strong Republicans, Weak Republicans, and Independent Republicans were regarded as consistent if they evaluated the Republican party more highly than the Democratic party. The opposite convention applied to Strong Democrats, Weak Democrats, and Independent Democrats. Independents were excluded from these scales.

The Index of Partisan Issue Consistency was constructed from the responses to five issue items and the associated perceptions of the candidates. The issue items included were:

Welfare payments ought to be increased.

The police ought to be given more authority.

TABLE A–6

Candidate, general	0009, 0036, 0201, 0223–0224, 0427–0430, 0443–0455, 0457, 0497–0498, 0505, 0701–0711, 0721–0722, 0797
Record—incumbency	0217, 0553, 0554, 0611
Experience	0211–0212, 0215–0216, 0218–0221, 0297, 0313, 0314, 0425–0426, 0456
Management	0311–0312, 0407–0408, 0601–0602, 0605–0610, 0612, 0697, 0841–0842
Intelligence	0413–0422
Trust	0213–0214, 0307–0308, 0309–0310, 0401–0404, 0431, 0432, 0603, 0604, 1010–1020
Personality	0301–0306, 0315–0320, 0411–0412, 0423–0424, 0433–0442, 0459–0460
People in party	0001–0008, 0010–0035, 0037–0097, 0502–0504, 0508, 0541–0542
Party affect	0101–0197, 0500–0501, 0506, 0507, 0597
Issues—general	0509–0512, 0515–0518, 0531–0536, 0551–0552, 0720, 0801–0828, 0843–0897, 0900, 0934–0935, 0997, 1297
International involvement	0513–0514, 0519–0520, 1101–1172, 1175–1177, 1179–1197
Economic management	0901–0904, 0911–0913, 0926–0933, 0936–0941, 0952–0958, 1007–1009, 1201–1214
Social benefits	0905–0910, 0914–0925, 0965–0967, 0994–0996, 1001–1003, 1219, 1222, 1227–1228, 1233–1234
Civil liberties	0405–0406, 0946–0951, 0968–0993, 1173–1174, 1178, 1217–1218, 1223–1226, 1229–1232
Natural resources	0959–0964, 1004–1006
Agriculture	0942–0945, 1215–1216
Missing data	9001–9002, 9996–9999, 0000

America should spend whatever is necessary to have a strong military force.

We must have peace in Vietnam.

Busing should not be used to desegregate schools.

Each respondent answered these questions by placing a card containing the statement in one of seven positions on a Sort Board ranging from Strongly Disagree to Strongly Agree. Each of the five items was adapted so the respondent could similarly indicate his perception of the two presidential candidates. For example:

McGovern as president would increase welfare payments.

Nixon as president would increase welfare payments.

For each item, a respondent was given a score of 1 if he or she perceived his or her own party's candidate as being closest to his or her preferred position, a score of 0 if she or he perceived the opposition candidate as closer to her or his preferred position, and a score of .5 if the candidates were perceived as being equidistant from the preferred position. The respondent's score on the Index of Partisan Issue Consistency was the average of these item scores for the items on which the respondent expressed a preference and reported perceptions of both presidential candidates.

The Index of Partisan Attitude Consistency is based on the open-ended questions that were used to analyze information level and presidential vote choice. A score of +1 was assigned to each comment that favored the respondent's own party or criticized the opposition party. A score of −1 was assigned to each comment that favored the opposition party or criticized the respondent's own party. The sum of these scores was divided by the total number of comments. This produced a raw Index that varied between +1 for complete partisan consistency and −1 for complete partisan inconsistency. The raw scores were then adjusted to bounds of 1 for complete consistency and 0 for complete inconsistency so as to be comparable to the Index of Partisan Issue Consistency.

A–10.1 MEDIAN POSITIONS OF VARIOUS PARTY GROUPINGS

Responses to card-sort items were used to calculate median scores for electoral activists, citizens, and members of the White House staff. Items and policy areas in which they were grouped in this analysis, were:

International Involvement
    The government should help countries all over the world.
    We should bring all American troops back from foreign countries.*
    America should spend whatever is necessary to have a strong military
        force. (R)
    We must have peace in Vietnam.*
Economic Management
    Wages and prices should not be controlled by the government. (R)
    Government spending should be cut. (R)
    The government should act to stop pollution.
    The federal government is getting too powerful. (R)
Social Benefits
    The government ought to help pay everyone's medical bills.
    Welfare payments ought to be increased.
    Social security benefits ought to be increased.*
Civil Liberties
    I favor letting Negroes move into white neighborhoods.*
    Busing should not be used to desegregate schools. (R)
    The police ought to be given more authority. (R)

Note: Designations * and (R) are explained later in the text.

All 14 of the items were given to citizens and to the electoral activists. Ten of the items were included in the interviews with members of the (White House) Domestic Council staff. The four that were omitted from the Domestic Council interviews are indicated with asterisks. There were some minor variations in wording in four of the stimulus items given to the Domestic Council staff members. The most important of these concerned the foreign aid and busing items. These were phrased "The United States should help countries all over the world" and "Busing should not be used to achieve a racial balance in schools" in the White House interviews.

In computing the scores by policy area, strong agreement with the item was given a score of 7 (that is, most liberal) and strong disagreement a score of 1 (that is, most conservative) in eight cases. In six cases, all indicated with an (R), strong agreement was given a score of 1 and strong disagreement a score of 7.

The score for the representatives was based on roll call votes cast in each policy dimension, and were arrayed on scales ranging from 10 to 30 by Aage R. Clausen. Professor Clausen kindly made these scales available, and they were converted to a 1 to 7 range for purposes of comparability. It is appropriate to use these to compare with the attitude scores in other institutional domains because congressmen are customarily judged by their behavior. One would also expect that congressmen would have more extreme scores because of institutional tendencies (Republicans voting with Republicans, and Democrats voting with Democrats) toward bifurcation.

The median scores underlying Table 10–1 are shown in Table A–7.

TABLE A–7

Party Grouping	Policy Area			
	International Involvement	Economic Management	Social Benefits	Civil Liberties
Democratic representatives	3.6	6.0	6.7	4.2
Democratic electoral activists	4.9	4.4	5.9	6.0
Democratic citizens	4.2	3.9	4.7	3.3
Republican citizens	4.1	3.5	4.1	2.9
Republican electoral activists	4.0	3.8	3.6	3.5
Republican White House staff	3.4	3.1	3.3	3.1
Republican representatives	1.7	2.4	2.6	2.5

Bibliography

Abramson, Paul R. 1975. *Generational Change and the Decline of Party Identification.* Lexington, Mass.: Lexington Books.

Adrian, Charles, and **Press, Charles.** 1968. "Decision Costs in Coalition Formation." *American Political Science Review* 62 (June): 556–63.

Aldrich, John H., and **Cnudde, Charles.** 1975. "Probing the Bounds of Conventional Wisdom: A Comparison of Regression, Probit, and Discriminant Analysis." *American Journal of Political Science* 19 (August): 571–608.

Aldrich, John H.; Gant, Michael; and **Simon, Dennis.** 1978. "To the Victor Belong the Spoils: Momentum in the 1976 Nomination Campaigns." Paper prepared for the 1978 meeting of the Public Choice Society.

Aldrich, John H. 1979. "A Dynamic Model of Pre-Convention Campaigns." Paper prepared for the 1979 meeting of the Midwest Political Science Association, at Pick Congress Hotel, Chicago, April 19–21.

Aldrich, John H. 1980. *Before the Convention: A Theory of Campaigning for the 1976 Presidential Nomination.* Chicago: University of Chicago Press.

Alexander, Herbert E. 1972. *Political Financing.* Minneapolis: Burgess.

Alexander, Herbert E. 1976. *Financing the 1972 Election.* Lexington, Mass.: D.C. Heath.

Apple, R.W., Jr. 1976. "The Ethnics Vote in the States that Really Count." *New York Times,* October 10, p. E1.

Arrington, Theodore S. 1975. "Some Effects of Political Experience on Issue Consciousness and Issue Partisanship among Tucson Party Activists." *American Journal of Political Science* 19 (November): 695–702.

Arterton, F. Christopher. Forthcoming. *Media Politics: The News Strategies of Presidential Campaigns.*

Asher, Herbert B. 1980. *Presidential Elections and American Politics: Voters, Candidates and Campaigns*

Since 1952. Rev. ed. Homewood, Ill.: Dorsey Press.

Axelrod, Robert. 1972. "Where the Votes Come From: An Analysis of Electoral Coalitions, 1952–1968." *American Political Science Review* 66 (March): 11–20.

Axelrod, Robert. 1978. Letter to the Editor: "1976 Update." *American Political Science Review* 72 (June): 622–24.

Barber, James David. 1974. *Choosing the President.* Englewood Cliffs, N.J.: Prentice–Hall.

Barber, James David. 1978. *Race for the Presidency: The Media and the Nominating Process.* Englewood Cliffs, N.J.: Prentice–Hall.

Bennett, W. Lance. 1977. "The Growth of Knowledge in Mass Belief Systems: An Epistomological Critique." *American Journal of Political Science* 21 (August): 465–500.

Bibby, John F. Forthcoming. "Party Renewal in the National Republican Party." In *American Party Renewal: Theory and Practice,* ed., Gerald M. Pomper. New York: Praeger.

Bishop, George E.; Tuchfarber, Alfred J.; and Oldendick, Robert W. 1978. "Change in the Structure of American Political Attitudes: The Nagging Question of Question Wording." *American Journal of Political Science* 22 (May): 250–69.

Bone, Hugh A. 1971. *American Politics and the Party System.* New York: McGraw–Hill.

Brams, Steven J. 1978. *The Presidential Election Game.* New Haven, Conn.: Yale University Press.

Broder, David S. 1964. "Johnson Creates a Campaign Style." *Washington Star,* October 13, p. 1.

Broder, David S. 1970. "Reporters in Presidential Politics." In *Inside the System,* eds., Charles Peters and Timothy J. Adams. New York: Praeger.

Brody, Richard A. 1977. "Stability and Change in Party Identification: Presidential to Off-Years." Paper prepared for delivery at the 1977 annual meeting of the American Political Science Association, Washington, D.C., Sept. 1–4.

Burnham, Walter Dean. 1970. *Critical Elections and the Mainsprings of American Politics.* New York: Norton.

Burnham, Walter Dean. 1975. "American Politics in the 1970's: Beyond Party?" In *The American Party System: Stages of Political Development,* 2d ed., eds., William N. Chambers and Walter Dean Burnham, pp.308–57. New York: Oxford University Press.

Campbell, Angus; Gurin, Gerald; and Miller, Warren E. 1954. *The Voter Decides.* Evanston, Ill.: Row, Peterson.

Campbell, Angus; Converse, Philip E.; Miller, Warren E.; and Stokes, Donald E. 1960. *The American Voter.* New York: Wiley.

Cannon, James M. 1960. *Politics, U.S.A.: A Practical Guide to the Winning of Public Office.* Garden City, N.Y.: Doubleday.

Chester, Lewis; Hodgson, Godfrey; and Page, Bruce. 1969. *An American Melodrama: The Presidential Campaign of 1968.* New York: Viking.

Clarke, James W. 1970. Personal communication.

Clausen, Aage R., and Cheney, Richard B. 1970. "A Comparative Analysis of Senate and House Voting on Economic and Welfare Policy: 1953–1964." *American Political Science Review* 64 (March): 138–52.

Clausen, Aage R. 1973. *How Congressmen Decide: A Policy Focus.* New York: St. Martin's.

Comparative State Election Project. 1973. *Explaining the Vote: Presidential Choices in the Nation and the States.* Chapel Hill, N.C.: Institute for Research in Social Science.

Converse, Philip E. 1964. "The Nature of Belief Systems in Mass Publics." In *Ideology and Discontent*, ed., David W. Apter. New York: Free Press.

Converse, Philip E. 1975. "Public Opinion and Voting Behavior." In *Handbook of Political Science*, Vol. 4, eds., Fred I. Greenstein and Nelson W. Polsby. Reading, Mass.: Addison–Wesley.

Converse, Philip E. 1976. *The Dynamics of Party Support: Cohort Analyzing Party Identification*. Beverly Hills, Cal.: Sage.

Converse, Philip E., and Markus, Gregory B. 1979. "Plus ça change . . . : The New CPS Election Study Panel." *American Political Science Review* 73 (March): 32–49.

Corwin, Edward S. 1948. *The President Office and Powers, 1787–1948: History and Analysis of Practice and Opinion*. 3d rev. ed. New York: New York University Press.

Costain, Anne N. 1978. "An Analysis of Voting in American National Nominating Conventions, 1940–1976." *American Politics Quarterly* 6 (January): 375–94.

Cotter, Cornelius P., and Hennessy, Bernard C. 1964. *Politics Without Power: The National Party Committees*. New York: Atherton.

Cotter, Cornelius P., and Bibby, John F. 1979. "The Impact of Reform on the National Party Organizations: The Long-Term Determinants of Party Reform." Paper prepared for delivery at the 1979 annual meeting of the American Political Science Association, Washington, D.C., Aug. 30 to Sept. 2.

David, Paul T.; Goldman, Ralph M.; and Bain, Richard C. 1960. *The Politics of National Party Conventions*. Paperback ed. Washington: The Brookings Institution.

Downs, Anthony. 1957. *An Economic Theory of Democracy*. New York: Harper & Row.

Drew, Elizabeth. 1977. *American Journal: The Events of 1976*. New York: Random House.

Eldersveld, Samuel J. 1964. *Political Parties: A Behavioral Analysis*. Chicago: Rand McNally.

Epstein, Leon D. 1974. "Political Parties." In *Handbook of Political Science*, Vol. 4, eds., Fred I. Greenstein and Nelson W. Polsby. Reading, Mass.: Addison–Wesley.

Fiorina, Morris P. Forthcoming. *Retrospective Voting in American National Politics*. New Haven, Conn.: Yale University Press.

Fishel, Jeff. 1977. "Agenda Building in Presidential Campaigns: The Case of Jimmy Carter." Paper prepared for delivery at the 1977 annual meeting of the American Political Science Association, Washington, D.C., September 1–4.

Flanigan, William H., and Zingale, Nancy H. 1979. *Political Behavior of the American Electorate*. 4th ed. Boston: Allyn & Bacon.

Fogel, Norman J. 1974. "The Impact of Cognitive Inconsistency on Electoral Behavior." Unpublished Ph.D. dissertation, Ohio State University.

Ford, Gerald R. 1979. *A Time to Heal*. New York: Harper & Row.

Fortune. 1935. "The Democratic Party." April, p. 136. Cited in Herring (1940), p. 265.

Frankel, Max. 1968. "Seek to Counter Survey's Impact." *New York Times*, October 9, p. 34.

Gatlin, Douglas. 1973. "Florida." In Comparative State Election Project, *Explaining the Vote: Presidential Choices in the Nation and the States, 1968*. Chapel Hill, N.C.: Institute for Research in Social Science.

Gerston, Larry N.; Burstein, Jerome S.; and Cohen, Stephen S. 1979. "Presidential Nominations and Coalition Theory." *American Politics Quarterly* 7 (April): 175–97.

Graber, Doris A. 1976. "Press and TV as Opinion Resources in Presidential Campaigns." *Public Opinion Quarterly* 40 (Fall): 285–303.

Graber, Doris A. 1980. *The Mass Media and Politics.* Washington: Congressional Quarterly Press.

Greeley, Andrew M. 1974. *Building Coalitions: American Politics in the 1970's.* New York: Franklin Watts.

Greenstein, Fred I. 1974. "What the President Means to Americans." In *Choosing the President,* ed., James David Barber. Englewood Cliffs, N.J.: Prentice–Hall.

Guylay, L. Richard. 1960. "Public Relations." In *Politics, U.S.A.: A Practical Guide to the Winning of Public Office,* ed., James M. Cannon. Garden City, N.Y.: Doubleday.

Hanushek, Erik A., and Jackson, John E. 1977. *Statistical Methods for Social Scientists.* New York: Academic Press.

Hart, Gary W. 1973. *Right from the Start: A Chronicle of the McGovern Campaign.* New York: Quadrangle/New York Times Book Co.

Heard, Alexander. 1960. *The Costs of Democracy.* Chapel Hill: University of North Carolina Press.

Herring, Pendleton. 1940. *The Politics of Democracy: American Parties in Action.* New York: Rinehart.

Hershey, Marjorie R. 1977. "A Social Learning Theory of Innovation and Change in Political Campaigning." Paper prepared for delivery at the 1977 annual meeting of the American Political Science Association, Washington, D.C., September 1–4.

Hess, Stephen. 1974. *The Presidential Campaign: The Leadership Selection Process After Watergate.* Washington: The Brookings Institution.

Hinckley, Barbara; Hofstetter, Richard; and Kessel, John H. 1974. "Information and the Vote: A Comparative Election Study." *American Politics Quarterly* 2: 131–58.

Hoagland, Henry W. 1960. "The Advance Man." In *Politics, U.S.A.: A Practical Guide to the Winning of Public Office,* ed., James M. Cannon, Garden City, N.Y.: Doubleday.

Hofstetter, Richard. 1976. *Bias in the News: Network Television Coverage of the 1972 Election Campaign.* Columbus: Ohio State University Press.

Holcombe, Arthur N. 1950. *Our More Perfect Union: From Eighteenth Century Principles to Twentieth Century Practice.* Cambridge, Mass.: Harvard University Press.

Howell, Susan E. 1976. "The Psychological Dimension of Unity in American Political Parties." Paper prepared for delivery at the 1976 annual meeting of the American Political Science Association, Chicago, Sept. 2–5.

Huckshorn, Robert J. 1976. *Party Leadership in the States.* Amherst: University of Massachusetts Press.

Ivins, Molly. 1976. "Liberal from Goldwater Country." *New York Times Magazine,* February 1, pp. 12–33.

Jackson, John E. 1975. "Issues, Party Choices, and Presidential Votes." *American Journal of Political Science* 19 (May): 161–85.

Janeway, Michael C. 1962. "Lyndon Johnson and the Rise of Conservatism in Texas." Unpublished honors thesis, Harvard College History Department.

Jenkins, Ray. 1968. "Wallace Team Gears National Effort Toward Election Day." *Christian Science Monitor,* September 17, p. 3.

Jennings, M. Kent, and Zeigler, Harmon. 1966. *The Electoral Process.* Englewood Cliffs, N.J.: Prentice–Hall.

Jennings, M. Kent. 1966. Personal communication.

Johnson, Loch K., and Hahn, Harlan. 1973. "Delegate Turnover at National Party Conventions, 1944–68." In *Perspectives on Presidential Selection*, ed., Donald R. Matthews. Washington: The Brookings Institution.

Johnson, Lyndon B. 1971. *The Vantage Point*. Paperback ed. New York: Popular Library.

Keech, William R., and Matthews, Donald R. 1976. *The Party's Choice*. Washington: The Brookings Institution.

Kelley, Stanley, Jr. 1956. *Professional Public Relations and Political Power*. Baltimore: Johns Hopkins University Press.

Kelley, Stanley, Jr.; Ayers, Richard E.; and Bowen, William G. 1967. "Registration and Voting: Putting First Things First." *American Political Science Review* 61 (June): 359–77.

Kessel, John H. 1968. *The Goldwater Coalition: Republican Strategies in 1964*. Indianapolis: Bobbs–Merrill.

Kessel, John H. 1974. "The Parameters of Presidential Politics." *Social Science Quarterly* 55 (June): 8–24.

Kessel, John H. 1975. *The Domestic Presidency: Decision-Making in the White House*. North Scituate, Mass.: Duxbury Press.

Kessel, John H. 1977. "The Seasons of Presidential Politics." *Social Science Quarterly* 58 (December): 418–35.

Key, V.O., Jr. 1949. *Southern Politics in State and Nation*. New York: Knopf.

Key, V.O., Jr. 1964. *Politics, Parties, and Pressure Groups*. 5th ed. New York: Crowell.

Kingdon, John W. 1968. *Candidates for Office: Beliefs and Strategies*. New York: Random House.

Kirkpatrick, Jeane. 1976. *The New Presidential Elite: Men and Women in National Politics*. New York: Russell Sage Foundation and Twentieth Century Fund.

Kraus, Sidney. 1962. *The Great Debates: Kennedy vs. Nixon 1960*. Bloomington: Indiana University Press.

Kraus, Sidney. 1979. *The Great Debates: Ford vs. Carter 1976*. Bloomington: Indiana University Press.

Kruskal, Joseph B., and Wish, Myron. 1978. *Multidimensional Scaling*. Beverly Hills, Cal.: Sage.

Ladd, Everett Carll, and Hadley, Charles D. 1978. *Transformations of the American Party System*. 2d ed. New York: Norton.

Ladd, Everett Carll. 1978. *Where Have All the Voters Gone? The Fracturing of American Political Parties*. New York: Norton.

Lamb, Karl A. 1966. "Under One Roof: Barry Goldwater's Campaign Staff." In *Republican Politics: The 1964 Campaign and Its Aftermath*, eds., Bernard Cosman and Robert J. Huckshorn. New York: Praeger.

Lane, Robert E. 1973. "Patterns of Political Belief." In *Handbook of Political Psychology*, ed., Jeane M. Knutson. San Francisco: Jossey–Bass.

Lazarsfeld, Paul F.; Berelson, Bernard; and Gaudet, Hazel. 1944. *The People's Choice*. New York: Duell, Sloan & Pearce.

Lelyveld, Joseph H. 1976a. "The Selling of a Candidate." *New York Times Magazine*, March 28, p. 16ff.

Lelyveld, Joseph H. 1976b. "President's New TV Commercials." *New York Times*, October 29, p. 22.

Lelyveld, Joseph H. 1976c. "Iowa Woman, 79, Who Met a 'Nobody' in '75, Is Tickled by Carter Victory." *New York Times*, November 4, p. 51.

Lengle, James, and Shafer, Byron. 1976. "Primary Rules, Political

Power, and Social Change." *American Political Science Review* 70 (March): 25–40.

Levin, Eric. 1977. "How the Networks Decide What is News." *TV Guide*, July 2, pp. 4–10.

Levinson, Daniel J. 1978. *The Season's of a Man's Life*. New York: Knopf.

Lomax, Louis. 1964. "The Basic Issues in the Presidential Campaign." *Washington Star*, October 4, p. C3.

Lydon, Christopher. 1972. "How McGovern Rose to Top in Long Campaign." *New York Times*, June 11, p. 40.

Macrae, Duncan, Jr. 1970. *Issues and Parties in Legislative Voting*. New York: Harper & Row.

Marvick, Dwaine. 1973. "Party Organizational Behavior and Electoral Democracy: The Perspectives of Rival Cadres in Los Angeles from 1963 to 1972." Paper prepared for delivery at the Ninth World Congress, International Political Science Association, Montreal, Canada, Aug. 19–25.

Matthews, Donald R., and Prothro, James W. 1966. *Negroes and the New Southern Politics*. New York: Harcourt, Brace.

Matthews, Donald R. 1973. *Perspectives on Presidential Selection*. Washington: The Brookings Institution.

Matthews, Donald R. 1978. "Winnowing: The News Media and the 1976 Presidential Nominations." In *Race for the Presidency: The Media and the Nominating Process*, ed., James David Barber. Englewood Cliffs, N.J.: Prentice–Hall.

McClosky, Herbert; Hoffman, Paul J.; and O'Hara, Rosemary. 1960. "Issue Conflict and Consensus among Party Leaders and Followers." *American Political Science Review* 54 (June): 406–27.

McGinniss, Joe. 1969. *The Selling of the President 1968*. New York: Trident Press.

McGregor, Eugene B. 1978. "Uncertainty and National Nominating Coalitions." *Journal of Politics* 40 (December): 1011–42.

McKelvey, Richard, and Zavonia, William. 1969. "A Statistical Model for the Analysis of Legislative Behavior." Paper prepared for delivery at the 1969 annual meeting of the American Political Science Association, New York City, September 1–8.

Michelson, Charles. 1944. *The Ghost Talks*. New York: Putnam.

Miller, Arthur H. 1974. "Political Issues and Trust in Government: 1964–1970." *American Political Science Review* 68 (September): 951–72.

Miller, Arthur H., and Miller, Warren E. 1977. "Partisanship and Performance: 'Rational' Choice in the 1976 Elections." Paper prepared for delivery at the 1977 annual meeting of the American Political Science Association, Washington, D.C., September 1–4.

Miller, Warren E., and Levitin, Teresa E. 1976. *Leadership and Change: Presidential Elections from 1952 to 1976*. Cambridge, Mass.: Winthrop Press.

Moley, Raymond E. 1960. "Collaboration in Political Speech Writing." In *Politics, U.S.A.: A Practical Guide to the Winning of Public Office*, ed., James M. Cannon. Garden City, N.Y.: Doubleday.

Moore, Jonathan, and Fraser, Janet. 1977. *Campaign for President: The Managers Look at '76*. Cambridge, Mass.: Ballinger.

Mueller, John E. 1973. *War, Presidents, and Public Opinion*. New York: Wiley.

Munger, Frank J., and Blackhurst, James. 1965. "Factionalism in the National Conventions, 1940–1964: An Analysis of Ideological Consistency in State Delegation Voting." *Journal of Politics* 27 (May): 375–94.

Naughton, James M. 1976. "Ford Hopes Linked to Catholic Vote." *New York Times*, September 5, pp. 1, 26.

Neisser, Ulrich. 1976. *Cognition and Reality*. San Francisco: Freeman.

Nelson, Forrest D. 1976. "On a General Computer Algorithm for the Analysis of Models with Limited Dependent Variables." *Annals of Economic and Social Measurement*, pp. 493–509.

Nelson, Forrest D. and Olson, Lawrence. 1978. "Specification and Estimation of a Simultaneous-Equation Model with Limited Dependent Variables." *International Economic Review*, October.

Nexon, David. 1971. "Asymmetry in the Political System: Occasional Activists in the Republican and Democratic Parties, 1956–1964." *American Political Science Review* 65 (September): 716–30.

Nie, Norman H. and Andersen, Kristi. 1974. "Mass Belief Systems Revisited: Political Change and Attitude Structure." *Journal of Politics* 36 (August): 540–91.

Nie, Norman H.; Verba, Sidney; and Petrocik, John R. 1976. *The Changing American Voter*. Cambridge, Mass.: Harvard University Press.

Niemi, Richard G. and Jennings, M. Kent. 1968. "Intraparty Communication and the Selection of Delegates to a National Convention." *Western Political Quarterly* 22 (December): 29–46.

Niemi, Richard G., and Weisberg, Herbert F. 1976. *Controversies in American Voting Behavior*. San Francisco: Freeman.

Nimmo, Dan, and Savage, Robert L. 1976. *Candidates and Their Images: Concepts, Methods and Findings*. Pacific Palisades, Cal.: Goodyear.

Ogden, Daniel M., and Peterson,

Arthur L. 1968. *Electing the President*. Rev. ed. San Francisco: Chandler.

Orren, Gary R. 1978. "Candidate Style and Voter Alignment in 1976." In *Emerging Coalitions in American Politics*, ed., Seymour Martin Lipset. San Francisco: Institute for Contemporary Studies.

Page, Benjamin I., and Brody, Richard A. 1972. "Policy Voting and the Electoral Process: The Vietnam War Issue." *American Political Science Review* 66 (September): 979–95.

Page, Benjamin I. 1978. *Choices and Echoes in Presidential Elections: Rational Man and Electoral Democracy*. Chicago: University of Chicago Press.

Parris, Judith H. 1972. *The Convention Problem*. Washington: The Brookings Institution.

Parry, James M. 1977. "AMDAHL Speaks: Carter Really Won the Election." *National Observer*, February 12.

Patterson, Thomas E., and McClure, Robert D. 1976. *The Unseeing Eye: The Myth of Television Power in National Politics*. New York: Putnam.

Patterson, Thomas E. 1978. "Assessing Television Newscasts: Future Directions in Content Analysis." In *Television Network News: Issues in Content Research*, eds., William Adams and Fay Schreibman. Washington, D.C.: George Washington University Press.

Petrocik, John R. 1974. "Intransitivities in the Index of Party Identification." *Political Methodology* 1 (Summer): 31–48.

Polsby, Nelson W., and Wildavsky, Aaron. 1976. *Presidential Elections*. 4th ed. New York: Scribners.

Pomper, Gerald M. 1968. *Elections in America: Control and Influence in Democratic Politics*. New York: Dodd, Mead.

Pomper, Gerald M. 1977. "New

Rules and New Games in the National Conventions." Paper prepared for delivery to the 1977 annual meeting of the American Political Science Association, Washington, D.C., Sept. 1–4.

Rabinowitz, George B. 1975. "An Introduction to Non-Metric Multidimensional Scaling." *American Journal of Political Science* 19 (May): 343–90.

Ranney, Austin. 1975. *Curing the Mischiefs of Faction: Party Reform in America.* Berkeley: University of California Press.

Ranney, Austin. 1978. "The Political Parties: Reform and Decline." In *The New American Political System,* ed., Anthony King. Washington, D.C.: American Enterprise Institute.

Raskin, A. H. 1972. "All Over Lot in '72 Campaign." *New York Times,* August 20, pp. E1–E2.

Republican National Committee Chairman's Report. 1979. Washington, D.C.: by the Committee.

Riker, William H. 1962. *The Theory of Political Coalitions.* New Haven, Conn.: Yale University Press.

Robinson, Michael J. 1976. "Television News and the Presidential Nominating Process: The Case of Spring." Unpublished manuscript.

Rosenstone, Steven J., and Wolfinger, Raymond E. 1978. "The Effect of Registration Laws on Voter Turnout." *American Political Science Review* 72 (March): 22–45.

Rubin, Richard L. 1976. *Party Dynamics: The Democratic Coalition and the Politics of Change.* New York: Oxford University Press.

Safire, William 1975. *Before the Fall: An Inside View of the Pre-Watergate White House.* Garden City, N.Y.: Doubleday.

Schlesinger, Joseph A. 1965. "Political Parties." In *Handbook of Organizations,* ed., James G. March. Chicago: Rand McNally.

Schlesinger, Joseph A. 1975. "The Primary Goals of Political Parties: A Clarification of Positive Theory." *American Political Science Review* 69 (September): 840–49.

Schram, Martin. 1976. *Running for President 1976: The Carter Campaign.* New York: Stein and Day.

Sears, David O. 1977. "The Debates in the Light of Research: An Overview of the Effects." Paper prepared for delivery at the 1977 annual meeting of the American Political Science Association, Washington, D.C., September 1–4.

Sears, David O., and Chaffee, Steven H. 1978. "Uses and Effects of the 1976 Debates: An Overview of Empirical Studies." A chapter prepared for inclusion in *The Great Debates, 1976: Ford vs. Carter,* ed., Sidney Kraus. Bloomington: Indiana University Press, forthcoming.

Semple, Robert B. 1968. "Two Nixons Emerge in '68 Race: Stump Sloganeer, Radio Thinker." *New York Times,* October 17, p. 38.

Shively, W. Phillips. 1977. "Information Costs and the Partisan Life Cycle." Paper prepared for delivery at the 1977 annual meeting of the American Political Science Association, Washington, D.C., September 1–4.

Shively, W. Phillips. 1979. "The Development of Party Identification in Adults." *American Political Science Review* 73 (December): 1039–54.

Simon, Herbert. 1952. "Comments on the Theory of Organization." *American Political Science Review* 46 (December): 1130–52.

Sorauf, Frank J. 1980. *Party Politics in America.* 4th ed. Boston: Little, Brown.

Sorenson, Theodore. 1965. *Kennedy.* New York: Bantam Books.

Soule, John W., and Clarke, James W. 1970. "Amateurs and Professionals: A Study of Delegates to the 1968 Democratic National Convention." *American Political Science Review* 64 (September): 888–98.

Soule, John W., and McGrath, Wilma E. 1975. "A Comparative Study of Presidential Nominating Conventions." *American Journal of Political Science* 19 (August): 501–17.

Sperlich, Peter W. 1971. *Conflict and Harmony in Human Affairs: A Study of Cross-Pressures and Political Behavior.* Chicago: Rand McNally.

Sperling, Godfrey, Jr. 1972. "Steelworkers Wary on McGovern." *Christian Science Monitor,* September 20, p. 3.

Sterling, Christopher, and Haight, Timothy. 1979. *The Mass Media: Aspen Institute Guide to Communication Industry Trends.* Queenstown, Md.: by the Institute.

Stevenson, Robert L. 1978. "The Uses and Non-Uses of Television News." Paper prepared for the International Society of Political Psychology Meeting, New York City, September 1978.

Stimson, James A. 1976. "Public Support for American Presidents: A Cyclical Model." *Public Opinion Quarterly* 40: 1–21.

Stokes, Donald E.; Campbell, Angus; and Miller, Warren E. 1958. "Components of Electoral Decision." *American Political Science Review* 52 (June): 367–87.

Sullivan, Dennis G.; Pressman, Jeffrey L.; Page, Benjamin I.; and Lyons, John W. 1974. *The Politics of Representation: The Democratic Convention 1972.* New York: St. Martin's.

Sullivan, John L.; Piereson, James E.; and Marcus, George E. 1978. "Ideological Constraint in the Mass Public: A Methodological Critique and Some New Findings." *American Journal of Political Science* 22 (May): 250–69.

Tillett, Paul. 1962. *Inside Politics: The National Conventions, 1960.* Dobbs Ferry, N.Y.: Oceana Press.

Truman, David B. 1971. *The Governmental Process.* 2d ed. New York: Knopf.

Van Wingen, John R., and Valentine, David C. 1978. "Partisanship, Independence, and the Partisan Identification Index." Paper prepared for delivery at the 1978 annual meeting of the Midwest Political Science Association, Chicago.

Verba, Sidney, and Nie, Norman H. 1972. *Participation in America: Political Democracy and Social Equality.* New York: Harper & Row.

Weisberg, Herbert F. 1978. "Evaluating Theories of Congressional Roll Call Voting." *American Journal of Political Science* 22 (August): 554–77.

Weisberg, Herbert F. 1979. "A Multidimensional Conceptualization of Party Identification." Paper prepared for delivery at the 1979 annual meeting of the Midwest Political Science Association, Chicago, April 19–21.

White, F. Clifton. 1965. "Selection of Delegates to the 1964 Republican Nominating Convention Related to the Thirteen Western States." Paper prepared for delivery at the 1965 meeting of the Western Political Science Association, Victoria, B.C., March 19.

White, F. Clifton. 1967. *Suite 3505: The Story of the Draft Goldwater Movement.* New Rochelle, N.Y.: Arlington House.

White, Theodore H. 1961. *The Making of the President 1960.* New York: Atheneum.

White, Theodore H. 1965. *The*

Making of the President 1964. New York: Atheneum.

White, Theodore H. 1969. *The Making of the President 1968.* New York: Atheneum.

White, Theodore H. 1973. *The Making of the President 1972.* New York: Atheneum.

Williams, Daniel C., et al. 1976. "Voter Decisionmaking in a Primary Election." *American Journal of Political Science* 20 (February): 37–49.

Wilson, Woodrow. 1884. *Congressional Government.* New York: Meridian Books, 1956, Meridian edition.

Witcover, Jules. 1977. *Marathon: The Pursuit of the Presidency:* New York: Viking.

Wolfinger, Raymond E. 1972. "Why Political Machines Have Not Withered Away and Other Revisionist Thoughts." *Journal of Politics* 34 (February): 365–98.

Wolfinger, Raymond E., et al. 1977. "The Myth of the Independent Voter." Paper prepared for delivery at the 1977 annual meeting of the American Political Science Association, Washington, D.C., Sept. 1–4.

Wooten, James T. 1976. "Carter Strategy from the Start: 1976 Was the Year for a Gambler." *New York Times,* June 10, p. 42.

Yarnell, Steven. 1975. "The Measurement of Perceptual Accuracy: A Methodological Note." Unpublished paper, Ohio State University.

 Index

*This book has been set Linotype in 10 and 9
point Palatino, leaded 2 points. Part numbers
and chapter numbers are 24 point and 20 point
Palatino italic. Part and chapter titles are 20
point Palatino. The size of the type page is 27
by 45½ picas.*